CONCEIVED WITH MALICE

Louise DeSalvo

A DUTTON BOOK

DUTTON
Published by the Penguin Group
Penguin Books USA Inc., 375 Hudson Street,
New York, New York 10014, U.S.A.
Penguin Books Ltd, 27 Wrights Lane, London W8 5TZ, England
Penguin Books Australia Ltd, Ringwood, Victoria, Australia
Penguin Books Canada Ltd, 10 Alcorn Avenue,
Toronto, Ontario, Canada M4V 3B2
Penguin Books (N.Z.) Ltd, 182–190 Wairau Road, Auckland 10, New Zealand

Penguin Books Ltd, Registered Offices:
Harmondsworth, Middlesex, England

First published by Dutton, an imprint of Dutton Signet,
a division of Penguin Books USA Inc.
Distributed in Canada by McClelland & Stewart Inc.

First Printing, November, 1994
10 9 8 7 6 5 4 3 2 1

 REGISTERED TRADEMARK—MARCA REGISTRADA

LIBRARY OF CONGRESS CATALOGING IN PUBLICATION DATA
DeSalvo, Louise A.
Conceived with malice: literature as revenge / Louise DeSalvo.
p. cm.
Includes bibliographical references (p.) and index.
ISBN 0-525-93899-0
1. English literature—20th century—History and criticism.   2. American
literature—20th century—History and criticism.   3. Characters and characteristics
in literature. 4. Creation (Literary, artistic, etc.) 5. Authors—Friends and
associates. 6. Authors—Family relationships. 7. Revenge in literature.
8. Authors—Psychology. 9. Livres à clef. I. Title.
PR471.D47 1994
823'.91209353—dc20   94-9927
                                                                              CIP

Printed in the United States of America
Set in Palatino
Designed by Eve L. Kirch

For
Ernest J. DeSalvo,
Elizabeth Harlan,
Frank McLaughlin,
and Geri Thoma

CONTENTS

5.
"A DESPERADO OF LOVE":
Henry Miller, June Miller, and *Crazy Cock*
275

6.
AFTERWORD
353

Notes
357

Sources
399

Acknowledgments
421

Index
429

Every creative act is a declaration of war.

—HENRY MILLER
Henry Miller's Hamlet Letters

1

INTRODUCTION:

Literature as Revenge

Henry. Overbury thought her immoral, and believed she was exerting a pernicious influence upon his friend.

Of course, it was also true that her influence upon Rochester had undermined Overbury's, so his motives for opposing the liaison were surely not selfless. He wanted nothing to stand in the way of his power, and the Countess of Essex was doing just that. The countess, too, would tolerate no impediment to her desires. They were poised for battle.

Overbury's weapons were his pen and his poem, which became the talk of the court. The countess, convinced that revenge was the motive behind Overbury's poem, saw "The Wife" as part of a power play on his part to undermine her position. She believed he had written it to sully her reputation and to make her a laughingstock. She read "The Wife" as a deliberate, ironic contrast to her licentious life, for it described the kind of wife she most assuredly was not—"a pure and virtuous Woman." If Overbury continued to defame her through his work, her influence upon Rochester, and at court, would be seriously and perhaps permanently undermined.

And so she fought back. She convinced the King that Overbury was dangerous and should be jailed. Though he lacked knowledge of the personal nature of her vendetta, the King complied with her wishes for his own reasons. Nor did he realize that the countess was planning murder.

In September 1613, Overbury died, the victim of a lethal suppository, the countess having become impatient with waiting for slower-acting poisons to do their work. Overbury was buried hurriedly. Court gossip held that he had been murdered because of the countess's "revenge on Overbury for defaming her character" in his poem. His revenge prompted her retaliation. But hers killed him.

Two months after Overbury's death, the Countess of Essex and Lord Rochester (now the Earl of Somerset) married. More than a year later, the plot that had led to Overbury's death was uncovered and the countess's accomplices were executed. The intervention of the King himself spared the countess's life.

Sir Thomas Overbury paid with his life for writing a work of literature that the Countess of Essex believed was motivated by revenge. Perhaps no more dramatic an example exists in the world's literature of the issue I take up in this book—that writers create works of literature prompted not by the most sublime and exalted

Many of us believe that writing literature, and reading it, are uplifting experiences. Many theories of literary creativity portray the writer as an inspired being, different from, and better than, the rest of us.

But that isn't necessarily true. Take, for example, the strange case of the murder of the writer Sir Thomas Overbury.

In 1613, Overbury, author of such eminently forgettable literary works as the "Character of a Noble Spirit" and "Noble Housekeeper," lay dying in terrible agony in the Tower of London. The cause of the mysterious illness that would soon kill him? Accomplices of the Countess of Essex were poisoning him, slowly, by placing doses of copper vitriol in his food. The reason? She believed he had made fun of her in a poem of his called "The Wife," which members of the Court of King James, to which they both belonged, were reading and commenting upon.

When read today, laden as it is with sententiousness and piety, it is difficult to imagine how this insipid work could have offended anyone. But the Countess of Essex believed Overbury wrote "The Wife" to get back at her.

The countess was in the midst of an adulterous love affair with Overbury's close friend and confidant Lord Rochester. Rochester was also a favorite of the King—in effect, the King's private secretary. Overbury had been highly critical of Rochester's involvement with the young, exceedingly beautiful, thoroughly spoiled and self-willed countess, whose first lover, at sixteen, had been Prince of motives (William Wordsworth's notion that a work of art results from emotion recollected in tranquillity, for example), but by what we hold to be among the basest of human motives: revenge.

I conceived the idea of writing this book after I attended a pre-publication reading, in the 1980s, of a novel-in-progress by a famous American male novelist. After an upsetting sexual scene in which the writer's vicious yet artful prose demeaned a woman character, he looked straight at the audience, smirked, and said, "I really got *her* back with that one." Many members of the audience laughed. Before attending that reading, I had been a writer of literary biography, familiar with the complicated ways in which writers incorporate and transform their lives into their works of art, but I had never before heard so direct an admission that the written word can be used as a weapon, that a novel can be used to humiliate and excoriate a victim—that literature can be a powerful and enduring form of retaliation.

As I was driving home after the reading, I realized how stunned I was by the novelist's blatant admission of revenge as a motive for that scene. In part, it was because he challenged my idealized vision of writers. It was also because he was so satisfied with himself. I wondered whether "she" would find out what he had done to her in his work, and whether he would get away with it—or whether, when she found out about it, she would fight back. I hoped she would fight back.

When I became interested in revenge as a motive for writing fiction, I was writing a book on Virginia Woolf as a survivor of incest. Through the years, every time I came across an account that a writer had written a work of literature inspired by a desire for revenge, rather than by purer and finer motives, I took a note or clipped the article. Not surprisingly, my first examples came from the letters and diaries of Virginia Woolf. A writer ever alert to anything that smacked of scandal or personal intrigue, Woolf scribbled brilliant, riveting accounts about the negative portrait of her friend Ottoline Morrell in *Women in Love* by D. H. Lawrence: "I am reading . . . , lured on by the portrait of Ottoline. . . . She has just smashed Lawrence's head open with a ball of lapis lazuli—but then balls are smashed on every other page." Woolf also described how Hugh Walpole sat on the edge of his bed, one sock on, one sock off, reading, with fascination and horror, the cruel and malicious portrait of himself as Alroy Kear in Somerset Maugham's *Cakes and Ale*. (Walpole later retaliated against Maugham in two novels: *Captain Nicholas* and *John Cornelius*.)

Woolf herself was not above the practice she observed with such delight, but also with empathy for its victims. In *Orlando*, she set off a few volleys aimed at Vita Sackville-West, her former lover. In that mock-biography, in which Vita/Orlando changes sex from a man to a woman, Woolf attacks Sackville-West's promiscuity. Smarting from having been thrown over for younger, more stimulating partners, Woolf communicates her rage in her letter to Sackville-West describing the book's completion: "ORLANDO IS FINISHED!!!" she announces. Then: "Did you feel a sort of tug, as if your neck was being broken on Saturday last at 5 minutes to one? That is when he died." To which Sackville-West replied, "You absolutely terrified me by your remarks. . . . Well, I'll tell you one thing: if . . . Orlando is dead, you shall never set eyes on me again. . . . I *won't* be fictitious."

The examples I found in Woolf's papers didn't surprise me. At first, I thought members of Woolf's set were uniquely vicious and I was collecting material about an interesting, rare phenomenon that might challenge romanticized notions about a writer's motives in creating a work of art. In time it became clear that this was no singular phenomenon practiced among the Bloomsberries. It was far more widespread than I had imagined.

I learned of other examples when, as a member of a biography seminar at New York University, I discussed the question with other members. I asked Deirdre Bair, then working on her landmark biography of Simone de Beauvoir, whether Beauvoir or her friends did this kind of thing. "All the time," she replied. She told me about Beauvoir's portrait of her lover Nelson Algren in *The Mandarins*. When Bair's *Simone de Beauvoir* came out, I read the account with great interest.

Beauvoir's *The Mandarins*, like Woolf's *Orlando*, was written when her love affair with Algren was over and he would not see her. He had wanted a more permanent relationship than she could allow because of her relationship with Jean-Paul Sartre. Algren decided their affair was " 'going nowhere,' and that he no longer loved her." She wrote about it "almost literally, almost word for word" in describing the relationship of Anne and Lewis.

Beauvoir had promised Algren that she would not use their love affair as a subject for her art. He was an extraordinarily private man and hated the way she and Sartre carried on their lives in public. Despite her promise, she transposed her affair into her novel, at first not telling him about it. When he read the work in English, he was furious. What made him even angrier was her description of their relationship in her autobiography, *Force of Circumstance*. She could never understand why Algren could have felt "betrayed" by her writing "what was essentially the truth."

Elizabeth Harlan, at work on a biography of George Sand, told me about Curtis Cate's account of Sand's vindictive portrait of Chopin in her novel *Lucrezia Floriani*. In that novel, Sand attacks Prince Karol's (Chopin's) obsessive jealousy: "One day Karol was jealous of the Curé who had come to collect the money. Another day he was jealous of a servant who, being much spoiled . . . , answered with a boldness which struck him as unnatural."

Not content to use the written word alone, Sand subjected Chopin to public readings from the work at her estate in Nohant. The painter Delacroix, who was a guest, "listened appalled, as this experiment in literary vivisection unfolded itself relentlessly. He kept looking from George Sand to Chopin and back. . . . 'Executioner and victim.' " Sand was at it again later in life when she excoriated her former lover Alfred de Musset in *Elle et Lui*. Musset's brother Paul retaliated on his brother's behalf with another version of the liaison, *Lui et Elle*.

Every biography and autobiography I read while working on this project described revenge operating as an important motive in the creation of a literary work, and it seems a nearly universal phenomenon in the lives of writers. Richard Aldington, H. G. Wells, Rebecca West, Anthony West, Anaïs Nin, Violet Trefusis, F. Scott Fitzgerald, Ernest Hemingway, Roy Campbell, Christina Stead, Antonia White, Colley Cibber, Alexander Pope, Fyodor Dostoyevsky, the prime-minister-turned-novelist Benjamin Disraeli, Henry Gauthier Villars, Colette, John Cheever, Mary Cheever, Jean Rhys, H. H. Munro ("Saki"), Ford Madox Ford, Violet Hunt, Henry Fielding, Bernard DeVoto, Marcel Proust, Anne Sexton, Gustave Flaubert, Nathaniel Hawthorne—all wrote one or more literary works to take revenge. Readers will surely be able to add their own examples to this list.

The temptation to tell *all* these stories is great—how, for example, Richard Aldington avenged himself against what he saw as Nancy Cunard's lack of ethics in "Now Lies She There," which portrays her as using sex to make her way. How the poet Roy Campbell, after discovering the love affair his wife, Mary, had with Vita Sackville-West, got back at his rival in *The Georgiad*. How Violet Trefusis revenged herself on her lover Vita Sackville-West for jilting her in *Broderie Anglaise*. How John Cheever took out his rage on his wife, Mary, for developing a life outside their home, in a series of short stories, such as "The Geometry of Love," in which a husband dies of his wife's selfishness, and how she paid him back, addressing him as "Gorgon I" in her poems in *The Need for Chocolate*. How Ford Madox Ford took his revenge on Violet Hunt after the collapse of their relationship in *nine* of his novels, most dramatically in *Parade's End*, where she appears as Sylvia, the manipulative wife of Christopher Tietjens. How Jean Rhys vented *her* rage at Ford in her novel *Quartet* for what she believed was his victimization of her when she went to him for help after her husband had been jailed. How Ernest Hemingway skewered Sherwood Anderson and other friends in *Torrents of Spring*, motivated, in part, by a desire for revenge for perceived slights. How Hemingway savaged his friend Harold Loeb via the character Robert Cohn in *The Sun Also Rises*. The portrayal so infuriated Loeb that some said he carried a loaded gun and was looking to murder Hemingway; rumors began to circulate in Montparnasse after its publication that Hemingway's friends would get *their* revenge by writing a novel called *Six Characters in Search of an Author—with a Gun Apiece*.

Otto Rank told his patient Anaïs Nin: "Revenge is necessary. To reestablish equilibrium in the emotional life." He was urging Nin to break with her father, and to get back at him for abandoning his family, for his physical abuse and ridicule of her. Instead of confronting him directly, as Rank had urged, she took a different tack. She retaliated against him in her art: "I never go to the very end of my experiences," she wrote into her diary. "I stop somewhere to write the novel. The novel is the *aboutissement*. I did not go to the very end with my father, in an experience of destructive hatred and antagonism. I created a reconciliation and I am writing a novel of hatred." The story of her "reconciliation," an incestuous love affair, has been disclosed in a recently published volume of her diary, *Incest*. Nin saw her novel *Winter of Artifice* as her retribution against her father, "thought out, instead of wreaked upon others."

* * *

Conceived with Malice: Literature as Revenge explores in depth four literary figures working in England and the United States in the twentieth century who used the writing of a work of literature as a weapon of revenge. I describe Leonard Woolf writing about his wife, Virginia, in *The Wise Virgins* (1914), shortly after their marriage; D. H. Lawrence writing about his friend Ottoline Morrell in *Women in Love* (1916); Djuna Barnes writing about her family in *The Antiphon* (1937 to 1958); and Henry Miller writing about his wife, June Miller, in *Crazy Cock,* a work never published in his lifetime that was the prototype for his life's work about her.

I have chosen to concentrate upon the writing of a single work—I do not describe every work of revenge written by every writer I study: a whole book, for example, could be devoted to D. H. Lawrence's and Djuna Barnes's vindictive use of the novel. I have told the story of each writer's life before the writing of the work, each one's relationship with his/her target, the creation of each work, and its consequences, in some detail, to illustrate the complexity of the phenomenon of retaliation through writing. I do not mean to suggest that revenge is the only motive for creating a work of art, but I do believe it is a far more common motive than we think.

I have taken my title, *Conceived with Malice,* from Anthony West, son of Rebecca West and H. G. Wells, who said he was "conceived with malice," that his mother became pregnant with him to solidify her relationship with Wells. Anthony West himself, of course, wrote a well-known example of revenge literature, his novel *Heritage,* which savagely attacked his mother and described the private hell he had lived through as her child. "Conceived with malice" aptly describes the motive for the writing of the works discussed here. As John Gardner said, "Good fiction has come from the writer's wish to be loved, his wish to take revenge, his wish to work out his psychological woes, his wish for money and so on. No motive is too low for art."

When I told people about my interest in writing about literature as revenge, they invariably responded that it was a "great idea," and that it sounded like fun. Almost everyone smiled or laughed at the thought. When I gave a public lecture on Virginia Woolf, and the person introducing me mentioned that I was currently working on revenge, very often the whole audience would laugh. I, too, at first naively thought that working on revenge would be a change from the pain of working on incest, neglect, and emotional and physical abuse in Virginia Woolf's family.

It took me some time to realize that although the idea of revenge may be satisfying and may prompt laughter, there is nothing funny about it. The laughter I was hearing, I came to understand, was more the laughter of tension and emotional release than the laughter of joy. Although thinking about revenge may be pleasant, enacting a revenge fantasy can shatter lives. Researching and writing about revenge was going to be painful. Not as painful, surely, as incest. But painful in its own way and for many of the same reasons.

Incest is a terrible betrayal, with devastating and long-lasting consequences. Happily, current therapies and support groups are helping survivors of incest deal with its impact. Revenge, too, always involves betrayal. There is always a victim. It always involves shattered hopes, and pain. Sometimes that pain has its roots in a childhood of sexual or emotional abuse and suffering, as the lives of the writers I take up in this volume show. In reading and writing about revenge, I found myself entering much the same emotional terrain I had explored in my book on Woolf and incest.

The pain inflicted by the written word can be devastating. A graphic illustration is the "gruesome suicide" of the poet John Holmes's first wife. Despondent, she arranged the manuscripts of his poems—writings that had hurt her—on his desk, slashed her wrists, and bled to death all over his work.

But the pain that triggers a revenge piece is often unbearable. Anaïs Nin put it this way: "The writer is the duelist who never fights at the stated hour, who gathers up an insult, like another curious object, a collector's item, spreads it out on his desk later, and then engages in a duel with it verbally. Some people call it weakness. I call it postponement. . . . For he preserves, collects what will explode later in his work."

She should have known. She was in the midst of a tempestuous love affair with Henry Miller and knew that his writing "issued from [the] violence" he wanted to unleash against his wife, June Miller, for the pain she had inflicted upon him. As Nin put it in her diary, "He talks of beating June, but he would never dare. . . . All his life Henry will assert his manhood by destruction and hatred in his work; each time June appears he will bow his head." Nin herself wanted to harm her rival June, and she did, by writing of her as "Alarune," an "extremely beautiful, but diabolically depraved creature."

The budding novelist Esther Greenwood in Sylvia Plath's *The Bell Jar* says, "I decided I would spend the summer writing a novel. That would fix a lot of people. . . . My heroine would be myself, only in disguise." Plath herself, ever the dutiful, attentive, adoring daughter in her letters home to her mother, Aurelia Plath, "fixes" her mother in *The Bell Jar* even as Esther Greenwood, her fictional analogue, plans to do the same. Plath said nothing to her mother about the autobiographical subject of her novel-in-progress, the tortured period in her life preceding and including her first near-fatal suicide attempt. In a letter to her mother, she only said breezily that she had finished writing *"a batch of stuff."*

That "batch of stuff" exploded with rage against Aurelia. The only response Esther's mother (based on Aurelia) can muster to her daughter's descent into suicidal despair is to try to convince her to do something practical with her life, to study shorthand. One evening her mother drags up an old blackboard from the cellar and scribbles "little curlicues in white chalk," demonstrating her prowess and the pleasures in store for her daughter. Esther attends dutifully, trying to imagine what her life as a shorthand expert will be like, when what she really wants is to be a writer. She tells her mother she has a terrible headache and escapes to sleep. During the night, she hears her mother's snoring—they share a bedroom. She thinks the only way to stop the noise would be "to take the column of skin and sinew from which it rose and twist it to silence between my hands."

Plath published *The Bell Jar* under the pseudonym Victoria Lucas. Nonetheless, the "unrelieved venom" of the portrait of her mother that she left behind in that novel contributed to the pain and confusion Aurelia Plath had to endure after her daughter killed herself.

The character Nora in Djuna Barnes's *Nightwood* observes, with good reason, that "one should be careful into whose mind one gets." Nora, a writer, says that although she wants her faithless lover, Robin Vote, to die, she has conceived an even more powerful reprisal. By writing a novel about Robin, she can instead enact "an eternally recurring murder." Barnes did not intend to immortalize Thelma Wood and others by writing them into her work. Instead, according to her biographer Andrew Field, writing, for Barnes, was "execution without blood."

Djuna Barnes based her character Robin Vote upon Thelma Wood, her lover of eight years. Barnes prowled the bars of Paris in search of Wood, who was forever out cruising. Similarly, Barnes's fictional creation Nora searches for Robin and finds her going from "table to table, from drink to drink, from person to person." Although Wood apologized to Barnes for her "brutishness," for the "rotten time" she had put her through, Barnes retaliated nonetheless. Writing *Nightwood* was her "terrible vengeance." One of her cruelest strokes was portraying Robin/Thelma not as sexual, but as bestial. In the novel's most savage and humiliating moment, Robin/Thelma is bending over, about to be sodomized by a dog.

Thelma Wood found her portrait in Robin Vote "all too accurate," and she went to much trouble to keep her friends from reading the novel. When Barnes first read her excerpts from the nearly finished manuscript, Wood became so angry she hurled a teacup at Barnes and punched her in the mouth. Wood waited patiently for forgiveness from Barnes for mistreating her. It was not forthcoming. Writing the novel exorcised Wood's demon: "the revenge of *Nightwood* freed her surprisingly quickly from her lover."

Why artists use their art as weapons of retaliation is understandable only in the context of the writer's life, of that complex constellation of wishes, dreams, needs, and desires that provides the motivation to undertake a work of art. Nonetheless, a need to take revenge always entails profound, if unacknowledged and unexamined, feelings of loss, powerlessness, helplessness, hopelessness, and betrayal. These feelings may be engendered by present relationships, but they often have their roots in infancy and childhood.

In Elizabethan life, revenge was a serious issue. Elizabethan thinkers rigorously analyzed the feelings provoking it; their findings are worth noting even today. Each work taken up in this volume was provoked by one or more of the motives set forth in Elizabethan treatises on revenge. One such feeling was an admixture of anger and pain stemming from personal wrongs; taking revenge was thought to dissipate this anger. Jealousy was an extremely dangerous feeling precipitating revenge, for it could easily turn into hatred, then into frenzy, and finally into madness; in a state of extreme jealousy, a person can commit acts "beyond all common sense and reason"; revenge, so motivated, was usually self-destructive. Pride and ambition often figured in acts of revenge and finally envy—the envious person could inflict harm even without provocation, for the motive was internal, and it always involved an innocent victim.

Taking revenge entails a need to take action, which will restore our sense that we are agents, and not just passive victims. Writing a revenge piece engages the writer in an activity that is complex, so that involvement in the intricacies of the work diminishes the effect of negative feelings. Yet writers who compulsively settle scores through their works—D. H. Lawrence, Ford Madox Ford, John Cheever, Jean Rhys, Ernest Hemingway, Anaïs Nin—seem far more miserable and unhappy than other writers. Writing out a revenge fantasy often exacerbates rather than quells rage: "venting anger often makes us feel angrier."

There is often very little recognition that the emotional satisfaction derived from writing the work might be only temporary, that the feelings of powerlessness and loss that prompted the work might return once it is completed. The writer often fantasizes that the victim will be so completely disabled that s/he won't seek retribution, thus demonstrating an unwillingness to understand the ramifications of becoming engaged in a vendetta.

A revenge piece is always act of aggression for the artist. Revenge is a specialized form of aggressive behavior, activated by an overt threat, but also by "fear, frustration, and deprivation." The writing of a revenge piece is a way to regain something of the self that has been lost. This is accomplished by attacking the person who has frustrated the artist or deprived her/him of something that s/he wanted. Aggression can be positive. It can operate in the interests of self-preservation, which "demands . . . the potential for aggressive action, since the natural world is a place in which hostile threats must be overcome or evaded if life is to continue." As Henry Miller put it, "The writing may have seemed monstrous (to some) for it was a violation, but I became a more human individual because of it. I was getting the poison out of my system." Physiological changes which accompany aggression release an "invigorating sense of purpose" and well-being. As the fiction of D. H. Lawrence illustrates, opponents may be sought out for the express purpose of releasing these enjoyable feelings; throughout his life, "Lawrence eventually used most of his friends as models for characters in his fiction," settling old scores in one work after another.

Aggressive acts often establish separation and independence and routinely occur among people in close relationships. Closeness involves dependence, which, in turn, evokes feelings of vulnerability. Aggression often acts as a way to assert autonomy in a relationship that feels too close, and it sometimes flares up without warning and seemingly without provocation, as with Plath's fantasy of strangling her mother in *The Bell Jar*. Here, as in other cases, the revenge piece might be a way of asserting autonomy.

When erotic relationships or close friendships sour, passionate love makes "passionate hostility" a real possibility. Because love is an important source of self-esteem, the failure of a relationship can be felt as an "attack upon the self." The hatred felt for a former love is "self-preservative," an assertive rather than a depressive response to an attack against one's integrity. The more dependent a person is upon the love of another, the more threatened, and therefore hostile and aggressive, the person will become if love is withdrawn. When the spurned lover begins writing a revenge piece, s/he is repairing the damage done to the psyche, as much as retaliating against the lost lover—this was true of Ford Madox Ford and of Djuna Barnes. If both parties in a relationship are writers, the termination of a relationship often results in a volley of revenge pieces: after the collapse of Jean Rhys's marriage to Jean Lenglet, she wrote *Quartet* and he wrote *Barred*.

Just as in the animal kingdom, where there is often a substitution of threat and display for actual combat, so it is with artists. Artists and writers are no more or less capable of murderous feelings than the rest of humankind. Nor are they exempt from overt acts of violence: witness Pablo Picasso's repeatedly knocking his teenage lover Marie-Thérèse Walter into a state of unconsciousness; Jean Rhys's assault on her neighbor, which landed her in Holloway Prison; Samuel Johnson's notorious brawls, including his beating the bookseller Tom Osborne, "using as the weapon his own famous—and hefty—dictionary"; Norman Mailer's stabbing of his wife, Adele, after a party in their Manhattan apartment.

Nonetheless, as I have looked at the lives of many writers and artists, I have noticed how often descriptions of murderous or suicidal feelings have preceded the creation of a work of art. Anne

Sexton put it this way: "I'd rather be doing something productive [writing poetry] than sitting around thinking about killing myself—or killing myself." Sometimes, the creation of a retaliatory work seems to substitute for a more overt act of violence or self-destruction. My chapter on Henry Miller, "A Desperado of Love," will examine this issue in detail, but here one example will illustrate.

When Lee Miller threatened to leave the surrealist painter and photographer Man Ray for the man she eventually married, Ray threatened her life and told some people that he had a pistol he might use to kill her. There is no doubt that he considered murder. But he was also suicidal. He and another photographer, also abandoned by a lover, assumed and photographed many suicidal poses. This was not just a charade. At one point, Ray held a gun to his head; his friend did not know whether it was loaded. The moment passed, and he did not take his life.

Instead, not too long after, when he realized that Lee Miller would not come back to him, Man Ray began "defacing drawings of her image with erratic scrawls and scribbles. He retreated into 'breaking her up' by fragmenting the visual representation of her body. Her eye was a favorite target."

In *This Quartet*, Man Ray published an important image of his career that was an outgrowth of his defacing Lee Miller. It was "a drawing of a metronome with a cutout photograph of Lee's eye clipped to the stem. The instructions in the caption to the drawing, called *Object of Destruction*, ... told the whole story: 'Cut out the eye from a photograph of one who has been loved but is seen no more. ... Attach the eye to the pendulum of a metronome and regulate the weight to suit the tempo desired. ... Keep doing to the limit of endurance. ... With a hammer well-aimed, try to destroy the whole at a single blow.' "

In this way, Man Ray channeled all the self-hate, self-loathing, powerlessness, and despair that might have culminated in his suicide, and all the violence he felt toward Lee Miller that might have resulted in his murder of her, into a work of art. It became one of his major works and one of the most important icons of the surrealist movement.

Writing a work of literature motivated by revenge always has consequences, both for the writer and for the subject, that can be extraordinarily severe, even if the writer has not anticipated them. Saying that a work of art can have adverse consequences is different from arguing that it should be suppressed. Writers are, of course, free to write what they choose, within the limits of law, despite the consequences. Writers, however, very often know exactly what they're about, and what they're about is often none too pleasant.

Because it can be read by many people, the novel is a public form of humiliation that can provoke profound shame. The work of art, composed in private, can ruin reputations when it becomes a public document, if enough of its readers know the story behind the story.

As these narratives will illustrate, people who have become victims of their friends' or lovers' works of art often become depressed, disorganized, and disoriented, just as if they were the victims of physical abuse; they often feel violated; they often undergo something like post-traumatic stress disorder, although they may not fully recognize the extent of their trauma. A revenge piece seems to function as a special form of assault, somewhere between verbal abuse and physical violence.

Contemporary libel laws might seem to offer some measure of protection for the subjects of writers out to even a score. Occasionally, works such as D. H. Lawrence's *Women in Love* have been suppressed or held up by threats or fear of prosecution. This is not a deterrent to most writers. And sometimes, even if a libel suit *is* threatened, the victim has read drafts of the novel or advance copies, and psychic damage has already been done.

Sometimes victims of revenge pieces take no action in retaliation. Turgenev, the butt of Dostoyevsky's pen, never fought back. He just wrote Dostoyevsky, "You have hurt me more deeply than anyone," and pleaded with him to "forget my existence," to spare him further abuse. But people who are attacked in works of art very often fight back: Colley Cibber and Alexander Pope spent the better part of their careers savaging one another in print; the battle culminated in Pope's *The New Dunciad*, a "concentrated assault on Cibber's intelligence"—"Nonsense precipitate, like running lead," Pope wrote of his longtime enemy, "slipp'd thro' cracks and zigzags of the head."

* * *

The massive, ongoing study of creativity by Albert Rothenberg, M.D., is extraordinarily valuable in understanding revenge as a motive in the creation of art. His work shows that the creation of art is more often than not the product of *conscious* thought. His recent *Creativity and Madness* concludes that jealousy, hatred, and revenge often decide the theme and content of a work of art. Artists' desires to "hurt, maim, humiliate, even to annihilate other persons often provide fuel for the creative process." The process that structures these concerns into great art is healthy, not pathological. And the creative person is fully aware of what s/he is doing. The subject does not spring from the unconscious, but from a logical and detailed chain of thought. Personal conflict—recognizing and working through destructive feelings—is an important motivating factor in the making of a work of art.

Writing the work sometimes frees the writer from overwhelming negative feelings, from a painful psychological past, although this is not always the case. Writing the work also enables the writer to attain insight and to acquire wisdom. Dealing with personal material can cause anxiety, but it usually dissipates when the work is completed.

Sigmund Freud believed that the writer creates a work of art to alter, or to substitute through fantasy the dissatisfactions of the real world. The work of art occurs because the writer is either unhappy or dissatisfied. Though it has its origins in the writer's life, the work is also an escapist or corrective fantasy. It compensates for something missing in the writer's life.

An assumption underlying Freud's view of art is that the real world should provide all the satisfaction a person requires. Having fantasies or creating a work of art is an indication that a person's life is unsatisfactory: dissatisfaction is necessary for the creation of art. The better adjusted, the more mature, the less infantile the person, the less s/he will need to create. In Freud's view, the writing of a revenge piece would be seen as an infantile, regressive, escapist way of dealing with a failure in the writer's life. The work of art substitutes for an inadequacy in the writer's life; the work substitutes for an interaction the writer cannot or will not undertake in life.

Freud also believed that the real hero of every daydream and every story created by a writer is the invulnerable hero, or "His Majesty the Ego." Creative writing originates in the writer's need to be invulnerable and invincible. Writing, then, "fixes" the ego. It corrects an attack the ego has endured; it heals an injury the ego has sustained. In their work, then, writers fulfill their wish for invincibility. Too easily affected by what has occurred in their lives, they write fantasies that correct wrongs they have endured. They express them in works of art rather than more directly, Freud believed, because they are ashamed of them.

The writer creates characters by separating the conflicting parts of the ego. Each character in a novel personifies "conflicting currents of his own mental life." In creating characters, the writer gives shape to the conflicting aspects of her/his inner being so that they can be examined. In this way, the turmoil in the writer's life can be understood.

That internal turmoil, although stimulated by something that occurs in the present, is inevitably, for Freud, linked to something that occurred in childhood: "A strong experience in the present awakens in the creative writer a memory of an earlier experience (usually belonging to his childhood) from which there now proceeds a wish that finds its fulfillment in the creative work. The work itself exhibits elements of the recent provoking occasion as well as of the old memory."

And what of the reader? Why would a reader find pleasure in reading a work like *Tropic of Cancer* by Henry Miller, filled as it is with rage and vindictiveness? One component of our satisfaction comes from recognizing the "purely formal" aspects of the work of art, its order and internal logic. Our deeper pleasure, though, comes from "a liberation of tensions" resulting from the reader's recognition that the writer shares the same feelings as the reader. The reader, then, will be less likely to feel "self-reproach or shame" concerning these feelings. In reading a revenge piece, then, the reader discovers that others share his/her most carefully concealed wishes.

In his monumental work *The Act of Creation*, Arthur Koestler stated that the creative act is compelled by deeply felt aggressive and empathic needs. On the one hand, through humor, satire, and exaggeration, we can ridicule an enemy and vent our aggression. Paradoxically, the act of creation forces us to step into our enemies' shoes, reversing roles with them even as we criticize them. Through the act of creation, we try to understand what has impelled them to hurt us, even if we ultimately reject what we discover, and sometimes, in the writing, we discover that we, too, have harmed them. Through the act of re-creating them on the page, we become reunited with them, giving us back what we have lost, while simultaneously we push them away, often for what seems to be our own good.

Our act of creation transfers our attention away from ourselves and our present pain to another time, another place. This is an act of "self-transcendence." The work performs a cathartic function, similar to a rite of purification. Writing becomes a regenerative or self-healing process: the traumatized psyche heals itself through making art. Henry Miller phrased it this way: writing "is almost like the sewing up of a wound."

Writing releases rage less harmfully than if it had been more overtly expressed. In the process, the writer comes to accept the pain of the loss, rather than denying or escaping from it. Organizing and expressing experience prompts a feeling of mastery, supplanting a feeling of victimization. The artist, strengthened through pain, achieves insight as a concomitant to healing.

The creation of art possesses dramatic curative possibilities. Anthony Storr observed that if Ludwig van Beethoven had been unable to sublimate his hostility into the creation of music, he "might have succumbed to a paranoid psychosis." This is true, as well, for some writers.

One should not, however, inflate the positive effects to be derived from pursuing creative work. Writing about pain is painful. Henry Miller once admitted that by writing, "All I accomplished was to reopen the wound that had been inflicted upon me. The wound still lives, and with the pain of it comes the remembrance of what I was." There are cases of "mental illness actually intensifying subsequent to a creative accomplishment."

Sir Francis Bacon, in his famous essay "Of Revenge," wrote that he believed revenge is a "wild" form of justice that must be eradicated if civilization is to survive. Even if the impulse to take vengeance for wrongs committed against us is natural, it will be far better for our own sake, and for that of society, if we do not. If we take revenge, one evil simply begets another. The cycle of wrongdoing is not arrested but continues unabated. If we eschew revenge, we become the moral superior of our enemies.

It is far better for our psychic well-being if we do not take revenge. One of Bacon's most compelling observations is that a person who needs to get even is a person preoccupied with the past. Because revenge commits us to looking backward rather than ahead, our lives will, necessarily, turn out to be "unfortunate."

For Bacon, this is revenge's greatest danger. Revenge mires us in the past. Being preoccupied with old wrongs prevents us from paying attention to the present, erodes our capacity for pleasure, and forestalls our ability to grow beyond our pain into a future bright with possibility. Revenge, even as it tries to right a wrong, even as it tries to effect change, has as its psychic concomitants hopelessness and despair.

Revenge does not allow us to grow beyond the boundaries of what we have experienced before. It locks us into a continuing relationship with those who have wronged us, when it would be far better, and wiser, for us to let go, to move on. For if they have wronged us once, they will probably wrong us again. And if they have acted against us, perhaps without our provocation or awareness, what will they do to us once we have acted against them?

Revenge ensures that old wounds will not heal, and that new hurts will be added to old ones. In Bacon's words, "a man that studieth revenge keeps his old wounds green, which otherwise would heal and do well." Revenge, for Bacon, is a disguised form of self-abuse.

Yet Thomas Moore's important work *Care of the Soul* suggests that, for all its seeming perversity, writing a work of revenge might be a very important way for writers to care for themselves and, in the process, to become more soulful. Instead of trying to obliterate their feelings of rage, instead of hiding from them or pretending they weren't there, the writers I discuss here took time to nurture their vengeful impulses and fantasies, to stare them down, and to write them out. In doing so, I believe, it became possible for them to grow beyond their pain—perhaps to develop a sense of guilt that, in turn, led to the development of a generosity of spirit formerly lacking; to a temporary truce with rage and violence; to self-understanding or self-acceptance; to serenity; to wisdom. As Moore has said, "It is not easy to visit the place in ourselves that is most challenging and to look straight into the image that gives us the most fright; yet, there, where the work is most intense, is the source of the soul."

Taking revenge through writing a work of literature occurs when reconciliation seems impossible, when more direct forms of communication break down, when a wrongdoer refuses to accept responsibility for hurtful behavior, when a more direct form of re-dress cannot be negotiated, when amends cannot be made. Taking revenge through writing fiction occurs when a writer's present circumstances trigger memories associated with unresolved problems from the past. The person who becomes the object of the artist's rage often becomes the unwitting substitute for a rage that is infantile and, therefore, not easily amenable to resolution. Taking revenge through writing occurs when the writer's ability to control rage becomes impossible, when forgiveness and indifference are no longer options.

2

"THAT STRANGE PRELUDE":

Leonard Woolf, Virginia Woolf, and *The Wise Virgins*

When I contemplate the jungle of human relations, I feel that here are savageries and hatreds— ... which make the tiger and the viper seem gentle, charitable, tender-hearted.

—LEONARD WOOLF
Sowing

Saragossa, Spain
September 4, 1912

Leonard Woolf sat in a red plush chair, across from his wife, Virginia Woolf. Leonard was writing a novel. They were on their honeymoon. They had been married for less than a month, and they were making their way across Europe slowly, heading toward Venice. They were spending a few nights in each of their many stopovers along the way—Avignon, Barcelona, Madrid, Toledo, Valencia, Marseilles, Pisa—traveling by train and by cargo boat.

During the morning hours, they wandered through back streets. In the afternoons, they wrote and read. This was his second novel; he had completed his first, *The Village in the Jungle*, before their departure. She had finished a version of her first novel, *The Voyage Out*. Unwilling or unable to create a new work while leading such an unsettled life, she spent her writing time on letters to friends, describing their meanderings and the progress of her and Leonard's sexual relationship. During the long, hot afternoons in Spain, while her husband wrote fiction, she spent time reading "with fury" one hefty volume after another—Dostoyevsky's *Crime and Punishment*, Scott's *The Antiquary*, Lawrence's *The Trespassers*, Young's *Yonder*, Yonge's *The Heir of Redcliffe*.

After dinner, until eleven or so, they sat in cafés, engaged in exciting conversation. After that, there was "the proper business of bed." It had, more than once, been interrupted by swarms of mosquitoes. It had not yet been an unqualified success. The pleasures to be derived from the orgasm, Virginia Woolf had already concluded by the third week of her marriage, were "immensely exaggerated," suggesting she had not yet had that experience. Yes, she had lost her virginity, but she believed that people made too much of a "fuss" about the whole business of "marriage and copulation." It was her advanced age (she was thirty), possibly, that made it less of a "catastrophe" for her than it was for younger women. If it had not been for the patience and good cheer of her husband in putting up with her anger at the whole business, she believed that their marriage might never have been consummated at all, and she might very well have remained Miss Virginia Stephen instead of becoming Mrs. Leonard Woolf.

Leonard, apparently, had told her that he was writing a novel about the suburbs, a social satire about Putney, where he grew up. He had moved there with his mother and eight siblings after his father's death had drastically reduced his family's economic circumstances. Although his novel did contain a fictional portrait of the suburban environment in which he had grown up, what Virginia Woolf did not yet know, what she would find out in time, was that the novel that her husband was writing during their long, hot honeymoon afternoons also contained a vicious fictional portrait of her.

Trinity College, Cambridge
1900–1901

The first time Leonard Woolf was introduced to Virginia Stephen was at a tea party when she was eighteen or nineteen years old. It was a summer's day, and she had come up to Trinity College, Cambridge, with her sister, Vanessa, to visit their brother Thoby. The Stephen sisters were wearing white dresses and large hats, and they were carrying parasols. They were so astonishingly beautiful that they took his breath away. Coming upon them together in his friend Thoby's rooms had the same shocking effect, Leonard thought, as coming face to face with a great painting—Rembrandt's portrait of his wife or a Velázquez portrait of an infanta. It would have been impossible "for a man not to fall in love with them." And so he fell in love, at once, with both of them.

Leonard might have caught a glimpse of the Stephen sisters the year before when they had come up to Cambridge for May Week. The dance had been something of a disappointment. The Stephen sisters had arrived late at the Trinity Ball, the largest ball of the springtime festivities. Everyone's dance card was already filled, and their brother Thoby didn't know very many people, so they didn't dance very much, although he did introduce them to one of his good friends, Clive Bell. The spectacle of Bell walking through Great Court "in full hunting-rig" complete with a hunting-horn had attracted considerable attention at Cambridge. His posture as a country gentleman concealed his passion for literature and his fine mind. Meeting Clive Bell proved to be important, for in 1907, after Thoby's death from typhoid fever, Vanessa married him.

After a time, Virginia found a kind of platform to sit on, which allowed her to look out over the dancers and to watch their movements "without being disturbed." Awkward and graceless in social situations, she was much happier observing rather than participating in such proceedings. She and Vanessa usually came into a room, exchanged a few pleasantries, and then sat in a corner, looking "like mutes who are longing for a funeral."

These dances had very little meaning for her. She did not want to marry, though she suspected that in time she might have to. She wanted to "found a colony where there shall be no marrying," where there would be "nothing but ideal peace and endless meditation." There were, Virginia believed, far more important things than social success. Like music and books. Like Latin and Greek, which she had discussed with Charles Eliot Norton, professor of the history of art at Harvard. Like seeing the words forming as she pushed her pen across the pages of her journals, describing a sunset or a summer holiday or a fantasy of herself as a Norseman whose boat had become frozen in polar ice.

Leonard Woolf spent no time alone with the Stephen sisters at their first meeting. They were the "most Victorian of Victorian young ladies." In 1900 or 1901, it was improper for them to be alone with a man, even to visit their brother in his rooms unaccompanied. According to the mores of the time, their reputation and chastity had to be protected. Their chaperone was their cousin, the eminent Miss Katherine Stephen, principal of Newnham College. Ironically, each Stephen sister had been sexually molested by their half brothers, George and Gerald Duckworth, Virginia beginning when she was six years old. Their half brothers' continuing "male-factions," as Virginia called them, had not ended even as the Stephen sisters sat in their white dresses at Cambridge, chaperoned by their cousin.

Leonard Woolf was uncomfortable in the presence of young women. Like his friend Lytton Strachey, he thought it "one of the best facts in modern English life" that there were "no women" at Cambridge. He and Strachey shared an Aristotelian friendship. And he harbored an extremely strong affection for Thoby Stephen. He thought women a different, inferior species, incapable of thought.

Virginia believed she was more "susceptible to female charms" than to those of men; so, too, did Leonard Woolf prefer the company of men to that of women. Walking late at night in spring through the Cloisters of Nevile's Court in Trinity College with Thoby Stephen, Lytton Strachey, and Clive Bell was a high point in his life at Cambridge. On that night, with his friends, he saw the willows and the River Cam washed with moonlight, listened to the nightingales, and chanted Swinburne's poetry as they walked along: "We have drunk of things Lethean, and fed on the fulness of death."

Leonard was nervous in the presence of the Stephens. When he was nervous he trembled so violently that he couldn't bring a cup of tea up to his mouth without spilling the tea all over himself, without the cup rattling so noisily that everyone in the room could hear. Whatever opinion the principal of Newnham College expressed, she uttered as if it were "one of the Ten Commandments." It was a "sticky social situation," this meeting with the Stephen sisters and their chaperone, yet not one of the Stephens made an effort to put Leonard at his ease. The young people sat and said nothing to one another. So Leonard did not, at this time, tell Virginia or her sister, Vanessa, of his love of reading, which equaled hers, of his admiration for *War and Peace*, *The Brothers Karamazov*, *Madame Bovary*, and *Hedda Gabler*, or that he made a habit of reading 120 books a year. Or of his wish to write "the great poem" that still "fluttered helplessly" at the back of his mind, or "the great novel rumbling hopelessly in some strange depths" inside him.

Never sure of himself under ordinary circumstances, Leonard, surrounded by four members of an important family of England's intellectual aristocracy, was at a complete loss. He had already made the personal contacts that led to his election in 1902 to the elitist secret society the Cambridge Apostles, but he still believed he was an outsider. He was a scholarship boy, descended from merchants and tailors. His father had elevated their social status considerably by becoming a barrister, but from the time of his father's death, when Leonard was eleven, his family had been poor. He was both proud and ashamed of being a Jew. (We can be sure that Virginia Stephen never, during tea, expressed her belief that Jews were "repulsive objects.")

In the long and awkward silences between the principal's pronouncements, Leonard Woolf intently studied the demeanor of the Stephen sisters. Although they appeared demure, he wasn't fooled. They reminded him of the most dangerous kind of horse: the kind that appears to be friendly, but that has a look in its eye warning you "to be very, very careful." It was a look of "great intelligence, hypercritical, sarcastic, satirical."

Given his insecurities, it is no wonder that the Stephen family appeared "formidable, and even alarming." Virginia Stephen herself believed that any ordinary person would be "ground to a pulp" after just a week with the Stephens.

Leonard had already met Sir Leslie Stephen, the aged patriarch of the family, when Sir Leslie came up to Cambridge to see his son Thoby. He was a widower, a distinguished biographer, historian, literary critic, and editor of the *Dictionary of National Biography*. Leonard thought him less alarming than his daughters, a beautiful old gentleman, "of exquisite gentility and physical and mental distinction." On his face, all the sorrows of the world were etched in "indelible lines of suffering nobility."

Leonard and Sir Leslie had a great deal in common, and it is no wonder that Leonard found him so appealing. Leonard's strong resemblance to her father was a primary reason that Virginia would find Leonard worth marrying, though she would remain largely unaware of their fundamental similarity. Both were intractable and strong-minded; they worshipped "reason"; they had violent tempers; they suffered no fools; they were impolite and self-centered and found it impossible to apologize, even to imagine that their actions had caused pain. Though on the surface they might seem self-possessed, both harbored feelings of anxiety, helplessness, failure; they viewed the world with a sense of "profound, passive, cosmic despair." There was a major difference between them: in troubled times, Leslie Stephen demanded comfort and care from the women in his life, while Leonard Woolf retreated into himself, behind a "carapace," for self-protection.

Virginia Stephen had heard stories about Leonard Woolf from her brother Thoby even before she met him. After Thoby went up to Cambridge, he regaled his sisters for hours on holidays with stories of the "amazing character and exploits" of his closest friends. On long walks through the moors, or sitting by an open fire in Virginia's bedroom, Thoby would portray them as mythic, heroic, godlike creatures, or the greatest of poets.

The exploits of these fantastic creatures her brother knew fascinated Virginia, still living the carefully circumscribed life of a Victorian young lady, confined to her household except when in the company of a chaperone. Lytton Strachey, "the essence of culture." Clive Bell, "a perfect horseman." Saxon Sydney-Turner, a "prodigy of learning." She asked "endless questions" about them. She gave them characters. She made up stories about them and they became as much inhabitants of her very active imagination as they were her brother's friends.

One day, Thoby had told her about Leonard Woolf, an "astonishing fellow, who trembled perpetually all over." When Virginia asked her brother why Leonard trembled, Thoby replied that it was "part of his nature." He was "so violent, so savage." He "despised the whole human race."

46 Gordon Square, Bloomsbury
November 17, 1904

The second time Leonard Woolf saw Vanessa and Virginia Stephen was the evening of November 17, 1904, the day before he set sail for Ceylon for a six-and-a-half-year stint in the civil service. The Stephens were giving him an intimate farewell dinner. He was the first of Thoby's inner circle of Cambridge friends to take on the mantle of adult responsibility by becoming a wage-earner, the first to leave England. The Stephens solemnized this significant moment by a formal leavetaking in their new home.

The dinner took place at 46 Gordon Square, in Bloomsbury, to which the Stephens—Virginia, Vanessa, Thoby, and Adrian—had moved just a month before, after the death of Sir Leslie Stephen. There is no record of what transpired between Leonard and the Stephens, of what he said to Virginia or Vanessa as they saw him to the door, into the square. With "the lamps lit and the light on the green," Virginia believed the square "a romantic place." But we know that he was far more interested in Vanessa than in Virginia. He thought her the more sensitive, serene, beautiful, womanly of the two; to him, she had "something of the splendour of Aphrodite, but also Athene and Artemis" about her. He was sustained by her memory during his first months in Ceylon.

Before Leonard departed for Ceylon, Thoby told Virginia about a dream of Leonard's. In the dream, Leonard was "throttling a man." The dream was so real, and so violent, that when Leonard awakened, he realized that he had "pulled his own thumb out of joint." Virginia was "inspired with the deepest interest in that violent trembling misanthropic Jew who . . . was about to disappear into the tropics."

We do not have a record of their conversation, but we know that in this household, the Stephens tried something new, something radical: a commingling of the sexes. This dinner for Leonard was a precursor of the future. They were living in the "springtime of a conscious revolt" against everything their parents had held sacred; they were the vanguard of a "new society which should be free, rational, civilized, pursuing truth and beauty." These two young women were "less constrained in their thinking processes" and had "quite different points of view" about "Truth, Beauty, Goodness" than the doctrinaire Cambridge beliefs of these self-assured, pompous young men. Virginia and Vanessa were not required to engage in polite social conversation; the Cambridge set, committed to honesty in interpersonal encounters, were overt, blunt, and even cruel in stating their opinions. Sitting over cocoa and biscuits after dinner, with Virginia joining the men in puffing on a pipe, they might fall into silence and say nothing at all.

Through his years in Ceylon, Leonard would receive spirited reports about the lives and loves of the Stephen sisters from his good friend and principal correspondent, Lytton Strachey. As the years passed, the image of this London drawing room would fade. Leonard would wonder whether he would ever return to London. If he did, he wondered whether he could ever reestablish the passionate friendships of his Cambridge years, and whether he would be welcomed back into convivial drawing rooms like the one at 46 Gordon Square. His years in Ceylon would change him utterly; they would change his views about work, society, colonialism. About women and sex, his attitude remained the same: any relationship with a woman that involved carnality "absolutely degraded" him.

To Virginia, the house at Gordon Square was "the most beautiful, the most exciting, the most romantic place in the world." Unlike the darkness, dankness, and red-plush-and-black-paint gloom of the Stephen home at 22 Hyde Park Gate, the house at Gordon Square was light, airy, and filled with white and green chintz.

It was possible to stand at the drawing room window and look down into the tops of the trees in the peaceful square. Vanessa, who supervised every detail of the decorating, had the walls distempered, left the windows unadorned to let the sunlight into the high-ceilinged rooms, and decorated sparely so that the beauty of the precious family possessions she had salvaged—paintings by Watts, Dutch cabinets, blue willow-patterned china, Indian shawls—would not be lost amid too much clutter.

It was essential for Virginia to have privacy, and this the house at Gordon Square provided. She had important work to do. She believed that "self respect & purity" came from work and that it was a "blessed peace" that "deadens sorrow."

Until this time, the most important person in her life, outside her family, was Violet Dickinson. Violet was born in 1865, the daughter of a Somersetshire squire, and she lived much of her adult life at Welwyn with her brother Oswald. Virginia and she had been intimate friends since the summer of 1902, when Violet joined the Stephens on their holiday. Virginia wrote Violet impassioned, teasing, playful letters, reminding Violet of "a long embrace, in a bedroom," telling her she had stirred up "hot volcano depths" in Virginia, demanding of Violet all manner of sensual stimulation—pettings, strokings, lickings—and promising the same.

Violet had given her an inkpot for a gift, and she intended to use it. Frederic Maitland, who was writing a life of Sir Leslie Stephen, invited Virginia to contribute a note to his volume. More exciting still, Violet had contacted Margaret Lyttleton, editor of the Women's Supplement to *The Guardian*, on Virginia's behalf. Lyttleton commissioned Virginia's first book reviews and an essay on her visit to the Brontë parsonage in Haworth; they were published by the end of the year. And so Virginia Stephen, aged twenty-two, began to earn her living by her pen. She needed to supplement her income; she had overdrawn her passbook in paying her doctor bills. Her career had begun in earnest.

Each sister, for the first time, had not only one room of her own, but several. A private sitting room. A huge drawing room. A studio for Vanessa to paint in. A study for Virginia to write in. "I wish you could see my room," Virginia wrote to Madge Vaughan, "—all my beloved leather backed books standing up so handsome in their shelves, and a nice fire, . . . and a huge mass of manuscripts and letters and proof-sheets and pens and inks over the floor." For now the Stephen sisters had control of how they would spend their time. Each moment, to Virginia, was "an exquisite joy."

She wanted a "good large ambitious subject" to work on for the next ten years. Though she thought she might become a historian, she found her project in the writing of a novel.

She began to write fiction, at first tentatively. Walking the downs at the edge of the sea at Manorbier in Wales, where she spent time after her father's death, she had conceptualized a novel. She had begun writing it down in a green notebook. It was about marriage, about the several courtships of her fickle character Roger Brickdale. He believes that his charms are irresistible; that whomever he asks to marry him will unquestioningly become his bride. He becomes engaged to Hester Fitzjohn, but her family considers him an objectionable suitor.

Virginia's creation Hester Fitzjohn is an extremely nervous lover, a woman poised to repel the advances of her fiancé. When "he sat close beside her," on a sofa, she "moved to the farthest end . . . 'You must not touch me' she said nervously."

It had been a very difficult year for Virginia, but also a year of hope and change. In the aftermath of her father's death, she had tried to commit suicide by throwing herself from a window. When Leonard came to dinner, she had emerged from the most "wretched 8 months" of her life; the voices urging her to do wild things had quieted. She had begun teaching at Morley College, and knew now that writing was her "natural means of expression."

It had taken Sir Leslie a very long time to die. During those years when he became increasingly enfeebled by cancer, he became less virulent in his rages. Virginia grew increasingly fond of him, so his death was a shattering blow, something for which she felt responsible. She believed she had not done enough for him through the years. She cherished a ring he had given her.

During her father's illness, her half brother George's incestuous attentions continued; after her father's death, she complained that he "never lets one alone a moment." Now that her father was dead, she felt more unprotected than ever in her household, so "tangled and matted with emotion."

Violet Dickinson cared for Virginia during her recuperation. Violet's loving maternal attentions surely saved her life.

Vanessa dismantled the family home at 22 Hyde Park Gate. It had been the site of everything wonderful in Virginia's childhood—the free rein allowed her in her father's library at the top of the house, storytelling sessions under a table with Vanessa. It had also been the site of experiences that scarred her for life—her father's mistreatment of her half sister Laura, who was eventually locked away in a separate part of the household and then put into an asylum; Virginia's incestuous abuse by her half brother George, who would creep into her room late at night and throw himself upon her.

Vanessa, who had borne the brunt of her father's rages, was relieved when he died. At last she could get on with her life, without the responsibility of running her father's household. It was she who arranged for Virginia's care, who put a stop to George's sexual abuse of Virginia by telling a family doctor what had been transpiring. It was she who arranged the move to Bloomsbury. Theirs was to be an unusual household: there would be no chaperones to impede them. Their dour Stephen relatives, and many of their friends from the Hyde Park years, were horrified. Most important, there were no half brothers in residence; they had found accommodation elsewhere.

Leonard Woolf, like Virginia, had been through a very bad time when the two met for the second time in 1904. Taking the post in Ceylon represented the collapse of his hopes and dreams. At Cambridge, secure and sequestered, he and his friends believed they were the "mysterious priests of a new and amazing civilization." His present life, though, was fulfilling none of those hopes and dreams; it was "made up of the pain of desires & the ache of regrets." For a time, he was in such despair that he considered suicide. But he decided against it because he felt himself to be "dead & rotten already."

He was not going to Ceylon by choice, and he was terrified and disappointed by the turn his life had taken. On the eve of his departure, he felt like a small boy, standing on the top of the high diving board, looking down at the water so far below, bracing himself for the plunge. He had hoped for a career as a classicist, one of his life's ambitions. But he had taken only a second in the classical tripos at Cambridge, which foreclosed that possibility. He would have preferred to cast in his "lot with Literature"; he had already published a review of a biography of his beloved Voltaire. His privileged friends could rely on annuities or family support while they took the time to establish themselves as writers, but Leonard had learned that his family's financial situation was far more precarious than he had thought, and that he needed to support himself and to contribute to the running of his mother's household.

Before he decided to go to Ceylon, he had explored other, more attractive alternatives. He was terrified of "rotting" in a colonial outpost; he was afraid that in seven years' time he would become hopelessly out of date. But he had prepared himself inadequately for the rigorous civil service examination. He congratulated himself for his efforts when he put in five hours a day for two days running. In part, it was his arrogance that stood in his way. After all, he was a Cambridge Apostle; he had known the "best & the highest"; he had heard "the music of the spheres." He thought it was impossible for him not to succeed.

He did very poorly on his examination, which meant that he would not be offered a post in the home civil service in England. His poor showing made him question his competence. For a time, he considered becoming a teacher, which would permit him to remain in England. He wondered whether parents would "allow their sons to be taught by Jews." He managed to secure an appointment as an assistant teacher, but decided against it: it seemed a dead-end position, and a humiliating one. His family urged him to take the post in the colonies with its greater pay, and he complied with their wishes. His sister Bella, sensing his bleak spirits, told him not to take the post unless he wanted it. Although money was a problem, she would pay for him if he felt he could throw himself into study for the bar, but he declined her offer.

In the weeks before his departure, he turned to Burton's *Anatomy of Melancholy* for consolation. He took lessons to perfect his horseback riding, shopped for tropical garments, arranged for special passage for his dog Charles, packed his bags. He took along ninety large, beautifully printed volumes of Voltaire—the 1784 edition, in Baskerville type. They were something from home that would sustain his spirits in his new life in the jungle. He bought himself three bright green flannel collars, considered very bad taste in London but thought "dashing" in Ceylon.

Just a short time before, he had been discussing the meaning of beauty, truth, and love with his friends at Cambridge. Now all he could think about was his bottom, which was "raw from riding." He was trying desperately, and without success, to get used to the ludicrous but necessary outfit that he would have to wear in the tropics: "My balls," he wrote to Strachey, "are in a suspensory bandage with four straps round my legs & hips, . . . my belly in a cholera belt."

When he walked up the gangway of the S. S. *Syria* for his voyage out, he was leaving everything and everyone he knew. Watching his ship in the Channel from shore, Strachey believed that "all was lost" now that his friend had "vanished": "the kisses that I never gave you, your embraces that I have never felt, they are all that remain— . . . the external ghosts of our desires and dreams."

Leonard Woolf would celebrate his twenty-fourth birthday at sea. But he felt that he had "already become middle aged."

Jaffna, Ceylon
July 1905

Leonard was lonelier than he had ever been in his life, and steeped in melancholy. The monotony of his life appalled and enraged him. His days were spent signing letters, issuing licenses, "trying and fining miserable wretches, answering petitions," deciding questions about the harvesting of salt and about irrigation, settling family quarrels. It was a land of "blood & mange," a land where people hacked the heads off chickens, then tried to catch the fluttering, headless bodies spewing blood; where mad dogs were stoned to death; where he had developed an "intolerable rash" on his thighs and scrotum that made even walking about a torture; where many natives were just "skeletons, covered in sores." Some men, though, were "extraordinarily beautiful"; this accounted for the "rampantness of sodomy."

But in the evenings, after a hard day's work, he would enjoy the exceptional beauty of his surroundings. He would go for a walk at sunset by the side of a lagoon, and revel in the beauty of the rice paddies, the palms, the sea, "every shade of blue," the sky, "every shade of red & yellow." Reading Shakespeare, too, helped him forget his "aching bones."

He lived in a bungalow, little more than a one-room hut, thought to be haunted, shaded by an enormous banyan tree. At night, thousands of crows, whose rustlings never ceased, inhabited it. He slept under a mosquito net, with bats flying around him. There were so many that by morning his watch, the floor and the netting would be thick with bat dung. He shared this habitation with a police magistrate who, for twenty years, had been trying to perfect his poetry about elves and fairies.

Leonard opened his most recent letter from Lytton Strachey, who had corresponded with him regularly during the eight months he had been in Ceylon. It described Clive Bell's courtship. "He's wildly in love," Strachey wrote, "—and with Vanessa."

The news was a shock. "It's rather sad," Leonard responded, "for I always said that he was in love with one of them—though strangely I thought it was the other. In a way I should like never to come back now." Clive Bell, like Leonard himself, had been attracted to both Stephen sisters. But Leonard thought Bell preferred Virginia, while Leonard himself preferred Vanessa. Leonard was not heartened to hear from Strachey that Vanessa had rebuffed Clive's initial proposal, or that Clive's "small lascivious body oozes with disappointed lust."

Leonard had been in Vanessa's company only twice in his life. He had never uttered a word about his feelings to her, or to anyone else, including his very best friend, Lytton Strachey. He had even told Strachey that he was not in love with "any individual of the species—yet." He had imparted to Strachey his belief that love is "a good deal of what is beneath the girdle," but there had to be something "above the girdle" to interest him. This, given what Leonard believed to be the inferior minds of most women, it was almost impossible to find. He would have to resign himself to the inevitable, to losing Vanessa. How could he compete with Bell from such a distance?

Leonard did, finally, admit to Lytton that he, like Clive, was "wildly in love" with Vanessa. He had fallen in love with her, he confessed, the first time he saw her when she came up to Cambridge that May term. What attracted him in the first place, Leonard admitted, was her strong resemblance to her brother Thoby. Unlike Virginia's finely chiseled features, Vanessa's face—the deep-set, heavy-lidded eyes, the full, sensuous lips—was the female version of Thoby, nicknamed the Goth. "She is so superbly like the Goth. I often used to wonder," Leonard wrote, "whether . . . I was in love with her, because [I was in love] with the Goth."

Thousands of miles from Gordon Square, in the jungle of Ceylon, Leonard admitted that the source of his love for Vanessa was his unacted-upon homoerotic attachment to her brother. Strachey had regaled Leonard with story after story about his adventures as a sodomite, but Leonard's admission of his love for Thoby took Lytton by surprise, though Lytton wished there might be something of the "female" about Leonard. "It's really scandalous," Lytton wrote. "Also, how very, very wild." With no Vanessa to return to, Leonard might as well stay on in Ceylon. London was in another universe, and, locked into his seven-year stint in Ceylon, he was powerless to traverse the distance, to return to Gordon Square, to challenge Clive.

Jaffna, Ceylon
Autumn 1905–Winter 1906

With Vanessa seemingly spoken for, Leonard entered a period of "purely degraded debauch." He lost his virginity in Jaffna, but he lost a great deal more. Before Strachey's letter, he had been able to imagine himself returning to Gordon Square and taking up his relationship with Vanessa, the idealized woman of his fantasies; but after, that dream shattered.

He admitted an "unhealthy obsession with sex." When he had been a young schoolchild at Arlington House, sex had been explained "luridly" to him by a small boy with "the dirtiest mind in an extraordinarily dirty-minded school." All his life, Leonard remembered the "corruption" of this school, whose atmosphere was that of a "sordid brothel," suggesting that the boys used one another sexually. Whether Leonard was the subject of unwanted sexual advances he leaves unsaid. But at a very early age he developed a belief in his powerlessness in the face of a hostile universe, perhaps because of his experiences at Arlington House. When he was twelve years old, he lost his "chastity": he became sexually excited when he read an explicit description of a rape in *The Scottish Chieftains*.

In his friendship with Strachey, it was possible to talk of sodomy and of Aristotelian love between men. When discussing women, it was their inferiority, the meanness and coarseness of their minds, the repulsiveness of their bodies that they described.

Vanessa was in a separate category; she wasn't a woman, she was a goddess. With that goddess unavailable to him, he began a campaign to prove to himself that women were beasts, and that any intercourse with a woman would debase him. It was a desperate, self-destructive, horrifying plunge. He learned that he had given up the idealism of his youth, and that, according to his standards, he had become a failure. His capacity for sordidness appalled him; he "felt he was in the bottommost pit."

Before his letter from Strachey, he had disparaged his fellow colonials for talking about prostitutes. Now he wore himself out with a half-caste whore; copulated with "a burgher concubine" in vast and empty rooms, smelling of bats and damp, with paint and plaster peeling off the walls; entered a relationship with an "unmarried, ugly but terribly & femininely violent" woman that was nothing but "degraded stupidity." The sexual aggression he discovered in women appalled him.

The madness and bitterness of life stunned him. He wondered whether he could endure the "monotony of perpetual work, the glaring & scorching heat," the flies crawling over him all day long. He plunged into a "deeper and deeper depression." One night, he took out his gun, made his will, and prepared to shoot himself.

Nor did Strachey's letters, which had been an emotional lifeline to him, offer any consolation. Strachey, too, had become corrupted. All Cambridge, with Strachey leading the way, had broken out into "an interminable series of reciprocal flirtations," even into "open sodomy." As disgusted with his friend as he was with himself, he wrote Lytton, "You have corrupted Cambridge just as Socrates corrupted Athens."

46 Gordon Square, Bloomsbury
Autumn 1905–Winter 1906

"Cambridge youths," Virginia Stephen wrote to Violet Dickinson, "are a great trial. They sit silent, absolutely silent . . . ; occasionally they escape to a corner and chuckle over a Latin joke." She wondered whether one of them was falling in love with her sister, Vanessa, but she didn't think any of them were "robust enough" to feel.

Contemplating these sorry specimens, Virginia concluded that though her sister might succumb to male charms, "women are my line."

She had read a biography of Kate Greenaway, the illustrator of children's books. It described her and Violet's intimate friendship, their "incessant" correspondence, their incongruous appearance when together—Violet was more than six feet tall and slim; Greenaway was "noticeably short and stout." More than just a trifle jealous, Virginia teased, "You have had a past my Violet."

Her passionate friendship with Violet, she knew, was fading, and there was no one in her life to replace her. Violet's long absences bothered her. "Don't tell me you mean to stay away," Virginia wrote, "or I shall take the pledge never to get on kissing terms with women [any]more."

Another source of conflict was Violet's criticism of Virginia's work, which had become irritating. She suspected that, though Violet had helped her initially, she did not want Virginia to become independent of her. "I shall send things straight to the editors, whose criticism is important," she concluded.

Early in the year, her doctors had pronounced her "normal,"

and she began to develop the habits that would last her a lifetime. Hers was a disciplined, well-proportioned life. It centered on work, self-development (she learned Greek and Spanish) and daily physical activity. It also included much pleasure—an active social life, attendance at cultural events.

The only morning she stayed in bed late was Sunday. Otherwise, she was up early and at her desk and at work by nine-thirty or ten. She wrote every morning, then ran errands (often including a trip to old-book shops or to the London Library). She took her dog for a walk in Regents Park when her day's writing was complete. After lunch, she read her review books, had guests for tea, then read and wrote in her diary or answered letters until dinner. In the evenings, she went to hear music at Queens Hall, or to the theater, or entertained guests in her home. When pressed, she used her evenings to complete a review or essay.

She was very busy, teaching an English composition class at Morley College and reviewing and writing regularly for publication. In 1905, about thirty of her pieces appeared. She published reviews of works by Edith Wharton, Winston Churchill, and Henry James, and essays on her dog Shag, street music in London, and the value of laughter.

She was earning money regularly, and she was proud of it. Usually abstemious, she would occasionally permit herself small treats—a book stand, a pedestal for a lamp. "I have earned the right to buy," she told herself.

Jaffna, Ceylon
December 1906

Leonard Woolf had received news of Thoby Stephen's death from Lytton Strachey. He was "overwhelmed, crushed." The worst part was that he was alone. He had no one with him in Ceylon from Cambridge with whom he could speak of Thoby's impact on him, of how he had been "an anchor."

Leonard had received a letter from Thoby just recently, which made his death even more unreal. Thoby had written of his disgust at the abandonment of Cambridge ideals and his fear that the sexual antics of John Maynard Keynes and Strachey would cause a terrible scandal.

Thoby was the one person who had stood firm, who had not collapsed into degradation after Cambridge. Now he was dead, and Leonard was alone in Ceylon with no one to share his grief.

Before the news of Thoby's death, Leonard had lapsed into "the vegetable state of the East," and had forgotten how to think, even how to converse. But Thoby's death had torn a chink in Leonard's armor. All day long, Leonard saw Thoby before him, heard his voice. Only with his death did Leonard realize what his influence had been. "He was above everyone in his nobility," he wrote Strachey. When he heard that Vanessa had asked Saxon Sydney-Turner to choose mementos for Thoby's friends, Leonard asked for Thoby's copy of John Milton.

Idealized by Leonard in life, Thoby became even more venerated in death. Leonard cherished Thoby's letters, rereading them from time to time. They made him weep. But he realized that he would not appreciate the full impact of Thoby's death until he returned to London.

A few days after he learned of Thoby's death, Leonard received still more bad news. It, too, came from Strachey.

"Please be ready for something, which, after all, perhaps you have already guessed. Vanessa and Bell are engaged. . . . Poor Virginia! And Adrian! They must set up house together now. The mind recoils. . . . Oh, tears! tears! I saw them yesterday, and you can imagine that it was awful. . . . I could only think of Bedoe's poem—A Wedding-robe and a winding-sheet,/A bridal bed and a bier."

Too worn out from his grief over Thoby, Leonard could barely react. He had tried to bury his grief at the likelihood of losing Vanessa for many months. Ever the gentleman, though, he wrote to Clive Bell, "I send you many congratulations, & through you to Miss Stephen."

29 Fitzroy Square, Bloomsbury
1906–1907

After Thoby's death, Virginia Stephen walked the streets of London in grief, chanting lines from Alfred Lord Tennyson's *In Memoriam*. For years, Thoby had been her intellectual companion, the sibling with whom she discussed Shakespeare and the Greeks, the person who showed respect for the quickness of her mind, with whom she first engaged in equally matched heated intellectual argument. In losing him, she lost the young man who had provided her with access to the world beyond the home to which she had been confined.

Losses never came singly in her life. After her father's death, she lost her Hyde Park Gate home and her sanity. After Thoby's death, she lost her sister, Vanessa, to marriage, and she lost the home at Gordon Square that she loved, that Vanessa had made for them. (Clive and Vanessa Bell lived there after their marriage.) During Thoby's illness, Vanessa had been sick too, as had Violet Dickinson, all in the wake of a trip they had taken to Greece. The responsibility for supervising the doctors, giving orders to the nurses—chores usually undertaken by Vanessa—fell to Virginia.

She considered Thoby's doctor incompetent, though the doctor persuaded her not to consult someone else. Thoby's typhoid had been misdiagnosed as pneumonia; there had been a botched operation. Virginia blamed herself for his death; she wished she had been the one to die. She wrote Violet Dickinson: "The amount of pain that accumulates ... grows every day."

At first, she had no feeling for Clive Bell but jealousy and repulsion. Compared to the beauty of the men in the Stephen family, he was a funny creature. In marrying Vanessa, he was taking away more than just her sister; Vanessa was mother, sister, lover, protector, and savior to Virginia. Soon, though, she began to recognize his virtues, and that he (initially at least) made her sister happy. Virginia found him "honest and unselfish and scrupulous; ... clever, and cultivated— ... very affectionate." He had a "gift for making other people shine."

After Vanessa was engaged, Virginia realized that she would rarely, if ever, see her sister, except in the presence of Clive. Although she tried to accept it, it made her so furious that she often couldn't stand the sight of the young couple. Once, seeing them standing "like husband and wife before a great log fire," she lost her temper "and went out to trample it into the mud." On the eve of her sister's marriage, Virginia wrote her a letter saying she hoped Vanessa would marry *her*. Having developed no independent life of her own, she spent much time in the company of Clive and Vanessa. She traveled with them on outings to Bath, spent her summer holidays with them in Rye (Sussex), and journeyed with them, after their marriage, to Italy.

Virginia was furious at her friends' insistence that now that her sister was marrying, she, too, must marry. For a time, she entertained the attentions of Walter Headlam, a forty-year-old Greek scholar whose "real passion in life . . . was for little girls." Her chief complaint about him was that he knew nothing about her family—she expected the man she married to know her family intimately.

She felt "desperate" at the thought that she would have to begin setting up house all over, this time with her brother Adrian, with whom she never really got along. She could not imagine managing a home without Vanessa to help her.

At Fitzroy Square, she found a home for them. It had been Bernard Shaw's. It was within walking distance of her sister's home. The family furnishings had been left behind for the new couple at Gordon Square. Compared with the warm, intimate beauty of Gordon Square, Virginia's new home was at first scarcely habitable; they had practically no furniture; she had moved in without even a bed or a washstand. Soon, though, she had plans for double-glazing the tall windows to soundproof the room so that she could work; she began to arrange her books, to shop for curtains.

Vanessa married in February 1907. Virginia saw in her sister's life hope and possibility; Vanessa in love was "tawny and jubilant and lusty as a young God." Yet Virginia felt herself "not quite alive, nor yet suffered to die."

In October, still very much missing her sister, she was seriously writing fiction: "I can think of nothing but my novel," she wrote Vanessa. She had bought a desk at which she stood to write, adopting this unusual posture in imitation of her sister's posture as a painter.

Living separately from Vanessa prompted the most significant change in her life. Although she continued to review books, write essays, and keep a journal, she began to imagine that she might become a novelist. She wrote Violet Dickinson that in her life, she might be "miserable, or happy," but she hoped that she would become "a writer of such English as shall one day burn the pages."

Jaffna, Kandy, and Hambantota, Ceylon 1907–1909

During the two years after the death of Thoby Stephen, Leonard Woolf hardened his heart "against the past and against regret for the past." He tried to put Cambridge and his life in England behind him. When he first arrived in Ceylon, he wrote Strachey as many as seven letters a month. In time, their correspondence slowed to a trickle. During some months, he didn't write at all.

He became "almost fanatically interested" in the country, and began to accept the position in which he found himself. In time, the country got into his heart, "its austere beauty, its immobility and unchangeableness." He tried to better the lives of its people through the building of schools and irrigation facilities, the modernization of the salt and pearl industries, and the control of rinderpest, the highly infectious disease which afflicts cattle and sheep.

He had learned the "happiness of complete solitude"; he "acquired a taste for it," and realized that it could purge him of his passions. From childhood, he had protected himself with a "carapace"; here that hardened into a lifelong habit of withdrawal.

Although he grew to despise imperialism, he was now a "model imperialist." Required to be present at hangings and floggings, he developed a fierce hatred of such punishments. He came to believe that flogging with a cat-o'-nine-tails was "the most disgusting and barbarous thing"; the man's back was "literally flayed" open. In Ceylon, he developed the political and moral attitudes that became the basis of the fervid socialist politics of his maturity.

He worked incessantly, and prided himself on being a fair and evenhanded administrator of justice. Without the strict enforcement of law, he believed that life for everyone would become, in Hobbes's words, "poor, nasty, brutish, and short," and he was for the most part respected. His superiors had recognized his talents, and in 1908 Leonard took over the administration of his own district, Hambantota. All members of the native population did not appreciate his rigid standards; an entry in a local paper read: "Mr. L. S. Woolf deserves to be shot."

Unlike many of his fellow countrymen, he learned Tamil and Sinhalese, and traveled to find out about the districts he ruled. Among his favorite moments were those spent camping out, in complete solitude, by a watering hole in the jungle, watching the animals come out of the undergrowth to drink. He learned the beauty of wild animals and grew to despise hunting for sport. But he did not romanticize the jungle: he realized it was "hostile, dangerous."

The first time Leonard proposed to Virginia, he was still living in Ceylon. It cannot be said that he was in love with her when he proposed. In 1908, Strachey had written Leonard speculating on who might, in time, marry Virginia; the letter alluded to Leonard; Leonard's response was receptive. Under these circumstances—discussing the wedding of Virginia—Lytton and Leonard resumed their correspondence on a more frequent basis. Leonard could take a leave to visit England after 1910, and so his thoughts turned again to his homeland, to which he retained a fierce loyalty.

He did not put an actual proposal forward until 1909, and then it was under tangled circumstances. While he was talking of proposing to Virginia long-distance, he became involved with two Englishwomen, Gwen, when he was in Jaffna, and Rachel, when he was in Kandy.

His first platonic love affair had occurred in Jaffna. At night, his duties completed, he would meet Gwen. A "gentle, languid, and pleasant melancholy" pervaded the atmosphere after the brutal heat of the day. Leonard and Gwen wandered on the beach at the edge of the lagoon, then lay "on the seaweedy sand platonically . . . in each other's arms."

But if he was in love with anyone (besides the memory of Thoby Stephen and the idealized, phantom image of Vanessa Bell) when he began to think about an alliance with Virginia, it was with an Englishwoman named Rachel, whom he met when he moved from Jaffna to Kandy to take up a new appointment. As they walked in the hills of Kandy, he and Rachel slipped into long silences. When they came upon a broad ledge from which one could see the jungle and the sea, a "strange, painful feeling" enveloped him. He believed he was being "tempted," that she was showing him "all the kingdoms of the earth." But he could not declare himself. He stood beside her in "miserable silence."

He knew he was in love with Rachel. Yet he wrote Strachey that it was not "pleasant because it is pretty degrading." He knew he wouldn't marry her, so he didn't know how to behave toward her. Besides, he thought he was merely in love with "silly intrigue & controlling a situation." Looking at Rachel's "big cow eyes" puzzled him. He thought she could never understand "anything which one said." Yet he believed the look in her eyes conveyed that she "understood everything that has ever been, is or will be."

Although he had fallen in love, he had not gotten over his disgust at the female body. As a magistrate, he visited a hut in which a woman had been kicked to death by the man she lived with because she did not have his dinner ready. His only sentiments were that most women "naked when alive are extraordinarily ugly, but dead they are repulsive."

When he left Rachel behind to move to Hambantota, it was with regret. But it was also with a profound sense of relief.

On February 1, 1909, Leonard Woolf received a letter from Lytton Strachey. Leonard was in Palatupana, living in a hut in a jungle, on his way to a game sanctuary. All he could think about was shooting a deer for his dinner so that he could have something other than sardines or chicken, his usual diet. Into this setting Lytton dropped a thunderbolt of a letter. It raised the possibility that one of them should marry Virginia.

Lytton's love life was in a tangle as usual. He vacillated between loving Duncan Grant and "Virginia and Sicilian prostitutes and chastity." He was terrified that he might undertake an action that would ruin his life and just as terrified that he would never do anything at all. In one fantasy, he tore Leonard away from his "blacks" and his "executions," and he and Leonard lived happily ever after in a small but comfortable flat in London.

Leonard wrote:

> The most wonderful would have been to marry Virginia. She is I imagine supreme & then the final solution would have been there. . . . Of course I suppose it is really impossible for the reason (if for no other) that I cannot place you in it. . . . It is undoubtedly

the only way to happiness, to anything settled, to anything not these appalling alternations from violent pleasures to the depths of depression. . . . [S]omething or other always saves me just at the last moment from these degradations—their lasciviousness or their ugliness probably—though I believe if I did I should probably be happy. Do you think Virginia would have me? Wire to me if she accepts. I'll take the next boat home; & then when I arrived I should probably come straight to talk with you.

Leonard included in his letter a poem he had written about his love—it is unclear whether for Rachel or for Gwen:

> When I am dead & you forget
>   My kisses: in the stirring air
> Will you not shudder when my touch,
>   Grown nothing now, just stirs your hair?
>   . . . You will not know that you have kissed
> A dead man. Only there may come
>   A memory of a foreign land
> Of wind & sun & how you lay
>   By the salt marshes in the sand
> With someone. . . .

On February 17, before Leonard's letter arrived, "despite a heavy cold," which usually incapacitated him, Lytton gathered his courage and journeyed across London to Fitzroy Square to propose marriage to Virginia. His proposal was a desperate attempt to escape his family, to put the sordidness of his involvement with both Duncan Grant and Maynard Keynes behind him. In effect, he was trying to renounce his homosexual identity.

Even as he proposed, Lytton realized how abhorrent the whole idea was to him: "I saw it would be death if she accepted me. . . . I was in terror lest she should kiss me," he wrote Leonard. But accept him she did.

On February 19, Lytton received Leonard's letter offering a marriage proposal to Virginia. He answered:

Your letter has this minute come—with your proposal to Virginia. . . . You are perfectly wonderful, and I want to throw my arms around your neck. . . . I'm rather ill and excited—by your letter. . . .
  The day before yesterday I proposed to Virginia. . . . I think

there's no doubt whatever that you ought to marry her. You *would* be great enough and you'll have the immense advantage of physical desire. . . . If you came and proposed [she would] accept. She really would.

The solution to the problem had presented itself in Leonard's letter. On the twentieth, realizing the impossibility of marriage to Virginia and buoyed by Leonard's proposal, Strachey met with Virginia and withdrew his proposal. But he did not mention Leonard's offer. Virginia admitted that though she would have married Lytton, she was not in love with him. They mutually agreed to revert to the relationship they had had before. Lytton believed he had managed "a fairly honourable retreat" from this difficult situation.

After his meeting with Virginia, Lytton wrote Leonard to tell him all about it, also telling him that he had told Vanessa to "hand on your proposal." Vanessa, whom Leonard had first loved, and perhaps still loved, was to deliver a proposal of marriage to Virginia, whom Leonard had seen but twice in his life, just after his best friend had proposed to her.

Nothing came of this first proposal. Bella Woolf, Leonard's sister, no doubt hearing some of this talk of marriage, wrote to her brother. She advised him that he should marry only if he found a very special type of woman, one who was "strong-minded & clever," one who could "hold her own" against him, yet be good-tempered. With a deep understanding of her brother's capacity for dominance and sadism, Bella warned her brother that if he married a woman who was weak or fragile, "you'll squash her."

In the summer of 1909, nearing the end of Leonard's fifth year in Ceylon, Lytton and Leonard were still tossing around the possibility of Leonard marrying Virginia. "Your destiny is clearly marked out for you," Lytton wrote in August. "You must marry Virginia." And, with no evidence to support his statement, he stooped to a familiar Stracheyesque maneuver. Wanting to stir things up, he inflamed Leonard by writing something that was simply not true, though Leonard had no way of knowing it: "She's sitting waiting for you. . . . [B]ut if you're not careful you'll lose the opportunity." Lytton told Leonard that Virginia was "young, wild, inquisitive, discontented, and longing to be in love."

The strategy worked. Leonard replied: "To imagine . . . Virginia exist[s]! . . . Of course I know that the one thing to do would be to marry Virginia. I am only frightened that when I come back in Dec 1910 I may." He suspected that once "everything was completed & consummated, life would probably at last be supreme." The "horrible preliminary complications, the ghastly complications . . . of virginity & marriage altogether appall me," he admitted. If that weren't the case, he would have telegraphed a firm proposal at once. But his pondering those horrible possibilities prevented him from doing so; he saw himself, at forty, married to a "widow . . . or an exprostitute."

29 Fitzroy Square, Bloomsbury and St. Ives, Cornwall April 1908–1911

Clive Bell, like Leonard Woolf, had fallen in love with both Stephen sisters. "Vanessa & her sister, the two people I love best in the world," Clive wrote to Virginia. In 1908, after the birth of the Bells' first child, Clive and Virginia began the most passionate heterosexual relationship of Virginia's lifetime, her first freely chosen foray into loving a man. George Duckworth had incestuously abused both Vanessa and Virginia. While they were still girls, they were introduced to the heated passions of taboo triangular sexual relationships, which they now re-created.

Virginia was furious that Clive had taken away her sister by marrying her, and she expressed her rage at Vanessa by trying to steal her husband's affection. By loving her sister's husband, Virginia was reenacting the hypersexualized, incestuous hothouse atmosphere of her past.

Her experience as a survivor of incest was very much on her mind as she began her flirtation with Clive. In April 1908, she was writing a long remembrance of the Stephen family, which she gave to Clive and Vanessa to read. Simultaneously, she worked on her first novel, which she was calling *Melymbrosia*. In *Reminiscences*, she described how George Duckworth violated both her and Vanessa after their mother's death. She described how the memory of her mother's death combined with the memory of the heat of the bay at Freshwater, on the Isle of Wight, where the family grieved; commingled with the luxuriant lushness of the vegetation there; how these, in turn, became mixed with other memories—memories of hot rooms and prolonged silences—so that Virginia felt as if she were choking.

In *Melymbrosia*, she was writing the emotional history of Rachel Vinrace, a young woman troubled by her inability to consummate a heterosexual relationship. Rachel has a deep-seated terror of men and an unconscious desire not to marry that is so profound that she is willing to die rather than to wed. Virginia Stephen, as she embarked upon her emotional, adulterous relationship with her brother-in-law, was rendering, in fiction as well as through memoir, the emotional aftermath of abuse.

Virginia sent both works to Clive and Vanessa to read. She used both documents to tell her sister's husband about their shared incestuous history. In *Reminiscences*, she was also telling Clive that she had been Vanessa's first lover, and that the love the members of the Stephen family bore one another superseded all other relationships.

She wrote him telling him to kiss her sister, "most passionately, in all my private places—neck, and arm, and eyeball, and tell her—what new thing is there to tell her? how fond I am of her husband." He responded, teasingly, "It is just because women are so deliciously soft in some places that they are so exquisitely hard in others; and you who are as feminine as anything . . . are too much of a genius to believe in your own sex."

Virginia joined Clive and Vanessa in St. Ives, Cornwall, in April 1908. While Vanessa cared for a squalling baby (which made Virginia sure she would never have one), Clive and Virginia walked on the cliffs, looked at the sea with its "strange shivers of purple and green," talked about her work, and testified to their love. When she returned to London, she wrote him:

> Why do you torment me with half uttered and ambiguous
> sentences? my presence is 'vivid and strange and bewildering'. . . .
> I was certainly of [the] opinion, though we did not kiss—(I was
> willing and offered once—but let that be)—I think we 'achieved
> the heights' as you put it. But did you realise how profoundly I
> was moved, and at the same time, restricted, by the sight of your

daily life.... When Nessa is bumbling about the world, and making each thorn blossom, what room is there for me?

There were, however, kisses, and perhaps more. Clive and Virginia continued to protest their love for one another, to steal moments together away from Vanessa for passionate embraces. This lasted through the period of Lytton Strachey's marriage proposal to Virginia in 1909, and continued until 1911 or so, when Leonard Woolf returned to London from Ceylon. In a photograph of Clive and Virginia taken on a beach, Virginia, in swimming costume, is laughing at his antics. He hunches his shoulders, slackens his bathing suit, trying to conceal his all-too-obvious penis. She looks happier than in any other photograph.

Clive supported her decision to become a novelist and critiqued her novel-in-progress, offering advice about style and substance. Yet Virginia realized that their behavior had drastically altered her sister's marriage. Before her affair with Clive, Virginia described Vanessa as surrounded in a sea of wedded bliss, basking "like an old seal on a rock." After, Vanessa and Clive drifted apart. Vanessa controlled herself and only on occasion expressed an urge to "shake" her sister for interfering with her marriage. In time, Vanessa turned her attentions elsewhere, to Roger Fry, and then to Duncan Grant, the father of her daughter, Angelica. In 1909, Clive Bell continued an adulterous affair with Mrs. Raven-Hill, who had initiated him into sexuality when he was eighteen. He was still pursuing Virginia and writing her passionate letters. He also wrote Virginia about how "delicious" Mrs. Raven-Hill was as a lover.

Clive and Virginia's affair was, ultimately, dangerous and damaging, not only for Virginia, but also for Vanessa. Clive Bell and his friends at Cambridge—Lytton Strachey and Leonard Woolf—had, in the tradition of G. E. Moore, their philosopher-king, dedicated themselves to pursuing "truth and beauty," to eliminating "hypocrisy and cant" from their lives. Nothing was hidden; everything was open—they talked about affairs, adulteries, sexual encounters. What they achieved was not ideal, but rather something far different, something pernicious. Behind the cloak of Moore's philosophy, the Bloomsberries raised personal betrayal to an art form, and insisted that its members hide their pain.

For Virginia and Vanessa, this behavior perpetuated the Stephen incest script, and it had serious consequences. Entangled with

Clive, Virginia experienced a loss of control, a loss of her sense of self. She wrote Lytton Strachey about a recurrence of her lifelong fantasy of suicide by drowning: "I had begun to doubt my own identity—and imagined I was part of a sea-gull, and dreamt at night of deep pools of blue water, full of eels."

After Virginia's affair with Clive, Vanessa plunged into a life-threatening two-year depression; she thought she was "losing control of her mind." Clive and Virginia blamed absolutely everything but their behavior. Vanessa was overworked. She was feeling the aftermath of childbirth. She was exhausted from traveling. She had had a miscarriage. Responsibility for Virginia was proving too much for her.

The affair became a sore spot in Virginia's conscience, and had long-term psychic consequences. Virginia, too, required a month-long "rest cure" in 1910 because of the agitations the affair caused her. Years later, she admitted "my affair with Clive and Nessa . . . turned more of a knife in me than anything else." The immediate effect of her affair was to postpone her separation from her sister, to postpone her establishment of an independent life.

By 1911, she had grown tired of this life, lived on the periphery of her sister's, and could foresee no future for herself if she continued this way. "I could not write," she wrote her sister in June 1911, just as Leonard Woolf returned to London, "and all the devils came out—hairy black ones. To be 29 and unmarried—to be a failure—childless—insane too, no writer."

London, Cambridge, and Dartmoor
June–December 1911

Leonard Woolf was thirty-one years old when, in June 1911, he returned from Ceylon. He felt himself even more locked away inside the carapace that he used to protect himself from the world than when he had left England nearly seven years before. He believed he was embarking on "Scene I, Act I" of a "quite new play." He had no firm plans; he thought that after his yearlong leave he might return to Ceylon again, to try to make Hambantota into one of the best-governed districts in the British Empire. Apart from his position in the colonial service, he had no way of supporting himself. Unless he could find work in London, he was obliged to return to Ceylon.

The first person he wanted to see when he returned was Lytton Strachey. After visiting his mother and family for three days in Putney, Leonard headed straight for Cambridge, where Strachey was living. Strachey marveled at the physical change in Leonard, at his "long, drawn, weather-beaten face." His manner, too, had changed, but not for the better. He reminded Lytton of someone who had just died.

Leonard dined at the high table in Trinity College, saw Bertrand Russell and Rupert Brooke, and reentered the life he had left behind. He saw that although he himself had been changed dramatically by his life in Ceylon, "all the eternal truths and values" of his youth were going on, as before, at Cambridge. This reassured him, but no doubt made him envious.

He joined Lytton and his mentor, G. E. Moore, on a trip to Dartmoor. Lytton was writing his *Landmarks in French Literature;* G. E. Moore, his *Ethics.* Both were groaning, complaining about the effort that went into their projects. Moore sat in the garden, his panama hat on his head, perspiring. He was mentally constipated: when he wrote down a sentence, "he saw that it was just false or that it required a sentence to qualify the qualification." His friends were embarking on important work that would prove that their belief in themselves as England's intellectual elite had not been unfounded.

Strachey, Moore, and Woolf took long walks together over Dartmoor. They stripped themselves naked and swam in deep, black, frigid pools of water. Moore continually posed his favorite question: "What exactly do you mean by that?" He insisted, as he always had, on honesty and truth in interpersonal relationships.

Leonard had realized while living in Ceylon that he would only feel the full impact of his loss of Thoby when he returned to London. On July 3, three weeks after his return from Ceylon, he dined with Vanessa and Clive Bell at 46 Gordon Square. After dinner, Virginia and Duncan Grant came for coffee and conversation.

Leonard discovered that everything at Gordon Square, except the furniture and the Stephen sisters' beauty, had changed. What he found so "new and so exhilarating" was the freedom of thought and speech that manifested itself there. And, for the first time in his experience, women were truly included in conversation.

No subject, not even sex, was out of bounds, although the most frequent topics of conversation were the differences between younger and older generations and between painters and writers. He sensed a deep intimacy; he saw that they had swept away older, more formal ways of behaving.

It was only the third time Virginia and Leonard had met. The woman he encountered at her sister's home in 1911 was very different from the one he had seen just before his departure for Ceylon in 1904. While Leonard had been away, Virginia had become an important and influential presence in English letters, a tastemaker, reviewing works of established writers and those of her contemporaries; she had published more than a hundred reviews and essays since embarking upon her career in 1904. She had completed a draft of her first novel. She had traveled widely, to Spain, France, Italy, Greece, Constantinople, regularly publishing articles about her travels.

Yet she had suffered the emotional consequences of her entanglement with Clive. She was, at twenty-nine, not altogether sure she wanted to marry; yet she felt herself a failure for not having married. She had been a professional writer for close to seven years; yet she had struggled for so many years with her first novel that she did not believe herself a success.

Lytton Strachey had kept Leonard informed of Clive's entanglement with Virginia and Vanessa while he was in Ceylon. After the threesome embarked on a trip to Italy, Lytton, always delighted to convey news of a *ménage à trois*, wrote Leonard: "Don't you think it's the wildest romance? That that little canary-coloured creature we knew . . . should have achieved that? The two most beautiful and wittiest women in England! He's certainly lucky."

Strachey was always eager to exchange proof with Leonard of the corrupt nature of women. Although Strachey admired both Vanessa and Virginia, Virginia's affair with Clive proved that Virginia was not virginal. She, too, was susceptible to seduction. This placed her in a dangerous category in Leonard's mind, for Leonard despised such women. He himself had seduced the wife of a colleague in Ceylon, but soon felt "degraded" by the escapade.

Strachey's information—that Virginia was seriously flirting with Clive Bell—probably obsessed Leonard. He could not help comparing the way she behaved toward him with the way she had behaved toward Clive. Once Leonard knew of this affair, Virginia could not emerge unharmed from a relationship with him, given his beliefs about women and his self-loathing. If she behaved less amorously to Leonard than she had to Clive, Leonard would see himself as a failure, and he hurt those who made him feel that way. If Leonard became sexually aroused by her, she also would be at risk. Leonard told Lytton that he believed that love was "99/100ths . . . the desire to copulate"; but he also believed that the desire to copulate with a particular woman was "no less degraded than a general" urge to do so. So if Leonard felt the "desire to copulate" with Virginia, he would inevitably feel degraded by it. If *she* became erotically aroused, that was also fraught with danger, because he believed that in a woman the desire to copulate was proof that the woman was corrupt.

No matter how Virginia behaved toward Leonard, once he became interested in her the consequences inevitably would be disastrous. But Virginia had no way of knowing this.

Leonard and Virginia's meeting at Gordon Square must have provoked her interest. Perhaps it was that, in conversation, his "brilliant light-blue eyes would fix, as he listened, with a severe intensity of expression." Less than a week later, on July 8, she invited him to join her for a weekend at her country cottage. She had dubbed it "Little Talland House," in imitation of her childhood country home, Talland House, in St. Ives, Cornwall. In reality, it was an ugly suburban villa in the village of Firle in the Sussex countryside.

"Dear Mr Wolf," she wrote, misspelling his name, as she would repeatedly, "Would you come down . . . for a week end?"

He was unable to accept this first invitation. He had other plans. During the first six months after his homecoming, he entered a period of serene contentment. He experienced more pure pleasure than he ever had in his life or ever would again.

He had returned to England during an exhilarating period in its history. Not only was the society at Gordon Square different. Victorianism, it seemed, had been completely cast aside. For the first time in history, governments were considering the "rights of Jews, cobblers, and coloured men." In the period preceding World War I, it seemed that "militarism, imperialism, and antisemitism" were on the wane. There was the excitement of the motorcar and the airplane; the revolution in knowledge due to the work of Freud, Rutherford, and Einstein; the impact on the arts of Ibsen, Shaw, Cézanne, Matisse, Picasso, and the Russian ballet. "It was exciting to be alive in London in 1911."

Shortly after he met Virginia again, Leonard embarked upon a trip to Sweden with his brother Edgar. While gliding on a steamer through the fjords and lakes, he gloried in the sunshine and in rereading *The Brothers Karamazov*. He confided to his brother his difficulty in summoning up the courage to propose to Virginia. He had, apparently, decided to propose the first time he saw her upon his return. His prospects, he told his brother, were dim; he had heard reports that Virginia had turned down "one suitor after another." In the months before Leonard's official proposal, Virginia was courted by Walter Lamb and Sydney Waterlow (just separated from his wife) and chased by Jean Thomas, who had developed a frantic lesbian passion for her when she cared for Virginia during a rest cure.

Clive Bell, perhaps because he sensed Virginia was distancing herself from him for her own protection, in the months following Leonard's return carried on a campaign to besmirch her reputation. Clive had cornered Lamb and treated him to a recital of Virginia's faults; he repeated his allegations to Lytton, with whom he argued about Virginia's character. Lamb told Virginia that she was difficult to love because of this, because she lived her life in the middle of a "hornet's nest," and because intrigue complicated her life. His analysis of Virginia's character at this time was astute: she encouraged the ritual of courtship, though she was not necessarily interested in partnership; she encouraged people to pursue her, and then withdrew from them; she encouraged many people to compete for her affection.

Leonard and Virginia spent time together in September and October at Little Talland House, walking the South Downs in Sussex and enjoying the "physical loveliness" of the landscape, sitting deep in conversation until late in the night. In London, his interest in her grew as she accompanied him to performances of *Das Rheingold*, *Siegfried*, and *Götterdämmerung*.

In November 1911, Leonard decided to take rooms in a house that Adrian and Virginia were letting at 38 Brunswick Square. He had saved enough money to support himself for two years without working, and he drew upon this stash to pay his way. He was at work on his first novel, *The Village in the Jungle,* which drew upon his experiences in Ceylon, and he needed a place to live and work. He was unsure of his future; his new life was pleasurable, but the idea that he could return to Ceylon if he chose was comforting.

The living arrangement Virginia proposed was that for a weekly fee Leonard, together with Maynard Keynes and Duncan Grant, could have a bedroom, sitting room, and meals. The establishment would be run like a boarding house. "Inmates," as she called them, would have maximum freedom and privacy. Their lodgings were grander than any of them could afford individually, and they shared servants who would prepare meals and keep house.

Leonard moved from his mother's house to Brunswick Square on December 4. A few days later, he began keeping a diary in cypher, in a combination of Sinhalese and Tamil characters. In it he recorded his interactions with Virginia and his observations of her behavior.

Living together, Virginia and Leonard began seeing one another constantly; by the end of 1911, he knew he would propose marriage. Even so, his love for her, he believed, was hopeless, even dangerous; he thought love was "always a danger which is never really worth the risk." Lytton Strachey, too, observed that a relationship for Leonard would be a danger—but not to Leonard. Strachey believed that, like Swift, Leonard would "murder his wife."

38 Brunswick Square, London
Asheham House, Sussex
January–February 1912

It was a very strange courtship. On January 11, Leonard proposed to Virginia. She had shown him no sign of affection. He told her he had never realized how much he loved her until they discussed his return to Ceylon. He spoke of his love for her in Wagnerian terms: he saw himself inside "the ring of fire."

Unsure whether she would accept him, he had begun to see a

woman who was the daughter of friends of his family. He continued seeing her throughout his courtship of Virginia; he ended the relationship only when he was sure Virginia would accept him.

Immediately after the proposal, he listed all his faults. He told Virginia he was "selfish, jealous, cruel, lustful, a liar & probably worse"—he knew he would not make a good husband. He confessed that he had intended never to marry because he suspected he would not control these urges with a submissive woman. With her, he lessened the risk of acting on his evil impulses. He could not promise her that he would control his cruelty; instead, he thought marrying her lessened the risk of his being cruel. He knew that no woman "ought" to marry him, yet his desire for her was blinding.

She parried with a list of *her* faults, of the reasons *she* didn't want to marry. She was "vain, an egoist, untruthful." Rejecting his proposal, she told him she wanted to continue their friendship. She would keep his proposal a secret, though she would tell her sister. She asked Vanessa, with good reason, not to tell Clive.

The day after Virginia rejected Leonard's proposal, Vanessa wrote two very different letters, one to him and one to her sister. She advised Virginia not to marry unless she was in love, but not to let Leonard's "Jewishness" stop her; she could imagine Leonard as Virginia's husband.

To Leonard, she was much more favorable: she encouraged his suit, despite what her sister had said. He was the only person she could imagine as Virginia's husband (she had said something similar when Lytton had asked Virginia to marry); she urged him not to go back to Ceylon. Though she had seen him a very few times, and knew him hardly at all, she trusted her instincts that he was the right husband for her sister. Vanessa's encouragement was self-serving: Virginia had become a maddening responsibility, and Vanessa herself wasn't well. Not only had Virginia carried on with Clive, but after Vanessa began an affair with Roger Fry, Virginia had also acted seductively to him. Vanessa wanted her sister settled with someone, anyone. Having Virginia married would give Vanessa some peace.

After Virginia declined Leonard's proposal, they spent time together in the company of others, within the guidelines Leonard had agreed to. On weekends, they traveled to Sussex, to Asheham

House. It was a romantic yellow house with french windows and towering elms in the Ouse River Valley, overlooking fields, the valley, and the downs. Virginia and Leonard had discovered it on one of their rambles; Virginia had decided to lease it immediately, giving up the less well-situated Little Talland House. They lived a primitive life there, walking four miles from the railway station with backpacks filled with provisions, pumping their water, using candles and oil lamps for lighting.

Leonard joined Virginia at Asheham for a weekend housewarming party early in February. It was a disaster—the pipes froze, birds starved to death outside their windows, and one of the guests got chicken pox.

Though Leonard had promised not to pressure Virginia, she felt unwell in the wake of his proposal. She saw herself as an "anemone at the bottom of an aquarium"; she had a recurrence of her fantasies of drowning. What provoked her illness is unclear. Perhaps it was Leonard's attentions; perhaps it was the strain of the hornet's-nest life she was leading; perhaps she discovered he was also courting another woman.

More likely, though, Leonard's cruelty precipitated her illness. He gave her his collection of letters from Lytton Strachey, the ones Strachey had written to him in Ceylon. He gave them to her perhaps to punish her, or to carry on in the spirit of ruthless honesty with which they had begun their intimacy. This was his first act of unmitigated cruelty to her.

And what a collection it was! Virginia learned that Leonard had had a homosexual attraction for her brother Thoby. That he had fallen in love with Vanessa. That he believed Vanessa was more beautiful, more womanly, more desirable than she was. That he had had a series of sordid affairs because the news that Vanessa was marrying Clive devastated him. That *Lytton* had come up with the idea that Leonard propose to her. She learned that, despite Leonard's recent protestations of long-standing love for her, he had loved her brother and her sister before he had loved her. He had even loved another woman in Ceylon. He had warned her that he was a liar; now he proved it.

She also learned that Leonard thought loving a woman was degrading. That having sex with a woman was the ultimate depravity. That marriage was a sordid affair.

* * *

In the middle of February, Virginia had a breakdown and entered Jean Thomas's nursing home at Twickenham for a rest cure. She was having trouble working. In 1911, she published only two reviews; in 1912, just another two. Work on her novel proceeded slowly or not at all. Romantic entanglements were not helping her work. Why, after the beginning of a courtship that impeded her work and that landed her in a nursing home, she encouraged Leonard further, is a question that can be answered with the most cursory look at her family history. Cruel and sadistic men, men who used sex to demean and degrade women, had been commonplace in her life.

Burley, Cambridge Park, Twickenham
38 Brunswick Square, Bloomsbury
Asheham House, Sussex
March–May 1912

Jean Thomas's nursing home in Twickenham was a less than ideal setting for Virginia to recuperate from the strains of her intimacy with Leonard. Jean Thomas ran an establishment that forced food and drink upon her patients and shut them up in dark rooms for periods of enforced rest. She gave them sleeping draughts and sedatives to ensure their compliance. Yet her patients were sometimes able to wander about. One patient routinely pulled up the roses in the flower beds and walked into the village to attend church services. Virginia, on a previous cure, had wandered around in the garden wrapped only in a blanket; and Vanessa spoke of having heard that Virginia had been busy "seducing" the entire household. Jean Thomas, infatuated with Virginia, routinely pursued her, and spoke of her with "tears in her eyes."

Virginia described her stay to Leonard when she returned to London in March. He had sent her books to read, and she had read them and liked them, but she had been forbidden to write a letter thanking him. She had had long conversations about religion, and she had summoned "a conclave, and made a proclamation about Christianity"; the "lunatics" had elected her "King"; her stay had been filled with adventures and with disasters; she had taken up knitting to calm herself. Now, back in London, she felt "clear, calm," though she moved slowly, after her forced weight gain, like one of the "great big animals at the zoo." She was taking sleeping draughts regularly, and they made her feel as if she had been "knocked on the head."

On March 21, Leonard paid a visit to George Savage, Virginia's doctor, to discuss her health. He did this without her knowledge, but the visit shows that he would pursue his suit despite (or even because of) her precarious health. His interest in her despite her illness separated him from other suitors, like Lamb, who had expressed dissatisfaction with anything seemingly abnormal.

While at Twickenham, Virginia had done some thinking about marriage, and she had concluded that she was not altogether against it. Young married couples appalled her, but so did "melancholy old maids." Neither a safe and sober marriage nor the single life suited her. Her loneliness frightened her. Early in life, she had had a "tremendous, absurd, ideal of marriage" that she had had to reject because most of the marriages she had observed "disgusted" her. For a time, she thought marriage was "a very low down affair." In time, she had become more realistic about what marriage could afford; she realized that she would be very difficult to live with, given her "intemperate and changeable" nature; but she believed that she could enter into an alliance with a man who made her "vehement."

Leonard was not giving up. Though she did not encourage him, she did not discourage him either. She no longer felt responsible for accepting his proposal because she suspected he would choose to stay in London whether or not she accepted him.

During her illness, Virginia realized that her poor health was a liability few men would accept. Her choice of husbands was limited to those who could withstand and endure her attacks of instability. She understood, too, that she required special care during these episodes, and she realized that Vanessa, whose life had become increasingly complex, would no longer provide it.

Leonard always felt himself a failure. He felt less so in the presence of someone so obviously damaged. His ability to care for someone ill buttressed his fragile sense of self. Virginia's illness also leveled the inequality of class that might have remained a barrier to their alliance.

During his furlough, Leonard had consulted doctors about his own nervous condition. His interest in Virginia's health proceeded in part from empathy, though he surely wanted to know what a life with her would entail. In his relationship with Lytton Strachey, he had often acted the role of the nurse when Lytton was sick; it was a role that agreed with him. In helping a friend, he felt masterful. He had listened intently to Strachey's descriptions of his excited states, and had written him loving letters, urging self-control, when Strachey required rest cures. He repeated this behavior with Virginia.

Leonard envied people like Strachey and Virginia who were excitable: he believed it was a sign that Strachey *lived* life rather than being "a mere spectator," watching life with his hands in his pockets instead of participating in it. The closer Leonard could get to these special people, the more alive he felt. In Virginia, he found the perfect replacement for Lytton Strachey. The more severe her symptoms, the more tender and attentive he became.

After she was released from Twickenham, Virginia read some of her novel, *The Voyage Out*, aloud to him. He thought it "extraordinarily good," and he told her. Although Clive Bell had read her work, his praise had been qualified; he told her what needed to be changed, rather than how well she was doing. Leonard's was the first clear, unequivocal encouragement she received for her fiction, and it marked a turning point in their relationship. As cruel as he had been to her, as many faults as he possessed, he valued hard work, as she did, and he was generous in his praise of work well done. This fine quality in him would, in time, seem far more significant than his obvious and problematic faults.

He had written an analysis of her character, which he showed her. He watched her read it as they sat in front of a fire. While recognizing the complexity of her character, he praised the quality of her mind. In this, he was like Thoby. Virginia began to fix upon his similarity to her dead brother. With Leonard, she could have again what she and her brother had shared. Leonard called her "Aspasia," and this name showed his surprise at and respect for her power over words. In *The Dialogues of Plato*, Menexenus tells

Socrates, "I marvel that Aspasia, who is only a woman, should be able to compose such a speech, she must be a rare one."

"I am in love with Aspasia," Virginia read. "When I think of Aspasia I think of hills . . . ; there is snow upon them which no sun has ever melted & no man has ever trodden. But the sun too is in her hair, . . . & in the glow of her mind. . . . [H]er mind is so astonishingly fearless, there is no fact & no reality which it does not face, touch frankly openly. She is one of possibly three women who know that dung is merely dung, death death & semen semen. She is the most Olympian of the Olympians. And that is why perhaps she seems to take life too hardly. She does not really know the feeling—which alone saves the brain & the body—that after all nothing matters. She asks too much from the earth & from the people who crawl about it."

"I don't think you have made me soft or lovable enough," Virginia replied after reading of herself.

She continued to invite him down to Asheham for country weekends throughout the springtime, which was "gorgeous." They worked together on home improvements; they lolled in the sun on the terrace; they sat by fires, telling stories of their past. But his praise of her work had marked a turning point in their relationship, and she again felt able to write. His praise meant so much to her that by May she was writing at *The Voyage Out* regularly, writing five hundred words a morning.

The intimacy of living with Virginia at Asheham House in Sussex and at Brunswick Square inflamed Leonard's desire, rather than mitigating it. Virginia was adept at keeping people interested in her if they manifested signs that their ardor was abating. On April 29, Leonard wrote her a letter, pouring out his feelings. He composed it after he decided to resign from the colonial service, no matter what her response to him might be. It was nearly three o'clock in the morning when he finished it.

He had read two more of her manuscripts, and he believed she "might write something astonishingly good" one day. He was unhappy because something in her seemed to turn against him. He wanted to assure her that he found great happiness in being with her, "mind to mind," "soul to soul." He contradicted himself. He told her that physical desire was the least important aspect of his feeling for her; he found her lovable in so many other ways. He

envied. It was a match that provided him with access to the powerful and influential people she knew. Soon after the marriage, he acted as secretary to Roger Fry's Second Post-Impressionist Exhibit at the Grafton Galleries. Because Virginia had an independent income, about which Leonard knew—he helped her with her accounts soon after moving into Brunswick Square—he wouldn't have to worry about earning much of a living: they could live very nicely on her annuities if both of them earned a little extra. This removed one of the biggest burdens he faced. If he hadn't married a woman with an independent income, it would have been impossible for him to marry so soon.

Her illness seemed not to bother him; if anything, he regarded her care and coddling as a challenge, even during their engagement. "I've been rather headachy, and had a bad night," Virginia wrote Violet Dickinson, "and Leonard made me into a comatose invalid." Like Vanessa before her, Virginia, during her engagement, became increasingly unwell. Leonard's fervor in setting about nursing her requires scrutiny. Though he would come to appreciate her real strengths, he seemed to prefer her when she was ill. In this, he was like her mother, who believed that the relationships between the sick and the well were easier to manage than those between people who were well.

And he had grown to love her.

On the warm summer day when Virginia agreed to marry Leonard, they took a train to Maidenhead, rowed to Marlow, and dined at a riverside restaurant. They felt the "strange happiness of being for a moment alone together in an empty universe." That happiness was to be extremely short-lived.

London
August 10, 1912

Leonard and Virginia Woolf were married on August 10, 1912, in the midst of a violent thunderstorm, which continued unabated during the early days of their honeymoon. They were married in Bloomsbury at the St. Pancras Registry Office, which looked out over a cemetery. During the ceremony, Leonard looked out the window and saw the tombstones; the words " 'til death us do part" became especially significant to him.

The registrar who married them was deformed and nearly blind; he mixed up the ceremony, thinking it was Vanessa and not Virginia who was marrying Leonard. The ceremony was interrupted again when Vanessa decided she would take this opportunity to enquire how she might change her son's name. "One thing at a time, please, Madam," the registrar chided her.

Attending the ceremony, or the "very odd lunch party," celebrating the marriage, besides Vanessa (wearing Turkish silk), were Clive Bell (who was trying to persuade himself to love Virginia's husband, too), Virginia's Aunt Mary (on crutches, wearing widow's weeds), George and Gerald Duckworth (in frock coats), and Duncan Grant (looking like a ragpicker).

Leonard had not invited his mother; he probably thought she would embarrass him, acting inappropriately in front of his friends and new family. Her behavior often irritated him; he never seemed to please her; he believed she liked him the least of her nine children.

Marie Woolf never forgave him. He was the first of her sons to marry. Attending the ceremony, she wrote him, "would have compensated me for the very great hardships I have endured in bringing you all up by myself. . . . To leave out one's Parent, must strike one as an unheard of slight."

In marrying Virginia, Leonard was trying to leave Putney and everything it represented far behind. He was marrying into a family he envied, but also into a way of life he already had come to despise. Before meeting Virginia, despite attending Cambridge, he had known very little about the ways of upper-middle-class professionals, only what he learned through Lytton Strachey's family. During their engagement, Virginia introduced him to her friends and relations. On their visits to her Aunt Anny, the Vaughans, and the Duckworth brothers, he became aware of the sense of entitlement and assuredness the members of this class possessed. It was very different from his sense of inferiority and shame. "They lived," he observed, "in a peculiar atmosphere of influence, manners, respectability . . . so natural, they were unaware of it." It could only be a matter of time before Leonard began to despise Virginia for those values.

Virginia told all her friends that marrying Leonard made her happy, and that, under his care, she couldn't possibly become ill again. But she was putting up a brave and false front. Years later, she wrote: "How I hated marrying a Jew—how I hated their nasal voices, and their oriental jewelry, and their noses, and their wattles—what a snob I was." When Leonard had taken her to meet his family in Putney, she had found their ways "queer." She had talked to his mother about why the Woolfs, as Jews, didn't eat "Ham or bacon or Shellfish": "Because it says in the Scriptures that they are unclean creatures." Virginia, the agnostic, couldn't comprehend a life lived according to Scripture. But that was not all. She noticed how "commonplace" the family's surroundings were, how "hideous" their furniture and decorations. She was surprised that Marie Woolf served potted-meat sandwiches for tea—one didn't serve meat sandwiches for tea. Marie Woolf's manners were suspect; they didn't conform to the ways of Virginia's class. Meeting Leonard's family lowered him in her opinion.

She must have communicated something of this repulsion, something of her rabid anti-Semitism, something of her sense of his inferiority to Leonard. She delighted in satire, in caustic commentaries about people who didn't measure up to her standards, and she ridiculed his family's strange ways throughout her life. She described a visit to the Woolf home in Putney as if it were a trip into a foreign, repellent country. Never one to spare words, she probably let Leonard know how "queer" she thought his family was, and he probably sensed her disappointment in marrying him.

The Plough Inn
Holford, Somerset
Late August 1912

Their problems started almost immediately after the ceremony. In March 1923, Leonard Woolf had a conversation with Gerald Brenan, a mere acquaintance, about what had transpired on his honeymoon.

They had spent a few nights at Asheham House, returned to London, and traveled from there to the Plough Inn in Holford,

Somerset, for the first part of their honeymoon. The weather was dreadful; it rained the entire time and it was as cold as winter. They had come for the beauty of the countryside, but it was impossible to see the Quantock Hills through all the mist. Nonetheless, they ventured out in the rain and did some climbing. The rest of the time they spent inside, hunched by a fire, reading.

Leonard told Gerald Brenan that on their honeymoon he had tried to make love to Virginia, but "she had got into such a violent state of excitement that he had to stop, knowing as he did that these states were a prelude to her attacks of madness." Leonard portrayed himself as a "strongly sexed man," who quickly "had to give up all idea of ever having any sort of sexual satisfaction" in his marriage. He was prepared to do this, he told Brenan, because his wife was "a genius."

Leonard blamed the sexual failure of their marriage on his wife's frigidity. But his remarks to Brenan and other contemporary letters suggest that something other than Virginia's refusing him had occurred. He told Brenan that he had given up the idea of having sexual satisfaction with her, but not because she was "frigid" and resisted his advances. He said he *stopped himself* because she had gotten into "a violent state of excitement" and he assumed that if she was sexually excited, she would go crazy.

Sexually demonstrative women had terrified Leonard Woolf all his adult life. From Ceylon, he had written Lytton Strachey a string of letters about how he had "degraded" himself by his sexual behavior. He described his need to end a relationship with a woman who was falling in love with him: the reason was that she had become "terribly & femininely violent" in their lovemaking. His sexual intercourse with her, rather than drawing them closer, had made him feel "beyond the pale of being."

Leonard's language about Virginia's response was much the same. Her violent excitement probably aroused that same sense of degradation that had been an all-too-common feature of his sexual life. He stopped himself with Virginia because, perhaps, he feared that sexual intercourse with her would make him hate her, as it had made him hate every one of his sexual partners in the past.

How did his resistance to her excitement make *her* feel and act? One can imagine that, given her history as a survivor of incest, anything less than loving, gentle understanding would have been problematic. Leonard repeatedly referred to the violence of his desire even as he avowed to Gerald Brenan that the violence of her desire stopped him. Years later, Virginia told her lesbian lover Vita Sackville-West that her sexual relationship with Leonard had been "a terrible failure, and was abandoned quite soon" after their marriage.

In telling Brenan that he was an ardent man and that he chose to give up a life of sexual fulfillment with Virginia, Leonard was muddying the waters: he was not giving up anything he had ever had. His relationship with Rachel, the young Englishwoman he had met in Kandy, had "degraded" him because she tempted him. The single relationship that had given him fulfillment in the past, despite his self-portrait as an extremely ardent man, was the chaste, quasi-platonic affair he had with Gwen in Jaffna. His most cherished memories were of the hugs and kisses they shared, lying on the sand by the lagoon in the moonlight.

He turned his marriage with Virginia into something similar. Perhaps he believed it would be unmanly to admit he preferred a life of sexual abstinence, and so he blamed her frigidity, not his needs and inclinations, for the celibacy in their marriage. He needed a marriage to Aspasia, in her guise as the snow maiden. Over the years, Virginia blamed herself and blamed her lack of self-control for the sexual failure of their marriage, and Leonard allowed her to believe this.

While the Woolfs were on their honeymoon, Vanessa Bell wrote Virginia and Leonard describing her pleasure at hearing about the "internal warmth" the newlyweds had been experiencing, in contrast to the cold weather that prevailed outside. The launching of their marriage had been promising and mutually satisfying, she trusted, but she wanted the newlyweds to send on a full report about their sexual life—she was bored and wanted a good story. She wanted to know whether Virginia was really as "promising" a sexual pupil as Leonard had suggested.

Leonard obliged Vanessa by sending on a full report of "his night with the Ape [Virginia]," which Vanessa then described, in detail, to Virginia! It couldn't have been an altogether satisfactory report, for Vanessa said she pitied Leonard "sincerely" for what he had to endure from Virginia. Vanessa and Leonard were banding together already to critique Virginia's sexual performance and to tell her about her supposed failings.

The most personal and private of human encounters quickly became the stuff of letters and confidences exchanged between Vanessa and Leonard. Under the guise of Apostolic honesty, under the rubric of complete openness in human discourse, Vanessa and Leonard were each punishing Virginia for different reasons.

Just as Virginia could not stand to see her sister in the presence of Clive, Vanessa, too, felt confused and excluded by her sister's marriage, which she wanted immediately to penetrate. Vanessa had found it "bewildering & upsetting"' to see Virginia and Leonard together. Leonard's sense of self-worth must have been seriously damaged when, for whatever reasons, his sexual relationship with Virginia presented problems. The two of them discovered that talking about Virginia relieved their sense of isolation; they quickly became allies, in league against Virginia.

Vanessa had to endure Clive's philandering very soon after their marriage had begun, first with Virginia and then with Mrs. Raven-Hill. But the collapse of Vanessa's marriage began when Virginia and Clive started their affair. Although at the time of Virginia's marriage, Vanessa was having an apparently satisfactory affair with Roger Fry, Clive's sentimentality at losing Virginia to marriage must have stirred up old resentments. To pay her sister back, what better method could Vanessa have chosen than flirting with Leonard just as Virginia had flirted with Clive, all the while claiming a sisterly interest in Virginia's marriage, just as Virginia had carried on her outlandish behavior with Clive amid protestations of unflagging sisterly devotion?

Turning the tables, Vanessa began to seduce Leonard. Confessing that she was sexually inadequate, she suggested that Leonard might want to give *her* a few lessons in the fine art of lovemaking. It was a very dangerous game, not only because Leonard had loved Vanessa first, but also because it stirred up a maelstrom of rivalrous and incestuous emotions in the two sisters.

Vanessa also wanted Leonard to know something that Virginia had probably not confessed: she and her sister had been sexually intimate; they had been lovers since their time in the nursery; they had shared mutual pettings and fondlings; they knew how to satisfy one another. Virginia had told Clive of their intimacy at the time of Vanessa's own marriage; but Leonard's attitude toward women who claimed their right to sexual pleasure was persecutory, whereas Clive's was not.

Vanessa wanted to share with Leonard expert information on

how he might satisfy Virginia sexually. Referring to Virginia as "the ape," a pet name, and using a male pronoun, Vanessa told Leonard: "As long as the ape [Virginia] gets all he wants, doesn't smell too much & has his claws well cut he's a pleasant enough bedfellow for a short time." Referring to Virginia's incestuous past, Vanessa suggested that if Virginia was an "apt pupil" it was because "he's been so much used." Referring to Virginia's lesbian history, she wondered whether Virginia "really feels more attracted by the male than by the female figure. Does he like manly strength & hardness?" She wanted Leonard to tell her *honestly* how her sister's sexual performance compared "to all the others" Leonard had slept with. She warned Leonard that there might be sexual problems in store for them. "The whole question," she wrote, "is what will happen when the red undergrowth sprouts in winter?"

The Wise Virgins
September 1912–June 1913

Leonard began writing *The Wise Virgins* less than a month after his marriage to Virginia. Each morning, and then again between tea and dinner, he methodically took up his pen and wrote at it—during his honeymoon in Europe, upon their return to London as they set up house in rooms at Cliffords Inn, during his trips to the Midlands and the north for the Women's Co-operative Guild, and during his and Virginia's stays in Sussex. By springtime, as he and Virginia worked together in the garden at Asheham House, as they burned nettles, planted foxgloves and wallflowers, fought moles and rabbits, and talked about having children, he had finished writing about half the novel.

It was a very good, productive time for them both, and it seemed to observers as if their marriage had gotten off to a good start. Virginia had finished her first novel, *The Voyage Out*. It was accepted for publication in April. Leonard's first novel, *The Village in the Jungle*, had been published, and reviewers were comparing his work favorably with that of Rudyard Kipling. Both were writing for *The Times*, and they were talking about jointly starting "the best magazine the world has ever seen." They were leading a very social life, seeing her cousins Marny and Emma Vaughan; Lady Ottoline Morrell, who was full of plans for Garsington, the fifteenth-century manor house she had just purchased, and who tried to wheedle confidences that Walter Lamb, one of her lovers, might have shared with Leonard; and Virginia's onetime suitor Sydney Waterlow, who came to recuperate from the effects of his divorce. Anyone who joined them at Asheham was handed a shovel and asked to dig with them in the garden.

But there was the problem of their sexual relationship. In December, Virginia and Leonard consulted Vanessa about Virginia's "coldness"; Vanessa blamed Virginia, telling Leonard that her sister had never been sympathetic to "sexual passion in men."

And there was the problem about children. Virginia wanted to have children; Leonard said he had come to believe that her having them would be too dangerous, that a pregnancy would result in another bout of madness. He aired his views both with Virginia and Vanessa. Although all agreed that after her marriage, Virginia seemed healthier than ever before, Leonard insisted on consulting four doctors about her, and Jean Thomas too. Some believed that childbearing would help Virginia. But Leonard persisted until he found a doctor willing to confirm his own position.

His fears might have been inflamed by a mysterious event that occurred on their honeymoon. On September 14, a little more than a month after their marriage, while the couple were touring Italy, Vanessa wrote her sister a curious letter. She told Virginia that because she hadn't written, she was "convinced" that Virginia "was having a miscarriage or something & now your letter came & I see that I was not altogether wrong."

What had happened to Virginia? The letter she wrote describing the event has not survived; presumably, it has been destroyed. Virginia and Leonard seem to have lived through a gynecological scare that incapacitated Virginia—Vanessa, in her letter, refers to Leonard's "treatment" of Virginia sounding "sensible."

If Virginia was to be permitted to have children, it meant that the couple would have to continue their sexual relationship, inadequate or terrifying as it was. Virginia was willing to continue their sexual life under these circumstances to have children; Leonard was not. Only a decree from a doctor forbidding Virginia's pregnancy would rule out sexual relations permanently. That was what Leonard wanted. He used a doctor's prohibition against his wife's pregnancy as a shield behind which to conduct his sexual life in a way that suited him, and what suited him was celibacy.

Behind Virginia's back, he enlisted Vanessa's support for his position, enumerating the emotional differences between the two sisters, suggesting to Vanessa that she was far more womanly than her sister, far more able to handle life's crises. Either he did not know, or ignored, that Vanessa had had her own breakdown in the wake of her first child's birth. Buttressed by Vanessa's support, he became intractable. Virginia must have suspected that he and her sister were conspiring. Once Vanessa learned of Leonard's decision, she circulated the story through Bloomsbury.

Early in 1913, when these events were transpiring, Virginia showed signs of stress. In January, Leonard showed Vanessa a draft of *The Wise Virgins*. In the novel, he blamed Virginia by innuendo for the sexual failure of their marriage, depicting her as a frigid snow queen, utterly incapable of sexual intercourse, even incapable of love.

The Wise Virgins is a vicious novel. Writing it was the most sadistic act, with the most tragic consequences, of Leonard Woolf's life.

Prompted by the betrayal he thought his marriage was, unaware of his failings, racked by self-hatred, pained by the virulent anti-Semitism he encountered in his wife and her family and friends, Leonard began writing a book that struck out at all those who had harmed him and that tried to repair his injured sense of self. He had endured significant blows to his pride since he began wooing Virginia: marrying a woman above his class had made him feel more, not less, inadequate.

The novel was intended to harm, although Leonard could not have anticipated the extent of the pain it would cause or the irreparable damage it would inflict. He knew it would be published. Inspired by the good notices for his first novel, his publisher was eager for his second effort. It was a *roman à clef*, transparent in its meanings to anyone who knew any of its major players—Leonard himself, Virginia, Vanessa, Clive Bell, Leonard's mother and sister.

The Wise Virgins concerns the amatory and sexual misadventures of a young Jewish Londoner, Harry Davis (Leonard himself), a self-styled Byronic hero. Davis is an art student from a conventional middle-class family, residing in Richstead (the Putney of

Leonard's youth). He travels in two very different social circles—the middle class and the affluent upper class, whose members he envies and loathes. He has become acquainted with upper-class society through Camilla Lawrence (Virginia), a fellow art student.

In the novel, Davis is tempted to desert his class; he is fascinated by Camilla and her sister Katherine (Vanessa), and Katherine suggests that Camilla marry him. His mother, though, arranges a meeting with Gwen Garland, a neighbor's daughter, that erupts into something more than a mere acquaintanceship.

Much of Harry's unhappiness springs from his feeling himself an outsider no matter where he is: his education renders him incapable of appreciating life in Richstead; his Jewishness and their anti-Semitism lock him out of acceptance in the drawing rooms of upper-class intellectuals in Bloomsbury; though he is invited to their homes, they deride him. Although he is drawn to Katherine and Camilla Lawrence, it will be his destiny to marry Gwen, his inferior, who both adores him because he is an artist, and fears him because he shows her the most vicious parts of his nature. With Gwen, he can feel masterful.

Before his honeymoon had ended, Leonard had begun a novel describing himself as a man who was violent, sadistic, lacking in self-control, yet immensely virile, with an ungovernable desire to debauch naive, innocent young women. A novel describing his wife Virginia (in the guise of Camilla) as an ice maiden, hopelessly frigid, locked into delusory imaginings, and beyond the possibility of experiencing satisfying sexual love. A novel confessing to his continuing, unrequited passion for Vanessa (in the guise of Katherine), the more beautiful, more sensuous of the two sisters. A novel describing that only Vanessa, of the two sisters, could love a man. And the fantasy that, had he married Vanessa, he could have had a good sex life with her, "and a calm life of marriage."

It was a novel that explored and decried the sisters' "curiously strong love" for one another, yet that exposed Vanessa's need to thwart Virginia's relationships. He wrote out his disgust at Virginia's relationship with Clive (in the person of Arthur), at Virginia's flirtatious ways, at her excitement at being desired by more than one man. His contempt for Virginia's family and her class. His own self-loathing. His equation of sexuality with violence. His belief that his love for Virginia had originated in his need to possess her, as one would possess a valuable object. His shame about his own family and their coarse, vulgar, and ignorant ways. His fury at his mother's chronic criticism of him.

In writing the novel, Leonard spared no one in his immediate circle except Lytton Strachey. During his years in Ceylon, he had come to crave solitude, to prefer a life lived in isolation. Writing *The Wise Virgins* would keep everyone in Leonard's life at a safe distance for a long time.

His major target was Virginia. He spared her nothing. He attacked her for everything—the way she looked, talked, and thought. Nothing they had experienced together was sacred. He used the troubled, pained, confusing conversations they had shared, the letters she had written to him during their courtship, sometimes paraphrasing them but sometimes reproducing her exact words. He used his letters to her, and the letters to and from Lytton Strachey discussing his love for Vanessa, which he had shown her. He lifted chunks from his portrait of her as "Aspasia." He stole the name of one of her characters in *The Voyage Out*. He took scenes straight from her novel, but satirized them, or rewrote them, from his point of view. He used their boat trip to Maidenhead on the day she said she would marry him. Their conversations on the terrace at Asheham House. Their evenings together in the company of the Bloomsberries. He even used their most intimate moments and significant moments—their wedding ceremony, and abortive attempts to make love.

One of the worst blows that Virginia faced in reading *The Wise Virgins* was that Leonard rewrote the outcome of his courtship; in fiction, he undid his marriage. In the novel Harry (Leonard) *does not marry* Camilla (Virginia). Though enlightened by the experience of having known Camilla Lawrence and her circle, he realizes that the members of her class are vacuous do-nothings. He understands that Camilla Lawrence is hopelessly damaged, and that she lives her life in the equivalent of a "sick-room."

He decides, instead, to marry Gwen Garland, a woman of his class, though marriage to her will not be satisfying either, and he hates her cowlike eyes. Leonard described Harry's knowledge that marriage to Camilla would have been a disaster; he knew that "the foulness" of his thoughts could not coexist in a marriage with "such purity of beauty." Harry saves himself from certain pain: He realizes that his appearance of "coldness and hardness," a defense against his bestial nature, repulses Camilla, though she is tempted by him because she senses that under "the crust" of his nature, there was "something intricate and perhaps violent." But he must live with a woman to whom he does not feel inferior, who is not put off by his nature, who will allow him to assert mastery over her, who will allow him to abuse her. In a telling conversation with Gwen about the similarity between women and dogs, Harry says that the "more you beat them the more they love you. . . . They say it's the same with . . . a woman."

The Wise Virgins exposed Leonard's confusion about sex and about women, reiterating points of view he had expressed over the years in his letters to Lytton Strachey. Another character in the novel maintains that unless women "are loose and vile they have no passions": sexual passion makes men "noble" but makes women base. Virginal women, like Camilla, "don't know," nor can they ever know, "what desire is. What they want is to be desired—that's all." Once a man desires them, they marry, but it will be his fate in such a marriage "to be disappointed." If a woman has a mind and sees the world clearly, as Camilla does, "what she really wants, only she doesn't know it, is to be a man"; this unacknowledged envy of men makes her undesirable as a woman.

When Camilla touches Harry's hand, his heart beats "violently," but he remembers his "trembling disgust" during an encounter with a prostitute. He can't imagine Camilla desiring him, so she reminds him of a prostitute who goes about her business without passion. When Harry proposes to Camilla, she perceives it as a threat (she is correct, as his subsequent proposal to Gwen illustrates), and she refuses. But her refusal makes him feel so inconsequential, so meaningless, that he lashes out in a fury at the disgusting nature of her gender:

> He saw women as he had never seen them before—ridiculous, grotesque, repulsive. The monstrous shapes of them . . . ! One imagined that "forked animal" woman—a poor, thin, soft white body, forking out into two long, weedy white legs like one of those white clammy turnips, which you sometimes see forking grotesquely into two legs.

The place between a woman's legs makes Harry sick.

If this is how Harry thinks about women he perceives as snow-covered mountains, his behavior to hot-blooded women is no better. After he gives Gwen a copy of *The Master Builder* to read and she admits that she felt she was a new Hilda and that he was *"her* Master Builder," she tells him she wants to start living, to start following her instincts, "to prove herself by some daring act or noble passion," instead of merely existing: she wants to change her life.

Though Gwen suspects that Harry is cruel, she tries to change her life by asserting her passion for him. She puts her arms around him, and there is an encounter that sounds just like what Leonard Woolf told Gerald Brenan about his lovemaking with Virginia:

> He felt her body on his. He took her in his arms, and began to kiss her. She returned his kisses passionately, pressing herself against him. Her violence and her tears surprised him; he half drew away, but she held him to her. He allowed her to lie quietly in his arms.

He feels "sudden fear and horror," and responds to Gwen's passion by calling her "child." Her sexual assertiveness leads him to believe that she "might do anything; she was mad."

When Gwen confronts him again, in his bedroom, Harry feels a "little movement of desire," but it is "cruel and brutal." They share a night of "madness and passion," which initially makes Harry feel satisfied: "he seemed to be all body." And in a scene that sounds as if D. H. Lawrence might have written it, Harry caresses himself: "He ran his hands down the firm flesh, felt and saw the short curves of the muscles, and thought to himself, proud and half-amused: 'Thank God, I'm a man!' " The feeling doesn't last long. Almost immediately, he finds himself walking "with the spring of a fresh young *mare"*: sexual intercourse unmans him; it makes him hate her "soft, childish face and body and mind"; it reminds him he lives in a "foul and fetid world." When he thinks again of Gwen, he sings himself a ditty about her being the "queen of pleasure" and him being the "king of pain."

Gwen tells her mother and his mother what has happened. Harry decides he might as well marry Gwen. He thinks she will become "his chattel, his wife, his dog."

Just after his marriage to Virginia, Leonard used the art of fiction to contemplate what his life might have been if he had married the other woman in his life, the friend of his family whom he had courted while courting Virginia. In *The Wise Virgins* he was saying that he had made a mistake, that he had made the wrong choice. If he could have done it over, he would have done it differently. In this way, he paid Virginia back for what he saw as the failure of his marriage.

Yet Harry's marriage is also seen as a trap. In the novel, Leonard scripts an attitude toward marriage that raises all the objections Virginia raised during their courtship. But Harry's marriage shows his contempt for women, and Gwen fares no better than Camilla would have fared. Any astute reader of the text would have realized the latent message: that whether a woman was sexually assertive or passive and virginal, Harry would hate her because Harry hates and fears women.

Leonard provided the most transparent clue to his state of mind toward Virginia in the name he chose for her in the novel: Camilla. The name shows the distance he had traversed in his feelings toward Virginia since he dubbed her "Aspasia," friend and colleague of man, during their courtship.

Camilla appears in Virgil's *Aeneid*. She represents the enemy of man, the Amazon whose power must be destroyed if men are to rule. Aeneas falls under Camilla's influence, and she unmans him and subverts his will. By getting him to build "her city instead of his own," she deflects his purpose. Camilla must be murdered so that her power can be destroyed and Rome can "be born."

Until Virginia, one of the greatest readers in literary criticism, read the manuscript of *The Wise Virgins*, she had no indication that Leonard was so dissatisfied with her, that there was no way for her to behave that would mollify him. Outwardly, all seemed well. Inwardly, like his creation Harry Davis, Leonard was seething with murderous fury.

13, Cliffords Inn, Fleet Street and Burley, Cambridge Park, Twickenham June–September 1913

"Marriage—yes?—What about marriage?" Virginia Woolf wrote. "I married Leonard Woolf in 1912, . . . and almost immediately was ill for 3 years."

The trouble started in late July, as Leonard was finishing work on *The Wise Virgins* and as she herself was reading proof for *The Voyage Out*. According to Leonard, she had become "much too nervous" about herself: she couldn't work; she couldn't sleep; she wouldn't eat; and she was extremely depressed. He persuaded her that it would be best if she entered Jean Thomas's nursing home at Twickenham for a rest cure.

According to Thomas, though, Virginia's panic and fear at the thought that she had exposed herself in her novel, and that "everyone would jeer at her" once it was published, precipitated her illness. Thomas believed her illness "*ought*" to have been avoided. Virginia was, no doubt, also afraid of what would be said about her portrait in *The Wise Virgins*. Rather than quieting her fears, rather than alleviating her anxiety, the people in her life—Clive Bell and Vanessa—"did the wrong thing & teased . . . & she got desperate." When she entered Twickenham, she was "a wreck." In true Bloomsbury fashion, weakness was ridiculed. The Bloomsberries knew how to launch an attack when any of its members showed weakness.

When Leonard visited her at Twickenham, she told him she suspected that she had caused him pain, and that he wasn't altogether happy with her. He declined the opportunity she provided to discuss the problems in their marriage. Instead, Leonard, the Cambridge Apostle committed to total honesty, denied her charge, telling her that she had done nothing but bring him "the most perfect happiness," a claim that would be impossible to prove to any reader of *The Wise Virgins*.

She was responding, with anger and disappointment, to their marriage. He would not permit her these feelings. Instead, he tried to persuade her that her response to him was unfounded—he loved her unconditionally; what she perceived about his dissatisfaction with her was untrue. He enlisted Vanessa's support. Vanessa told

Virginia that she would get better when she let herself, suggesting that Virginia was making herself sick. Vanessa implored Virginia not to make Leonard's life "difficult"; Vanessa told Virginia she "must take it on trust" that they were right about what was wrong with her. Only when she was "mad" could she express the depth of her rage at him for his betrayal of her.

After his visit, Leonard wrote a series of frantic letters, filled with reassurances about the splendor of their love and protestations that nothing would ever come between them. He wrote them in baby talk and love patter, using their nicknames—Mandril (the largest, most hideous, most ferocious of the baboons) for Virginia, Mongoose (a ferretlike creature known for its superior ability in driving out and tormenting its prey) for Leonard:

> My dearest Mistress Mandril, . . . you do know what a happy year we've had together. . . . I believe, Great One, you do want to take on your mongoose in service for another year—& if you'll only let him grovel before you & kiss your toes, he'll be happy.

Unable to face the problems in their marriage, Leonard built the fantasy of a perfect union, which he clung to throughout the near-tragic events of the coming months, while also writing his daily quota of words of *The Wise Virgins*. He let her know that if she told him "dreadful things," he wouldn't believe them. Unable to persuade Leonard that there were serious issues they needed to consider, knowing that he would think she was lying if she expressed displeasure, Virginia began blaming herself for whatever had gone wrong.

At the beginning of August, when Leonard visited her, she suggested that they separate because she had dissatisfied him. He begged her not to persist: "Surely you must know what you mean to me," he wrote her, "—to be really separated from you would be absolutely unbearable." He assured her that he had never been anything but honest with her, and told her that there was no "reason in the world why you should reproach yourself with anything or think that you have done anything to be laughed at." He asked her to tell him whether he had done anything to displease her, promising that he would "do anything to change any beastliness in myself, if I knew how it had shown itself."

She said he was not to blame. He had been "absolutely perfect." Whatever problems they had were all her fault.

The Wise Virgins is never mentioned in these exchanges as a cause of Virginia Woolf's pain, but her fears that she would become even more of a laughingstock were surely rooted in her knowledge of what Leonard had written in the novel. He was going public with a story that would make her a target, that would expose her to further scorn and ridicule.

After the forced rest at Twickenham, Virginia was somewhat better. When she felt her symptoms abate, she insisted on leaving. Leonard took her off to Asheham House for a fortnight to continue her cure of quiet and rest.

During this period, as his wife was trying to recover, he finished *The Wise Virgins*.

Her recuperation was interrupted because Vanessa wanted the use of the house for a house party and callously insisted that Leonard and Virginia depart. Leonard, realizing that he couldn't take Virginia back to London in her agitated state, decided instead to take her on a holiday to the Plough Inn in the Quantocks, the site of the early days of their honeymoon.

The trip to the Plough Inn was a "nightmare." It cannot have been reassuring or restful for Virginia. She knew Leonard had finished his novel and that he intended to publish. She was in a state of near-panic and agitation; she felt she was being mocked and scorned. She realized that her sister cared more for her own pleasure than for her well-being; a party was more important to Vanessa than Virginia's recuperation. Now Virginia's care was entirely in the hands of her husband, a man who had re-created her as Camilla in *The Wise Virgins*.

With almost no emotional resources left, she packed her belongings, endured another long and uncomfortable train journey, and revisited the Plough Inn, the site of the sexual debacle of the early days of her honeymoon. After a week at the Plough Inn, she was far more depressed than when she had arrived. She refused to eat; she couldn't rest. As always, Leonard gave her veronal when she had trouble sleeping, and it exacerbated her depression.

Leonard, however worried he may have been at his wife's ever worsening condition, was eating magnificently. While Virginia was starving herself, he began his morning with "bread, butter, cream, and eggs and bacon." He enjoyed his evening meals of "beef, mutton, and lamb . . . always magnificent and perfectly cooked." To accompany his daily repasts, he indulged himself in local "beer and cider" that he found "delicious."

He persuaded her to return to London to consult a doctor of her own choosing to decide the state of her sanity. He had secured the services of a friend, Ka Cox, to help him bring Virginia back to London when it seemed he would have trouble managing her alone. He never told her that he had already sought medical advice before their journey. He wanted her to admit that she was seriously ill; he wanted her to admit her insanity.

Virginia was now altogether alone. In her pain, she found she could count on no one, not Vanessa or Clive or Leonard. No matter how severe her suffering, no matter how desperate she felt, her husband continued to work on his novel, and her family would not help her. When they saw her suffer, they jeered at her, and then they told her that her feelings of being laughed at were "delusions." They knew she was insane, and she should admit it. What she sought, but never found, was a state of "immunity"; she wanted to feel "apart from rubs, shocks, suffering."

They made the agonizing journey back to London on September 8. On the train ride back, Leonard and Ka Cox kept Virginia under constant surveillance. She was in "blackest despair." They were sure she had become suicidal and they were afraid she would try to kill herself by throwing herself off the moving train.

38 Brunswick Square, Bloomsbury
Tuesday, September 9, 1913

Leonard and Ka took Virginia to spend the night at Vanessa's home in Bloomsbury.

The next day, September 9, a Tuesday, some time after taking her tea, Virginia tried to kill herself. It was a very serious suicide attempt. While Leonard was out and she was in Ka's care, she had found and taken "100 grains of veronal and also an immense quantity of an even more dangerous drug—medinal."

On the morning of September 9, Leonard had accompanied Virginia to see Dr. Wright and then Dr. Head, both of whom told her that "she was ill," and that she would need a prolonged period of rest to recover. After, when they returned to Brunswick Square, Virginia conversed with Vanessa. Leonard was relieved to see her more "cheerful & rested."

Leonard left Virginia in Vanessa's and Ka's care while he took care of some business at their rooms in Cliffords Inn. He returned to Brunswick Square to have tea with Virginia, but again left her to arrange a consultation between the two doctors. It was a beautiful, sunny day, and during the late afternoon, Leonard and Vanessa met in Regents Park and sat together, discussing Virginia.

Leonard had another appointment to keep, later in the day, with Dr. Savage. Ka Cox phoned Savage's office to report that Virginia had fallen into a deep sleep. Leonard sensed danger and rushed back to Brunswick Square by taxi. Virginia "seemed unconscious." He telephoned Vanessa to bring a doctor; she brought Dr. Head, who brought along nurses to help work on Virginia.

Leonard and Dr. Geoffrey Keynes (Maynard Keynes's brother) rushed to a nearby hospital for a stomach pump. Head, Keynes, and the nurses worked until twelve-thirty, when Leonard went to sleep. He confessed that he could always get a good night's rest, even under the most trying circumstances.

With Leonard sleeping, Virginia reached a crisis at one-thirty. No one awakened him. By the next morning, the doctor pronounced her out of danger. Vanessa came in to him at six in the morning to tell him the good news.

Virginia Woolf did not recover consciousness until Friday.

Leonard believed the suicide attempt was his fault. The reason he gave was that he had forgotten to lock the case containing Virginia's medications and had left it in the room in which she would be resting.

Although he was willing to admit his guilt, he confessed he felt no remorse about what he had done. He was a person "unable to feel remorse for something which has been done and cannot be undone." He was "mentally and morally unable to cry over spilt milk."

In the months following his wife's suicide attempt, as she recuperated at Dalingridge Place, George Duckworth's country estate, in the care of four nurses, and then at Asheham House in Sussex, Leonard sent copies of *The Wise Virgins* around to members of his family and friends to ask what he should do about the novel. Most thought it was either not good enough to publish, or a misguided effort that would do his family and Virginia harm. His mother, Marie Woolf, warned that if he published the work, with its "ridicule, contempt and pity" of the family, there would be a "serious break" between them. His sister Bella wrote him a nine-page letter condemning the work: "You have dipped your pen in pessimism & it sticks to everyone." His brother Edgar's pain in reading the work was still keenly remembered forty years later when he wrote Leonard: "As a boy you were mean & a bully. . . . You showed what a cad you were when you published the Wise Virgins."

Leonard decided he was willing to risk all to publish the work, telling the "whole lot of them to go to Hell," but only if it was a good book, one worth publishing. He enlisted Lytton Strachey's help in ascertaining the worth of his effort and sent along the novel.

Lytton Strachey's largely negative critical commentary was eight handwritten pages long. Strachey believed the novel was unconvincing in describing the motivation of Harry "after the fucking of Gwen"; he thought the general conception of the novel was off the mark; he advised Leonard to put it aside for six months, but to keep writing at something else. Privately, though, Lytton did not believe his old friend had the makings of a novelist: "Perhaps he should be a camel merchant," he told Lamb, "slowly driving his beasts over the vast plains of Baluchistan. Something like that would I'm sure be more appropriate than his present occupations."

After soliciting Strachey's opinion, Leonard polled just about everyone he could. Before publication, he elicited opinions from Vanessa Bell, Adrian Stephen, Janet Case (Virginia's former Greek teacher and close friend), and Margaret Llewelyn Davies (of the Women's Co-operative Guild, with whom Leonard was working). Leonard was circulating the portrait of Virginia as Camilla throughout Bloomsbury even before the novel's publication, after Camilla's prototype, Virginia, had very nearly killed herself. Most comments were negative. Vanessa's, though, were not. She thought that though the story would offend, Leonard should publish anyway— "feelings," she wrote, "after all, *arent* [sic] very important."

Despite the majority opinion, Leonard sent his novel on to his publisher with a letter expressing "hesitation about publishing the manuscript." His publisher replied that the novel showed "further evidence" of Leonard's "powers as a writer."

This decided Leonard. He agreed to the work's publication despite the risk to his personal relationships and to his wife's health. Soon after, he himself had a "nervous breakdown." He recuperated for a time with Lytton Strachey, writing Virginia daily bulletins describing the state of his health and asking about hers. "You can't realise how utterly you would end my life for me if you had taken that sleeping mixture successfully or if you ever dismissed me," he wrote.

How the Woolf marriage survived this betrayal and its consequences and went on to become one of the most important working partnerships in the history of English letters is the subject of another narrative. Despite what her husband had done to her in print, Virginia Woolf never viciously struck out at him in a work of literature. Instead, she sought to understand what had happened to them at the beginning of their marriage. Her life's work contained a few portraits of Leonard. He appears as Ralph Denham in *Night and Day*, as Louis in *The Waves*, as Peter Walsh in *Mrs. Dalloway*, but always the portraits are complex and sympathetic, though they may be sharp and critical. In *Night and Day*, the novel Virginia wrote once her recuperation was complete, she takes up the same essential subject that her husband had traversed in *The Wise Virgins*—the subject of marriage across class and culture. The heroine thinks about her forthcoming marriage:

> [S]he took up her knitting again and listened, chiefly with a view to confirming herself in the belief that to be engaged to marry some one with whom you are not in love is an inevitable step in a world where the existence of passion is only a traveller's story brought from the heart of deep forests and told so rarely that wise people doubt whether the story can be true.

Virginia's recovery was not simple and straightforward. It took years, and she did not lead a comparatively normal life until 1916. For months, her life followed the routine of the invalid: "Bed—walk—bed—walk—bed—sleep." Years later, she described herself in those days as "creeping about, like a rat struck on the head."

In 1915, during a period when she appeared to be getting better, she reread *The Wise Virgins* in its entirety. She entered some favorable remarks about it in her diary (which Leonard had access to and read, so they were, perhaps, not honest), calling it a "remarkable book," a "writer's book." Soon after, though, she entered the most violent and angry phase of her illness. Again she required the services of nurses. She hurled "terrific outbursts of abuse" at Leonard; she was "violently hostile" to him; she wouldn't talk to him or allow him to come into her room. At one point, she refused to see him for two months. Nor did she spare Vanessa or Clive.

Both Leonard and Vanessa believed Virginia's rage was caused by her illness, that it was an irrational feature of her madness. Her illness, though, seems to have been a classic case of post-traumatic stress disorder.

Leonard and Vanessa never linked Virginia's rage with their betrayal of her. Vanessa, describing her sister's behavior, wrote: "She won't see Leonard at all & has taken against all men. She says the most malicious & cutting things she can think of to everyone and they are so clever that they always hurt." The malicious and cutting things Virginia said hurt Vanessa and others, no doubt, because what she said was true.

In time, Virginia broke the cycle of revenge and betrayal Leonard had initiated through her capacity to forgive him for what he had done. He, too, though he maintained that he was incapable of remorse, from this time forward dedicated his life to her care: he had, no doubt, realized his potential for cruelty, and it changed him. In October 1915, in the month when *The Wise Virgins* was published, after he had taken her for an outing to Brighton, she gave him a gift that carried a twofold message: of pain, but also of the possibility that their life could again be joyful. It was a copy of Fyodor Dostoyevsky's *The Insulted and the Injured* in which she had written: "A Memory of the grand treat; Brighton."

Although he was irritable, difficult, and often irascible, during the remainder of their life together Leonard never again inflicted major harm upon Virginia. Once she recovered, she did not again suffer a major illness for twenty-four years, and this was due, in part, to his care.

Leonard Woolf became a staunch feminist, a socialist, a pacifist, an ardent critic of imperialism, genuinely interested in the well-being of humankind. After its initial phase, he lived his moral and ethical principles in his marriage, and became his wife's most faithful supporter, the first reader of her work, her copublisher, her soul mate, and her friend. Instead of children, the two brought forth, through their joint effort, starting in 1917, the publications of the Hogarth Press, one of the most important and successful publishing ventures in history, which Virginia called "that strange offspring." At first, they did all the setting up and printing themselves, by hand; they mended their marriage as, side by side, they built their press. Virginia, who was dyslexic, very often set type backward or upside down. Their first publication was a joint effort: her "Mark on the Wall" and his "Three Jews."

Publishing *The Wise Virgins* had serious consequences for Leonard. He had always wanted to be a novelist. The novel shows as much promise as the early work of D. H. Lawrence, E. M. Forster, and Virginia Woolf herself. All Leonard said about the novel in his autobiography was that it was published "simultaneously with the outbreak of the war," that the "war killed it dead," and that all he earned from it was twenty pounds. The reviews were generally poor. Harry Davis was seen as an obnoxious character, Camilla and her family as depressives.

After the debacle of *The Wise Virgins*, though he started a work of fiction called "The Empire Builder," he soon abandoned it, and he never wrote another novel. Suffering from the criticism he received from family and friends, Leonard told Lytton Strachey that he was abandoning fiction because of his experience with the novel: "I shall never write another book after these damned Virgins," he remarked. His self-esteem suffered. He saw himself as a failed novelist. When he became literary editor of *The Nation and Atheneum*, he did not regard it as an honor. Instead, in thinking back to the novels he had written and musing on the novels he would now never write, he believed he had "sunk to the last rung."

In 1933, for artistic reasons, to refresh her memory of World War I, Virginia Woolf went back and read her diary. She read of the life she had shared with Leonard at the time, and wrote:

> How close the tears come, again & again; as I read of L. & me . . . : our quarrels. . . . Well we are very happy. Life buds & sprouts all round us. . . . I think we live in a rich porous earth. I think we live very fully, freely & adventurously. In short, what we made of that strange prelude is good.

❧ 3 ❧

"LIKE A LION RAGING AFTER ITS PREY":

D. H. Lawrence, Ottoline Morrell, and *Women in Love*

One sheds one's sicknesses in books—repeats and presents again one's emotions, to be master of them.

—D. H. LAWRENCE
October 1913

Greatham, Pulborough, Sussex
February 1915

L ady Ottoline Morrell stepped down from the old four-wheeler
that D. H. Lawrence had sent to the train station to meet her,
into the Sussex countryside, wearing purple velvet and all her
pearls. He would remember until the end of his life how she
looked as she made her way across the meadows when she came
to see him in his borrowed country cottage on this sunlit day in
February 1915, with the war raging in France, on the other side of
the English Channel. He had hoped it would be a fine, sunny day
for her, and it was. She would recall the spareness of his cottage,
the long refectory table, his delightful talk, and that he himself
cooked her lunch.

She was the half sister of a duke and, as Lytton Strachey
phrased it, the daughter of a thousand earls, and he was "the son
of a Nottinghamshire miner." He believed at first that she belonged
to a special breed of woman, that she was like Cassandra or one of
the great saints. He hoped she would become the center of a new
community he envisioned. It would rise from the ashes of the war,
and integrity of character, not wealth or heredity, would take pri-
macy. She thought, after so many disappointments, she had found
a friend, one whom she could talk to openly, without "fear of being
thought silly." She felt that her true vocation was to "enhance the
lives of people she admired," and she admired him. To seal their
friendship, he painted a little wooden box for her. On the cover
was a phoenix, the emblem of his new community.

At first, they shared much: memories of the Nottinghamshire

countryside, where, though from different classes, each had grown up. He spoke to her in the Nottinghamshire dialect she loved. They talked of Sherwood Forest, the darkness of the miners' villages, the lives of colliers and their families, which had fascinated her since she was a child. They loved nature, and felt with the same intensity the rush of the wind and the vivid beauty of flowers when they came into blossom.

They were house-proud—perfectionists who stitched their own curtains, who thought carefully about where they should place their furniture. She inherited her furniture from her forebears. He bought his in jumble sales, or chose carefully among the discards of fishermen's wives at flea markets, or he made by hand the things he needed—a dresser, bookshelves. They were careful, too, of the colors they painted their rooms. Distemper stained with just a touch of pink. A translucent sea-green that gave the impression of water flowing.

Her rooms were in grand, beautifully proportioned buildings, and his were in converted outbuildings, even in cattle sheds, like the ones he was living in at Greatham. Often, he borrowed them from friends.

They liked to be surrounded by the smell of flowers. He waited for them to bloom each spring—sea-pinks, foxgloves, bluebells, primroses—and he placed vases of flowers he had grown in his garden where he could see them as he wrote. She planned and planted an elaborate Italianate garden at Garsington Manor, her Oxfordshire estate; indoors, she preferred her flowers dried, as pot-pourri, filling the warm air of her cluttered, gracious rooms with an intermingling of what some guests believed were too many heady scents.

They liked beautiful, colorful things. He decorated "pots and jars with bright designs in stripes and spots," took a discarded cupboard and painted it a brilliant blue. She had her artist friends paint murals on her walls, though she obliterated their work by whitewashing when she grew tired of them. She hung portraits of herself painted by her artist friends and lovers—Augustus John and Duncan Grant—where she could see them.

Each was a hopeless romantic. Each had steadfastly adhered, through much disappointment, to a belief in the redemptive power of love. Each believed "that love is all," though they had loved unwisely and either too much, or not well enough. Their marriages had become compromises, and their friends knew it, though they staunchly maintained that their marriages were successes.

They went for long walks together when she visited him in Sussex, into the woods and then up onto the Downs. After a long climb, they could see Arundel in the distance, and the brilliance of the sea. He brought his friends up there to see this view to test their characters. He wanted to find out whether they felt as passionately as he did about the beauty of this piece of England. He was afraid their walks were too much for her, and that he had tired her and made her uncomfortable, but she assured him he hadn't. Although she thought she wanted to experience a simple life, she was not used, as he was, to sleeping in such intense cold.

In the woods, with the trees still bare of leaves, he pulled down a branch and showed her the buds.

"See," he said to her, "here is the little red flame in Nature."

She looked at him as he spoke, and thought, but did not say, "In you, too, there certainly dwells that flame."

He was hard at work on *The Rainbow,* the novel that many would later describe as his masterpiece. She was exhausted from the effort of creating Garsington, her country estate just outside Oxford, which was her supreme accomplishment. There, as in her home in Bedford Square, Bloomsbury, she would bring together everyone she knew—the prime minister, writers, pacifists, mathematicians, musicians, philosophers, Japanese actors, dancers, refugees, the very famous and the unknown, for their mutual benefit. She had hopes that Lawrence and her current lover, Bertrand Russell, would become friends and share political ideas, and, for a time, they did. Enriching the lives of people she admired, introducing them to one another, and helping them "develop" canceled her fear that her life had been entirely without merit.

D. H. Lawrence came to understand Ottoline Morrell, and this was dangerous. He recognized that they were very much alike, and he thought she possessed many qualities he despised in himself—a passionate intensity in his relationships, alternating with an overwhelming need for solitude, which caused a flight from them; a will to control the way his friends behaved and the way they thought. He made a habit of using what he learned about people against them, both in his relations with them and in his work. She, too, could be vicious in her mockery. A friend once remarked that Lawrence tried to direct his friends' lives as if they were his literary creations, but when they resisted, he " 'took his revenge' ... by working 'his will upon them' in his books." And what was her hope to improve her friends but another way of saying that they didn't please her as they were and so they must change?

She might have held back from him, but that was not her way. She should have, for he had warned her that he might hurt her. She believed that because she understood him, she could control the way he treated her. She was mistaken. Lawrence had a history of using the women he knew and loved in his work. "If I need any woman for my purpose," he told a friend, "I shall use [her]. Why the devil should ... any woman come between me and the flowering of my genius?" Once, when a friend objected to Lawrence's using his friends in his work, he responded, "How can anyone complain so long as the narrator tells the truth? And suppose their puny feelings are hurt, or, what is probably nearer the mark, they get a pain in their pride, what does it matter so their lesson is given to the world and they shall have taught others to avoid the mistakes they made?"

Lawrence told Ottoline not to make too much of him, nor to expect too much from him, lest he disappoint her as she had been disappointed before. In a letter early in their friendship, he wrote, "they say comprendre c'est pardonner," that "to understand is to forgive." But no, he thought, it really should be "comprendre c'est vouloir pûnir." "To understand is to want to punish."

And punish her he did in his vicious portrait of her as Hermione Roddice, in *Women in Love,* which he began to write in April 1916, a little more than a year after they had been so happy together, when she came to see him in Sussex wearing purple velvet and all those pearls.

"The Daughter of a Thousand Earls"

1.

Ottoline remembered herself as a joyless child. She was the youngest of five children, born in London on June 16, 1873, and named Ottoline Violet Anne Cavendish Bentinck. Her father was Lieutenant-General Arthur Cavendish Bentinck, colonel of the Seventh Dragoon Guards. Her mother was Lady Bolsover, Augusta Mary Elizabeth, his second wife, who had Anglo-Irish connections.

Ottoline seemed born into a privileged world. Her family had a house in London and another in the country. They had servants, and a nurse for Ottoline. Hers was a world of lace dresses, pink sashes, and curled hair, of pony rides with her father, proudly and protectively beside her, laughing and taking pleasure in her company.

The family was very well off. Her father was the heir of the aged and failing fifth Duke of Portland. Upon his death, he would become the sixth duke, inheriting the family seat at Welbeck Abbey in Nottinghamshire and other properties.

When she was four and a half, though, Ottoline's father died unexpectedly of a heart attack, and the dukedom passed to her father's son from his first marriage. Ottoline's mother became bereft and depressed; she worried about her future. To lessen her overwhelming sense of loss, she turned to Ottoline for relief and comfort.

Ottoline became her mother's constant companion and her major source of emotional support. Ottoline remembered always being by her mother's side, walking with her hand in hand. She slept in her mother's room, her small, hard bed pulled directly up against her mother's. Through the night, Ottoline witnessed her mother's grief. No wonder that as an adult she tried to take care of her friends, to make other people's lives better. It was what her mother had demanded of her.

When Ottoline was six, her half brother came into his inheritance, becoming the sixth Duke of Portland. She was treated to a shopping spree in Cremer's toyshop in Regent's Street before she and her family took up residence in Welbeck Abbey, one of England's most eccentric residences.

The fifth Duke of Portland, though rumored to be simply eccentric, had, it seemed, gone completely berserk. To meet some inner and compelling need, he had undertaken a bizarre renovation of Welbeck Abbey. He had lopped the tops off the trees; taken up all the floorboards in the house; torn up the paths and the driveways; littered the property with mounds of rubble; dug trenches everywhere, as if in preparation for battle with the forces of an invading army.

He had employed as many as six hundred people to carry out

the most peculiar of his plans: the building of a series of subterranean rooms and tunnels, which gave him his nickname, the Burrowing Duke. He seemed to want to live underground, out of sight. One tunnel stretched a mile and a half and was so wide that two carriages could have been driven through it side by side.

The duke had been a private man; he had never had visitors, and no one had seen him for some time before he died. Each of the many guest rooms at Welbeck was empty of furniture, except for a water closet in the corner. He communicated his orders to servants through double letter boxes cut into the doors so that he would not have to see them.

Ottoline's half brother, in despair at the sight of the place, thought, perhaps wisely, that it would be best to shut it up and return to his far more congenial rooms in London. Ottoline's mother persuaded him that his duty was to restore the Abbey's former glory. Closing the house, she argued, would harm the two thousand people who were dependent upon Welbeck. She would become his housekeeper, in the most important sense of that word, sorting through the Abbey's treasures. It would give her something to do and ensure that she and her children would have a place, though a peculiar one, to call home.

During her childhood at Welbeck, Ottoline remembered opening a trapdoor that led to a tunnel going nowhere, and a door that opened onto a never-used ballroom, with pink walls, chandeliers, and mirrors. She played with Henry VIII's ruby-studded dagger, the pearl drop from King Charles's ear. She locked up her letters in a "casket given by King William the Third." She watched her mother slowly, patiently, bringing order out of chaos. No wonder, as an adult, Ottoline insisted upon beauty. No wonder she developed an eccentric taste in interior decoration, cluttering her rooms with a staggering array of "oriental cloths, old embroideries, Italian damasks, painted silk." How could she not have developed an eccentric style, growing up in Welbeck Abbey?

As a child, Ottoline was never relieved of the responsibility of being her mother's companion. In adulthood, she wrote in her "Thought Book": "I have suffered very much from not having made friends in my youth." She had no friends her age. She never learned how to spend time alone happily and productively. She never learned that the welfare of others was their responsibility, not hers.

Paradoxically, she was both deprived, and pampered and indulged. Her only companions, other than her family, were servants who gave in to her every whim. She grew used to having her way and never learned that she was not the center of the universe. As a child, she never learned how to dress herself, to comb her hair, to buckle her shoes. Although she learned the Scriptures, embroidery, and reading and writing, she was taught nothing about literature, science, or politics. She never developed a sense of competence and mastery. She never took her potential seriously. Though she wished it otherwise, she was raised with no ambition but to marry an aristocrat.

2.

When Ottoline was sixteen, her brother married; her mother left Welbeck and became ill. Ottoline spent three years nursing her and living an ascetic life. She read Thomas à Kempis's *The Imitation of Christ* every day, and continued to observe its instructions: "all desire for food must be constrained, pleasant books put away, everything soft and pleasing renounced." As an adult, Ottoline counted these years of nursing her mother as the "happiest of her life," and she kept a lock of her mother's black and gray hair with her always.

Ottoline's mother had trained her to be her "willing slave," to toil without hope of reward, and to reap, for her efforts, betrayal. Though Ottoline did not know it, while she patiently acted as her mother's servant, her mother cut her out of her will. (The pattern her mother taught her of thankless selflessness, betrayal, and the idealization of her persecutor, Ottoline reenacted in her relationships with men throughout her life. She repeated it as well in her relationship with her daughter, Julian, whose needs she ignored. Ottoline sent Julian to live elsewhere so that Julian would not interfere with Ottoline's affairs, yet Julian was punished when she wanted independence.)

After her mother died, Ottoline traveled through Europe with chaperones, and was changed by her first taste of freedom. She especially relished her travel through Italy: "I drank . . . of the elixir of Italy. I drank so deeply of it that it has never left me," she wrote.

She was developing a love for autonomy; she steadfastly refused to consider marriage. After her travels, she studied logic for a time at St. Andrews University in Scotland.

In the summer of 1898, when she was twenty-four, Ottoline had her first serious relationships with two middle-aged men: Herbert Asquith, who would become prime minister (throughout his life, he preferred young women), and Axel Munthe, who would become a society doctor in Rome. Her experiences with Munthe set the pattern for her later relationships. At first, she became his "willing captive," obsessed with a need to "pour love into this man." Then he reproached her for holding back from him, even as she declared their hearts had "mingled." They parted because, so far as he was concerned, she was neurotic: "I have quite enough nerve cases among my patients," he told her. "To have one as my wife would be too much."

3.

After a period of studying Roman history and political economy at Somerville College, Oxford, as a way to improve herself, and to make up for the "poor schooling" she had had as a child, Ottoline met and, two years later, in 1902, married Philip Morrell. He recalled the first time he saw her in Oxford, riding a bicycle slowly past him. She was so beautiful, she took his breath away: "She was dressed entirely in white and her pale face had a set and rather anxious expression as if concentrated on the art of riding a bicycle; but the most striking part of her appearance was the mass of deep copper-coloured hair."

Both were "to some extent failures and misfits." Both were liberals in Tory families. Like hers, his health was not good. His confessions to her about his deep unhappiness and about his troubled psyche stirred her interest. He told her he suffered from a nervous disorder; that he could not recover from his brother's suicide.

Philip had wanted to study literature, but his parents insisted that he study law, which he hated. He had not yet found his mission. During their courtship, she confessed all her faults to him: "she was strongwilled; she had a mind of her own." He was timid with her and not inclined to dispute what she wanted; with him, she could live life her own way. Still, she knew the road of marriage to him would be "rough and steep," and that she would have to bear its burdens "alone." At their wedding, one of her brothers took Philip aside and said, "I'm glad I'm not in your shoes. I wouldn't undertake her for anything."

4.

As an adult, Ottoline reproached herself for never having found the secret of enjoying life, for never having made anything of it. "Life," she wrote, "lived on the same plane as poetry and as music, is my distinctive desire and standard. It is the failure to accomplish this which makes me discontented." Once, when Virginia Woolf asked her why, with her passion for literature, she had never written, she responded, "Ah, but I've no time—never any time."

Ottoline spent much time concerning herself with the needs of others. She would think about the perfect color for a scarf for Siegfried Sassoon; she decorated a set of rooms where Bertie Russell could be comfortable and produce his great work. She acted as the manageress of Garsington. Her ungrateful guests treated her home as if it were a large hotel providing entertainment—concerts, plays, picnics, masked balls. They acted as if they were entitled to three meals a day, clean linen, and towels for bathing.

To distract herself from her lifelong sorrow, Ottoline surrounded herself with people. She began new friendships and new love affairs frequently. Her search for the perfect man, who would make her life worth living, and her inability to value men's love once they gave it, would continue throughout her life. Perhaps she was seeking someone like the heroic father of her memory, who had adored her.

Her first adulterous affair was with John Cramb, an older man, "shaken with passion and fire," as she put it. He was a professor of modern history, and helped Ottoline better her mind by introducing her to Balzac, Diderot, Rousseau, Turgenev, and Carlyle, among others. Using the pseudonym J. A. Revermort, he wrote a novel, *Cuthbert Learmont,* about their affair, in which she appeared as Mary Fotheringham. It was Ottoline's first appearance in fiction.

Throughout her life, Ottoline subjected herself to life-improving regimens she had begun as a young woman: she practiced asceticism, thought control, and rituals of self-mortification and self-denial. Yet she was chronically ill, always ready to undertake the most drastic, painful cures, always ready to enter a nursing home.

She believed her unhappiness had something to do with how sickly she had been as a young woman; she had suffered chronic bouts of "headaches, excessive fatigue, nervous skin rashes and distorted vision." Her sorrow and her lifelong battle with depression were probably linked to her mother's, which had antedated her father's unexpected death. Then, too, there was her mother's overdependence on Ottoline when she was a child.

When she met Lawrence, Ottoline had settled into a life of caring for other people, helping Philip with the political career she had urged upon him, helping him "strengthen and improve" himself, and committing adultery. Neither partner in the Morrell marriage now found the other physically attractive; Ottoline and Philip were "comrades," more like brother and sister than husband and wife.

5.

Ottoline Morrell was irresistibly drawn to men who were passionate, to men who frightened her. If a man was an artist, or a thinker, or a writer, and was either married or involved with another woman and troubled or melancholy besides, then she would surely become interested in him and make him take notice of her. She would send along a letter of effusive praise for something he had written, in a hand that was an "arabesque of dots and flourishes," on large sheets of beautiful handmade paper. Or she would give him a manuscript book to compose in, bound in orange vermilion, with end papers of brocade, in a pattern of blue and marigold, or a handmade coverlet, doused with the scent she wore, or a book he wanted to read—Chapman's *Homer, The Brothers Karamazov*. Or she would give money, unasked for, that could either be repaid or not, as he saw fit.

The men who became her intimates and lovers were among the most powerful and talented of their time: Herbert Asquith, Augustus John, Roger Fry, Bertrand Russell, Henry Lamb, Siegfried Sassoon, Aldous Huxley, Lytton Strachey, and D. H. Lawrence. She chose men who needed to be nurtured, who were not sure what they wanted to do next or whether they possessed the talent or the courage to realize their dreams. These were men who needed to be assured that they were geniuses, and that, yes, they were on the brink of the major breakthroughs of their careers. She liked it when they were intensely, almost demoniacally, engaged in the struggle to create.

She had an eye for outrageous men who commanded attention by their appearance. Augustus John affected a cape and wore his hair in a fringe across his forehead, had "sea-anemone" eyes, and looked as if he might have been a "Macedonian king or a Renaissance poet." She had a taste for imposing men, like Bertrand Russell, who looked like a severe God on the Day of Judgment. She admired eccentric men, like Lytton Strachey, who loved a good gossip above all things, who took forever to settle his endlessly long, cadaverous limbs into a chair, who twittered in a high falsetto whenever he was amused, which was often. She enjoyed shy, young and beautiful, doomed men, like the soldier-poet Siegfried Sassoon, who, she feared, would be "too soon blown to atoms" in World War I.

It was impossible not to take notice of her, difficult to resist her advances. She was both incredibly generous and extremely meddlesome. It was as if her giving entitled her to interfere in the lives of her friends, to decorate their rooms, to read their mail, to force friendships, to arrange liaisons, to harangue them into giving up their virginity.

That most astute of observers, Virginia Woolf, commented upon Ottoline's immense, engaging vitality, her "indomitable spirit," her "bursts of shrewdness." D. H. Lawrence, near the end of his life, admitted that there was "only one Ottoline," that she had been "an important influence in lots of lives," in his life, and that she had moved men's imaginations.

She was very, very tall. "She had the slim swaying figure of a Lombardy poplar," Woolf said. She commanded attention when she entered a room. She was often accompanied by her pack of pug dogs, and she held herself like a blueblood, "magnificently upright" and with assurance. But when she walked on the street, she had a "feeble mincing step," like a "cockatoo with bad claws." She wanted people to look at her, and so painted the angles and hollows of her face with brilliant color. She wore outlandish outfits: pale pink Turkish trousers, enormous hats like parasols with cockatoo feathers covering her marmalade-colored hair. It was difficult to forget the impression she created.

She needed to be in a state of desire, to batter her wings against the cages into which men locked themselves, to try to force herself in. If she was bruised and wounded in the process, if she cried out in agony, so much the better. That was the destiny of those few who loved as completely and as unselfishly as she. The joy of personal contact that came after the battle was, for her, the greatest excitement one could hope for in life. Wooing and winning men and loving them in this way, she knew, was the only genius she possessed.

No matter that she became worn and weary while giving so much. No matter that she became disappointed, for every person she chose to love soon showed that he was not her perfect "wished-for person." Her despair over each one's inadequacies meant that she could begin, with hope, her quest for a new, more nearly perfect prospect who would surely satisfy her.

He had to be grateful (but not too grateful) for her lavish gifts, her support, and her attentions, but only when she was willing to give them. If he became too available, like Bertrand Russell, she would lose interest: it was the chase she adored, not the conquest. He could not become either so demanding or so slavishly dependent upon her that he threatened her independence, her need for solitude, or her marriage to that "weak amiable long suffering man," Philip Morrell. Philip let her go her own way and defended her behavior, no matter how outrageous it seemed to others, perhaps because he was finding satisfaction elsewhere.

"The Son of a Nottinghamshire Miner"

1.

David Herbert Richards Lawrence, the fourth of five children, was born on September 11, 1885. (Ottoline was twelve years old at the time and living at Welbeck.) He was the son of Arthur John Lawrence, a collier who worked the pits at Brinsley. Arthur Lawrence had been sent out to work at seven years old. He was a robust man with black hair, a full black beard, and dark, flashing eyes. In his youth, he was jovial, high-spirited, good-humored, and an excellent dancer. Although he could barely read and write, he wooed Lydia Beardsall, who had aspirations of becoming a school-teacher. In courting her, he used the "thee" and "thou" idiom of the rural people. For a time, she found his outgoing nature, such a contrast to hers, captivating. Although he was so unlike her people, she chose to marry him.

She was small and slight, with clear blue eyes. She came from the lower bourgeoisie and spoke the King's English without accent, unlike her husband. As a young woman, she had written verses, some of which she had published in magazines in her district. She wrote a fine Italian hand and was forever reading. She eagerly discussed religion and philosophy with the preacher when he visited, and she was an active member of the Women's Co-operative Guild. She was a deeply religious woman, contemptuous of vanity and frivolity, who never wore jewelry, and who dressed only in the somber tones of black, white, and gray. At times, though, her speech could become "amusingly racy." She claimed, but did not possess, a class superiority to her husband. There was much similarity between Lydia Lawrence and Ottoline Morrell—their religious faith, belief in self-improvement, and desire to control the lives of those they loved.

Soon after the Lawrences married, Lydia became revolted by the grit and grime in which her husband lived. He came home from the pit covered in coal dust, but he would not wash until after he had his supper—a habit among miners who returned voraciously hungry from their long, hard day's work. He had the reputation for being a good though troublesome miner; he was a "butty," which gave him some authority and control over his work, but he questioned the authority of the colliery officials and resented their interference. Lydia Lawrence believed herself superior to this coarse man, who, she believed, took too many drinks with his mates in the pub.

D. H. Lawrence spent his childhood in Eastwood in Nottinghamshire, which, though he grew to despise it, he called "the country of my heart." Apart from the mines, which he saw as "an accident," an unfortunate scar on the landscape, he thought the countryside was "extremely beautiful," though he later would call Eastwood, without explaining why, "that insipid Sodom."

Lawrence's mother never liked living in the Breach, the community built in the valley for miners. She hated the view from the back of the houses over ashpits, the noise, the smoke, the clanking headstock. There were, as compensation, a brook, hedges, trees, and open farmland nearby.

When Lawrence was six, the family moved to another house, with a bay window facing a "wonderful view." It had an ancient ash tree opposite, around which the Lawrence children played.

In time, Lydia Lawrence shut her husband out of the Lawrence children's lives. She taught her children to ignore him, and he spent much of his time in the household in solitude. She wanted a better life for them, and feared his capacity to influence them. As a child, Lawrence despised his father. As an adult, he believed Lydia had been wrong to turn them against him.

The Lawrence children remembered their parents' "everlasting quarrels." Lawrence was afraid his father would hurt his mother; as a child, he was unable to sleep for fear. In a poem, "Discord in Childhood," he wrote of a woman's "she-delirious rage," and of a "male thong booming and bruising" inside a house, which forced a woman into "a silence of blood."

Lydia Lawrence always worried about not having enough money to clothe and feed her children as well as she wished, and she never concealed her anxiety from them. From their mother, the Lawrence children learned the "terrible indignity of poverty" and the injustice of inequity, which "embittered" D. H. Lawrence "so much." To supplement their income, she unsuccessfully tried to sell linen and lace, baby clothes and ribbons. She turned the front room of her small house into a shop, proudly displaying her wares in the window.

Lydia Lawrence always saw to it that there was something special about her home, that it was a corner house, that it had a bay window, that it had a separate entry or an extra bit of garden. She knew quality. She was proud of the well-made mahogany and horsehair suite of furniture in her parlor. She preferred to do without rather than to surround herself with anything vulgar, second-rate, or poorly made.

She had high expectations, first for her elder son, Ernest, then, after his death, for David Herbert. He was sickly as a child, "a puny, fragile little specimen," and so thin she was afraid he would die. Like Ottoline, he was pampered and spoiled. He became something of a monster, unaware of the effect his behavior had upon others. He moved through the world as if it owed him something. He became enraged if people did not do what he wanted or think the way he wanted. In time, he believed he was "afflicted by a perversity amounting to minor insanity."

From the first, he preferred the company of girls. He was called a "Mardy" boy, babyish and effeminate. Yet he always believed he was superior, and "gave himself airs." The neighborhood boys chased after him, chanting, "Dicky Dicky Denches plays with the Wenches." He detested the games boys played, and preferred dancing, playing at charades, singing, inventing games and rules for others to follow. As a child, he was often "morbid" and would burst into tears for no apparent reason. When asked why by his irritated mother, he answered, "I don't know," and continued to sob. When he grew older, he called his gloomy fits his "Hamlet moments."

He was devoted to his mother, and felt as if he never really had a father. Like Ottoline's, his mother depended upon him for satisfaction and fulfillment. "To see them together," a neighbor remarked, "was to imagine them fond lovers." His strong feeling for her admitted no rival while she was alive. His strong attachment to her persisted even after her death. In adulthood, he described his "mother-love" as "a demon," drawing him away from the other women he loved.

He saw his mother's love as emotional incest, and wrote about it in *Fantasia of the Unconscious*. He described a woman, unhappy in her marriage, beating about "for her insatiable satisfaction, seeking whom she may devour." She "turns to her child." Her love becomes "a final and fatal devotion" that is "poison to her boy." She "serves him," she "stimulates him," and becomes "wife-submissive" to him. For a time, the son feels singled out and special. This changes when the son is "faced with the actual fact of sex necessity," which has been "mother-stimulated." Such a man will never be sexually satisfied, for the object of his desire is unavailable. His "carnal love" for another woman can never match the "high" he felt for his mother. Although he may look to women for comfort, he will always regard them with suspicion and distrust, and, in the end, withdraw from them, or persecute them.

Those who knew Lawrence as a boy remembered his violence. A childhood friend called him *"vengeful"*: he projected "jagged waves of hate and loathing." Often, with no provocation, he lashed out against others, and sometimes against himself. A friend said Lawrence's violence had roots in "the constant and bitter quarrels" of his parents and "the teasing and contempt of his schoolfellows." Then, too, there were the "violent thrashings" children were given in the school Lawrence attended.

Once, he flew down the street after one of his brothers and forced him down flat on his face, beating him on the back of his neck. Another time, he jumped back and forth across the pouring water of a millrace, terrifying his friends—if he had fallen, he would have drowned. He once smashed a woman friend's stone carving to pieces with a heavy coal pick; he was jealous of the man who had given it to her.

His violence was not only physical. In his relationship with Jessie Chambers, his childhood sweetheart (they met when Lawrence was fifteen and Chambers fourteen), he developed a pattern he repeated in his adulthood with both women and men. Like Ottoline, he identified some special potential he thought his friend should cultivate. He told them how they should behave, what their role in life should be. He said if they didn't do as he said, they would remain a worthless creature, and he would have no further use for them. He subjected her to what she called "the process of internal dismemberment." His behavior, though, was above reproach. It was to be neither questioned nor criticized. "With *should* and *ought*," he told Jessie Chambers, "I have nothing to do." She believed, though, that his arrogance was a "mask for his own wretchedness."

But he could also be immensely charming, funny, lively, and kind and helpful. He was charismatic, and had the gift of revitalizing people, especially new friends, and of "making them blossom with new ideas, new enthusiasms, and new hopes." When his meanness and violence exploded into a relationship, it took people by surprise. They would forgive him until he became so horrible that there would be a permanent break. He went through life shedding relationships like so many snakeskins. He maintained that he despised the human race. As others fell "in love" or even "in like" with their friends, he generally "fell in hate."

2.

At sixteen, Lawrence experienced what he later described as "perfect love." It was, as far as we know, his first and most important homosexual love affair, and it was with "a young coalminer."

The "more perfect love" men have for men became the subject of his first novel, *The White Peacock*. His complex feelings about his homosexuality were a lifelong source of pain.

One important trauma occurred when Lawrence was seventeen and working at the factory job he described in *Sons and Lovers*. A group of "rough" girls cornered him in a downstairs storeroom at the factory, "pounced on him," and tried to strip him to expose his genitals. It amounted to gang sexual assault. He fought them off, but "was left breathless and disgusted and retching." In the aftermath of the attack, he developed pneumonia. A friend believed "this shock" caused Lawrence's illness. The assault no doubt colored his attitude toward women and heterosexuality: images of women as sexual predators dominate his work. As we now know, one such incident can have lifelong emotional and physical effects.

3.

D. H. Lawrence did not endure years of thankless toil as a writer. His work was discovered early, in 1909, when he was only twenty-four years old. Jessie Chambers had sent his work, without his knowledge, to the *English Review*. In November 1909, six of his poems appeared. Ford Madox Ford, their reader, recalled that when he read Lawrence's "Odour of Chrysanthemums," he believed he had discovered a "genius." What excited him most was that Lawrence came from, as he put it, a "completely different race"—that of the "unskilled labourer," whose voice in literature until that time had been unheard.

When Ford met Lawrence, the breadth and depth of Lawrence's knowledge impressed him; it had been made possible, Ford thought, by the schooling Lawrence had received because of the Education Act. Lawrence, though "a miner's son ... moved amongst the high things of culture with a tranquil assurance." What Ford did not understand was the impact Lawrence's mother (and the self-betterment efforts of the Women's Co-operative Guild) had had on him. As a young man, he and Jessie Chambers spent Saturday evenings discussing Verlaine, Baudelaire, Nietzsche, Wagner, Marx, and Darwin, while tending to his mother's bread baking in the oven. Ford thought Lawrence's formal education far better than his. Ford did not understand that, unlike members of his class, Lawrence deeply valued knowledge.

Lawrence subsequently showed Ford *The White Peacock*, which he had written while teaching at the Davidson Road School in Croydon. Ford thought it, too, displayed genius, and sent it on to William Heinemann, who published it in 1911 almost unaltered—only four lines in the novel required fixing. Lawrence's career as a writer of fiction was launched. After resigning from teaching in 1912, he supported himself by his book earnings and the money given him by friends or advanced to him by his agents or publishers.

After the novel's publication, Lawrence was immediately invited to gatherings in London of the literary luminaries of his time—H. G. Wells, Ezra Pound, William Butler Yeats. He made an unforgettable impression. Even the literary greats found him mesmerizing, in part because his behavior was shockingly different from theirs. When asked what he thought, he answered directly, and often brutally. He did not believe in good manners, but in honesty.

He held a very high opinion of himself and his work, and a low one of almost everyone else's. Yet he could be eager to please people he considered his betters: as John Middleton Murry observed, "initiation into the dress-suit world was for him a serious and ritual affair." Once, when invited to the home of H. G. Wells, he annoyed Murry with the obsessive care he put into making a good appearance. He bought an expensive dinner jacket, which he couldn't afford. He had grown into a striking young man; he was tall, very thin, with a "shock of dark hair," and wore a "small ginger moustache"; his steel-gray eyes, which seemed blue, were captivating. He had long thin fingers and fragile, expressive hands. When he was enraged, which was often, he flailed them about.

Lawrence believed that his work would, like H. G. Wells's, earn him a fortune, and that soon he would be earning two thousand pounds a year by his pen. He fancied he would have a footman, that he would climb the social ladder, and that he would share an easy intimacy with "lords and, particularly, ladies." He believed he was entitled to this because of his and his mother's suffering.

Though working-class, he was a "terrific snob" and imperious, a trait associated with the privileged classes. He believed he had a right to moral support and physical care because of his talent and his genius, but he often grew to despise those who helped him. Yet, he was often awkward in society. At a party at Violet Hunt's (she was Ford's lover), Lawrence asked the maid, who was serving dinner, which knife he should use for the asparagus.

4.

Lawrence put a copy of *The White Peacock* into his mother's hands as she was dying; he suspected she doubted its value, since he had written it. His father "struggled through half a page." When he heard that his son had earned fifty pounds for his novel, his father said, "Fifty pounds! An' tha's niver done a day's hard work in thy life." Because of his family's response, Lawrence said he "put [the novel] aside, and I never wanted to see it again."

Lawrence's mother suffered from a lingering illness and died in 1910, when he was twenty-five. He believed that while she was still alive, he could not love another woman. He thought her death would free him. In 1914, he told a woman he met that "he had actually killed his mother," as his fictional counterpart, Paul Morel, does in *Sons and Lovers*. "You see *I* did it—I gave her the overdose of morphia and set her free."

After Lydia Lawrence's death, Lawrence became very ill. His world "began to dissolve," and he, too, "almost dissolved." Her death prompted a series of poems, among them "The Virgin Mother" and "The Bride." He wrote: "I must go, but my soul lies helpless/Beside your bed."

He could not bear "the stress of a life alone," and "needed to be married," and so made a sudden and "irresponsible engagement" to Louie Burrows, which estranged him from Jessie Chambers. He told Jessie he had loved his mother "like a lover," and that was why he could never love her. He told her he had a desperate need for sex, but he could never love a woman who gave him sex.

He used his early life, and the story of his affairs with Jessie and other lovers, as the basis for *Sons and Lovers*, the novel he began after his mother's death. His description of their affair was a blow from which Jessie Chambers believed she never recovered.

5.

When Lawrence met Frieda Weekley in 1912, she was married, the mother of three small children. Frieda's aristocratic heritage— she was a Baronin von Richthofen—was of "tremendous significance" to Lawrence, though the disparity of their social class caused problems. Once Frieda showed him her embroidered handkerchief, with her initial and a crown. He drew her *his* coat of arms: "a pickaxe, a school-board, a fountain pen with two lions rampant."

She felt stuck in a boring middle-class marriage to Ernest Weekley, an English professor and one of Lawrence's teachers. Lawrence met Frieda when he came to see Weekley for a letter of recommendation. She enchanted him; he thought her the most captivating woman in England, to which she replied that he musn't know many. When she watched the tenderness with which he played with her children, she believed she was falling in love.

She asked him to have sex with her, but he was morally opposed to adultery. He believed Frieda should leave her husband; he saw nothing wrong in openly taking a man's wife away, "if love compelled him."

Frieda had had one very important affair, with Otto Gross (who was also her sister's lover), while she was still married to Weekley. It introduced her to the beliefs and practices of the erotic movement in Germany. Gross was a drug addict, and persecutory in his relations with women. Frieda described her experience with him in euphoric terms; in all likelihood, it damaged her as well.

Gross had been cast out of Freud's movement for practicing "orgiastic therapy" and "sexual immorality," which he believed would be sufficient to smash apart the patriarchal state. He had a "savage contempt for democracy, rationalism, and liberalism," which he shared with Frieda, who in turn shared it with Lawrence. The orgies Gross organized gained him notoriety, as did the suicide of two of his mistresses. He was diagnosed as schizophrenic and institutionalized for a time. He ended his life as a cocaine addict, living on the street.

Lawrence and Frieda eloped just six weeks after they met. At the beginning, she was not sure she wanted to be with him: "fancy marrying again," she wrote, "it gives me [the] creeps." But she ran away with him anyway, and gave up her husband and children to throw her lot in with this man whom she hardly knew. She traded a comfortable bourgeois life to walk through Europe with Lawrence, wearing mud-stained skirts and sleeping in barns.

Lawrence wooed her by sending her poems of complaint he had written about earlier lovers, telling her, "I would never write that to you. I shall love you all my life." He wrote her about how unsure he was that they were doing the right thing.

One belief of Gross's that Frieda brought into their relationship was the idea of woman as *Magna Mater*, a great mother. Her function as a woman was fulfilled by her inspiring men, who couldn't "do things alone." Women fulfilled their nature simply by "being."

The *Magna Mater* principle seemed to allow Frieda to stay in bed all day and to insist that Lawrence serve her, which he did. From the start, he took on all the housework. When Frieda met him, she had no housekeeping skills; the work of her household had been done by servants. She couldn't use a telephone. She couldn't brew a decent cup of coffee. Lawrence even had to teach her to arrange her clothing in neat piles.

But part of Frieda's expectation that she had a right to be served came from her privileged background. In a sense, she turned Lawrence into her servant, and though her helplessness revolted him, she made almost no significant ongoing contribution to the relationship. He was used to hard physical labor, though he was always frail, and thought nothing of doing it.

He brought her breakfast in bed, made all their living and travel arrangements, decorated their cottages, painted their walls, planted their gardens, scrubbed their floors, cooked their meals, washed their dishes, earned their money, shopped for bargains, and scrubbed their pots clean, on the outside as well as on the inside, as his mother had taught him. And he did all this while writing.

6.

It is said that the Lawrences' sexual life together was, for some time, a success, that he gave himself "body and soul" to Frieda. Yet when they left for Europe, there was no sexual passion between them. And many of his poems to her, from the earliest days, describe feelings of failure, violence, and revulsion. He condemned foreplay in sexual relations, and women who sought sexual satisfaction disgusted him, so his marriage to a woman who saw herself as the embodiment of the erotic principle was bound to fail.

They traveled to Europe because Lawrence felt he couldn't breathe while they were in England. Their affair initially made him feel "shaky," as if he and Frieda were adrift on "a rather flimsy raft."

They went to Germany, met Frieda's family, then walked through Switzerland and Italy and settled for a time in Gargagno, Italy. She described how unhappy he was; he behaved like "a perfect agony," she wrote a friend; the "crucifixes here seem joyful . . . compared to him. I wanted love, now I have more than I can bear."

In Gargagno, Lawrence finished *Sons and Lovers*. As he read it to Frieda, they fought "like blazes" over it. Toward the end of the project, she got so disgusted over his obsession with his mother that she wrote a skit called "Paul Morel, or His Mother's Darling." It mocked Lawrence's attachment to his mother, which Frieda knew was an important impediment to their relationship. Still, she felt "responsible" for his writing such an important, revolutionary novel.

Four months after Frieda and Lawrence met, she seduced a friend, Harold Hobson, who traveled with them for several days. She believed that a woman should act on her erotic impulses, a tenet of the erotic movement which caused much trouble between her and Lawrence.

Her affair pained him deeply, though he maintained her right to satisfy herself. After a quarrel about her freedom, she swam across a river "to where a woodcutter was working, made love to him, and swam back." In this way, she asserted her right to take her sexual pleasure whenever and wherever she chose, and to prove to Lawrence that he didn't own her. In time, he saw her as the worst manifestation of the *Magna Mater*. She became "the devouring mother," and once he saw her this way, it was hard for him "to recover."

He attacked her sexuality, and its impact on him, in a number of poems published in *Look! We Have Come Through!* which, he said, was a history of their emotional relationship. In "In the Dark": "There is something in you destroys me—" In "Mutilation": "It aches in me for her/Life the agony of limbs cut off." In "Winter Dawn": "This love so full/Of hate has hurt us so." In "A Bad Beginning": "but if I am cruel what then are you?/I am bruised right through." But perhaps most forcibly in "Rabbit Snared in the Night": "Why should I want to throttle/you, bunny? . . . /It must be you who desire/this intermingling of the black and monstrous/fingers of Molock/ . . . already I am implicated with you/in your strange lust."

His friend John Middleton Murry believed that Lawrence was a "sexual failure" and that this was the primary cause of the Lawrences' unhappiness. Sexuality, to Lawrence, was "always sin." Frieda believed it was because he was consumed with love for his mother; her work with him on *Sons and Lovers* had proved it. Opposite a draft of his poem "My Love, My Mother" Frieda wrote: "I have nearly killed myself in the battle to get you into connection with myself and other people, sadly I have proved to myself that I can love, but never you. . . . You are a sad thing, I know your secret and your despair. . . ."

7.

Despite their frequent quarrels, they were married upon their return to England, on July 13, 1914. John Middleton Murry and Katherine Mansfield, who had become close friends, attended the ceremony. Their marriage continued the complicated tug-of-war already begun.

Frieda said, "Lawrence *is* wear and tear. . . . [He] chases my poor emotions till they drop like panting hares." Much in their relationship was abusive. Their battles were serious, even life-endangering. In their years together, she smashed him over the head with a heavy plate; he broke gramophone records over her head one by one; threw wine in her face; called her a dirty slut when she sat with her legs open; tried to choke her, and often threatened her life. Later, Mabel Dodge Luhan recalled seeing Frieda's naked body covered with bruises when they were swimming together.

Because Lawrence saw heterosexual relationships as a battleground, and because this was the way his parents had behaved, he did not think his war with Frieda was unusual.

When Lawrence and Ottoline met, the Lawrence marriage was foundering over the subject of Frieda's missing her children and wanting to see them. Her longing for her children made Lawrence "ill." He wanted no rival for her affections, and he believed she should simply forget them. Yet, despite his cruelty, Frieda felt herself bound to him; she had made herself completely dependent upon him. She had no friends other than his; she had no way to support herself; she was, as a friend observed, "amazingly incapable and . . . deeply afraid." No matter how badly he treated her, she thought it was her "job to see [Lawrence] through to the bitter end."

Frieda believed herself to be a "nitwit." Yet she was convinced that Lawrence had achieved his potential as a writer only because of her. *She* was responsible for the flowering of his talent; she had made him into a genius. She spoke of him as her "possession." She knew that women envied and hated her because "he had come her way and not theirs." As inclined to battle as her husband, Frieda would fight any woman who threatened her influence over this man. He was her creation; "the last green shoot" on the otherwise sterile "tree of English civilization."

"Only One Ottoline"

1.

Lawrence had heard his first stories of Ottoline when he was still a boy, living in Eastwood, Nottinghamshire, the village where he was born. He had known some servants who worked at Welbeck Abbey. He had spent many hours taking tea with one of Welbeck's servants, Mrs. Orchard, whose room was cold and damp, for she could not afford to light a gas fire. He listened to her talk about the Burrowing Duke, and the present duke, and Lady Ottoline, and the goings-on of these aristocrats, who lived such different lives.

Lady Ottoline Morrell had come to know Lawrence in the way she liked best, through reading his works. She read and admired *The White Peacock, Sons and Lovers,* and *The Prussian Officer and Other Stories.* On New Year's Eve 1914, she wrote Bertrand Russell that she had been reading Lawrence, and that he had "great passion—and is so alive to things outward and inward," and that his work was far better than "that muddled stuff of Woolfe [sic]—" She had found reading *Sons and Lovers* a "comfort."

Ottoline especially liked his works set in Nottinghamshire. Reading his descriptions of the countryside of her childhood released a flood of happy memories, "which had lain dry and curled up." She remembered riding with her brother, flying along in a cart behind two tiny Shetland ponies, and the dark beauty of the forests surrounding her childhood home. These memories had "blossomed out as old Japanese flowers in a glass of water," she said.

Lawrence's work also reawakened Ottoline's youthful excitement—and anxiety—at seeing the colliers "on their way home from the pits." She remembered the "men, tall, black and mysterious." She felt they were "rather fierce and yet full of laughter and fun, joking together as they hurried pell-mell along the dark roads" in the "grey winter light, a gleam of setting yellow sun behind them."

As a young woman, Ottoline had often nearly stopped on the "black slimy road, to have a few words" with the miners as they passed. She always restrained herself. She could not imagine what to say: "The cords that hold us back from escaping our own herd," she wrote, "are very strong and take time to wear thin." She imagined following the colliers home to their humble cottages and talking to them over their tea. She wanted to know what life was like in those cottages.

Even as a child, Ottoline had the fantasy that life was freer and more intensely lived among working-class people. As an adult, she believed that working men were spontaneous and vigorous, jovial and comradely, and energetically sexual, unlike the men of her class. She believed, too, that they could be violent, but she saw their violence as an enviable lack of repression. Repression was what the members of her class suffered from, she thought, and she herself had tried to live a more emotionally open, less restrained life.

Ottoline believed Lawrence's works manifested the qualities working-class men possessed. They were wonderfully alive and energetic. Lawrence, she believed, would be sensitive to the "outward and inward" world, to nature and the emotions.

If she could meet him, she would be captivated, she knew. She valued passion, sensitivity, and spontaneity in men. These were qualities that her current lover, Bertrand Russell, an aristocrat, and her husband did not possess, qualities she had been trying for years, without much success, to help them develop.

After reading Lawrence's work, Ottoline decided she would pursue him, and she wrote him an effusive letter praising his work. They had already met at one of her parties in August 1914, but he had not made a favorable impression on Ottoline then, perhaps because, according to Katherine Mansfield, he had made himself "cheap" in aristocratic company.

In January 1915, Ottoline asked Gilbert Cannan to invite the Lawrences, who were living in a cottage at Chesham in Buckinghamshire, to her home in Bedford Square. Ottoline was forty-one and feeling "weary"; Lawrence was twenty-nine and in one of his winter funks when their friendship began.

He responded warmly to her overture, writing her that he was glad she liked his stories. He preferred the appreciation of "the few" to the praise of the mob. He assured her that he didn't hold her class against her; he believed life was "an affair of the aristocrats." He was "no democrat, save in politics." His motto was "Fierté, Inégalité, Hostilité." If he were an aristocrat like her, he wouldn't be ashamed, he'd be "proud as hell."

He told Ottoline they couldn't see her often because they were so poor they couldn't afford the train fare. He didn't mind being poor and unencumbered—he waved his "rags like the feathers of a bird of paradise." They would have to postpone their meeting because he had a "lingering miserable cold."

2.

From the first, Ottoline's friendship with Lawrence proceeded from her assumption that he would be exactly what she imagined a coal miner's son would be. She expected to meet a familiar, recognizable type—a free spirit. As she saw it, "He was not the child of an old cultivated family who inherits a natural restraint. . . . His old home was a small intense world where interests were passionate, direct and often violent. . . . [I]t was a life untrammeled by middle-class conventions or decorum; kindness, curiosity, anger, were all freely and frankly expressed."

How wrong she was. Lawrence's fundamental qualities eluded her. She was unprepared for how rigid and conventional (especially in matters of sexuality) he was, despite his marriage to the free-spirited Frieda. Ottoline was completely unprepared for how morally outraged Lawrence would become at her friends' (and, ultimately, her) behavior, and how he seemed to exempt himself from the rules he applied to others.

Ottoline had a history of romantic entanglements with men whose work she admired. She seems to have believed that Lawrence would quickly, easily, become her next and possibly her most interesting conquest. Perhaps she thought a man of his class would be grateful for attention from a woman of hers. She had never before known a man from the working class, and his allure was, in part, his exoticism. Perhaps together they could forge a new kind of friendship and bridge the chasm between their classes. She might have imagined what a passionate sexual relationship with him might be like.

When Ottoline met Lawrence, she was involved with Bertrand Russell; she was used to a complicated love life, with more than one man in her orbit. She had begun her love affair with Russell when she was involved with both Roger Fry and Henry Lamb. (Once, when a guest discovered her and Lamb in a passionate embrace, Ottoline surfaced, composed herself, and explained, "I was just giving Henry an aspirin.") She had managed a three-day idyll at Studland Bay on the Dorset coast with Russell early in their affair while putting off the attentions of Lamb, who waited for her nearby, and her husband, who would join her later. Russell described their early time together as "among the few moments when life seemed all that it might be." Despite Russell's involvement with Ottoline, he and Ottoline's husband, Philip, worked together on antiwar activities. Philip said he would tolerate Ottoline's affair with Russell so long as they never spent a night together.

Ottoline was used to juggling the simultaneous attentions of several men. She believed she had become an expert at it through the years. The more complicated things became, the better she liked them. Lawrence, though, as she quickly discovered, was not suited by temperament to becoming one of many. From the time he was a child, he was used to being the "supreme" object of a woman's attentions. He was used to having many women in *his* orbit.

Ottoline and Russell had been lovers since 1911. By the end of 1914, when she first became acquainted with Lawrence, their affair had cooled considerably. Her passion for Russell had long since vanished. At first, their affair had brought him a new sense of the power of his sexuality, and a respite from his habits of self-denial. And she was thrilled to be involved in a relationship with the most attractive, "alarming," and "supremely intellectual" man she had ever met.

Russell's looks had captivated her. She liked the shape of his head from the back, but she made him shave off his beard. Without the beard, she thought he looked like a cross between "Voltaire and an actor." He had transported her "into worlds of thought" she had not dreamed she could enter. For this she was grateful. Yet she had also felt "battered and scourged" by his attentions; he felt as if she had shut him up in a cage. Their meetings were frequently marred by her "terrible headaches" and by his bad breath, which had made their lovemaking a strain for her. She was too much the lady ever to complain. Things improved considerably after he had his gums treated.

When they went out for walks together, she noticed that when she became "ravished" by what she saw, he was never moved. Worse, he regarded her excitement as a "frivolous interruption" to the theory he was currently pondering. Since the war had begun, there had been less pleasure for them. More of their time together was spent "in great despair and unhappiness."

She wanted to go her way, to be free of him. She believed he was crushing the life out of her. Often, after a conquest, she would infuriate men by her abrupt shift into coldness. Russell believed this behavior had very nearly driven him mad.

Still, she had an obligation to him. And there remained moments of great physical passion: she wrote that their lovemaking could be "all passion that has been burnt white . . . and all the experience of our lives." She outfitted a comfortable room for him at Garsington, with a view across the Berkshire Downs. There he could work on his philosophy of politics, which would later be published as *Principles of Social Reconstruction.* They were bound together by their pacifist politics, by their opposition to the war. He and her husband were among the movement's prime movers. She had been a source of strength to Russell when he first decided to work against the war, and he still needed her to do his best work.

3.

On January 21, 1915, D. H. Lawrence and his wife, Frieda, came to see Lady Ottoline Morrell at her home at 44 Bedford Square, in Bloomsbury. They were escorted by Gilbert Cannan. Lawrence was over his cold and felt able enough at last, in this dark and dismal month which he hated, to accept Ottoline's overture of friendship.

Over the years, Ottoline had taken great pains to make her home into the most important gathering place in London for writers, painters, poets, and politicians. Many thought 44 Bedford Square "the most civilised few hundred square feet in the world."

Those who walked through the green double doors, as the Lawrences did on that day in January, would be invited into the wide hallway and up the long, curving staircase to the second-floor drawing rooms overlooking the square's private gardens. They would usually join twenty or more people who were also making cultural or political history—Henry James, William Butler Yeats, Max Beerbohm, Ramsay MacDonald, Herbert Asquith. At the center of it all was Ottoline. She was always eager to introduce her latest discovery to her old friends, to draw the newest of her friends into her circle.

The gray and yellow drawing rooms, filled with a profusion of yellow chrysanthemums, were comfortable places for conversation, the sofas piled high with cushions. Conversation was the art Ottoline encouraged, and because she was continually bringing new people together, one never knew what exciting and unforeseen turn the talk might take.

On this day, Ottoline was introducing the Lawrences to Duncan Grant, David Garnett, E. M. Forster, and Barbara Hiles (a student at the Slade Academy of Art). Ottoline was resplendent in a "Spanish dress with a high comb and a lace mantilla." She was nervous, "anxiously on the watch" to see that her guests were interacting and as happy as she could make them.

She seated Lawrence next to E. M. Forster, hoping that they would become friends, and seated Garnett next to Frieda. The conversation turned, as it always did at Ottoline's parties in 1915, to the war, to literature, and to art. Lawrence hated the war. He thought it was a "wicked mistake." Ottoline was filled with despair about its "dull, grinding agony" and its waste of young life.

She excitedly described Duncan Grant's work to the Lawrences, and when Lawrence showed interest, Grant invited the couple to his studio in Bloomsbury the next afternoon.

One of Ottoline's chief aims in life, to get her friends to become friends, she seemed to be achieving brilliantly. She hardly knew the Lawrences, yet she had already secured for them an important invitation.

After dinner, there was music—a Mozart quintet—and then dancing. The dancing got so violently improvisational, in imitation of Nijinsky, that the entertainments ended in chaos. Barbara Hiles leapt into the air and struck Garnett in the eye, startling him so that he bit down on his tongue. Duncan, dancing with Ottoline, caught his shoe in the train of her dress. His clutching at her to regain his balance sent the two of them crashing to the floor, which ended the dancing.

4.

The bruises Duncan Grant sustained that evening were nothing compared to what he suffered in his studio on the following afternoon when the Lawrences came to tea and to see his most recent work.

After tea, Grant pulled out a painting for the Lawrences to admire. It was a portrait of Ottoline, a three-quarter view of her head, with a string of cheap pearls around her neck, tacked onto the canvas. He also showed them other works, some large marionettes made out of cardboard, for Bloomsbury entertainments.

"Ah," Frieda chortled with each new work, "I like this one so much better! It is beautiful." Did she mean it?

Lawrence winced at his wife's remarks. But he also winced at every canvas. He paced, and thought.

As a finale, Grant brought out an experimental work for the experimental novelist to admire: a long swath of green cotton, on two rollers, in the manner of an Oriental scroll, featuring some "abstract shapes."

"Worthless," Lawrence said.

Grant said nothing. He sat in his chair, "his hands on his knees, rocking himself" back and forth. He and Lawrence were worlds apart. They would never understand one another.

A few days later, Lawrence wrote Ottoline. He and Frieda really liked Duncan Grant very much. But it looked as if he led a dissolute life, and Ottoline should tell him to change his ways. "He looks as if he dissipates, and certainly he doesn't enjoy it," Lawrence wrote. "Tell him to stop." She should also tell him to stop his "puerile . . . dabbing of geometric figures," his "silly experiments . . . with bits of color on a moving paper." Lawrence lectured Ottoline on the philosophy Grant should adopt if he wanted to do worthwhile work: "It is an Absolute we are all after . . . —the issue of progress through Time—and the return, making unchangeable eternity." Ottoline had a moral responsibility to enlighten Grant: she must pass on Lawrence's words: "*Do* rub this into Duncan Grant, and save him his foolish waste."

Grant's work and his sexual mores so infuriated Lawrence that he told Ottoline he had burned her letter discussing his work. This was the first of many disputes Ottoline and Lawrence would have about art, politics, class, and moral behavior. Lawrence was evolving the idea of a revolutionary role for art. Grant's work was safe, decorative, and derivative. In writing *The Rainbow*, Lawrence wanted to reshape the English novel, to create "a new thing in the world," "almost a new vision of life." He believed it was time to break into new forms of expression, and to imagine new ways of being. He insisted that everyone he knew, everyone he met, join him in this important endeavor in which he would lead the way.

5.

Introducing Lawrence to her Bloomsbury friends hadn't turned out the way Ottoline had anticipated. Even so, he had completely captivated her. She wrote her observations about him in her diary. He gave the impression of "someone who had been undernourished in youth." She thought he looked, and acted, like Van Gogh. His face was "overshadowed by a mass of red hair and a short beard." He was fragile and delicate. Although he was vehement in his works, in his attitude toward art, and in his conversations with her friends, to her he had remained "gentle and tender." She liked that his feelings were so "freely and frankly expressed." She herself so often felt deadened, unable to rouse herself to activity. How she admired this man who could shake his arm above his head, and shriek, and roar, in the face of a man he believed was a hypocrite. It wasn't that he was "really angry"; it was, she thought, his way of arguing, prompted by an excess of "exuberance."

She wrote in her diary: "Lawrence is the spirit of flame. He has indeed a fire within him, a fire which flames into excitement and conviction when a subject or a controversy strikes a light." He "is interested in almost everything. Few subjects bore him. And by his wonderful capacity of being absolutely natural he stimulates those round him to be the same."

"The Powers of Darkness"

1.

Lawrence was initially just as captivated by Ottoline as she was by him. He invited her to come to see him and Frieda when they moved to a cottage they were borrowing in Sussex. It would be nicer, more comfortable for her to visit them there than in the miserable, depressing cottage they were currently inhabiting. Their new living quarters would even have a bath, with "beautiful hot water," and a spare bedroom for her to stay in.

The time they shared in the very early days of their relationship, when she came to Sussex, their walking on the Downs, getting to know one another, reminiscing about Nottinghamshire, discussing their past, was the best in their friendship. He wrote a friend that she was *"really* nice—somebody to know in this scant world." He had always been intoxicated by the aristocracy, and was happy he had become her friend.

Before a month passed, serious problems began to emerge in their friendship.

At first, he was not too proud to accept whatever gifts she was willing to send his way. Sometimes, but not always, he politely refused her offers and gifts of money. He had a habit of making extraordinary demands on his friends (like asking them to pack up and ship the entire contents of his household in precisely the way he described), so he took Ottoline's generosity as his due. Here was a woman who seemed willing to comply with his every request.

Very soon after they met, Frieda presumed upon her friendship and upon her position. She wrote to ask Ottoline to act as intermediary with Ernest Weekley, her former husband, who lived in London; Frieda wanted Ottoline to write a letter entreating Weekley to allow her to see her children. He had denied her access to their three children after she ran away with Lawrence. Lawrence was convinced that Weekley would respond positively to a request by anyone of Ottoline's position in society. Frieda had spent three years trying unsuccessfully to persuade Weekley to change his mind.

Inadvertently, by using her power and position to help Frieda, Ottoline contributed to the Lawrences' furious battles about

Frieda's wish to see her children. Ottoline's letter hadn't resulted in a visitation, but now Frieda had hope, and the issue was reopened. Still, Frieda believed she had gained a "genuine confidante and ally" in Ottoline. "You have given me a generous helping hand," she wrote, "and I am so grateful to you that I could sing."

2.

Soon after Ottoline's first visit to the Lawrences in February, Ottoline proposed bringing Russell to Sussex. Lawrence was terrified, afraid that he would "stutter" in the presence of this highly regarded "philosophic-mathematics man." Ottoline had high expectations in bringing together these two "passionate men," for they were both in "a mood of bitter rebellion." She thought the two of them could "plan a 'revolution' and a 'New World,' and write manifestos together." At first, it seemed a success.

Russell was transfixed by Lawrence. He thought he had been in the presence of "Ezekiel or some other Old Testament prophet," and said of Lawrence, "he sees everything and is always right." He believed Lawrence and he were in fundamental agreement about how best to resist the war, and especially liked Lawrence's "habit of challenging assumptions."

Soon after meeting Russell, Lawrence told Ottoline he was writing some "philosophicalish stuff" that she would like. He wanted Russell, and Ottoline, not to treat him as a "*Wunderkind*," but to take his political ideas seriously; he expected that Russell, too, would join him for his revolution. He believed Russell's work was too rooted in the "temporal," and that Russell might learn from him to take a larger view.

As much as Lawrence liked Ottoline, and as much as he wanted her to become important in his life, he wasn't going to move within Ottoline's constellation. He was going to draw her into his. He had other, more important ideas for their relationship than attending her parties (which he didn't like) and meeting her friends. He wasn't going to trot after her like Russell or her pug dog Socrates.

In the autumn of 1914, before getting to know her, he had been in despair. By February 1915, though, she had become intertwined with his newfound hope for the future, with the belief that he could instigate changes in English society. She had become central to his plans. "My heart feels quite big," he told her, "with hope for the future." He hoped she would agree to become the nucleus of the outsider society he was planning, a small, select group of followers, from which a revolution in the state would be launched.

All property, he told her, would be seized and then nationalized. All property owners would be dispossessed. Land use, industry, communication, and public amusements would be nationalized. Everyone would be provided with a guaranteed annual wage so that money worries (like those that plagued Lawrence constantly) would vanish overnight.

Though his ideas were shifting and evolving, Lawrence was proposing a kind of communism mixed with democracy, a system that advocated "individual freedom and common effort towards good." It was a moral "goodness" he was after. But well-being would be based, "not on poverty, but on riches, not on humility, but on pride, not on sacrifice but upon complete fulfilment in the flesh of all strong desire, not on forfeiture but upon inheritance." Throughout this time, he elicited the support of everyone he met, keeping track of who was now with him "for the Revolution." (Murry, he said, "is with me.") Lawrence's biographer Paul Delany called this period, which lasted from the end of January through October 1915, "Lawrence's Messianic phase." It coincided with the beginning, and deterioration, of his relationship with Ottoline. During this time, Lawrence "imagined himself a prophet called to save England, and to build a new Jerusalem on the ruins of the old."

He called this new society "Rananim," and his proposing that Ottoline should be its center and that it should be launched from Garsington surely marks a curious moment in English literary history. Lawrence's proposal revealed how little he had learned about Ottoline. Much of what he believed he admired in her was based not upon who she was, but upon his idea of what she should become.

He expected that Lady Ottoline Morrell, the "daughter of a thousand earls," would act as the high priestess of his revolution, which, if it were to be successful, would dispossess people like her of their power, privilege, position, and worldly goods. Lawrence thought she, too, believed that the entire foundation of English society was bankrupt and needed to be destroyed, not reformed, to effect change. He believed that aristocrats with liberal inclinations, like Ottoline and Russell, would join him in a revolution against the very society that had afforded their class power, wealth, and privilege while the people of his class had remained poor and powerless. He thought aristocrats like Lady Ottoline and Russell would willingly and happily allow him to become a leader in politics and in political philosophy.

Though, at the beginning, the Lawrences believed Ottoline was a real friend to them both, it became clear in just a month that Ottoline tolerated Frieda so that she could see Lawrence. Though she helped Frieda see her children, she gave Lawrence the gift of an opal. The significance of this gift did not escape Frieda, nor did Ottoline's unwillingness to visit her if Lawrence wasn't at home. "I feel everybody against me," Frieda said, "but then I can stand up to it, thank God."

By the beginning of March, Ottoline suggested to Lawrence that he leave Frieda behind when he visited. He agreed. He thought there was no reason "why we should always be a triangle." Lawrence and Ottoline began to discuss the meaning of "passion." He urged her to revamp her life to put passion at its center (as if the pursuit of passion were not already at the center of her life): It is "the dark fire, the hidden, invisible passion, that has neither flame nor heat, that is the greatest of all passion," he wrote her.

Ottoline and Lawrence had begun what Frieda called their "soul mush," a connection she believed more threatening than adultery. Frieda wasn't worried about Ottoline and Lorenzo, as she called her husband, having a sexual affair. That, she believed, she could have tolerated. She wrote Ottoline: "I would not mind if you and he had an ordinary love affair—what I hate is this 'soul mush.' "

Frieda, I think, misinterpreted what Ottoline and her husband were about. She also underestimated her own capacity for reacting with pain and despair to Lawrence's extramarital involvements, as she was to discover later in their marriage. Lawrence and Ottoline's exchanges about passion suggest that Lawrence was flirting, and that Ottoline was receptive. Soon, Ottoline began writing Lawrence about her philosophy "that love is all." And he began to discuss how important it was to be true to the "animal" in oneself. They discussed "sensual lust." They moved on to the topic of when, and under what circumstances, adultery was permissible. Ottoline believed one went to lovers to fulfill different aspects of one's being;

Lawrence grudgingly admitted this might be permissible. Though Frieda might have seen it as "soul mush," their correspondence surely reads like foreplay.

Ottoline had started to wage her war for Lawrence against Frieda, and it was inevitable that Frieda would become her enemy. What Ottoline didn't realize was that penniless Frieda, totally dependent upon Lawrence, could be a very powerful adversary, and that she stood to lose a great deal from Frieda's rancor. Ottoline had her marriage, her affair with Russell, her class, her houses, and innumerable friends, and Lawrence. But Lawrence was all Frieda had.

When Lawrence was creating his idea for Rananim, Ottoline was preoccupied, not with politics, but with interior decoration. She was frantically renovating Garsington, donning overalls to join the army of carpenters, painters, stonemasons, and joiners who were making the estate over into a "lovely romantic place," a "fresh magic world." On the grounds, there would be peacocks and carefully planted Italianate gardens. Ottoline would invite high-ranking government officials and her artistic friends to commingle. There would be charades, dramas, masquerades, acrobatic dances on the lawn, swimming in the pool, Philip's pianola-playing, and sexual intrigue without end. Though it would be a place where pacifists could convene, its primary function was to be a retreat from the reality of the war.

Lawrence believed it was his mission to create a more significant purpose for Ottoline. He believed her tragedy was that she had "never found the god Apollo." *He* knew she could give herself over to this dream of "the new life" that he posited. *He* knew she possessed a central core of "burning darkness" that would provide energy for his new movement. He understood what her intrinsic nature was, though she herself did not yet know. She would fulfill herself, not as "the Salon lady and the blue stocking," not within the realm of society or of thought, but beyond it, as "the medium, the prophetess." For this was the role of the truly great woman, as he conceived it: to act as the wellspring of a man's power, as the source of his inspiration, not by what she did for him, but by what she was.

This was what he had thought his wife would become for him, but she still resisted his domination. Frieda complained that Lawrence always wanted "to treat women like the chicken we had the other day, take its guts out and pluck its feathers sitting over a pail."

Lawrence thought Ottoline might provide him and Frieda with material benefits. By the beginning of March, he hoped she would give them housing at Garsington (as she would give Russell), at little cost, ten or twenty pounds a year. He promised to pay promptly if his publisher advanced money for *The Rainbow*. Otherwise, he would be in her debt, and forever grateful. She could retain ownership of her cottage, for there was "something so limited and jealous" about ownership, but he wanted her permission to call it his.

He wanted nothing lavish or extravagant—just an old monastic outbuilding that she could convert cheaply to his specifications: a window, to face east, punched into the bedroom wall; a door to provide easy access to the stairs; a bathroom to avoid the clutter of washstands; a workroom. And she could also provide some furnishings. There he and Frieda could live, happily, like "cuckoos," pluming themselves in Ottoline's nest, which was the "nest of a fine bird."

3.

In March, Lawrence reluctantly agreed to visit Cambridge with Russell to meet John Maynard Keynes, G. E. Moore, and other influential Cambridge intellects, members of the Cambridge Apostles. In part, Lawrence agreed to go because he wanted to be with Russell; he had felt a "hastening of love" for him. In part, he believed he could share his ideas for the revolution at Cambridge and recruit followers.

Russell gave a breakfast party for Lawrence in his rooms in Nevile's Court. Lawrence was "morose" throughout and sat "crouching" on the sofa, with his head down. Nothing could have been more alien to him than Cambridge and its "rationalism," "cynicism," "libertinism," and class privilege.

The trip was a complete disaster. Lawrence described it as one of the major crises in his life. It prompted a very serious disagreement with Ottoline, and a breakdown on Lawrence's part. In the wake of the visit, he found he couldn't write, and he became ill. He became "sick with the knowledge of the prevalence of evil," obsessed with thoughts that evil was "an insidious disease" that was catching. He no doubt feared he had caught it.

What had prompted his response was John Maynard Keynes's coming out of his room in his pajamas.

> We went into his rooms at midday, and it was very sunny. . . . Then suddenly a door opened and K. was there, blinking from sleep, standing in his pyjamas. And as he stood there gradually a knowledge passed into me, which has been like a little madness to me ever since. And it was carried along with the most dreadful sense of repulsiveness—something like carrion—a vulture gives me the same feeling. I begin to feel mad as I think of it—insane.

Lawrence responded to the sight of Keynes in bedclothes with loathing and disgust. Perhaps Keynes's genitals were all too obvious through his nightwear. Keynes reminded him of a "rat, as it slithers along in the dark," which Lawrence "want[ed] to kill." Lawrence had probably learned of Grant's and Keynes's affair. Both Grant and Keynes became identified, for Lawrence, with homosexuality, with the "principle of evil" that made him "sick." To cure himself, he would have to stamp it out.

He wrote Russell that the experience obliterated his hope for the future: "Cambridge made me very black and down. I cannot bear its smell of rottenness, marsh-stagnancy. . . . How can so sick people rise up? They must die first." If the types he saw at Cambridge were the rulers, thinkers, and artists of England, then, he thought, there was something profoundly wrong with the country. "I think I can't stand this England any more: it is too wicked and perverse."

Ottoline tried reasoning with him that it was important to be tolerant, to understand rather than to condemn. But he could not be persuaded.

The Cambridge Apostles, of which Russell and Keynes were both members, had espoused for some time the principle of a homosexual elite, with Keynes and Lytton Strachey in the vanguard. Lawrence's outsider's attack on the power elite at Cambridge in all likelihood startled Russell and Ottoline.

After his visit to Cambridge, Lawrence had recurrent nightmares of loathsome black beetles crawling all over him, indicating his disgust for homosexuality, but also his identification with homosexuals. His stirring of love for Russell terrified him. No doubt

Russell's beginning to respond to him terrified him even more. "Lawrence is wonderfully lovable," Russell had told Ottoline after the trip to Cambridge. "The mainspring of his life is love. . . . I love him more and more."

Even more than a relationship with a woman, Lawrence had been casting about for a strong male friendship to replace what he lacked with Frieda. He believed he wanted a powerful bond with a man, including love, and the swearing of an oath of allegiance or blood-brotherhood, sealed by a ceremony involving some physical contact. But his homosexual inclinations revolted him. Even as he practiced homosexuality (and he practiced it only with men of his class), he described overt homosexuality in others as "a form of inward corruption, . . . as if it came from deep inward dirt—a sort of sewer."

For a time, Lawrence believed Russell was the man with whom he could attain this longed-for state, and Ottoline inevitably became drawn into the high drama of Lawrence's relationship with Russell. Lawrence must have learned at some point of Russell's adulterous affair with Ottoline, perhaps even of Russell's earlier love for Wittgenstein. Adultery was something Lawrence did not approve of, even if his wife had practiced it, even when he himself flirted with it, or, later, engaged in it. In wanting a blood-brotherhood with Russell, Lawrence would be competing with Ottoline for his attentions, and Ottoline did not like competition where her admirers were concerned. For his part, Lawrence was the most jealous of men, who could fly into rages, or write vengefully, when he believed he had been provoked into this most uncomfortable feeling.

Lawrence's friendship with Ottoline and Russell had quickly stirred up some of Lawrence's most dangerous demons. But he would blame others—Keynes, Russell, and Ottoline—and not his conflicting emotions for what he suffered. He wrote Ottoline that her friends made him "dream of a beetle that bites a scorpion. But I killed it—a very large beetle." He knew there was a Devil, and he was struggling with the "Powers of Darkness," he told her.

As for Russell, Lawrence had learned that he had a "powerful malignant will in him." Though it was bad to be evil, the "worst wickedness" was to "refuse to acknowledge the passionate evil that is in us. This makes us secret and rotten." Ottoline's job was to get

Russell to acknowledge his hidden rottenness. Lawrence told Ottoline he wished he himself could let go of his inhibitions, and "be really wicked—kill and murder—but kill chiefly. I do want to kill. But I want to select whom I shall kill. Then I shall enjoy it."

An "Old, Tragic Queen"

1.

Lawrence's first brutal outburst at Ottoline came in April 1915; they had known one another just four months. It was about her treatment of Maria Nys, a member of her household.

Maria Nys was a young Belgian refugee whom Ottoline had taken into her home. She was seen in later years as one of Ottoline's "protégées." Ottoline included her in the goings-on at Bedford Square, introduced her to everyone, and tried to provide her with an education. (Later in 1915, Maria Nys met Aldous Huxley at Ottoline's, and she married him in 1919.)

Maria developed an "adolescent crush" on Ottoline and followed her around "like a young calf," sitting adoringly at her feet while Ottoline embroidered. Ottoline had been warm, welcoming, and generous to Maria, but when Maria exhibited too much feeling, Ottoline withdrew. As Ottoline wrote in her diary: "I fly near other people but they never come to me or touch my essential self, and when they approach me I fly on." Maria's slavish devotion made Ottoline feel encumbered, and Ottoline decided that Maria should stay in London when she moved her household to Garsington.

Just after Ottoline told her that she wouldn't be living at Garsington, Maria tried to kill herself "in a moment of passionate grief." She walked into Ottoline's bedroom after swallowing poison, looked at her accusingly, and said "J'ai pris du sublime" before collapsing. A doctor was called in time, and Maria's life was saved, but her health was adversely affected. After, Ottoline gave in and allowed Maria to move to Garsington.

When Lawrence found out about Maria's attempted suicide, he lashed out at Ottoline.

I think it . . . [is] as if you, with a strong, old-developed *will* had enveloped the girl, in this will, so that she lived under the dominance of your will: and then you want to put her away from you, eject her from your will. So that when she says it was because she couldn't bear being left, that she took the poison, it is a great deal true.

Ottoline had forced Maria into dependency, treated her as a satellite, then cast her aside. Her treatment of Maria was not an isolated case, but a pattern: "Why must you always use your *will* so much, why can't you let things be, without always grasping and trying to know and to dominate," Lawrence chastised her.

He believed Maria's attraction to Ottoline was the result of Ottoline's seductive behavior. Since he maintained a lifelong repulsion for lesbian love, this was a serious accusation. It made him think Ottoline was evil: "I'm not sure whether you aren't really more wicked than I had at first thought you. I think you can't help torturing a bit." His remark suggests that he had already shifted from seeing Ottoline as a saint to seeing her as a sinner. Now it was just a matter of determining not whether she was evil, but just how evil she was.

Lawrence held that the "most fatal, most hateful of all things is bullying. But what is bullying? It is a desire to superimpose my own will upon another person." Bullying was what overbearing mothers did to their children, under the guise of loving them, he argued. Ottoline had treated Maria as a daughter, but she had also invited Maria's romantic attraction. But when Maria drew close, Ottoline pulled away. The situation between them replicated the worst features of Lawrence's relationship with his mother.

Lawrence lashed out at Ottoline in a fury that had its roots in what he had suffered from his mother's too ardent love and her dominance. Bullying children, as he believed he was bullied by Lydia Lawrence, as he believed Maria was bullied by Ottoline, led to "neurasthenia"—illnesses linked with depression, and "a living sort of half life." This had happened to him; this had happened to Maria Nys. In striking at Ottoline for her will, he was striking, too, at a deadly quality she and his mother shared.

Lawrence's outburst about Maria had something to do with the changes occurring in his relationship with Ottoline. He found himself in a position like Maria's. Like Maria, he had professed devotion to Ottoline, thought her the center of the universe, and had told her. As always, though in Lawrence's case with good reason, Ottoline was withdrawing from him as she had from Maria. Lawrence liked to control the level of intimacy with his friends; he was usually the one who withdrew. As with Maria, his independence and autonomy had become compromised, and Ottoline's changeable behavior had maddened him: at one point he wrote to thank her for sending him a "salve-box," but, in a telling slip, he wrote "slave-box." But when he didn't hear from her, he confessed to her that he became anxious.

Like Maria, Lawrence thought Ottoline would provide a home for him at Garsington. But the scheme in which he and Frieda would live in a converted outbuilding, which had so excited him, fell through. He was desperately poor, very nearly bankrupt, for he was charged for costs for Frieda's divorce. Ottoline had made tantalizing promises he had counted on, then had withdrawn them.

It was a living arrangement that never could have worked. Lawrence's attempts to live communally—with John Middleton Murry and Katherine Mansfield and, later, with Mabel Dodge Luhan—ended in bitterness and rancor on all sides. But it was Ottoline who called a halt to the fantasy plan, not Lawrence. She used her husband, Philip (as she often did), as an intermediary to do the unpleasant. She had Philip tell Lawrence that the costs of the proposed renovation were prohibitive.

Lawrence knew that Ottoline had reasons other than the expense, because she was willing to outfit very comfortable rooms for Bertrand Russell. Lawrence persisted after the initial rebuff, asking Ottoline for a few rooms in a gardener's cottage that she needn't renovate. That proposal, too, she turned down. Lawrence covered whatever disappointment he felt with a show of bravado. He said the cottage would have been "a log on my ankle," thanking God for keeping him free, imagining that he would now find himself a "tiny place on the sea." But he was humiliated, and to heal the damage to his soul, he struck back through the issue of Maria Nys.

The Lawrences now had no place to live. He and Frieda began to look for cheap lodgings in London. They were so poor that they asked friends to make contributions toward furnishings. Lawrence wrote Ottoline, asking for whatever she could spare to help them—an egg cup or a salt spoon, perhaps, nothing expensive. Having cast them out, with the Lawrences at their poorest, Ottoline nonetheless invited them to Garsington throughout the summer to witness the splendor she was creating there.

The purpose of Garsington for Ottoline was to provide a serene retreat from the problems of the war. This would have been seriously compromised with the Lawrences in residence. They battled continuously. And Lawrence was launching an increasingly bitter critique of English society and a call to revolution: "For I am hostile, hostile, hostile to all that is, in our public and national life. I want to destroy it," he wrote Russell. Though Ottoline wanted Garsington to be a center for liberal political thought and pacifist politics, Lawrence's politics were far too radical and his manner far too vitriolic for her aristocratic view of the way revolutions within England should be conducted.

Lawrence began to change his mind about the Morrells. He saw that he had held them in too high esteem. They were "not fighters or leaders." His feelings about Ottoline had become conflicted: he was attracted to her, and to her wealth, and he liked her attentions; but she had become repellent to him as well. He started referring to her as an object. She was no longer a saint, a mythic woman, or the potential center of his idealistic community; he started demeaning her by calling her "the Ottoline."

2.

The joy-filled, life-enhancing man whom Ottoline believed she had found in Lawrence to her chagrin had turned, overnight, it seemed, into a specter of gloom and violence. His letters to her (and other friends) were now filled not with hope and promise, but with apocalyptic fears. His visions of changing the world with Ottoline's help had been abandoned. Now he saw only a "corrosive darkness." He repeatedly and obsessively cursed everyone he knew, everyone he saw: Maynard Keynes and the Cambridge homosexuals ("I like sensual lust—but insectwise, no—it is obscene . . . one insect mounted on another—oh God!)"; Bertrand Russell (a creature with a "powerful malignant will in himself"); soldiers (they reminded him "of lice of bugs"); people in general ("they are dogs and swine, bloodsuckers").

Lawrence had become far more troubling to Ottoline than Bertrand Russell ever was. She thought he was seeing the world this way because his imagination had become "disordered." She didn't realize how dangerously unstable he had become, and that, for the next few years, he would be battling his sexual, murderous, and suicidal urges. But no, he told her. It wasn't him. Everything around him, all England, was "insect-teeming." She was wrong to have faith in humanity; it was time to confront her wickedness. The world had gone mad. The *Lusitania* had been sunk. There were anti-German riots in London. It was time, he thought, for the Lord to send another flood to cleanse the world. He wasn't sure whether he wanted to be Noah.

He was having terrifying dreams: that the stars were on fire and leaving the sky: that the ghosts of dead soldiers were "marching home in legions over the white, silent sea," taking their vengeance on all those who had stayed behind, killing them all. And he was suicidal. He thought it would be "pleasant" to "walk over the edge" of a cliff and into the peaceful world of water that lay below. This would release him from "this world" of "torture."

Whatever its origins in his life history or in his psychic makeup, Lawrence attributed the onset of this crisis to his visit to Cambridge with Russell. He had become contaminated by knowing Ottoline and her set.

3.

In late April, Ottoline was reading the final chunk of Lawrence's new novel, *The Rainbow*, which he had been sending her in installments. His financial well-being depended upon its successful publication, as he stressed to his agent. It had taken him three years to write. He believed it his best work, and he was eager to hear what Ottoline thought. He probably thought she would be sympathetic to its theme—the marital lives of three generations of women—and its explicit treatment of sexuality.

Ottoline didn't like it. She finished reading by the end of April, after Lawrence began criticizing her behavior, and perhaps she was now less inclined to like his work.

She was "shocked" by the novel, in which many passionate sexual encounters take place between wives and husbands. In a letter to Russell, she complained, "It is too *intensely* sexual." She thought the novel was "slapdash," "sloppy," and "amateurish." She believed there *were* memorable passages of "passionate beauty." But she did not like his "habit" of verbal repetition—she "counted the

word 'fecund' " at least "twelve times on one page." She believed
the novel illustrated Lawrence's deterioration as an artist; Frieda,
she believed, was responsible.

At the heart of the novel was Lawrence's notion that marital
love was the central, most important experience in life, and that
there were serious consequences if the conjugal bond was weak-
ened. It was an attitude that Ottoline did not share, though she
would find it threatening. Still, when the novel was published, she
wrote him a letter of praise. Hers was almost the only praise he received.

4.

In June 1915, Lawrence and Frieda were staying at Garsington
for Ottoline's birthday, which was the same day as his sister Ada's,
and he was doing some painting. His job, given to him by Ottoline,
was to line the flaming Venetian red panels of the dining room
with a gold border. Dressed in white coveralls, he was "creeping
slowly round" on the floor, an egg cup in one hand, a very fine
paintbrush in the other. Garsington was still not finished, and
Ottoline insisted that all the guests join in the work.

Although Lawrence and Russell were fighting, and Lawrence
and Frieda were fighting, and Ottoline and Lawrence were fighting, Ottoline insisted that because it was her birthday and a lovely
summer, they should all call a truce. They should be "nice and kind
to each other, and not quarrel."

Frieda, as always, was causing trouble. She would not help with
the painting. She sat in the middle of the room, perched on the dining room table, "swinging her legs and laughing and mocking."

Ottoline thought Frieda was jealous of her efforts to make
Garsington "nice." Frieda didn't even have a permanent place to
call home, and lugged her meager possessions around "in a few
trunks." She knew Frieda was jealous of the attention everyone
paid Lawrence. "She even said in a loud, challenging voice,"
Ottoline reported, " 'I am just as remarkable and important as
Lorenzo.' "

With Frieda around, it was like "sitting with a tigress" who
would "spring and rend" at any moment. Ottoline believed that
Frieda was always stirring up trouble, trying to turn Lawrence

against her. Ottoline wrote in her diary that Frieda appeared "to be a woman that Strindberg might have married and hated, and is what is called a 'clever fool.' "

But Ottoline recognized that Lawrence could never leave Frieda. He was too "timid and sensitive to face life alone."

On the last night of their visit, the Lawrences had "a violent quarrel in their room and objects were heard being thrown around." Frieda "went off in a high temper to London" the next morning. Lawrence couldn't figure out whether he should follow his wife or stay at Garsington. Meekly, he left. Frieda said she was having "ructions" with "the old Ottoline." To a friend she wrote: "She will say such *vile* things about me—and I think it's so mean, when she is rich and I am poor and people will take such a mean advantage of one's poverty." She confessed that at Garsington she felt like "a Hun and a nobody."

"Poor Lawrence," Ottoline thought, "how dreadful to be tied to her as he is by his need of some strong big woman. And how humiliating to have to follow her, like a whipped dog, even if he does manage sometimes to get in a snap and snarl!" You could see how "whipped, forlorn and crestfallen" Lawrence looked, so different from the way he behaved when he was alone.

The best times were those when Frieda wasn't there. Then Lawrence could be "quiet and natural" instead of exploding with rage at Frieda's instigation. During the summer, when he came without her, he would read poems in the evenings to entertain Ottoline and her guests, "generally poems from Swinburne." Or he would tell stories from his life, making the characters "comic, and kindly and real." Or he would go with Ottoline to visit Oxford. He thought it was a "dead and useless" place, although he lingered with pleasure over the illuminated books at the Bodleian library. Ottoline prompted the librarian to remove them from their cases so that he could inspect them carefully, for he wanted to make copies.

Ottoline believed that staying with Frieda would "kill" Lawrence's "gentle tender side." She blamed Frieda for the violence, and couldn't admit that Lawrence was equally culpable. She believed he could never fulfill his potential if he remained with Frieda. Her primary scheme for his development was to hasten the end of his marriage and to substitute Russell's and her influence over him.

Even Philip Morrell urged Lawrence to leave Frieda, possibly at

Ottoline's suggestion, because of the harm he believed the marriage was causing Lawrence. In time, Ottoline said she didn't have "room for Frieda" at Garsington, although she would always welcome Lawrence. Lawrence's relationship with Ottoline strained his deteriorating relationship with Frieda still further. It became inevitable that Frieda would force him to choose between his friendship with Ottoline and the glittering world of Garsington, and his marriage, troubled though it may have been, to her.

5.

In the summer of 1915, Lawrence became preoccupied, as he had been in the first days of his attachment to Frieda, with the destructive effects of lust. Only now it was Russell and Ottoline and the Cambridge homosexuals whom he used as targets. As the summer progressed, Lawrence met with Russell about a planned series of lectures on ethics and immortality. They never came off, because Lawrence realized he was "very shy" and couldn't speak in public, and because they quarreled. He had further opportunity to observe Russell and Ottoline and the goings-on at Garsington, and he began to view Russell primarily, but Ottoline, too, as creatures "full of lust."

Lawrence was, no doubt, so conscious of lust because he himself was attracted to Russell, and wanted to swear a blood-brotherhood with him, and he also found Ottoline's provocative behavior unsettling. Ottoline's biographer Miranda Seymour has described this period as an especially ardent time in Russell and Ottoline's affair, which they cannot have concealed from Lawrence. Ottoline and Russell had become inadvertently embroiled in Lawrence's moral and psychic crisis, in his confused and dangerous feelings about his thwarted desires, and it was psychically safer for him to attack them than to attack himself.

Frieda fought fiercely throughout her marriage against what she saw as the threat of Lawrence's homosexual proclivities. She hated Bertrand Russell from the first, ostensibly because of his politics, but also because she believed he patronized her. Still, she knew Lawrence was attracted to him. Russell and Ottoline presented a triple threat to Frieda: Russell because of Lawrence's desire for a man; Ottoline because she threatened Frieda's impact upon Lawrence's "soul" and his creative spirit; and both of them together because they were trying to end her marriage.

When Ottoline told Lawrence that Frieda was no longer welcome at Garsington, Lawrence and Frieda began to reconnect, and made temporary repairs in the rift of their marriage. Frieda's increasing jealousy over Ottoline prompted her to reassert her claim on Lawrence. She urged him to understand that the impact of Russell's and Ottoline's political and philosophical ideas on him was pernicious. She began to urge him to get as far away from them as he could. For better or for worse, she would have him to herself again.

In the coming months, Lawrence vacillated between making it clear to Ottoline that he would not come to Garsington without Frieda, and wanting to go to Garsington without her. When he tried to write to Ottoline, Frieda would seize the letter and tear it up, and he would threaten to hit her in the mouth. Soon Ottoline and Russell became the symbols of evil incarnate, as Lawrence idealized what his relationship with Frieda might become. It was a strategy that helped the Lawrences' marriage to survive. But the cost was enormous.

6.

It was July, and Lawrence wasn't in the mood for visiting Garsington. He told Ottoline he wouldn't come to see her unless Russell pledged to work *with* him, unless Frieda was again welcome.

Throughout the summer of 1915, a summer of "queer unsettled weather," Lawrence's relationship with Ottoline and Russell continued to deteriorate. Russell and Lawrence reached an irrevocable impasse in their politics and philosophy. Russell was advocating pacifism and resistance to the war, rooted in a fundamental belief in democracy and the rational nature of human beings. Lawrence believed that all forms of social criticism were conservative, for they implied that the existing order merely required repair rather than replacement.

Lawrence now wanted an aristocracy to rule the country, with an elected kaiser. He had developed a theory of knowledge based in blood-consciousness: "My great religion is a belief in the blood," he wrote, "the flesh, as being wiser than the intellect. We can go wrong in our minds. But what our blood feels and believes and says, is always true." Russell thought Lawrence's ideas were ridiculous. Later, he called Lawrence a proto-fascist.

Lawrence had begun to write down his philosophy as a way of working himself out of his deepening depression, but also to force Russell into changing his thinking. He had been writing it throughout the springtime, sitting in the sunshine, as the apple trees and bluebells came into blossom.

In July, Lawrence and Russell exchanged their work. Lawrence, proud of his "cleverness," sent copies of his work to Ottoline, believing that she would like it better than his novel. He "scribbled" all over Russell's manuscript, denouncing his principles of democracy. "NO! NO! NO! NO! NO!" he wrote. "This is *not good.*" Russell couldn't make "head or tail" of Lawrence's philosophy, and believed that his ideas were nothing but "bosh." Yet Lawrence believed they were near to swearing "Blutbruderschaft."

Ottoline and Russell, their class prejudice showing, wondered whether the son of a coal miner had the intellectual capacity to launch *any* attack against the ruling class or any other aspect of society. Lawrence began to see Ottoline and Russell as emblematic of upper-class decadence. He began to see the war as moving toward class warfare, as resolving itself into "a war between Labour and Capital" that would, in time, move to England. When that happened, he told Ottoline, they all would have to be ready "to direct the way." Ottoline thought the impasse between Lawrence and Russell over the issue of politics had occurred because of an "enmity between the natural, impatient, and not profoundly educated man of genius," and the man "who possessed a mind that was a fine and delicate instrument." But it came about because Lawrence's politics were revolutionary and Russell's were reformist.

7.

In August, the turning point came. Ottoline and Russell had told Lawrence that his work was worthless and that he couldn't think. He felt so soiled by his relationship with them that he had gone to the sea to wash himself clean. With his back to the land, looking out at the pale sand and the white foam of the sea and the few gulls that were about, he thought, "It is a great thing to realise that the original world is still there—perfectly clean and pure."

He wrote his friend Lady Cynthia Asquith an account of the rift:

> I've got a real bitterness in my soul, just now, as if Russell and
> Lady Ottoline were traitors—they are traitors. . . . They come to
> me, and they make me talk, and they enjoy it, it gives them a
> profoundly gratifying sensation. And that is all. . . . [A]s if I were a
> cake or a wine or a pudding. Then they say, I—D.H.L. am
> wonderful, I am an exceedingly valuable personality, but that the
> things I say are extravaganza, illusions. They say I cannot think.
> . . . They are static, static, static. . . . [A]ll my effort, which is my
> life, they betray, they are like Judas. . . .
> But I know them now, which is enough.

In September, Russell sent Lawrence an article he had written called "The Danger to Civilization," which Lawrence had solicited for *The Signature*, the little magazine he had started with Katherine Mansfield and John Middleton Murry. Lawrence responded to Russell's attack on his work with an attack of his own: "The article you send me is a plausible lie, and I hate it." But he also criticized Russell's psyche. He mentioned the word "lust" so often in his harangue that it seems he was attacking Russell, too, because he had become the embodiment of evil.

> You are too full of devilish repressions to be anything but lustful
> and cruel. I would rather have the German soldiers with rapine
> and cruelty, than you with your words of goodness. It is the falsity
> I can't bear. I wouldn't care if you were six times a murderer, so
> long as you said to yourself, "I am this." The enemy of all
> mankind, you are, full of the lust of enmity.
> . . . . Let us become strangers again, I think it is better.

Russell was so shaken by Lawrence's letter that he "sat without moving for a whole day." For twenty-four hours, he seriously contemplated suicide.

Lawrence wrote Ottoline that he had written "very violently" to Russell: "I am glad, because it had to be said sometime. But also I am very sorry, and feel like going into a corner to cry, as I used to do when I was a child. . . . And then, damn it all, why should one [cry]." Though Russell and Lawrence would continue to interact for a time, their friendship was over.

Lawrence had told Ottoline that he adhered to the belief "If thine eye offend thee, pluck it out." Russell had offended him; Russell was plucked out.

8.

The autumn of 1915 was a "terrible" one for Lawrence. His crisis worsened, and he began to believe that it was necessary for him to quit England if he was to survive—that if he couldn't leave, he would die. "It was the autumn of the Gallipoli failure, of the first large Zeppelin air raids," and increasing zealotry on the part of proponents of the war, with the Bishop of London calling the war "the greatest fight ever made for the Christian religion."

Lawrence's personal despair became exacerbated by the prosecution and suppression of *The Rainbow*, the novel upon which he had pinned so many hopes. The novel had been published on September 30, 1915, and he was excited by what he had accomplished in writing it. On November 13, copies of the novel were confiscated by court order, "ostensibly on the grounds of obscenity." Then the public hangman of London made a mound of more than a thousand copies of the novel outside the Royal Exchange, set it afire, and burned them all.

The courts had proceeded against the novel based on "complaints of the National Purity League" and two hostile reviews, condemning the book's "viciousness" and stating that such a work had "no right to exist in the wind of war" when young men were dying for their country. A reviewer called it "a greater menace to our public health than any of the . . . disease[s] which we pay our medical officers to fight."

The Obscene Publications Act of 1857 permitted the seizure of a book if *any* citizen lodged a complaint of indecency. That Frieda was German surely played a part, as did Lawrence's reputation as a writer who openly resisted the war and advocated revolution, although it was maintained officially that the book's obscenity was the sole reason for the action.

Though his relationship with Ottoline was in turmoil, Lawrence enlisted Philip Morrell's aid as a member of Parliament. "On 8 November, five days before the final hearing," Lawrence went to Garsington. To Ottoline, he seemed resigned. Instead of discussing the novel, he helped her plant irises above the pond, and they went on long walks into the countryside.

Philip Morrell did "all he could in the House of Commons to get the ban removed." He asked pointed questions on two separate occasions about the legality of the seizure and the author's rights in such a situation. "Does the right Hon. Gentleman not see that a grave injustice has been done to this man, seeing that he has no opportunity of defending his book against the charges brought against it?" he asked.

Lawrence was grateful for his efforts. But Morrell himself was in disrepute because of his antiwar stance; his effort came to nothing, and the book remained unavailable in England until 1926.

The Rainbow seizure forced Ottoline and Lawrence into a temporary and shaky truce that lasted for a time. But it reinforced Lawrence's belief that he had to get out of England if he was going to survive. Ottoline went to see him in Hampstead Heath. While they walked on the Heath, he told her that in England "life is dead, the land dead, the people are dead sapless sticks." He felt he had to leave before he, too, died. He became determined to go to America to "write for Americans." He would establish his Rananim in Florida, where he hoped his health would improve. As for those responsible for the suppression of his work: "I only curse them all, body and soul, root, branch and leaf, to eternal damnation." Ottoline felt he had come to resemble "an excited dog," rushing from one idea to the next, "barking and barking at an imaginary enemy."

Throughout the autumn, although they had tried to help him, Ottoline and Philip Morrell came to represent for him the terrible decay and depravity at the very core of English civilization. He wrote Ottoline telling her that he felt he had to shed "the old." He had to find a way "to be clear and true to my deepest self," and he always wanted them to be friends. He had seen a zeppelin in the sky, the "splashes of fire as the shells fired from earth burst." He thought it was time for "a new heaven and a new earth."

Garsington, which he had once believed would be the center for change, for his Rananim, he saw instead as the emblem of everything he needed to escape. "This house of the Ottoline's—It is England—my God, it breaks my soul— . . . the great past, crumbling down, breaking down." Ottoline, once seen as a prophetess, was now "an old, tragic queen" who had "exhausted" herself in an attempt to escape her past, but who had only "destroyed," not "created." Referring to the Book of Judges, he said Ottoline had pulled "the temple down," and "she lies exhausted in the ruins."

Lawrence shared none of these changing feelings with Ottoline. Instead, although he admitted problems with Russell, he protested his continuing devotion to her, though the tone of her letters had cooled. He told her that wherever he lived there would be "a bond" between them. They would be together, "in spirit, deep to the bottom," and she would be his "spiritual home in England." But she might have read between the lines when he sent her a long, effusive elegy to Garsington, depicting himself as a "drowning man" who "cannot bear" to look upon Garsington—the "old three-pointed house" whose interior is "fragrant with . . . remembered lustiness."

Ottoline, no doubt aware of the change in Lawrence, tried to work her way back into his esteem by sending presents: some flowers, a pair of boots, which he needed. And she planned to work an embroidery for them.

Still, his visits to Garsington continued. He even built her a rose arbor in the garden. After they planted the roses, he stood by, giving "orders to the roses to flower with all their essential and primitive Rose-Force as rapidly and abundantly as possible."

He tried to be a good guest, but he always "talked violently" and shouted "too loud," and this annoyed Ottoline. But he joined in with the evening's entertainments and participated in the masquerades. He picked out costumes from the "hundreds of exquisite rags, heaps of coloured cloths and things" that she kept about.

9.

In the middle of November, Lawrence asked Ottoline to join him on his trip to Florida, to come on "a cotton boat to these Semi-tropical seas." There, he told her, they could forget "these past days of destruction and misery." She said no, but sent him some money toward his expenses. To help him, she sent a letter to some friends, including George Bernard Shaw, asking for contributions: "Poor fellow," she wrote, "he is miserably depressed and hopeless and he feels that there is *no* opening for his work here and that he must go forth to new fields. It seems an awful pity that we should lose him as he is a real genius." Lawrence never made the trip. He postponed sailing because of business concerning *The Rainbow*. When he was ready to go, it was impossible to leave England.

Ottoline continued to tell friends she thought Lawrence was saintly for putting up with Frieda. Lawrence reported to Ottoline that though he remembered the "fine hours" they all had shared, the "friction" among them now seemed "inevitable." His status with Ottoline as "*a favorite*" to Frieda was "ignominious" and had made his wife hate him. Also, Frieda said Lawrence was "a traitor to her."

At a farewell party given for him in London, Ottoline was discussed. Everyone was "tearing O. to pieces." One guest cried out, "Stop! We must leave her just one feather!" Lawrence laughed "a high tinkling laugh, mischievous," and replied, "We will leave her just one draggled feather in her tail, the poor plucked hen!"

In December, Lawrence wrote Ottoline, telling her that the trip to America was off. He was visiting his sister for Christmas. Then, perhaps, he would go west, to Cornwall. His going away would be "a sort of retirement to get strength and concord in myself," he told her. He wanted "all knots . . . broken, all bonds unloosed, all connections slackened and released." He felt "a certain amount of slow, subterranean hope"; he was feeling "full and nascent."

10.

On a last visit to Garsington, Lawrence rewrote his own version of *Othello*, and acted the part of the Moor. In his rendition, he emphasized "the affair between a noble lady and an outcast male." In his costume of a "large straw hat and a real Arab coat," Ottoline said, "it was the only time I ever saw him look beautiful."

It was a role Lawrence must have relished: the self-righteous anger and justifiable revenge of the wronged man, his fingers around the throat of his unfaithful wife—made impure by her lust—choking the very life out of the woman who had betrayed him.

Looking on, enjoying the spectacle, was Ottoline. She felt "happy, fresh and gay." What she was watching, though, was a foreshadowing of what Lawrence would do to her in *Women in Love*.

"*Shooting Them with Noiseless Bullets*"

1.

At the end of 1915, D. H. Lawrence, feeling he was finished with the world and its people, exiled himself to Cornwall with Frieda. During January and February 1916, they lived in a borrowed cottage at Porthcothan, on the north coast of Cornwall, near the Bedruthan Steps. His despair over the suppression of *The Rainbow*, according to Frieda, had made him ill: "I'll never write another word I mean," he had told her. It had also turned him against her.

Frieda was very worried about him, his spirits were so low. And his health was very bad. She wanted "revenge" for the way they had been treated, for the way the world had persecuted them and suppressed his work. She believed that if she could get Lawrence to fight back, his spirits would brighten, and he would stop fighting her.

In his months in Cornwall, Lawrence underwent a moral and emotional crisis. His emotions hit bottom; for a time, it seemed as if he had become psychotic. He severed one friendship after another, in a deliberate program to seal himself off from everyone: "I had rather venture among lions and tigers," he wrote, "than among my abhorred fellow men, who fill me with untold horror and disgust."

Lawrence had not yet abandoned his plan to leave England, but as the war had progressed it had become harder to do so, and the threat of conscription hung over him. He had wanted to go west, to Florida, to see a new civilization, and to try to establish his Rananim with a few faithful followers. But now Cornwall was as far west as he could manage.

At first, Cornwall pleased him. He loved the old farmhouse he was living in and its "remote and desolate" situation—looking out over a "brow of land" at the "grey and shaggy" sea. He could hear the waves night and day, and the "strong and fierce wind," which never stopped blowing. He had given up all struggle and striving, and he wanted to be "like a thistle-down" on the wind, with "no connection" with anyone but Frieda. The right way, the only way, to be happy, he believed, was to fight to forge a "nucleus of love between a man and a woman, and let the world look after itself."

He had made friends with two young men—Philip Heseltine and Dikran Kouyoumdjian—who had joined him and were helping pay the rent. He saw them as the nucleus of a group of young people with whom he would one day found a colony. He had some hope that his friendship with them would be the "miracle" he needed to revitalize himself, though they seemed empty. Ottoline, who met them, thought Heseltine "degenerate" and Kouyoumdjian possessing "a certain vulgar sexual force." His new friends mirrored Lawrence's increasing preoccupation with sex during the Cornwall period. In time, he would come to believe they were "sick." Heseltine, though, stayed for two months, and typed the collection of poetry Lawrence prepared while in Porthcothan.

Lawrence hoped, too, that John Middleton Murry and Katherine Mansfield, who seemed like-minded, would come to live with them in Cornwall. Murry and Mansfield were in Bandol, France, but Lawrence wanted them to come when they could, to establish a scaled-down version of his utopian community. Murry became Lawrence's next candidate for a blood-brotherhood, replacing Russell.

In Cornwall, in what Lawrence saw for a time as a world untarnished by the worst of modern civilization, that "banquet of vomit," with reminders of King Arthur and Tristan all around, he would try to write his way out of despair. It was a strategy for survival that had worked for him in the past.

Predicting what he himself would do, Lawrence wrote Russell that, to save oneself during these times, "one must be an outlaw. . . . One must retire out of the herd and then fire bombs into it." No matter how poor or mad he was, he could "still write bombs." As he wrote to Ottoline, he saw himself as a "pirate or a highwayman." Writing was his way of attacking people, his "way of shooting them with noiseless bullets that explode in their souls." First, while living at Porthcothan, he wrote philosophy. Then, after he moved to Higher Tregerthen, he turned to fiction, to *Women in Love*. It was a bomb he lobbed back into the herd containing both Ottoline and Russell.

2.

It was a long winter "of weather and lovelessness and discontent and sadness." Heseltine and Kouyoumdjian had begun to irritate him, though Heseltine's affair with Puma, "a prostitute," who joined Heseltine at the end of January, interested him. Used to dominating, Lawrence didn't like the way his young friends "noisily assert[ed] themselves."

Lawrence spent much of January in bed with what he told friends was an inflammation in his chest. The right side of his body became paralyzed for a time. He was so ill, it was an "effort even to hold a pen to write."

Frieda realized he was seriously depressed. She was "thrown into a panic," and wrote Bertrand Russell in desperation, asking him to visit: "I am so worried about Lawrence. . . . He might just die because everything is too much for him." But Russell was doing antiwar work, and he no longer wanted that degree of intimacy with the Lawrences.

Maitland Radford had come to attend Lawrence at Frieda's request. He told Lawrence, "There is no organic illness at all, except the mucus in the bronchi etc are weak." Lawrence's major problem was "nervous stress," and it was necessary for him to "go somewhere and be very peaceful."

Nonetheless, by the middle of January Lawrence was working on his philosophy, promising to send it to Ottoline and Russell when he finished it. With the wind howling outside and the waves "thundering splendidly" in the cove below, he turned to work on the "destructive" phase of his philosophy. He was calling the work *Goats and Compasses*, and it was an angry and bitter treatise on the evils of homosexuality. In a few months, in his prologue to *Women in Love*, he would be writing of the allure of homosexuality. Now, though, he was creating a document that reiterated his idea that heterosexual love was good and homosexual relations evil.

Through his stay at Porthcothan, Lawrence continued his relationship with Ottoline and Russell. He wrote Russell that he thought about him "nearly every day," and that he wished Russell would come to see him. He wondered what Russell was doing, and how he was feeling, and said he wanted to hear from him. He was "launched" into the writing of his philosophy; he would send Russell a copy, which Russell "must read . . . with pleasure."

He hoped that, though the trip was long, Ottoline would come to see him. It was "essential" for her to see Cornwall. She should bring her maid, and something warm for her bed, as they were short of blankets. Two or three books for him—the *Homeric Hymn*, Petronius in French, "something a bit learned": about the Druids or Africa or the Orphic Religions or Egypt or fetish worship, or primitive customs, Dostoyevsky's *The Possessed*. And a "nice spirit" for Frieda.

The trip was postponed. Ottoline had become ill and couldn't travel. In what was by now a familiar refrain, Lawrence told her that she must "lie still, . . . as if you had no more will. . . . Then you will get well."

But Ottoline would never travel to Cornwall to see the Lawrences. Their relationship took another turn for the worse. When Ottoline was ill, Frieda wrote her a "disagreeable letter" because Heseltine and Kouyoumdjian had told her what Ottoline had said when they had stayed at Garsington about her, and about her marriage with Lawrence:

> I know in your heart you have been my enemy. You thought that Lawrence ought to leave me, that I am bad for him, that he does not care for me. . . . You have been very unfair to me, I think, you have tried to put me down as of no account.

Ottoline, when she showed the letter to Russell, said, "Isn't Frieda a mad woman!! She would send me mad too. I wonder why she makes this attack on me."

Lawrence hoped his wife and Ottoline could resolve their differences, that they could forget their troubles, but that never happened.

Ottoline, though, stayed in touch with him. She sent a selection of books. In February, more presents followed: a blue and black counterpane, food, more books, and medicines and preparations to increase his strength. She again offered him accommodations at Garsington.

Frieda and Lawrence had been amusing themselves by reading Ottoline's copy of Dostoyevsky's *The Possessed*. Lawrence took a "great dislike" to the novel. It treated something that had preoccupied him since his visit to Cambridge: "the pure mind . . . trampled . . . under the hoofs of secret, perverse, undirect sensuality." Frieda noted that Varvara, who was "tall and bony," with an "immensely long" face, "reminding one of a horse" was "[e]xactly" like Ottoline. Frieda had begun her campaign to extricate her husband from his friendship with Ottoline by mocking and caricaturing her, by suggesting that she sullied Lawrence. He in time succumbed. He used the image of the horse face to describe Ottoline's appearance in *Women in Love*. It was one of the kinder details he would employ to describe her.

Lawrence ruined Ottoline's copy of *The Possessed* by leaving it on a window seat on a rainy night. He didn't bother replacing it, he told her, because he knew she didn't like it.

3.

By the beginning of February, Lawrence had prepared a collection of his poems presenting a history of his emotional and sexual life (much of it unsatisfactory) from the ages of twenty to twenty-six. He titled it *Amores*. He decided to dedicate the work to Ottoline. The first poem in the collection was "Tease," about a man who seduces a woman into becoming "slave-like" in her submission to him. This was precisely the relationship he would create between his character and Ottoline's in *Women in Love*.

Perhaps he thought he could force his wife and Ottoline into a rapprochement if he showed Frieda he intended to maintain his friendship with Ottoline. If he had deliberately tried to make Frieda even angrier at and more jealous of Ottoline, he couldn't have chosen a better way of doing it.

"To Ottoline Morrell in Tribute to Her Noble and Independent Sympathy and Her Generous Understanding These Poems are Gratefully Dedicated" should be, he thought, the inscription in the volume. This to the woman Frieda knew had tried to destroy her marriage. Still, Lawrence had always enjoyed having women fight over him.

Russell's break with Lawrence came in February. In London, Russell was fighting conscription by giving his No-Conscription Fellowship lectures; his antiwar work eventually landed him in prison. He wrote Lawrence expressing doubt about whether his efforts were worthwhile and wondering whether he had any reason for living. Lawrence exploded over what he saw as Russell's preoccupation with "fussy trivialities" and his "obstinate" nature, which made him go his own way and kept him from being Lawrence's disciple. He wrote Russell an "impudent" letter.

What's the good of living as you do, any way. I don't believe your
lectures *are* good. . . .
    What's the good of sticking in the damned ship and
haranguing the merchant-pilgrims in their own language. Why
don't you drop overboard? Why don't you clear out of the whole
show. . . .
    Even your mathematics are only *dead* truth. . . .
    Oh, and I want to ask you, when you make your will, do leave
me enough to live on.

In closing, Lawrence wrote: "My love to you."

Ottoline tried to smooth Russell's ruffled feathers: Lawrence's
letter wasn't "beastly," as Russell thought, it was simply *"silly,"*
obviously written under Frieda's influence, and it showed that
Lawrence was really "quite unbalanced." But Russell's anger at
Lawrence was not to be assuaged; he wrote Lawrence: "Our ways
should be separate."

By February 25, Lawrence sent a section of *Goats and Compasses*
to Ottoline for her comments, telling her to read it only on a
"winter-dark" day to match its mood. Ottoline didn't like it, and
she told him. She realized that Frieda would "rejoice" at her disap-
proval, for it would give Frieda an opportunity to jeer at her to
Lawrence.

Ottoline wrote in her diary that she thought it was "deplorable
tosh"—Lawrence "at his very worst"—"perverted and self-
contradictory." He was writing a "gospel of hate and of violent in-
dividualism. He attacks the will, love and sympathy. Indeed, the
only thing he doesn't revile and condemn is love between men and
women." She believed the philosophy was surely "the outcome of
Frieda." She didn't realize the Lawrences' marriage was on the
verge of collapsing, and that Lawrence was desperately, hopelessly,
trying to persuade himself of the sanctity of the love between men
and women.

Years later, Ottoline saw the work as evidence of Frieda's triumph over Lawrence. His ongoing battle with his wife—"these two
violent creatures . . . tearing at each other"—had made Lawrence
"raw and bitter inside." He was now "filled with hate." Ottoline
believed Lawrence ended the fight by acquiescing to Frieda's dominance over him. She was right, and she was wrong. Like the war

that was raging across the Channel, the bloodiest phase of the war between the Lawrences hadn't yet begun.

Lawrence was beginning to wonder whether monogamy was necessary. He felt tempted by the sensuous nature of Cornish men, even as he proclaimed that he and Frieda were becoming "more and more truly married." Even as he fought Frieda, was unfaithful to her, and professed dominance over her, he tried to mend the rift in his marriage and to create the ideal marriage he wanted. This he did by seeing people as she saw them.

Lawrence never published *Goats and Compasses*. He burned a version of it before he left Cornwall. Its philosophy, however, became that of his alter ego, Rupert Birkin, in *Women in Love*.

Ottoline saw *Goats and Compasses* as an index that Lawrence had become dangerously antisocial. In this she was right. She thought it proved he was "not fit to deal with other human beings," and that he and Frieda were locked together in a *folie à deux*. They were alienating almost everyone and sealing themselves off "alone in an enclosure, where they could dance together, mocking and laughing at those outside, calling them fools or enemies." Ottoline believed Frieda and Lawrence supported and reinforced each other's distorted perception that everyone's behavior but theirs was vile and loathsome. In truth, she observed, their behavior was far more problematic than most people's.

Lawrence, as he told Ottoline, *had* decided to cut himself off as much as possible. He believed these dangerous times demanded radical strategies for survival. "As for me," he wrote, "as far as I can, I will save myself. . . . I don't care if sixty million individuals die." Heartless and megalomaniacal as it sounded, he had come to believe the war was a necessary cleansing of a degenerate society: "This world of ours has got to collapse now." He saw himself, though, as exempt from the fate awaiting others: "I will not live any more in this time." He had been reading histories of Babylon, Nineveh, Ashurbanipal; the destruction of empires, he understood, was nothing new and in the larger scheme of things did not matter.

Reading Lawrence's philosophy marked a significant shift in Ottoline's relationship with him; she understood that he was beyond Russell's influence, and beyond her power. Through the coming months, she cooled toward him considerably. There were no visits, fewer letters and presents.

Her affair with Russell having changed to a companionate relationship (because of his interest in other women—Vivien Eliot and Constance Malleson—which he did not tell her about), her friendship with Lawrence having foundered, Ottoline began to search for a new man who could become what she had hoped Russell or Lawrence would be. She was determined to live life fully, and that meant having a passionate man in her life.

By September, she had found him: the poet Siegfried Sassoon, "a young man who was both brave and imaginative, who loved nature . . . ; surely this was the kindred spirit she had been seeking all her life." Soon she began to lavish presents upon him—a "vellum-bound manuscript book," a statement about her "dream for Garsington," and, as with Lawrence, an opal. And much to her surprise, while on a visit to Garsington, Murry declared his love, while Mansfield seemed to be pursuing Russell!

Her "soul mush," or whatever it was that she had shared with Lawrence, was over. By the end of May, Lawrence noticed "Ottoline is *very cool*." Through the spring, summer, and autumn, when he was writing his novel, her remoteness triggered his retaliatory rage. *He* was supposed to determine how intimate their relationship would be. Through writing *Women in Love*, he would force her to take notice of him.

"Like a Lion Raging After Its Prey"

1.

The Lawrences left Porthcothan near the end of February 1916. Too poor to travel any other way, they walked south, "in the snow," looking for lodgings. Fifty miles away, they came upon Zennor. It was a tiny hamlet of seven houses and a church, set in "under hills all wild with gorse and great grey granite boulders, above the wide-stretching sea." At first, they moved into the Tinners Arms. Soon, though, they found a tiny cottage at Higher Tregerthen, "two rooms and a scullery," an outside privy, no running water, but a spring on a hillside. It rented for five pounds a year, a rate they could afford. He was economizing because he suspected he would be poor for some time to come. *Amores* had been "rudely rejected," and they had only fifty pounds saved, and no prospects for income.

Lawrence thought he had found the "Promised Land," a place where he could be happy. He was hoping Mansfield and Murry would join them by April: "I feel you are my only real friends in the world," he wrote them.

2.

With the return of spring, with the "gorse, all happy with flowers" and the lambs "leaping into the air, kicking their hind legs with a wild little flourish," Lawrence felt he was "getting really well."

He wanted to start working on something new, something other than philosophy, a novel. Fiction had always been his "major source of income," and he and Frieda needed money. For a time, he thought he might go back to a novel he had begun in Italy, *The Insurrection of Miss Houghton*, but he soon abandoned that plan, and turned to continuing the Brangwen saga he had begun in *The Rainbow*. "Soon," he wrote, ten days before beginning *Women in Love*, "I shall be like a lion raging after his prey, seeking whom he may devour."

Before beginning his novel, he made a comfortable home for himself and Frieda at Higher Tregerthen. He had found some isolated gray granite outbuildings that reminded him of a "little monastery." They were in a splendid situation, "under the moors," on the edge of "rough stony fields," overlooking the sea and the setting sun. There was a "little grassy terrace" outside where meals could be taken in fine weather, and space for planting vegetables and flowers. There was room for Murry and Mansfield. They would have separate quarters in a long house, with a tower, where Katherine could write. It was a stone's throw from the Lawrences, and would allow a good deal of intimacy.

Lawrence busied himself outfitting his new home. He sent to London for his furnishings—his mother's brass candlesticks, his rugs and cooking utensils, and his books. He set about painting, and sewing "buttercup yellow curtains with green blobs," and making furniture—a dresser, and shelves for books and for plates. And he and Frieda went to sales in St. Ives to buy "coco-matting" to use for rugs, and wicker chairs. Life, he thought, was "going to be wonderful."

He faithfully reported each detail of his interior decorating scheme to Ottoline; he knew she would be interested. Downstairs, he told her, he had painted his walls a "pale pale pink," his furniture a royal blue, and the ceiling and its beams white.

Upstairs was his writing room and bedroom. In this room, he told Ottoline, he had given pride of place to the embroidery and counterpane she had made for him. They made the room look "brilliant and gay." The embroidery was done from a drawing by Duncan Grant, one of Lawrence's least favorite painters—"a tree with big bright flowers and birds and beasts." His workroom had a "deep window looking to the sea," and another that faced the "hill-slope of gorse and granite." Finally, he felt that he had his "own home," and he was "content."

When he worked, the primeval and clean natural beauty he found so calming surrounded him. When the weather was fine, he went outside, onto the hill-slope, and sat in the sun. He braced himself against a pale gray granite outcropping and wrote with his notebook upon his knees. There, amid the sounds of birds and the wind and the sea, he would write his novel. Writing made him feel "safe and remote."

Mansfield and Murry came to live with the Lawrences at the beginning of April. At first, it appeared as if the scheme might work; Murry was impressed with Lawrence's "warm and irresistible intimacy" and his capacity for awakening "the feeling that there was something in you which could grow." Frieda and Katherine busied themselves making potpourri, painting boxes, taking walks. Just after they arrived, Lawrence turned to the writing of fiction. While there, Murry worked on his critical book on Dostoyevsky; Mansfield began the work that became "Prelude."

During this time, Murry observed, two issues preyed on Lawrence's mind. The war filled him with such revulsion that he would sit in a chair rocking and moaning. "War, more war!" he would chant. " 'Dies irae, dies illa', a monstrous disaster, the collapse of all human decency." And his relationship with Frieda, Murry believed, was making "a sick man" of him. Murry never saw, though, how deeply tormented Lawrence was by erotic desire for him, which he was writing into *Women in Love.*

Murry and Mansfield saw how physically abusive the Lawrences had become. Both sent reports back to Ottoline (whom they had only recently met) at Garsington, which she shared with her guests. To them, Frieda was *"monstrum, horrendum."* By this time, Garsington had become the lodging place for many conscientious objectors, and something of a free hotel for Ottoline's friends, so there were many people—among them Aldous Huxley, Lytton Strachey, Maynard Keynes, Ramsay MacDonald—gathered around the breakfast table to hear of the Lawrences' battles as Ottoline read the juiciest bits aloud from her latest correspondence.

Once, Murry reported, Lawrence chased Frieda around a long table, crying, "I'll *kill* her, I'll *kill* her!" Another time, Lawrence attacked Frieda with a knife, "roaring, 'I'll cut your throat, you bitch.' "

Lawrence had wanted Murry to come to Cornwall so that he could provide something that was missing in his relationship with Frieda, something he could never get from a woman. He began to urge upon Murry a "blood-brotherhood," and the celebration of "some pre-Christian blood-rite," which Murry evaded. This seems to have been Lawrence's attempt to force his increasingly urgent homosexual desires into a spiritual union.

Katherine Mansfield became so sick of what she regarded as Lawrence's obsession with sex during these months that she told him he should call his cottage "The Phallus." Frieda agreed.

3.

In early April, Frieda wrote Ottoline an enraged letter. Perhaps Murry and Mansfield had told her something Ottoline had said. Perhaps something in a letter Ottoline had sent had irritated her.

> Now for over a year I was ready to be your friend—but steadily and persistently you have treated me with arrogance and insolence! ... [Y]ou have tried to separate Lawrence and me because you wanted some sort of unwholesome relation with him. ... But I have had enough! Either you treat me with ordinary courtesy and respect or I wish neither to hear from you or see you again!

Lawrence wrote Ottoline that he was glad Frieda had "said what she feels." Ottoline foolishly mailed Frieda's letter to Murry and

Mansfield, but Frieda, who collected the mail from the postman, had seen Ottoline's handwriting and, suspecting mischief, had opened it.

Lawrence was beginning to see things Frieda's way. He told Murry that if he continued his friendship with Ottoline, it was "black treachery to him." Murry reported this to Ottoline. Lawrence was about to begin the prologue to *Women in Love*, about to develop the idea that Ottoline had wanted an "unwholesome relation" with him. This, and his belief that Ottoline, and other aristocrats, were "dead," would become a trait of Ottoline's stand-in.

4.

About April 19, Lawrence began work on a novel he was calling *The Sisters*—a sequel to *The Rainbow*. In time, he named it *Women in Love*. He first mentioned it in a letter to Mark Gertler on April 26: "I am much better in health," he wrote. "This last week I have felt really well, as I have not been for many months. So am very glad. And I began a novel. I will write only when I am very healthy. I will not waste myself." To Cynthia Asquith he reported that though the "world crackles and busts," while writing, he had "a certain order" in his soul. It made him feel "inviolable": "There one sits, as in a crow's nest, out of it all."

As he worked on the novel, he kept Ottoline informed of his progress, even as he was writing her into his work as a hateful character. He never told her he was creating her portrait. Yet he admitted he was writing a work that had no "hope of ever being published, because of the things it says."

First, Lawrence wrote the prologue. In it, he described his preference for homosexual love. He had by this time met William Henry Hocking, the young farmer with whom he would later become intimate. This would be Lawrence's first homosexual affair since adolescence. The Hocking family ran Tregerthen Farm, in the hollow just below the Lawrences' lodgings. In the prologue, Lawrence describes Birkin's "overwhelming physical desire to devour, absorb and satisfy himself on the handsome animal-like body of the Cornish type embodied in William Henry":

There would come into a restaurant a strange Cornish type of man, with dark eyes like holes in his head, or like the eyes of a rat, and with dark, fine, rather stiff hair, and full, heavy softly-strong limbs. Then again Birkin would feel the desire spring up in him, the desire to know this man, to have him, as it were to eat him, take the very substance of him. And watching the strange, rather furtive, rabbit-like way in which the strong, softly-built man ate, Birkin would feel the rousedness burning in his own breast, as if this were what he wanted, as if the satisfaction of his desire lay in the body of the young, strong man opposite.

Birkin (Lawrence) tries to understand why he feels so much "vindictiveness" toward Hermione (Ottoline), why he has been so "jeering and spiteful" to her. He has used her secrets to mock her, he has been instrumental in her "going mad," and he wonders why he has treated her this way. With uncanny prescience, Lawrence was predicting precisely the effect his jeering and vindictive novel would have on Ottoline: like Hermione, she, too, would become dangerously unstable.

Birkin knows that guilt over his unacted-upon "passion of desire" for Gerald Crich (Murry) has made him persecute Hermione. He uses his relationship with her to force himself into heterosexuality. After a night of love, though, he always becomes so "hollow and ghastly" that he "turned upon her savagely, like a maddened dog. And like a priestess who is rended for sacrifice, she submitted and endured." He couldn't "desire any woman"; this "was a real torture." But "he forced himself towards her" anyway. Unable to transcend his loathing for her, he becomes mired in self-hatred. He believes that mortifying himself in this way with her will lead to spirituality, but he is wrong.

Whether or not Frieda Lawrence had wanted to acknowledge it, Lawrence's relationship with Ottoline went far beyond the "soul mush" she claimed. Ottoline's history makes it likely that she acted seductively toward Lawrence. He struck out at her so forcibly because she tempted and revolted him. He *imagined* what a sexual relationship with Ottoline would be like, even if he did not engage in one. He did not like what he imagined. And he reacted violently to it.

Hermione nauseates Birkin, and he realizes it; he knows a woman cannot arouse him. It was "for men that he felt the hot, flushing roused attraction which a man is supposed to feel for the other sex." Birkin imagines the men he lusts for. They are "white-skinned, keen-limbed men with eyes like blue-flashing ice and hair like crystals of winter sunshine, the northmen, inhuman as sharp-crying gulls." Or they are "men with dark eyes that one can enter and plunge into, bathe in, as in a liquid darkness." It is not only Crich he desires, but many other men.

Frieda Lawrence said that in Cornwall, Lawrence's "homosexuality . . . was a short phase out of misery—I fought him and won." She was wrong. She never won, because she couldn't win.

Lawrence's battle was not the choice between having sex with women or having sex with men. He battled to force himself to have sex with a woman though it revolted him, and not to have sex with a man though he desired it. In *Women in Love*, Birkin's anal intercourse with Ursula is clearly a substitute for the consummation he wants with Crich. No matter how strong his feelings for men are, though, Birkin sees them as evil and dangerous: "I *should not* feel like this. . . . It is the ultimate mark of my deficiency, that I feel like this," Birkin says.

Birkin fights to expel his need for men; it is a battle he cannot win, for it goes against his true nature. Fighting Hermione for Birkin, like fighting Ottoline for Lawrence, became "the strongest movement in his life" because it screened the stronger, more dangerous battle: Birkin's/Lawrence's war against his homosexuality.

The prologue (which Lawrence removed from the work before sending it to his agent, and which Ottoline and other friends who read the novel in typescript never saw) tells us that in creating the character of Hermione Roddice in *Women in Love*, Lawrence was turning on Hermione/Ottoline all his self-loathing. No matter how awful the consequences for her, the outcome for him, he knew, would be equally devastating. In fighting her, he was on the "point of breaking, becoming a thing, losing his integral being, or else of becoming insane." To head off that inevitable breakdown, he would attack her even as he knew it would harm her.

On May 5, as Cornwall exploded with beauty—"tangles of blackthorn and solid mounds of gorse blossom, and bluebells beneath, and myriads of violets, and . . . ferns unrolling finely and delicately"—he wrote Ottoline that his new novel was "a thing that is a stranger to me even as I write it." By May 19, he was "half way through." The work had been "very easy," he wrote his friend, the

Freudian psychoanalyst Barbara Low: "I have not travailed over it. It is the book of my free soul."

On May 24, with the primroses and sea-pinks in flower, Lawrence described the progress he had made to Ottoline: "I have got a long way with my novel. It comes rapidly, and is very good." Within a month, he had written through Birkin and Ursula's marriage (more than four hundred printed pages). He explained to Ottoline that he was writing so quickly because the novel was coming straight from his soul: "When one is shaken to the very depths, one finds reality in the unreal world. At present my real world is the world of my inner soul, which reflects on to the novel I write."

This came close to admitting that the novel was an emotional autobiography, that the real world had become too much for Lawrence, that what he had lived through (though he did not describe it to Ottoline) had shaken him, and that he needed to withdraw to a world of his creation for stability.

Near the end of May, Frieda had a "great rumpus" with Ottoline. It was the final battle in their war. Murry believed that the fundamental cause for Frieda's rage, despite what she said, was that she felt herself "*déclassée*." When she had met Lawrence, it had seemed as if his literary star would continue to rise and his work would be financially successful. Now they were poor. Ottoline believed Lawrence was a saint for putting up with Frieda: "If only we could put her in a sack and drown her," she wrote Russell. Frieda had probably heard of Ottoline's blaming her for everything that was wrong with Lawrence; of Ottoline's belief that Lawrence had to leave Frieda to reclaim his soul.

Frieda, in a fury, wrote Ottoline that she would no longer tolerate Ottoline's interference in her marriage. Frieda also lashed out at the hypocrisy of Ottoline's liberal politics, at her support for the Irish Rising. She told Ottoline that "her spirituality [was] false, her democracy . . . an autocrat turned sour"; that her pretenses at "humanity and kindness" were really only "stunts" for someone "whose inside is frozen." Ottoline's splendid appearance couldn't hide her moral bankruptcy: "inside those wonderful shawls," Frieda told her, "there is cheapness and vulgarity." Lawrence used precisely these qualities of hypocrisy and spiritual decay in developing Ottoline's alter ego in *Women in Love*.

5.

Within two months, about June 19, Lawrence was almost done. The work had come "rushing out," and he felt "very triumphant in it." By June 30, he declared that he had "finished" with the handwritten draft; the work of typing was now before him. Preparing the typescript took on an urgency because he had only six pounds left; his agent, Pinker, when he learned this, lent him fifty pounds.

Lawrence had been writing at a ferocious pace. On some days, he wrote as many as three thousand words, and kept up this rigorous pace throughout its composition. He wrote in one small notebook after another, filling about fifteen notebooks—863 pages in all. On July 9, he wrote his devoted friend, reviewer and novelist Catherine Carswell, that he was "finished."

6.

In the middle of June, just before Lawrence finished the handwritten draft of *Women in Love*, Murry and Mansfield left Higher Tregerthen. They could no longer tolerate the Lawrences' violent relationship. The "saucepans and frying pans hurtled through the air." The "atmosphere of HATE between them." The beatings. The making up: Lawrence's bringing Frieda breakfast in bed, their singing together, and her twining flowers in her hair for him, the day after he had threatened to "cut her throat" if she went near him. Mansfield believed Lawrence had "gone a little bit out of his mind." If disagreed with, he flew into a "frenzy," saying, "You have gone wrong in your sex and belong to an obscene spirit," she reported to Ottoline.

One night, Murry heard Lawrence crying out, "Jack is killing me"; when Murry tried to placate him by telling him he loved him, Lawrence shouted, "I hate your love, I hate it. You're an obscene bug sucking my life away." Murry's blood ran "thin with horror"; he knew Lawrence had crossed over to insanity, and he "fled in terror." Through the months they lived together, Lawrence was writing Murry and Mansfield into the novel as the death-obsessed lovers Gerald Crich and Gudrun Brangwen.

General conscription having been announced, at the end of June Lawrence and Frieda walked to Penzance so that he could report to the authorities for his medical examination. He was sent on to

Bodmin, where he stayed for two days. He was declared "physically unfit for military service." He used the experience of his humiliating examination in his 1923 novel, *Kangaroo;* he knew that if he had been compelled to serve, he would have died.

After Murry and Mansfield left, Lawrence began his affair with an American journalist, Esther Andrews. Even as he was writing the conclusion of *Women in Love*—the triumph of the struggle for love between Birkin and Ursula—he was turning his attention to another woman. The affair was "a miserable failure." Yet it seriously threatened his marriage. Frieda was distraught over it, and Andrews remained an important woman in Lawrence's life until the middle of 1917.

7.

With a handwritten draft of the work completed, Lawrence turned by July 12 to the "labour" of typing the work himself on a machine the American poet Amy Lowell had given him. He was too poor to pay to have it typed and too poor to afford a new ribbon for his typewriter. Still, he turned the task of typing to his advantage, by revising, even recomposing, as he went along. The work proceeded slowly and got on his nerves; by the end of the month, he had managed only fifteen pages. He promised himself, though, that if the typing became too much of a struggle, he would find a way to have the manuscript typed.

During the warm summer days as he worked, "terrible battles were being fought at Verdun and on the Somme." By autumn, when he finished, more than half a million men had been killed in battle. While he worked, Frieda sunned herself, or walked into St. Ives to shop, sporting the brightly colored stockings—orange, pink, yellow, or green—she had taken to wearing. Lawrence had Ursula and Gudrun, too, wear them in *Women in Love.*

Once, she went to London to see her children. Lawrence seems to have begun his relationship with William Henry Hocking, which lasted until Lawrence left Cornwall the next year, at this time. Throughout 1917, Lawrence spent "much of his time" with the young farmer. Lawrence's turning "against her," to Hocking, made Frieda feel "utterly alone there, on that wild Cornish moor, in the little granite cottage." "Deeply hurt" by his infidelity, she turned for solace to an affair with the composer Cecil Gray, who was living at Bosigran Castle.

Lawrence typed out his novel in the tower room Mansfield had used. He kept at it through the end of October, when he couldn't bear doing the work anymore. The walls of the room were such a bright yellow, they hurt his eyes. He surrounded himself with vases filled with the flowers he had grown

To relieve the tedium of preparing the typescript, he often went down to the sea to swim. He let the waves, as high as mountains, lift his naked body. It was very dangerous, and he frightened himself. The shoreline was rocky, and when the waves crashed, he barely managed to avoid being seriously hurt: "It is so frightening," he wrote Amy Lowell, "when one is naked among the rocks, to see the high water rising to a threatening wall, . . . then bursting into a furious wild incandescence of foam."

On September 26, he wrote Ottoline that he would like to see her at Garsington when he finished. Though the early phase of the work had proceeded swiftly, he was now struggling: "I only want to finish this novel, which is like a malady or a madness while it lasts." His mood was grim, perhaps the result of his guilt over his relationship with Hocking. He felt he was living in Sodom: he had been to Zennor, and when he saw people there, he imagined killing them:

> I want to crouch in the bushes and shoot them silently with
> invisible arrows of death. I think truly the only righteousness is the
> destruction of man, as in Sodom. But they creep in, the
> obstructions, the people, like bugs. . . . Oh, if one could have but a
> great box of insect powder, and shake it over them.

"A Terrible and Horrible and Wonderful Novel"

1.

As Lawrence was writing his saga of the saving love Rupert Birkin and Ursula Brangwen move toward, he and Frieda were living through one of the most physically violent and unfaithful periods in their marriage. It seemed that the marriage would not survive, that one of the Lawrences would kill the other, that Lawrence would kill himself, or that he would never emerge from what surely was an acute psychotic episode. *Women in Love* is Lawrence's urgent attempt to persuade himself, and his readers, that the love he and Frieda shared was normal, that heterosexual love was good, and that he was able to practice it in a life-enhancing way. Much about the novel was fantasy, wish-fulfillment.

The novel's settings are Beldover, a small colliery town in the Midlands much like Lawrence's birthplace, Eastwood; Shortlands and Breadalby, the "great houses" nearby, which belong to the mine-owning Criches and the Roddices (he is a member of Parliament); and, later, the Alps. Its major theme is the obsessive power of desire and its lethal potential, if it is allowed to go unchecked. Lawrence/Rupert and Frieda/Ursula seem to accomplish this, whereas in life, this was not the case. Lawrence illustrates his theme by exploring the relationships of many sets of lovers. Apart from Rupert Birkin and Ursula Brangwen, there are Rupert Birkin and Hermione Roddice, based upon himself and Ottoline Morrell; Gerald Crich and Gudrun Brangwen, modeled after Murry and Mansfield (in an early version, he even gives Crich Murry's "black and orange" college blazer to wear); Loerke and Leitner; and Pussum and Halliday, based on Puma and Heseltine. There is, too, Birkin's thwarted relationship with Crich—his wish to have a "perfect relationship between man and man—additional to marriage."

In *Women in Love*, Lawrence misrepresented the life he and Frieda shared. Though he showed how all the other relationships in the novel were deadly, it was the Lawrences' that nearly killed both him and Frieda. He projected Frieda's violence onto Ottoline's character, Hermione; his and Frieda's sadism and masochism onto Murry's and Mansfield's Gerald and Gudrun; his obsession with what he saw as sexual perversity onto Crich, Gudrun, and Loerke. (Ursula and Rupert feel the allure of what is described as deadly, forbidden pleasure—anal intercourse—but they seem to reject this by the end of the novel.) Lawrence demonstrates how each couple fails to realize the novel's ideal, except one—Rupert Birkin and Ursula Brangwen—when in fact his marriage was at its nadir.

Richard Aldington (who saw it as "a book of retaliation") said that *Women in Love* was misnamed, that it should have been called

Everybody in Hate. The loathing and self-hatred, the attacks and counterattacks among the novel's so-called lovers, reflect Lawrence's disposition and behavior as he wrote it. Words like "foul," "deathly," "obscene," "perverse," "sordid," "soiled," "ugly," "filth," "loathsome," "corruption," "degenerate," "violated," "dread," "horror," "meaningless," "defiled," "repulsion," "violent," "murderous," "tortured," "mockery," "wounds," "vulnerable," "contempt," "torment," "humiliation" are used to describe the feelings each set of "lovers" share, and are the insults they hurl at one another. Rupert and Ursula are no exception; their "happiness" at the end of the novel is not a logical outcome of his battle to dominate her, but seems a hope, on Lawrence's part, that his troubled marriage could move into a less violent phase.

2.

As Lawrence wrote, he incorporated his experiences into the work. The novel begins in spring, with promise, as did his composition of it. An adder he saw on a walk became an image for Ottoline. He mined Ottoline's letters, Frieda's, and his own for descriptions and dialogue. Ursula and Rupert play out Lawrence and Frieda's fights about Ottoline. Rupert is given Lawrence's illness, and his need for blood-brotherhood. Both Rupert and Gerald have Lawrence's suicidal fantasies, and his world-weariness. Rupert and Ursula verbally abuse one another, as did Frieda and Lawrence. Gudrun and Gerald physically assault each other, as did Frieda and Lawrence: Gudrun slaps Gerald across the face. Lawrence's murderous behavior to Frieda is replicated in Gerald's choking Gudrun in an unsuccessful attempt to kill her. Gudrun fantasizes about Gerald killing her while they have sex; she sees it as the perfect consummation—the lover becoming the murderer.

Frieda once smashed a heavy dinner plate over Lawrence's head. "It was only lucky you didn't kill me," he told her. "You might have." This act is given to Hermione. But in keeping with Hermione's class, when she tries to murder Birkin she smashes a lapis lazuli paperweight over his head.

As Lawrence proceeded with the work, he and Frieda severed one relationship after another. Friends turned to enemies, and Lawrence wrote them into the novel as the embodiment of everything he detested, everything he considered evil. Frieda's lover, Cecil

Gray, commenting on this trait, said Lawrence created "abject little caricatures of his friends" when they resisted his control; he avenged himself by writing about them.

After Lawrence's breach with Russell, he wrote Russell into the novel as the foolish Sir Joshua Malleson (or Matteson—Lawrence used both names for the same character). Everything Lawrence had come to detest about Russell he used in his portrait of Sir Joshua, who resembles a "great lizard," who talks "endlessly, endlessly" in his "harsh," "rather mincing voice," saying absolutely nothing worth listening to. All his political discourse at Breadalby, about a new social order is, really, "quite useless and cheap."

At the end of April, Lawrence broke with Philip Heseltine, who became in *Women in Love* the decadent Halliday; Heseltine's lover, Puma, became the sex-crazed, pregnant prostitute, Pussum. After Mansfield and Murry left and Lawrence heard that Mansfield had taken another lover, he wrote Gudrun's affair with Loerke.

3.

But it was Ottoline Morrell who was most severely scapegoated. She had come to represent a woman who, though she appeared humble and subservient, really wanted to claim ascendancy over men "with horrible, insidious arrogance and female tyranny." Robert Lucas, Frieda's biographer, claims that Lawrence's "desire for revenge" against women was never rational; it was rooted in his fury at his mother's too ardent relationship with him as a child and young man. Ottoline became the repository for all the rage Lawrence felt toward his mother (which he made clear in the prologue)—for that which he felt toward himself and his wife during these torturous months in Cornwall. Ottoline/Hermione was a safer target than Frieda, Lawrence thought, and he used Hermione to attack what he detested in Frieda but couldn't say about her because he still hoped for a successful heterosexual relationship. Divorcing Frieda was impossible: they were partners for life. He used Hermione, too, to take his revenge on Ottoline for the humiliation he and Frieda had suffered by entering Ottoline's upper-class world, which he had never expressed to her directly.

In the novel, Hermione represented the kind of woman Rupert had to reject, the destructive love Birkin must give up, to find a saving, empowering love with Ursula. Hermione is a devouring monster-woman, a viper, who wants to dominate and so destroy her lover Rupert Birkin.

Lawrence's most vicious portrait in the novel was that of Ottoline Morrell as Hermione Roddice. Hermione, like Ottoline, believes her class position makes her invincible. "No one," she thinks, "could make mock of her, because she stood among the first, and those that were against her were below her. . . . So, she was invulnerable." In *Women in Love*, Hermione, like Ottoline, is bested by her social inferiors—Rupert and Ursula. Both use the weapons Lawrence himself used: mockery, insult, and caricature—the weapons of words. In the novel, Rupert says that if anyone had the courage to show Hermione what she looked like to others, it would destroy her. *Women in Love* did just that to Ottoline Morrell.

4.

Lawrence poured everything he knew, everything he observed, everything he detested about Ottoline into his portrait of her as Hermione Roddice: her offensive mannerisms: her "curious, sinister, rapt look"; the way she lifted her eyelids when she was "hurt and overwrought"; her turning away from people as they spoke to her. Her mind-control exercises. Her gift-giving, a way of forcing people into her debt. Her class superiority, despite her "curious pleasure" in pretending she believed in equality; her way of treating everyone not of her class as servants she could order about. The way she came up to inspect people "out of sheer curiosity, as if they were creatures on exhibition." Her paroxysms over beauty. Her habit of lapsing into Italian, whether or not her listeners knew the language. Her way of ignoring women when men were present. Her voice, which was a "sing-song." Her dresses, which were outlandish and forced people to look at her. Her trailing, heavily embroidered shawls. Her fur-lined cloaks. Her enormous hats. Her "gaudy" parasols. Her thick hair. The way she walked. "She looked striking, astonishing, almost macabre," an observer notes: little girls think she looks *"weird!"*

Lawrence attacked her politics, and Garsington, her relationships with men, and her treatment of Maria Nys, who appears as Miss Bradley, treated as a "subservient" with "cool almost amused contempt by Hermione, and therefore slighted by everybody." He mocked Ottoline's deepest fears about herself and her hidden desires, which she had revealed to him. Many of his sharpest barbs repeat her own self-analysis. She had allowed him to see into her heart, and he used her worst doubts and fears in his portrait.

One of his cruelest strokes was his portrait of her as a woman so empty that she believed herself worthless if she did not have the attentions of a man, no matter how miserably he treated her. He used what she had told him about her troubled love affairs to create a portrait of a woman whose "greatest reality" was "suffering" for men. Hermione's/Ottoline's credo was that "one must be willing to suffer" for a man "hourly, daily." Her ideal man was "bullying" and "insensitive."

In a wonderfully ironic thrust, Lawrence wrote Hermione/Ottoline as sick with love for Rupert Birkin, his alter ego in the novel. Without him, she slips into depression and morbidity.

Lawrence turned Philip Morrell's character, called Salsie, into Hermione's/Ottoline's *brother*. This was a snide comment upon what the Morrells' marriage had turned into, given Ottoline's (and Philip's, though it was not known at the time) adulterous liaisons. Although, like Philip, Salsie is a liberal member of Parliament, his most significant character trait is his pomposity.

5.

As the sisters Ursula and Gudrun Brangwen observe the wedding ceremony of Gerald Crich's sister, Hermione makes her first, unforgettable appearance in the novel, as a bridesmaid. She is a "tall, slow, reluctant woman with red brown hair." She walks with her "head held up, balancing an enormous flat hat of pale yellow velvet," adorned with "ostrich feathers." She is self-absorbed, out of touch with reality, and consumed by her troubled internal world. "She drifted forward as if perfectly aimless, her long blenched face lifted up, not to see the world"; she seems "almost drugged, as if a strange mass of thoughts coiled in the darkness within her, and she was never allowed to escape." Her appearance, at the wedding festivities, is "macabre"; she is a "lovely horror."

She is an ardent pacifist, and "passionately interested in reform." She acts as "a medium for the culture of ideas," but she never has any ideas of her own. Using lines lifted from Frieda's furious letter to Ottoline, Birkin thinks Hermione's belief in "democracy is an absolute lie," her "brotherhood of man is a pure falsity."

Hermione's real *raison d'être*, though, is not politics; it is having "various intimacies of mind and soul, with various men of capacity": she is "a man's woman."

Her most important aim in life is to make herself "invulnerable, unassailable, beyond reach of the world's judgment." She is defeated, though, by the school inspector Rupert Birkin, her social inferior. He toys with her, takes her affection and her lavish gifts—she helps him outfit a gorgeous set of rooms—but he controls her by playing a game of cat and mouse with her which makes her desire for him insatiable.

Hermione's/Ottoline's need for a man, no matter what the psychic cost, is the "chink in her armor." Rupert/Lawrence knows this, and he uses it against her. It is the reason her soul is "tortured." She has "no natural sufficiency, there was a terrible void, a lack, a deficiency of being within her."

She becomes the masochistic victim of Birkin's sadism. What she wants from a man is that he allow her "to be his slave!" She courts abuse, and she relishes it.

Hermione enters the church with "a little convulsion of suffering yearning," knowing Birkin will be there. When she doesn't see him, she feels "as if she were drowning." When she does see him, she doesn't feel complete unless her body touches his. He sees her looking at him and feels "acute pity for her."

Lawrence savagely describes Ottoline/Hermione as a "strange figure," "dazed," "gnawed as by a neuralgia," "tormented," with a look of "exhaustion" about her, as if "she had come out of some new, bizarre picture." She has trouble thinking and speaking: her face contorts, her brow knits as she becomes "twisted in troublesome effort for utterance"; her words are preceded by a "queer rumbling in her throat." The "darkness covered her, she was like a ship that has gone down."

In a schoolroom, where Birkin has gone to oversee Ursula's progress as a teacher, Lawrence has Birkin confronting Hermione and haranguing her about everything she stands for. Hermione has come to see Birkin as he works, so hungry is she to be near him. He shows her the female bud of the catkin, the "little red flame," which she has never before noticed. In a fictional transcription of his nature walk with Ottoline, Hermione develops a "strange, almost mystic-passionate attraction" for the female part of the flower, which prompts her to assert her belief that education ruins the instinctive self.

Birkin verbally assaults her in front of Ursula. Hermione is a hypocrite, acting as if she wants "[p]assion and the instincts," but she really only wants these through her "consciousness. It all takes place in your head, under that skull of yours." He thinks she is "decadent," the product of a civilization that began with the Renaissance, now, though, on the "road to death."

6.

Each moment Lawrence had spent at Garsington was mined for his scathing portrait of Breadalby, Hermione's house, in *Women in Love*. That which Ottoline had created with such love and care as a gathering place for artists and politicians, Lawrence exposed as a place of aristocratic decline, decay, and moral perversity, where the dead-in-life consorted.

Like Garsington, Breadalby looks across "the dip, where the fish-ponds lay in silence at the pillared front of the house." There is the pool guests use for swimming. Beautifully clad women walk around on the lawn and sit in the shade of an "enormous, beautifully balanced ilex tree." But the narrative insists, "what a snare and a delusion, . . . what a horrible, dead prison Breadalby really was."

It is to Breadalby that Hermione summons everyone she meets. In this, her world, she plays out her need to dominate, and she exercises her will and desire to control, under the guise of the good hostess. Here she grips "hours by the throat, to force her life from them." In time, Birkin realizes, "Such a will is an obscenity," and anyone who receives her gifts is in danger.

She has invited the sisters, Ursula and Gudrun, to Breadalby, and they have come because they are curious, though she represents everything they despise. They know they are better than she is, though Ursula is a teacher and Gudrun is an artist.

Through Ursula's (Frieda's) eyes, Hermione is even more grotesque than she appears through Birkin's. Her dresses, though they command attention, are "shabby and soiled, even rather dirty," making her look "sordid." Her presence is so oppressive that Ursula is relieved when she is at last allowed to be alone. Hermione has such a need for intimacy that she presses "herself physically upon one, in a way that was most embarrassing and trying. She seemed to clog one's workings." In one scene, she makes a sexual play for Ursula, indicating they should become lovers.

The invited guests assemble for conversation, which is utterly vacuous, though the participants, among them Sir Joshua/Russell, seem to think it is meaningful. The talk goes on "like a rattle of small artillery, always slightly sententious"; it was "a canal of conversation rather than a stream." Hermione's brother, Salsie/Philip Morrell, strides about, able to talk only of politics. Hermione works at her embroidery, as she "rumble[s] and ruminate[s]" in thought, but she is unable to utter anything meaningful. Always wanting her own way, she tries to force everyone to join her for a walk on the grounds. When Birkin refuses, she is furious: "It made her blood run sharp to be thwarted in even so trifling a matter." She calls him a "little boy" in front of everyone; he calls her an "impudent hag" under his breath.

Hermione is obsessed with sex. When she encounters a stag on the grounds, though she is in company, she talks to it as if it were a "boy she wanted to wheedle and fondle." She regales her guests with anecdotes about the sexual habits of swans. When she returns to the house, she must find Birkin instantly, or she cannot survive. Stimulated by her conflict with him, she sings out in her "high, small call: 'Ru-oo-pert! Ru-oo-pert!' "

She knows that a break is coming with him. Although she pretends to care for him and likes to have him "safe" with her at Breadalby, she harbors a "subconscious" and "intense" "hatred of him" because he doesn't need her. She finds him hard at work, copying a Chinese drawing of geese. Knowing that he is shutting her out of her life, she suffers "the ghastliness of dissolution, broken and gone in a horrible corruption. . . . [S]he was gone like a corpse."

At dinner, she is "strange and sepulchral"; she looks "ghastly," "uncanny and oppressive." She listens to her guests with "drugged attention."

After dinner, a servant appears with silk robes and shawls and scarves, costumes for the evening's entertainments. Throughout the enactment of "Naomi and Ruth and Orpah," Hermione's interest is piqued only when a woman exhibits "dumb helplessness" or becomes "manless." Birkin, no participant, watches the performance "like a hermit crab from its hole." At its conclusion, Hermione realizes that though this is her home, though she has directed the evening's pleasure, she is, nonetheless, always "out of it all."

At breakfast the next morning, Hermione appears "pale and ghastly." She is at her worst in the morning, and the moribund nature of Breadalby, of the English aristocracy, is then most obvious. Here they are—a famous hostess, a member of parliament, a famous philosopher, artists—gathered around the breakfast table at Breadalby/Garsington. More than anything else it resembles an Egyptian tomb. The guests and its inhabitants are corpses, "immemorial and tremendous."

After lunch and another political harangue by Birkin about the uselessness of democracy and everyone's inferiority (which makes Gerald Crich call him a megalomaniac), Hermione's hatred of Birkin reaches a climax. He goes after her, aware that his political arguments against her are a way of being violent, vindictive, and cruel to her. She knows he is destroying her: "Unless she could break out, she must die most fearfully, walled up in horror. And he was the wall. She must break down the wall."

She is electrified by this knowledge, and when he is alone, working on a drawing, she attacks him from behind and tries to kill him by beating him over the head with a paperweight. It was this scene that all Ottoline's and Lawrence's friends and enemies gossiped about. For during Ottoline's/Hermione's act of attempted murder, she has an orgasm:

> A terrible voluptuous thrill ran down her arms—she was going to know her voluptuous consummation. . . . Her hand closed on a large, beautiful ball of lapis lazuli. . . . Her heart was a pure flame in her breast, she was purely unconscious in voluptuous ecstasy. . . .
>
> Then swiftly, in a flame that drenched down her body like fluid lightning, and gave her a perfect, unutterable consummation, unutterable satisfaction, she brought down the ball of jewel stone with all her force, crash on his head. . . . But it was not enough. She lifted her arm high to aim once more, straight down on the head that lay limp on the table. She must smash it, it must be smashed before her ecstasy was consummated, fulfilled for ever.

Rupert fights her off. " 'No you don't, Hermione,' he said in a low voice. 'I don't let you. . . . It isn't I who will fail. You hear?' "

Surely these were cruel strokes: Hermione/Ottoline, who thought herself the kindest, gentlest woman, possessed by unconscious murderous rage! Hermione/Ottoline, orgasmic with rage! Hermione/Ottoline, vanquished by Lawrence! Hermione/Ottoline, abandoned by Lawrence, left to fester in perversity and self-hatred!

7.

In the novel, Lawrence described his and Frieda's quarrels about Ottoline's interference in their marriage, Frieda's feelings about her rival (her "rage and violence"), and her ultimatum that he end the relationship. Anyone who knew of the affair understood that not only did Frieda have her victory over Ottoline in life, but in fiction Lawrence humiliated the vanquished party. When Rupert and Ursula fight "to the death" about Hermione, Ursula explodes in fury over Hermione's sordid, depraved impact on Rupert.

When Ursula sees Hermione after not seeing her for a time, she thinks: "There was something of the stupidity and the unenlightened self-esteem of a horse in it [Hermione's face]. 'She's got a horse-face,' Ursula said to herself, 'she runs between blinkers.' " Ursula despises Hermione and sees her as a believer in "Mammon, the flesh, and the devil."

Ursula jeers at Rupert for being unable to immediately sever his relationship with Hermione. Everything Hermione stands for is "lies, it is false, it is death." She compares Hermione to a "corpse," to "vomit," and to "offal." Rupert is an "eater of corpses," a "scavenger" dog who feeds on offal—one who must "return" to "his vomit."

Ursula warns Rupert that he must choose: if he maintains his connection with Hermione, "you've nothing to do with me." In time, Rupert sees that Hermione stands for the "Flux of Corruption." Ursula, though, is the "Fiery Flame."

8.

In the autumn of 1916, with the "bracken withering," while German airships attacked London and the east, D. H. Lawrence was working at "phenomenal speed," finishing his novel. It had been a "cold and rainy" autumn, and he had suffered "repeated bouts of illness."

Working on the typewriter had been "a strain," so he had switched to "scribbling . . . in pencil" in small exercise books. When he finished the version, he didn't rest; he immediately started revising, enlisting Frieda's help in entering changes. As he worked, he knew that everybody would "hate [it] *completely.*" The novel was so "end-of-the-world," it frightened even him.

At the end of October, he sent the last half to his agent, Pinker, for typing. He warned Pinker: "It is a terrible and horrible and wonderful novel. You will hate it and nobody will publish it." Frieda wanted to call it *Dies Irae,* but by November, Lawrence had decided to keep the title *Women in Love.*

"Daniel in the Lion's Den"

1.

When Lawrence had begun the novel the previous spring, his mood had been hopeful. Throughout November, as he revised, his mood was savage, and the character of Hermione collected his rage. He went over the passages he had written about her and made her even "more unpleasant and grotesque" than before.

Though Frieda wanted to travel to London to see her children, Lawrence preferred to stay in isolation in Cornwall, where he had now been for a year: "I had much rather be Daniel in the lion's den, than myself in London," he wrote a friend. "I am *much* too terrified and horrified by people—the world—nowadays." Lawrence, who in writing his novel had seen himself as a lion stalking its prey, now felt himself the prey of lions.

His spirits were extremely low. He seemed paranoid, and he was seriously suicidal. He had believed that by writing this novel he had secured his freedom, that when it was finished he would knock a "loop-hole" in the prison of his bad feelings. "I have [done with] Lady Ottoline and all the rest," he wrote. "And now I am glad and free."

Writing had brought a measure of relief. But it lasted only while he was at work. His work, he now admitted, "nearly kills me." By writing this novel, which attacked so many of his friends, he was deliberately making enemies, walling himself off even more, and this was what he now wanted. "I have *no connection* with the rest of people," he wrote, "I am only at war with them, at war with the whole body of mankind."

2.

By writing the novel, Lawrence believed he had won a temporary though costly truce with Frieda. "Frieda and I have finished the long and bloody fight at last, and are one," he wrote to Murry. "It is a fight one has to fight—the old Adam to be killed in me, the old Eve in her. . . . Till the fight is finished, it is only honourable to fight. But, oh dear, it is very horrible and agonizing." Their fight, though, was hardly over.

Frieda was glad he had portrayed her as Ursula, a nice person. His portrait of her was a peace offering, just as his portrait of Ottoline was a spoil of war for Frieda, a way of saying that he had come around to her point of view about Ottoline, that Ottoline was evil. Frieda was happy to see her husband on the attack, rather than in the role of suppliant, currying Ottoline's favor. Ottoline had "played Salome" to her husband's John the Baptist. And, Frieda wrote, "I *hate* L. in that role."

Still, during the autumn, Frieda tried to make peace with Ottoline. She was afraid, with the winter approaching and Lawrence so ill, that she would need Ottoline's help. The Lawrences had alienated so many people that they were now very much alone. Frieda wrote Ottoline a letter, never mentioning what she knew of her portrait in *Women in Love,* asking whether Ottoline had, perhaps, forgotten her "nasty letter of the spring," asking whether they could be friends, telling her she was courageous to keep going on, though much in her life had caused her sorrow: "Very likely it was my fault to a great extent," Frieda apologized. Ottoline did not relent.

While he was at work, Lawrence had sent Ottoline a letter to tell her that he was writing about her in his novel. She was not troubled by the news. Lawrence probably told Murry that his portrait of Ottoline was unflattering. By late summer or early autumn, when Murry believed he was falling in love with Ottoline, he no doubt felt duty bound to tell her what Lawrence had told him.

3.

On November 20, 1916, Lawrence was at last finished, and he sent a typescript of his novel to Pinker. The agent intended to offer it to Lawrence's publisher, Methuen, which held the rights to Lawrence's next three novels.

It had taken Lawrence seven months of intense work to write *Women in Love*. The typescript ran to 666 pages, and he had accomplished three very different drafts since he had started in the spring. A letter to E. M. Forster shows his sentiments upon completion: "I get sick of giving people my books, or even of writing. People today want their senses gratified in art, but their *will* remains static. . . . There ought to be a flood to drown mankind, for there is no health in it. . . . The process of violent death will possess humanity for many a generation yet. . . . I am glad, for they are too corrupt and cowardly."

Lawrence sent another typescript to his friends Catherine and Donald Carswell, telling them in his enclosed letter that he was relieved to have finally gotten the work "out of the house." Whatever anyone else would say about it, he believed he had written a great book. He asked Donald Carswell, a barrister, to advise him whether any part was "libellous," and to "make any corrections necessary." But, he warned the Carswells, *"Don't let anybody else read it."*

He was worried about what he had written. But he told Carswell that the only portraits he had taken directly from life were those of two minor characters—Halliday (based on Philip Heseltine) and Pussum (based on Minnie Channing). "Nobody else at all lifelike," he claimed. Though he was asking Carswell to advise him about libel, he misrepresented the extent to which his novel was based upon his friends' lives; he subverted Carswell's ability to give him an accurate assessment of his legal culpability, particularly with respect to the more public figures in his work, the Morrells and Russell.

Donald Carswell dutifully read the work and noted in the margin that a description of the famous actress Eleanora Duse, "panting with her lovers after the theatre," among other descriptions, was "a grave libel" and would have to be changed. But Carswell made no objection to Halliday and Pussum, or to the characters of Hermione, Salsie, and Sir Joshua Malleson.

If Lawrence had wanted to safeguard his art, the wiser course

would have been silence. He should not have admitted to anyone—not even Carswell—that he had drawn upon his friends'
lives. This was inviting trouble, but during this period, many of
Lawrence's actions were irrational, ill considered, or impulsive.
And trouble was what he seemed to want. Because the work was
intended as an act of retaliation, Lawrence no doubt wanted his
victims to suffer by what he had done to them.

4.

Ottoline had learned about the unflattering nature of her appearance in Lawrence's novel by late November. She wrote to him
telling him what she had heard, but apparently she did not ask to
see the work.

At this point, if he had been behaving rationally and protecting
himself and his work, Lawrence would have had several options.
He could have stonewalled Ottoline; he could have referred her to
his agent; he could have written Donald Carswell for advice about
how to deal with her; he could have recalled his work and revised
it by blurring the obvious similarities between Ottoline and Hermione.

Instead, he acted injudiciously and self-destructively. He offered
to send Ottoline a copy of his novel. He wrote Catherine Carswell,
telling her, "I heard from Ottoline Morrell this morning, saying she
hears she is the villainess of the new book. It is very strange how
rumours go round.—So I have offered to send her the MS." He
asked Carswell whether she thought Ottoline would find the portrait offensive: "Do you think it would really hurt her—the Hermione? Would you be hurt, if there was some of you in Hermione?"
But, he said, the portrait wasn't really her, just suggested by her. "It
is probable," he wrote, "she will think Hermione has nothing to do
with her."

Throughout December, though he had told the Carswells to
keep the novel to themselves, he submitted to his friends' requests
to see it, compounding the trouble he would have with Ottoline.
When the novel arrived at Garsington, he had already given it to
Barbara Low, Esther Andrews, and the American poet Hilda
Doolittle, who was to send her copy on to Ottoline after she finished it.

Lawrence had fervently hoped that Ottoline would not take him up on his offer to show her the manuscript. But if he really did not want Ottoline to see it, he never should have offered to send it. Receiving a copy of a work that defamed her from another reader, and knowing that Lawrence's portrait of her was making the rounds before publication, surely compounded the blow to Ottoline's pride when she finally got her hands on the manuscript. But Lawrence was acting recklessly and ensuring that Ottoline would take action: she would have to.

5.

Lawrence had begun to think again of leaving England. He wrote Amy Lowell that he wanted to travel to Italy, if he could leave the country. Now that the "clever little Welsh *rat*" Lloyd George had become prime minister, Lawrence believed it was impossible to live with integrity in England, and he was sure the country would land "in a very big mess." Lloyd George did not share the ideals of Asquith, his predecessor, of "the old English *decency*, and the lingering love of liberty."

By the end of the year, the Lawrences' finances were in such bad shape that they couldn't afford the train fare to London. They desperately needed the money that would come from the publication of *Women in Love.*

It was a "bitter season" for Lawrence, an " 'ugly' and 'loathsome' Christmas." Still, he believed that with the new year there would come hope, and "we shall be able to begin something new."

"A Season in Hell"

1.

While Ottoline Morrell awaited the arrival of the manuscript of Lawrence's novel, she decorated Garsington for her Christmas party with "bright coloured paper garlands and evergreen swags and Chinese lanterns." The celebration marked the end of Garsington as a jovial gathering place for her friends.

Katherine Mansfield, Aldous Huxley, Maria Nys, Clive Bell,

Bertrand Russell, and Lytton Strachey were there. There was an enactment of *The Laurels*, a play written by Mansfield, and a fancy-dress dinner. Bell came costumed as a "fat repulsive old woman." Ottoline, in what proved a fitting and ironic move, was costumed as "a Masher," wearing her husband's evening dress and opera hat.

It was a troubled holiday. After Ottoline went to her room at bedtime, Mansfield held Russell rapt until early morning with her malicious talk about her hostess. At breakfast, Strachey had a temper tantrum. He berated Ottoline for not "providing him with sufficient breakfast," though it was difficult for Ottoline to procure food for her guests during wartime shortages; the next morning, she sent "six eggs, ham, fish, scones" up to his room, as much in an attempt to mock him as to please.

Throughout the festivities, Philip Morrell seemed detached. Ottoline's personal maid, Eva Merrifield, departed suddenly and without warning. Early in January, Russell told Ottoline he "needed to be free to form new relationships." Though she didn't know it, he had already begun a serious affair with Constance Malleson, and he had decided to "kill" Ottoline's love for him. He wanted a "clean break, a quick amputation," and he apparently told her so in a letter. Now in their platonic meetings, he could be cruel. As Huxley aptly noted, the "widowed state of the cosmos of Garsington" was "crumbling."

2.

Ottoline received a copy of *Women in Love* sometime in January. It was a "deep black, somnolent winter, now," she wrote, with "long dark days, blackness and cold."

She sat down to read the novel in her boudoir at Garsington, where she and Lawrence had exchanged the confidences he described in detail in the novel. She was shocked, hurt, and outraged. Nothing had prepared her for seeing herself portrayed as Hermione Roddice. She had persuaded herself that Lawrence's recent letters to her, which were "quite friendly," meant that he still liked her and so had no reason to humiliate her by writing about her unfavorably.

I read it and found myself going pale with horror, for nothing could have been more vile and obviously spiteful and contemptuous. . . . It was a great shock, . . . and I had no idea that he disliked me. . . . I was called every name from an "old hag," obsessed by sex-mania, to a corrupt Sapphist. He described me as his own discarded Mistress, who, in my sitting-room, which was minutely described, had tried to bash him over the head with a paper weight, at which he had exclaimed, "No you don't, Hermione. No you don't." In another scene I had attempted to make indecent advances to the Heroine, who was a glorified Frieda. My dresses were dirty; I was rude and insolent to my guests.

All this was offensive enough to me personally but it was made quite clear to anyone who read the book that it was meant as my portrait. There was an accurate description of the house, and garden and of Philip . . . and Maria, Bertie Russell and other friends who were in it.

On I read, chapter after chapter, scene after scene, all written, as far as I could tell, in order to humiliate me.

After she finished reading, Ottoline "acted like a scalded cat." She saw her portrait as an act of revenge, not on Lawrence's part, but on Frieda's. She wrote Russell:

Lawrence has sent me his *awful* Book. It is so loathsome one can not get clean after it—and a most insulting Chapter with *minute* photograph of Garsington and a horrible disgusting portrait of me making me out as if filled with cruel devilish *Lust*. Isn't it a shame. After having been friendly but it is of course Frieda's revenge.

She wrote Lawrence at length, "to protest." His only response, she said, was that "Hermione was a very fine woman."

She showed the manuscript to everyone staying at Garsington. It proved to be an ill-considered act. Philip, too, was angered, and took action. Katherine Mansfield agreed with Ottoline's interpretation that "Frieda is at the bottom of it"; she thought that "left to himself, Lawrence goes mad"; and she urged Ottoline to try to squelch publication—"I think it is really *fatal* that such books should be published."

Huxley, who was living at Garsington as a surrogate son, told Ottoline he was "horrified," but that the novel was "very bad." (However bad it was, it inspired Huxley to write *Crome Yellow*, his own derisive portrayal of Ottoline and Garsington life.) Clive Bell was living at Garsington with other conscientious objectors during the war, doing a modicum of farm work as a substitute for military service. He read it, too. Much to Ottoline's dismay, Bell began including lines from Lawrence's novel in his letters to her: "No you don't Hermione," Clive Bell wrote, "as I dare say you remember Lawrence's hero says."

What Ottoline didn't yet know was that Bell, who had observed her frenzy upon reading the work, was posting bulletins about her distress throughout Bloomsbury. David Garnett, Duncan Grant, and Vanessa Bell "thought very badly of Ottoline for suppressing *Women in Love.*"

By the end of February, Lytton Strachey wrote Virginia Woolf of the terrible changes that had come over Ottoline since she had read the novel. "Lady Omega Muddle," he wrote, "is now I think almost at the last gasp—infinitely old, ill, depressed, and bad-tempered—she is soon to sink into a nursing-home, where she will be fed on nuts, and allowed to receive visitors (in bed)."

3.

After she saw herself as Hermione, as Strachey reported, Ottoline went into a severe depression, a *"saison en enfer,"* a season in hell. Lawrence's view of her seriously eroded her self-worth.

"Was I really like that," she wondered. "For many months," she confessed, "the ghastly portrait of myself, written by someone whom I had trusted and liked haunted my thoughts and horrified me." The book, too, challenged her belief that friendship was important, eroded whatever confidence she had in her ability to judge people's characters, and so undermined her stability. "The bruise is inward," she wrote, "and makes a scar. . . . [U]nderneath I felt it very deeply, and naturally I thought what after all is the value of any more appreciation and friendship if it can be so easily and so perfidiously turned into such public mockery?" She felt battered by the book, almost as if Lawrence had physically assaulted her.

Lawrence's contemptuous view of life at Garsington was a sharp blow. He had claimed that it would be the center for his idealistic community; obviously, he had changed his mind, for he showed it as a gathering place for vapid incompetents. In the book, he mocked what Ottoline believed her most significant achievement, the creation, in her words, of a "fresh magic world, where all is blossom and spring and tranquility."

Ottoline's reading Lawrence's lampoon marked a significant shift that had occurred in English culture. In the past, members of the aristocracy, like Ottoline, had been protected from knowing what their social inferiors thought of them and their way of life: members of the working class, like Lawrence, had neither the access to places like Garsington nor the education to write critical portraits. Ottoline, because of her liberal political views, had invited Lawrence into her home; she had imagined that because she had been generous to the son of a miner, he would repay her with gratitude and would write of her with praise. What she did not foresee, what came as such a blow, was that she could not control the way Lawrence would interpret her life and the members of her class.

Ottoline now felt that there were "ghosts that haunt the rooms" at Garsington. She imagined them following her, clutching at her "with cold claws, whispering into my ear disillusionment and fear. . . . [They] assail me in the moonlight and invade my soul and faith." Lawrence's novel marked the beginning of the decline of Garsington as a gathering place for artistic and political figures. After Lawrence's satire, Ottoline believed that what she was doing was no longer meaningful; perhaps it never had been meaningful. Her guests now came not to celebrate, but to jeer.

4.

Lawrence's portrait prompted all London to talk about Ottoline with scorn, and she knew it. She was no longer respected: "waves of gossip and tittle-tattle surged up . . . leaving their dirty deposit at our door."

The Bloomsbury gossip-mongers, who loved to pounce upon a victim, especially once someone else had delivered the first blow, were hard at work. They were led, Ottoline thought, by Clive Bell. Their disloyalty, delight in her misfortune, and willingness to attack her when she most needed support made her feel "terrified and lonely."

The Lawrences, too, added fuel to the raging fire of abuse. They spread stories to Ottoline's friends that things at Garsington had been far worse than Lawrence had described them in *Women in*

Love. During their stays, Philip had patrolled the corridors outside the bedrooms every night, toting a pistol, ready to "shoot anyone who appeared." Frieda "claimed" that her husband based the portraits of Ottoline/Hermione and Lawrence/Birkin as lovers upon fact: Ottoline had in fact tried to lure a reluctant Lawrence into her bed. Ottoline's well-documented history of acting on her sexual impulses lent credence to Frieda's story. Many were inclined to believe that the two had become lovers. Ottoline, who heard it, probably felt that accusing a "Cavendish-Bentinck . . . of trying to entice into her bed the son of a local collier . . . [was] the unkindest slander of them all."

5.

Ottoline entered a nursing home in Royal Avenue, Chelsea, soon after she read *Women in Love.* Though she told people she was "undergoing one of her cures," she was trying to recover from the shock of the novel. She was trying, too, to retreat from the onslaught, and perhaps even trying to squelch the outcry by showing how severely she had been harmed.

While there, she received yet another, even more profound injury. On March 7, her husband, Philip, came to visit and told her that he had been unfaithful to her; that "he had two mistresses"— his secretary (Alice Jones) and Ottoline's former personal maid (Eva Merrifield); that *both* of them were pregnant; and that one was "threatening to disclose what had happened if she was not adequately supported." Given that Philip was a member of the House of Commons, a "sensational story" in the press and a scandal seemed likely.

Even worse for Ottoline, Philip (who she believed was sexless) admitted he had been consistently unfaithful to her since 1906. It was a blow from which she never recovered. Unfaithfulness she could pardon. Duplicity she could not. The bedrock of her life was their honesty with one another. She had told him about her lovers, and she believed he would tell her about his. "Don't, don't, oh don't ever again deceive me, I beg and entreat that," she wrote to her husband after learning the news.

In the wake of Lawrence's portrait, Ottoline wondered to what extent her behavior had contributed to that of her husband. Her depression worsened: "I lie like a lifeless body, quite still. I felt there was no life in my limbs. I knew what went on but it was all dim and of no moment. I lived in a dream world."

6.

Her depression lasted a full year, until the beginning of 1918, but it forever changed the way she viewed the world. Her husband's behavior was no doubt far more damaging to her pride than Lawrence's novel. Still, in her memoirs, it was the portrait of herself as Hermione that she acknowledged as the primary cause of her deepest despair. Talk, she reasoned, was ephemeral; her relationship with Philip could be mended (and, in large part, it was). But the effect of a pernicious work of art would last beyond her death. The world would remember her not as the creator of Garsington, not as a respected member of English high society, but as the sex-crazed old hag Hermione Roddice.

In time, Ottoline used these crises to reevaluate her behavior. She saw people "without the veil of illusion that I had clothed them in." She was changing, and her view of the world was changing: "I see that most people live in a steaming cauldron of resentments, irritation and dislike and envy and have only a varnish of decent behavior. This is all new to me and it has been a great shock." The most lasting effect of Lawrence's vengeful portrait was that he killed Ottoline's optimism, idealism, and hope: he forced upon her a vision of the world almost as unrelentingly hopeless and bleak as his. "I feel I have been caught in a whirlwind," she wrote in her journal, "down alone to a dark valley, where furies came grinning and mocking me, showing me all my foolish ideals, distorted, tattered."

7.

Ottoline did not feel herself emerging from her "season in hell" until January 1918. At last, she felt herself awakening from the life-in-death of the previous year. She had traversed a "land of swamps and mire and jungle and fever and horrors." It had been "a long journey," she wrote, but "still I have got through."

Lawrence's portrait of Ottoline had important consequences, not only in terms of her depression, but also in her diminished stature, and in the way artists and writers represented her in their works. It changed the way her friends and acquaintances saw her, and initiated a reinterpretation of her character. Although she had always been seen as odd and quirky, she had been respected, if sometimes somewhat grudgingly. She now lost any dignity she had possessed and became someone to criticize and caricature to those she counted among her friends, to whom she had been generous.

> Those who have turned on me and are abusive and contemptuous are those who professed . . . loyalty. . . . I am told by several people that many in London think me a dangerous and designing woman, immoral and unclean, and that no one likes me for myself, . . . and that they enjoy making fun of me. Naturally such things make me sensitive and self-conscious and I shrink from seeing people.

She believed that their ridicule echoed that of *Women in Love.* Subsequent fictional portraits of her, many published within years of Lawrence's, did rely upon the distorting lenses of Lawrence's imagination. There was Gilbert Cannan's portrait of her as Lady Rusholme in *Pugs and Peacocks.* In Aldous Huxley's *Crome Yellow,* Ottoline appears as Mrs. Wimbush, who dresses in silk and pearls, who loses a fortune betting on horses, consults her astrological chart before doing anything, and retires to the country to cultivate an "ill-defined malady." Huxley would caricature her again in *Those Barren Leaves,* in which she is Mrs. Aldwinkle, and also in *Point Counter Point,* in which she is Mrs. Bidlake, who indulges in "vague, unending meditations on 'God, Pinturicchio, dandelions, eternity, the sky, the clouds, the early Venetians, dandelions.' " There was Osbert Sitwell's in *Triple Fugue,* in which she is Lady Septugesima Goodley, distinguished by a "height that was over life-size for a woman, so that without looking a giantess she might seem an animated public monument." Russell's mistress, Constance Malleson, caricatured her as Magdalena de Santa Segunda in *The Coming Back.* Graham Greene lampooned her as Lady Caroline Bury in *It's a Battlefield.* One of the cruelest blows was Walter Turner's portrait of Ottoline as Lady Virginia Caraway in *The Aesthetes.* By reputation a closet murderess, having "killed the first American poet that ever came to England," Lady Virginia comes down to lunch with her head swathed in bandages because of her neuralgia, trailed by fifteen pugs. She records her sexual triumphs with creative men in her little orange diary: "He came to me a genius, he left me a man."

After leaving the nursing home and returning to Garsington, Ottoline tried to put the past behind her and take up her old life. She sat for a portrait by Dorothy Brett. When she saw the completed work, Ottoline was furious: Brett, she believed, had made her "look like a prostitute," like Lawrence's sex-obsessed villainess. Clive Bell saw the painting and "spread a rumour that Brett's 'Colossus' had turned out to be a cruel caricature 'au Lawrence.' " During a "row" with Brett, probably over the painting and her loyalty to Lawrence, Ottoline "flung" Lawrence's gift of "a little blue brooch" with a chalcedony stone at Brett in a rage. In April 1917, Brett wrote Ottoline: "I have not made a prostitute of you—I swear I haven't."

Though she had revered artists and writers, Ottoline now concluded that they were ungrateful and incapable of loyalty or friendship. They put their need to "scratch away at their 'little works of art' " before "love for humanity." It was best not to depend on anyone. If she could have, she claimed, she would have become a nun.

Once so careful about the appearance she made, Ottoline became a caricature of her former self, "her face almost entirely covered by peeling flakes of white chalk." Speaking of his portrait of Gertrude Stein, Pablo Picasso once remarked that if it didn't look like her when he painted it, in time she would grow to look like it. Ottoline Morrell grew to resemble Hermione Roddice. To her guests at Garsington, Ottoline seemed dazed and apoplectic. Upon seeing her in London, Lady Cynthia Asquith remarked that she was "looking like a nightmare."

Even Russell's doting concern, upon which she had always relied, had turned to cruelty. Parroting Birkin's description of Hermione, Russell told Ottoline she wasn't as attractive as she had once been—she looked old, and it was a pity her hair was turning gray. Befuddled and confused after he accused her of causing his unhappiness, she responded: "Perhaps after all Lawrence's view of me in his book is partly True. (It is a far worse onslaught on me than his Letter to you—and Trumpeted forth to the Public.")

The only happy moments Ottoline recalled during this difficult time were "an afternoon with Virginia Woolf, who was herself recovering from a mental breakdown" in the wake of her husband's vindictive portrait of her in *The Wise Virgins*. Ottoline, still scarred, had taken to obsessively "drawing up her lists of loyal friends" and revising them.

She invited Virginia Woolf to have tea with her. Woolf responded to her letter, telling Ottoline she had become "one of the romantic myths of my life." When Woolf saw her, she told Ottoline "how much everyone in London had missed her." There is no record of what these women, both savaged in fiction, said to one another. Later, though, in a letter to Woolf, Ottoline "complain[ed] of age & ugliness, . . . & the sadness of not being wanted."

In time, Ottoline came to believe that Lawrence's depiction of her as Hermione Roddice had very little to do with her at all—that it was, instead, "a pornographic image of his own mind." She reasoned that when Lawrence was in Cornwall composing his portrait of her, he was "very unbalanced." Still, as late as 1932, her feelings ran deep; she could recall with disgust the portrait of her as that "utterly horrible and disgusting" character, Hermione Roddice.

8.

Lawrence's portrait of Ottoline as Hermione Roddice marked the end of their intimacy. It caused her at first "to sever all ties" with her former confidant and friend, and after her response to him upon first reading the novel, she had nothing further to do with him for four years, until 1922. She refused to see him, though he "made several attempts" through mutual friends to see her. "I did not think," she wrote, "it would be possible for me to behave naturally or unself-consciously in his presence. The hurt that he had done me made a very great mark in my life." "Conversation, words," she knew, "may soon be forgotten but a printed book endures for centuries."

"Months and Years of Slow Execution"

1.

After Ottoline read *Women in Love,* she wrote Lawrence a very long letter detailing her "frenzy over the novel." It has not survived

—Lawrence probably destroyed it—but Clive Bell described it to his wife, Vanessa:

> Ottoline returned Lawrence his MS with an incredibly foolish reply, in spite of excellent counsel from me, and some desperate admonitions from Philip against falling into the depths of folly. Every line of her letter that I was allowed to hear revealed a wound: Lawrence must have rejoiced.

She probably insisted that he not publish the work, or that he change what he had written about her. She also commanded that he return her present of an opal. But, Bell reported, Lawrence "very sensibly, having sold it or pawned it, declined to do anything of the sort."

Replying to Ottoline in a February 1917 letter, Lawrence told her that her portrait as Hermione Roddice was "her own fault" and there was "nothing to be in a frenzy over." He no doubt also said that, despite her objections, he was "determined to publish."

Frieda Lawrence was delighted with Ottoline's response and believed she had gotten what she deserved, even if it meant the work would not be printed. She saw Lawrence's vindictive portrait of Ottoline, and her own portrayal as Ursula, as her personal victory: "I am *so* nice in L's new novel," she boasted.

2.

As determined as Lawrence was to publish, Ottoline was just as determined to keep the novel from being published. And Lawrence would soon feel the effect of her resolve.

When Ottoline read *Women in Love*, Methuen had already turned down the novel; Methuen also "cancelled their contract for the rights to Lawrence's next three novels." Lawrence asked Lady Cynthia Asquith whether she knew a powerful person to whom he might dedicate the novel, to ward off its suppression, which he believed was a possibility.

In mid-January, he learned that Duckworth, the house that previously published his work, had also refused the novel, as had Martin Secker (publisher of the novel in England in 1921). By the end of the month, Constable & Co. had turned it down because of its "expressions of antipathy to England and all forms of English civilisation" and its "destructive philosophy . . . unwelcome at the present time."

3.

After Ottoline heard that Lawrence would not change her portrait, she asked Philip to help her keep the novel out of print. The Morrells used both direct and covert measures to make sure that Lawrence's novel would not be published.

Ottoline's problem with Lawrence came at a most difficult period in the Morrells' marriage, though at the time she was unaware of it. (She found out in March.) Philip, carrying on surreptitious affairs with two mistresses, was feeling the stress of his predicament, which later led to his serious breakdown.

Unknowingly, Lawrence had given Philip a chance to act the role of devoted husband and protector when he was feeling like neither, when friends were catching glimpses of him in London in the company of a young woman. He seized the opportunity. Ironically, he was demanding that a fictional account of his wife's sexual behavior be kept out of print as one of his mistresses was threatening to expose him. Seeing his wife suffering from Lawrence's betrayal surely showed Philip the grief he would cause her when she found out about his.

In time, fighting to keep *Women in Love* out of print helped the Morrells mend the rift in their marriage, just as mocking Ottoline had helped the Lawrences'. In her memoirs, Ottoline wrote of Philip's acting on her behalf after Lawrence's attack as an action prompted by his devotion to her, by his wish not to have her reputation sullied.

Philip Morrell went to Pinker, Lawrence's agent, and told him that if *Women in Love* was published "as it stood," he would "bring an action against the Publishers for libel." Philip invited Pinker to visit Garsington, to show him that Lawrence's "character [was] his wife." Once Lawrence's champion and defender when *The Rainbow* faced censorship, Philip now found himself doing everything he could to keep Lawrence's work out of print.

After Morrell's visit, Pinker wrote Lawrence asking about the validity of the claims. In responding, Lawrence lied, which cannot have helped his cause, for Morrell had surely shown Pinker Lawrence's letter admitting that Hermione was based on Ottoline. Lawrence wrote Pinker:

> Really, the world has gone completely dotty! Hermione is not much more like Ottoline Morrell than Queen Victoria . . . Ottoline flatters herself.—There *is* a hint of her in the character of Hermione: but so there is a hint of a million women.

He told Pinker that Ottoline was "vindictive," and that her seeing herself in Hermione was an act of "vanity." He maintained that the Morrells "could make libel cases for ever," but "they haven't half a leg to stand on." Still, Lawrence realized he had dashed any hope of publishing the novel. "It is no use trying to publish the novel in England in this state of affairs," he told his agent. "The novel can lie by till there is an end of the war and a change of feeling over the world."

This proved prophetic. The threat of the Morrells' libel suit, and the action against *The Rainbow,* kept publishers from taking *Women in Love* until 1920.

In March 1917, Lawrence asked Pinker to send him a copy of the novel: "I would like to look at Ottoline Morrell's imaginary portrait again," he wrote. "I feel weary, and wish something better would come." He had received it by the end of the month, and, perhaps, made some changes in Hermione's appearance, changing the color of her hair from red to blond. Weary as he felt, hopeless as he was about the novel's publication, he continued to revise *Women in Love* throughout the year.

Though Pinker continued to act as Lawrence's agent, there can be no doubt that Philip Morrell's visit had an impact. Several years later, Lawrence discovered that "Pinker had not circulated the three copies of the typescript in his possession, ignoring Lawrence's instruction to send copies to prospective publishers." When Lawrence found out, he dropped Pinker as an agent.

Through the war years, Lawrence continued to try, but failed, to find a publisher who might be willing to take a chance and publish the work. He often sent on the novel himself. In 1917 alone, the work was offered to and rejected by Cecil Palmer; Little, Brown in America; Maunsel in Dublin; Fisher Unwin; Arnold Bennett; and John Galsworthy, who considered publishing it privately.

4.

Along with his publishing problems, Lawrence encountered serious difficulties with English authorities. These forced him out of
Cornwall and, after the war, caused him to leave England and to
engage in his "savage pilgrimage" throughout the world. Lawrence's feud with Ottoline exacerbated his problem: he had lost her
patronage and could not use Garsington as a refuge, as other pacifists did during the war.

Writing to Catherine Carswell in 1917, Lawrence assumed that
he and Ottoline would be "enemies for ever. I don't care," he
wrote. "I don't care if every English person is my enemy—if they
wish to be, so be it." He realized that having Ottoline for an enemy
meant having the Morrells' allies as enemies as well. He had a pre-
monition that there would be big trouble for him; he realized he
had burned his "boats."

Losing Ottoline's support meant that Lawrence could no longer
ask Philip Morrell to intercede for him when he had trouble with
the authorities, as Morrell did for many of their friends throughout
the war.

Lawrence persisted in cajoling his friends to ask Ottoline to relent about the novel. If there were no threat of a libel suit, he might
be able to find a publisher. She apparently would not change her
mind, so he accused her, to them, of being nothing but "old carrion," which surely hardened her resolve. "If I can publish," he
concluded, "I shall publish. But ten to one I can't."

By alienating Ottoline, Lawrence had foreclosed important ave-
nues of support when he and Frieda most needed them. Their mutual friend S. S. Koteliansky told Lawrence that "some of his
troubles might be relieved if he tried to make up with Ottoline."
Lawrence answered: "I know the Ot. is very nice. . . . But she is like
someone who has died." Acting as intermediary, Koteliansky
fetched Lawrence's manuscripts from Garsington, where they had
been left for safekeeping; thanking Ottoline for their return, Lawrence told her he was trying to hunt up something publishable in
"these days of leanness," he was "awfully sick of the world," and
perhaps they would meet "in some sort of Afterwards when the
laugh is on a new side."

Lawrence acted so as to guarantee the Morrells' continuing an-
imosity. In April 1917, he wrote their mutual friend Mark Gertler

asking whether he saw a resemblance between Hermione and Ottoline. "The Ott.," he wrote, "is really too disgusting, with her threats of legal proceedings etc. She is really contemptible. We have flattered her above all bounds, in attending to her at all." This surely made its way back to Ottoline.

In time, he realized that Ottoline "would go any length to do me damage in this affair," and that "all the Ott. crowd, are full of malice against me." Just as the Morrells could be powerful friends, so they could be formidable enemies. He had, after all, criticized Ottoline for her indomitable will. And Philip was a member of Parliament, with access to power.

Lawrence would have to wait out the war before the publishing climate would change enough to be receptive to *Women in Love*. "Whilst President Wilson coos and preens in New York, whilst Ottoline stinks at Garsington, whilst Clemenceau spouts in France," he wrote Koteliansky, "I am not worth a penny."

5.

Security on the Cornish coast was stepped up. Rumors circulated that German spies living on the coast might be signaling submarines. Frieda Lawrence, who never concealed her distaste for the English or her loyalty to Germany, and who continued to correspond with family members during the war, became a prime suspect. Lawrence, too, was placed under surveillance.

He had often expressed "his intention of initiating a disruptive, pacifist and nihilist campaign in the industrial North" to bring an end to the war. His publications revealed his contempt for England, and his writings in wartime were considered subversive. His essays, such as "Democracy," appeared in *The Word*, a pacifist socialist journal, and pacifists were carefully watched as the war progressed.

Lawrence and Frieda visited their friend Cecil Gray, the Scottish composer, at Bosigran Castle. On the cliffs near the castle, six men, armed with rifles, interrupted them while they were singing German folk songs and demanded to search the premises. A flickering light had been spotted in a window. They were suspected of signaling an enemy submarine that had been sighted off the coast.

The Lawrences' house was searched in their absence. They were ordered to "leave the area of Cornwall" and were prohibited from journeying to any port or coastal region. When Lawrence asked why, the officer replied, "You know better than I do."

He and Frieda were suspected of being spies. "I cannot even conceive how I have incurred suspicion," he wrote, "—have not the faintest notion. We are as innocent even of pacifist activities, let alone spying of any sort as the rabbits in the field outside. And we must leave Cornwall, and live in an unprohibited area, and report to the police. It is *very* vile. We have practically no money at all—I don't know what we shall do."

The Lawrences left Cornwall on October 15, 1917. Before departing, amid all his troubles, Lawrence nonetheless had managed to "altogether" rewrite *Women in Love*. He then put it aside until the war was over.

Frieda remarked that when they were "turned out of Cornwall something changed in Lawrence forever." He was in "intense distress" and "utterly at a loss to know what to do next." The only money he had was the prospect of an eighteen-pound advance for a book of poems. Leaving Cornwall also ended his affair with William Henry Hocking.

The Lawrences moved to London and lived on the generosity of friends and family. Because of his trouble with Ottoline, though, his "circle of friends shrank"—Catherine Carswell, Koteliansky, Mark Gertler, and Cynthia Asquith remained loyal. Lawrence was out of place in London, wearing his often-mended trousers, corduroy jacket, and canvas shoes, the only clothes he had.

After London, the Lawrences pressed on to Berkshire, the Midlands, Derbyshire (where Lawrence learned to his delight that George Moore thought *Women in Love* a great book), Essex, and Kent. They lived in borrowed cottages, lent by friends or paid for by Lawrence's sister. He filed an application for money from the Royal Literary Fund, but since he could not be polite on the form, he assumed he would get nothing. He visited Eastwood, the place of his birth, and learned that he had stopped hating it. He felt like "Ovid in his Thracian exile."

In February 1918, a year after the trouble with Ottoline had started, Lawrence declared that he was "at the dead end of my money." Desperately poor, he had to beg money from friends. He hurled curses at the "damned, mean, narrow-gutted, pitiful, crawling, mongrel world" that wouldn't "have a man's work and won't even allow him to live."

In July 1918, he begged Mark Gertler to intercede on his behalf with Ottoline, telling Gertler that he couldn't work, that he was "at the end of *everything*." He asked, "Do you think she would like to see us again?" Ottoline apparently refused. "To Hell with the Ott.— the whole Ottlerie—what am I doing temporising with them. . . . What in the name of hell do I care about the Ott's queases and qualms," he wrote Koteliansky after hearing that Ottoline was not receptive to his offer.

But he was not altogether chastened. He wrote Koteliansky that though he had suffered during "these months and years of slow execution, . . . I *should* like my revenge on the world."

6.

Lawrence and Frieda were in London on Armistice Day, November 11, 1918, for a Bloomsbury party attended by Diaghilev, Massine, Maynard Keynes, Duncan Grant, David Garnett, and others.

Lawrence's was "the only unhappy face in all that excited gathering." While others rejoiced, he made a dire prediction, his voice raised:

The crowd outside thinks that Germany is crushed forever. But the Germans will soon rise again. . . . Even if the fighting should stop, the evil will be worse because the hate will be damned up in men's hearts and will show itself in all sorts of ways which will be worse than war.

7.

In the summer of 1919, Lawrence turned again to *Women in Love,* and made some changes. With the war over, two publishers were willing to consider the work—Thomas Seltzer and Martin Secker.

In November 1919, Lawrence at last was able to leave England. Frieda was in Germany. It seemed as if their marriage, ravaged by the stresses Lawrence's relationship with William Henry Hocking had placed upon it, might not survive. Lawrence "seemed not to care if he ever saw her again."

He was making his way to Italy, and to the sun, "the fruitlands, the flowery valleys, the glowing seas." He was putting that "grey, dreary-grey coffin of England" behind him.

Though he would return to England for brief visits, he never again would live there. Each time he returned, he would find the place "hateful." He left England because England had persecuted him: it had burned his books, censored his work, taken him for a spy, forced him into exile. In his relationship with Ottoline and Philip Morrell he had learned firsthand the privilege of having the powerful as champions and the peril of having them as enemies. To a man who had hoped to found a society in which personal worth, and not power and position, would determine one's fortunes, the impossibility of achieving anything near this ideal in England meant that he had to turn his back on a country that he had once "loved so bitterly, bitterly."

D. H. Lawrence's expatriate years had begun.

"A Book the Police Should Ban"

1.

Women in Love was not published until 1920 in the United States, where it was privately printed by Thomas Seltzer. It appeared in 1921 in England, published by Martin Secker, more than eight years after Lawrence had started writing it, in an edition of 1,500 copies, for which Lawrence received a seventy-five-pound advance. When the novel finally appeared, Lawrence, in Baden-Baden at the time, "drank a bottle of beautiful Moselle to its luck: and dreamed of huge blue prosecution papers."

The dream was prophetic. Legal trouble came, but not from Ottoline, who did nothing to block its publication, believing that "legal action would bring more ridicule than satisfaction." She contented herself with thinking that because she had been upset, Lawrence had made major changes to satisfy her: "the setting of the house and garden were altered and some of the worst scenes expunged." As she read, she scrawled in the margin, opposite the worst parts of her portrait, "Frieda" "Surely Frieda," and "Frieda again." But she might have exercised her power indirectly to see that Lawrence received a negative review in the *Times Literary Supplement.*

Lawrence had heard through a friend that "Ott's nose [was] out of joint" because of the publication of *Women in Love.* He couldn't imagine why: he noted that in a generally contemptuous review of the novel in the *Times,* the reviewer said that "Hermione was a grand-sincere figure, among a nest of perverse puppies."

The *Times Literary Supplement* had chosen to write the review a young poet named Edmund Blunden, "a regular visitor to the Morrells at Garsington Manor" known for his "loyalty to Lady Ottoline," thereby virtually ensuring that the review would be negative. Not only did Blunden pan the novel, calling it a "dull, disappointing piece of work," he rewrote Lawrence's portrait of Ottoline in his review, maintaining that Hermione Roddice was a character of "immense dignity," the "one thing in the whole work which was worth Mr. Lawrence's powers." The power of Lady Ottoline Morrell and Philip had again made itself felt.

Virginia Woolf read the work with keen interest, disagreeing with the "stupid and unfair" *Times* notice and wishing she could have reviewed it instead. She would have critiqued it favorably, despite her friendship with Ottoline. She thought Lawrence's description of Garsington and its habitués was accurate: "Ott: is there to the life." Though there was something wrong with Lawrence's psyche which made him "brood over sex," she believed "he is honest, and therefore he is 100 times better than most of us."

2.

On September 23, 1921, Lawrence and Frieda, arriving in Fontana, Italy, in "a whirlwind and rain," found a number of letters which told of the trouble the publication of *Women in Love* was causing. He had received a copy of the bad review in *John Bull* and a cold letter from his literary agent saying that his new novel, *Aaron's Rod,* was libelous and couldn't be published. There was also a letter from his publisher, who was worried about the reviews, and worried, too, about the threat of a lawsuit by Philip Heseltine.

Under the banner "A BOOK THE POLICE SHOULD BAN. Loathsome Study of Sex Depravity—Misleading Youth to Unspeakable Disaster," W. Charles Pilley, writing in the sensationalist periodical *John Bull*, proclaimed that when a work like *Women in Love* was published, the "police should be . . . alert." Pilley asserted that the novel was "sheer filth" and "justly merits the fate of its predecessor." Lawrence's characters exhibited "every perverted instinct that ever vexed the mind of man or tortured the soul of woman." They were obviously "mad," and in real life "would be safely under lock and key." In fiction, they were free to harm young minds.

Hermione was the worst of the lot, a "female degenerate who half kills her lover in a fit of frenzy and as she strikes the blow feels 'a delirium of pleasure.' . . . We know well enough where this sort of thing leads to in real life." Pilley concluded, "The police must act" upon this "obscene abomination."

3.

When the novel appeared, Philip Heseltine threatened a libel suit against Lawrence and his publisher, Martin Secker, for Heseltine's portrayal as Halliday, and for Minnie Channing's as Pussum. He also tried to get the book suppressed by the Purity League. The dispute was quickly resolved, though circulation of the novel was temporarily suspended. Some "hush-money"—sixty pounds and ten shillings—was paid, and Lawrence, who was sent "marked passages from the novel," changed the characters' physical appearance, which he had taken from life, though he was irritated. Pussum became fair instead of dark; Halliday became dark instead of fair. Heseltine, though, was so infuriated by Lawrence's fictional portrait that he used a manuscript Lawrence had given him for safekeeping as toilet paper.

Lawrence, now in Taormina, was in "a hell of a temper" because of the problems his novel faced. "I've written such very spiteful letters to everybody that now the postman never comes," he admitted. "But it is a world of *Canaille*; absolutely. Canaille, canaglia, Schweinhunderei, stinkpots. Pfui!—pish, pshaw, prrr! They all stink in my nostrils. . . . If I hadn't my own stories to amuse myself with I should die, chiefly of spleen."

Women in Love was "his best, his favourite book, the one which contained the quintessence of his message to Mankind." Its reception broke his spirit. *Westminster Gazette*'s review "poked fun"; *Time and Tide* noted the novel's "incompetence"; the *Observer* spoke of the book's "ravings"; even his old friend John Middleton Murry, no doubt upset by his portrait as Crich, wrote in *The Atheneum* that it was "turgid, exasperated writing." A few positive notes were sounded, in the *Manchester Guardian* and in the *New Statesman*, by Rebecca West, who called it "a work of genius."

As a result of the novel's reception, Lawrence vowed to quit Europe forever, and soon began making plans to take up Mabel Dodge Luhan's proposal to move to New Mexico: "My heart and soul are broken, in Europe," he wrote. "It's no use."

At the beginning of 1922, Lawrence and Frieda were making plans to travel from Sicily to Ceylon, to Australia, and then to San Francisco. When they arrived, on September 3, a judgment had just been handed down in New York on *Women in Love*. The New York Society for the Suppression of Vice had taken Thomas Seltzer, Lawrence's American publisher, to court on obscenity charges, but Seltzer had "won with triumph," the judge finding the work not at all obscene, but "a distinct contribution to literature." Publicity from the trial "stimulated a huge demand for the novel." By the end of 1922, there were 15,000 copies in print in the United States and 13,000 copies in England. This marked a "decisive change in Lawrence's fortunes as a writer."

4.

Lawrence moved on to New Mexico, and for the first time in his life he was not destitute, or dependent upon the generosity of his friends. He had been able to stash five hundred pounds in the bank and was repaying debts and offering loans to friends in need. He used the profit from *Women in Love* to pay Ottoline back the money she had given him "so long ago."

Though in her memoirs Ottoline contended that she and Lawrence remained estranged because of the novel until near the end of his life, this is not entirely true. Though their intimacy had ended, in a generous and concerned gesture of support Ottoline sent Lawrence a letter after the suppression trial. He was apparently surprised, for he told a few friends, "I even had a letter from Ottoline." He probably did not answer her immediately, but contacted her at least once in 1923, when he sent her a card which he asked her to pass on to Katherine Mansfield.

"A Time to Laugh Over Our Old Quarrels"

1.

Frieda Lawrence saw Ottoline briefly when she visited London in 1926; she thought Ottoline looked "a little faded." Lawrence resumed a steady correspondence with her in the spring of 1928, when he heard from Aldous Huxley that Ottoline had undergone an operation for necrosis of the jaw in 1927, leaving her face badly scarred. She had become "so disfigured and repulsive," she thought, "that no eye could look on . . . without turning away in disgust."

Lawrence and Frieda were living in Italy temporarily, thinking about moving on to Switzerland, searching, as always, for a favorable climate for Lawrence, who suffered from what he described as flu. He was reluctant as ever to admit he had tuberculosis and was seriously ill.

Lawrence wrote Ottoline in May 1928 when he learned of her illness, telling her how sorry he was to hear she had been in pain, but pleased to learn that she was much better. He downplayed his own illness: "I consider people like you and me, we've had our whack of bodily ills," he wrote, "we ought to be let off a bit." He trusted that they would "meet again one day" because, through this "long lapse," he was sure that they had, nonetheless, remained "fond of one another."

She wrote back warmly, telling him about her pain, and that she felt her life was a failure. She asked whether his feelings still ran deeply; she told him she had given up Garsington, and wondered whether he missed it.

He responded characteristically, with a little lecture. She wasn't "self-keeping and self-preserving" enough, and her behavior had allowed the "microbes, which are the pure incarnation of invisible selfishness," to "pounce." Answering her questions, he told her that he still felt things deeply, but that he now knew that his habits of "bitterness" and "chagrin" undermined his health. Yes, he was "sad about Garsington." And, in the closest he came to an apology, he wrote that he wished he could have two lives: "the first, in which to make one's mistakes, which seem as if they *had* to be made; and the second in which to profit by them. If it could only be so, what a lovely Garsington we could all have, and no bitterness at the end of it!"

He hoped that they could now "start afresh . . . , in a quieter, gentler way," and they did, exchanging letters through the last year and a half of his life, reminiscing and mending the breach that had grown between them. Without drama, Lawrence gently, consistently made amends, undoing some of the damage he had caused. His last letters to Ottoline are among the most sensitive and generous of his life. Through them, he helped her recover some trust in herself. He was, she believed, "sorry and regretful for what had been done." Knowing he was near death, perhaps, had mellowed him: "It is so nice to feel peaceful and quiet with people one likes and can trust," he wrote. "I want no excitements or exaltations or extravagances."

He rebuked her for not feeling she had led a valuable life. "You've been an important influence," he wrote, "in lots of lives, as you have in mine: through being fundamentally generous, and through being Ottoline." She had "moved one's imagination," and *that* mattered, but she was so singular that "the so-called portraits of Ottoline can't possibly be Ottoline." This came close to admitting that his portrait of her had been a caricature.

He told her, as always, of his work in progress, of *Lady Chatterley's Lover*, which was about "phallic awareness and the old phallic insouciance" and the *"rapprochement* of a man and a woman." By the end of 1928, she had read an illicit copy of the novel, and had written him "sweetly" of it, but with some misgivings about the relentless sexuality in the work. But when customs officers confiscated the novel as "pornographic," she took up his cause.

Lawrence used his response to her problems with the novel to tell her something she needed to know about her sexual history. He said that he did not advocate "perpetual sex," as she suggested; he wanted to show that the "reason why the common people often keep—or kept—the good *natural glow* of life . . . longer than educated people, was because it was still possible for them to say fuck! or shit without either a shudder or a sensation." If a man could have approached the physical reality of her as a woman when she was young and in love, without recoiling, her whole life might have been different. This was his message: "If a man had been able to say to you . . . an' if tha shits, an' if tha pisses, I'glad, I shoudna want a woman who couldna shit nor piss—surely it would have been a liberation to you, and it would have helped to keep your heart warm." Her failings had not caused her painful sexual history: it was the upper-class male's fear of women. This was why Constance Chatterley could find sexual satisfaction, not with her privileged husband, but with a gamekeeper.

Throughout 1929, the last year of his life, Lawrence and Ottoline shared news about their health and their friends. They reminisced, discussed his work and friendship. He had sent her some poems, and he was glad to hear she thought they were among his finest. He was having an exhibit of his paintings in London: "Do go and look at the pictures," he wrote, "because some of them you will surely like."

Lawrence and Frieda were living in Bandol, in the south of France, where it was sunny even in winter, but Lawrence, ever restless, wanted to move on to Spain. He wished he and Ottoline lived close enough to resume their friendship: "I feel we might be friends now really," he wrote, "and with that stillness in friendship which is the best."

In one of her last letters to him, Ottoline asked whether he remembered when she had traveled to Greatham, in Sussex, to see him. He replied:

> Yes, I remember your coming to Sussex—stepping out of an old four-wheeler in all your pearls, and a purple velvet frock. . . . It is a pity something came across it all and prevented us keeping a nice harmony. But life does queer things to us, and it takes a long time to come to our real steady self.

2.

In the last year of Lawrence's life, there was a showing of his paintings at the Warren Gallery in London, which he had suggested Ottoline might enjoy. He was too ill to attend; he was also in danger of being arrested on his arrival in England for sending copies of *Lady Chatterley's Lover* through the mail. What transpired in the wake of the exhibition prompted Ottoline Morrell's last public display of support for Lawrence's work during his lifetime.

Dorothy Warren, founder of the gallery, was Ottoline and Philip's niece, and she had met Lawrence at Garsington. She persuaded him to mount an exhibition of his much sought-after paintings at her Mayfair gallery.

The exhibition opened on June 14, 1929. A "gay flag" with Lawrence's name hung outside. His pictures, according to Frieda, who attended, clutching a bunch of lilies as a symbol of her husband's purity, "looked a little wild and overwhelming in the elegant, delicate rooms of the galleries." But she never imagined that "a few pictures could raise such a storm."

Among the paintings Lawrence exhibited were many nudes. During the three weeks following the opening, more than thirteen thousand people saw the works. Some viewers were outraged and filed a complaint. The Home Secretary issued an order to seize the offending pictures. Six London policemen raided the gallery and carried off copies of the exhibition catalog and thirteen of Lawrence's paintings, among them *Accident in a Mine,* of naked miners tending to a stricken worker, and *Leda,* of the mythic figure's intercourse with a swan. The only paintings taken were those depicting pubic hair.

The authorities threatened to burn the works because they were obscene and a threat to public morals. Lawrence, hounded throughout his career by censorship, received a telegram about the event, and he couldn't understand how normal grown-ups could be upset by the sight of "normal pudenda"; he was forced to conclude that if the viewers were so upset, they couldn't be normal. He was also so deeply hurt that he lost his will to work. "All this persecution and insult, and most of all, the white-livered poltroonery of the so-called 'free' young people in England puts me off work," he wrote. "Why should one produce things, in such a dirty world!' "

After the seizure, Lawrence became gravely ill. A friend, responsible for him while Frieda traveled to London to attend the exhibition, believed he was dying. He "telegraphed in panic" to Frieda to return to Italy.

3.

On August 8, the trial of Lawrence's pictures took place. The courtroom was filled with his friends, supporters, and detractors, many lawyers, and members of the press, who covered the case avidly. A petition had been circulated protesting the action.

Ottoline Morrell, with Philip, turned out to support her old friend, though she did not now like to appear in public because of her disfigurement. She was there to protest the censorship of Lawrence's work, though she had done her best to keep *Women in Love* from publication.

Her "entrance created a stir in the courtroom." She still dressed to draw attention, but since her operation, she had taken to tying the veil of her huge hats "a little higher than before." The "proceedings halted as her tall, resplendent figure wove through the public gallery," trying to find a seat. Once settled, she listened to the arguments of Herbert J. Muskett, the prosecutor, who had been responsible for the destruction of copies of Lawrence's *The Rainbow*.

"These paintings, I submit to you," Muskett argued, "are gross, coarse, hideous, and unlovely from any aesthetic or artistic point of view, and are in their nature obscene."

When the prosecution suggested that if the paintings were judged obscene, they could be burned even if they were irreplaceable works of art, a rustling in the back of the room interrupted the proceedings. It was Ottoline Morrell, who was rising from her seat.

"Standing her statuesque height, with a long forefinger pointing at the Magistrate, she was gently intoning an incantation:

" 'He ought to be burned, he ought to be burned.' "

Though the catalog of the exhibition was ordered destroyed, the paintings were spared.

Lawrence surely heard of his old friend's dramatic gesture on his behalf. Frieda, breaking her silence of many years, wrote Ottoline that she appreciated her "bigness and real spirit."

4.

In the last months of his life, Lawrence continued to write and paint. He liked "to look at the sea and be quiet and happy." He had hoped that Ottoline would travel south to see him, and that they could have time for "a few quiet chats and laughs together." She, too, hoped they would have "time to laugh over our old quarrels, to disagree and argue, and to plan a new Elysian world." That time never came.

In 1929, as Lawrence approached death, Ottoline traveled to Aix-en-Provence. She had no intention of visiting the Lawrences, though they were less than a hundred kilometers away in Bandol.

In his last letter to her, written a few weeks before he died, Lawrence wrote of his bad health and said he would probably have to "go into a sanitorium." He regretted they had been "so near" one another, yet hadn't met. "It would have been so good to see you again," he wrote.

D. H. Lawrence died on March 2, 1930. Norman Douglas, whom Lawrence had lampooned in *Aaron's Rod*, claimed that no one who knew Lawrence well was sorry when he died. Most of the obituaries painted him as "a man morose, frustrated, tortured, even a sinister failure." Aldous Huxley sent Ottoline a telegram "saying that Lawrence died peacefully." The news, she wrote, "fell on me as a great blow."

5.

Ottoline Morrell's pain from *Women in Love* persisted after Lawrence's death, though she had tried her best to maintain a distant friendship with him in the last years of his life. But in 1933, with Lawrence dead and unable to respond, she had her chance to write about him, about her version of their relationship, and about why he had written his "wicked, spiteful" portrait of her. Just as he had mined her most intimate confidences for his portrait of Hermione Roddice, so she now drew upon his for her portrait of him.

Her "Recollections of D. H. Lawrence" was published in *The Atheneum* in 1933, and in her memoir. Working on the piece, she admitted, had stirred up her fury at Frieda for interfering in her relationship with Lawrence. Publishing the work allowed her to retaliate against him for what he had said about her, and to even the score to some degree. What she wrote was not pleasant: hers was a portrait of Lawrence as a deranged, uncivilized man, locked into a mutually abusive, destructive relationship with Frieda.

She wanted to impress her readers with her generosity of spirit in writing of "the friend whom one has lost." But she wanted to assure them that her impressions of Lawrence were "fairly true."

She wrote that he was a violent man, "naturally violent," she believed, since childhood. He was unsure of himself, primitive, untrammeled, and undisciplined. Whatever "lovely qualities" he had he turned into "spite and hatred." Through the years she knew him, "spiteful denunciation seems to have grown more and more an automatic habit of his mind."

Ottoline told how, when Lawrence met someone, at first "he was enchanting and sympathetic, friendly and easy." Then Frieda and he would talk, and the "duet of denunciation would begin."

> The schoolmaster Lawrence would whip out his cane. The prophet Lawrence would start his "Woe! Woe!" The novelist Lawrence would elaborate and invent fantastic, exciting nightmare tales about him, and a volley of words ... would come hurtling about the poor wretch's head, ... and conviction of the outcast's sin would form in the moralist Lawrence's mind, and he would then say he "hated" him.

This, in effect, was what had happened to her.

She believed Lawrence to be the least tolerant of men, "perfectly convinced that his vision was the only correct one." This was due, she thought, to "some inner discord"; his illness was a "soul illness." He had a "Messiah instinct," and turned against England because of his treatment during the war, and because his feelings had been hurt. "In this," she wrote, "he displayed his very feminine nature."

The more she thought, however, the more clearly she saw that Lawrence was "violent because he was afraid": his behavior was that of "a frightened dog." But, she reasoned, his violence was largely Frieda's fault. She was a "disastrous" mate for him, forever "goading him into a fury."

When Ottoline had first read the manuscript of *Women in Love*, she had noted that "all the worst parts were in Frieda's handwriting." Though Frieda had no doubt been entering Lawrence's corrections, Ottoline persuaded herself that Frieda had been largely responsible for the way Lawrence had portrayed her. In her "Recollections," Ottoline described what she believed had caused him to write of her with such vengeance. Frieda, she wrote, "lash[ed] him on to castigate, and was happy and triumphant when she could inflame him to flay the soul that had been laid bare to him in devoted friendship."

To stay married to Frieda, Lawrence had to turn on anyone who made Frieda jealous, and "blaspheme his own true feelings." To stay married to Frieda, he had to see the world her way, and so "real people, simple, kind and generous, . . . faded from his sight, and instead he [saw] these phantoms, distorted ghosts, . . . fighting and tearing and abusing one another." To stay married to Frieda, he even concocted a "Philosophy of Hate" that suited the "wild jungle of passion that she embodied." Frieda had carried Ottoline's friend Lawrence away from her and "into the heart of darkness."

More than fifteen years after first reading of herself as Hermione Roddice, Ottoline Morrell was still trying to understand why her friend D. H. Lawrence, to whom she had been so devoted, had turned on her with such vengeance. In blaming his nature, in blaming Frieda, she was exonerating him. And so she was able to preserve her memory of the deep and abiding friendship she still believed they had shared.

4

"JUSTICE, NOT REVENGE":

Djuna Barnes and the
Making of *The Antiphon*

I wrote *The Antiphon* with clenched teeth, and I noted . . . that my handwriting had changed, it was as savage as a dagger.

—Djuna Barnes to Willa Muir
July 23, 1961

5 Patchin Place
Greenwich Village, New York City
Early April 1958

Djuna Barnes sat in her one-room, rent-controlled Greenwich Village apartment, "a place shut away from time" but showing "the ravages of time." She sat amid its typical disorganized clutter—innumerable drafts of her work-in-progress; file boxes of letters from old friends in no particular order; an old set of English dictionaries; old bank statements; stubs of pencils with hardened erasers; empty ballpoint pens; aerosol cans of Hargate roach spray; an elegant walking stick; a broken doll, a present from her former lover Thelma Wood, smashed in an argument, staring down from the mantelpiece. Barnes was reading a letter she had just received from her older brother, Thurn Budington. She was sixty-six years old; he was sixty-eight. He had written in response to her play *The Antiphon*, which had recently been published in London and in New York.

He opened his letter "Dearest Sister," but he wrote to register a strong complaint.

> I am reading your play for the second time to try and understand what seems to me to be a fixation or sort of revenge for something long dead and to be forgotten. The writing itself is tremendous but . . . I can only wish the subject could have been different. One which could live as a monument to the genius of your mind.

It is no wonder that Thurn Budington complained, for the subject of his sister's play was incest. He had been reading a thinly disguised but graphic account of his own family history and the part he and other members of the Barnes clan had played in it. He had read how, throughout Djuna's childhood, he and his brothers, their father, and even an outsider had sexually assaulted their sister, while their mother did nothing to stop it. He had read how he and his brothers had mocked and scorned this girl whom they had brutalized; how her world had fractured, how she had lost a sense of life's meaning, how she had succumbed to despair. He had read how, when she vowed to write her story, the family tried to keep her quiet by committing her to an insane asylum; how she knew they all wanted her dead because then their secret would be safe—it would die with her.

Thurn Budington saw his sister's work as "revenge," as prompted by unclean motives. He believed that instead of writing about what she had experienced, she should forgive and forget, turn the other cheek. Let bygones be bygones. He saw her obsession with her betrayal by the entire family, not the betrayal itself, as a problem. It was a "fixation" that she should try to get over. He and other family members had been singing this song for a very long time. Djuna was a great writer. Djuna was a genius. But she should use that great gift on another subject, on any other subject but her favorite subject—their family.

Djuna Barnes saw things differently. She had been writing *The Antiphon* since 1949; the writing had taken her the better part of a decade. In the margin of a draft of the play over which she had labored for so long, she had written the words, "Justice, not revenge." For her, the issue of a "daughter's betrayal was not dead." For her, the only form of justice, the only retribution for what she had survived, was to tell her story. Her art was her weapon, not for revenge, she believed, but for justice. And her art was a powerful weapon; it was, she knew, "as savage as a dagger."

Gare d'Austerlitz
Paris
October 1939

It was late at night, and the Gare d'Austerlitz, so brightly lighted in peacetime, was in almost complete darkness now that war had broken out.

Djuna Barnes waited on the platform in the "terrible tension" of the station. She was waiting for the train that would take her to the ship that would carry her back to her family in New York City. She was in "terrible" shape, in a "complete state" of emotional and physical collapse. She was having another of what she called "my famous breakdowns." Like her many others, this one involved "severely heavy drinking." She had had the D.T.'s—saw things crawling on walls; had suffered fainting spells, sweats, and heart palpitations. Recently, one of her friends, the writer Antonia White, in exasperation at what Barnes's friends believed to be her self-defeating behavior, had asked her, "What do you really want, Djuna?" To which Barnes replied, "To die."

Her dream of a gay, free, and happy life in Paris, as a writer, far away from her family, had turned into a nightmare. She had come to Paris "during the heyday between the wars, when rent and food were cheap; alcohol was plentiful; and stimulating, sympathetic compatriots crowded cafés." Jimmy Charters, the most famous barman in Paris, who worked at the Dingo, which the expatriate crowd frequented, recalled that the "intoxication was in the drinks," but also in "the spirit of freedom from all the conventions and ties that bound these people at home." Among the freedoms of Parisian life was "the right to be homosexual, which was condoned in France at that time."

In retrospect, Djuna saw that she had made a "mess" of her life; she had written her friend Bob McAlmon that life had become "hell" for her. Her decade-long love affair with the artist Thelma Wood (whom Janet Flanner dubbed "the bitch of all time") had been "horrible." It had ended in near-disaster when Wood's fury turned murderous. Barnes admitted she was attracted to Thelma because she looked just like her grandmother Zadel, who had kept Barnes's abusive father from beating her too often with a whip, but who had abused her granddaughter as well.

The only home Barnes had ever owned, the home she had lived in with Thelma Wood, at 9 rue St.-Romain, had been broken up. The Venetian glass chandeliers, cherubim from Vienna, ecclesiastical hangings from Rome, a heart-shaped mirror, satin and tapestried chairs, a china virgin, a religious scene painted on glass—all these things, so lovingly chosen in the Les Halles marketplace, which had made the apartment look like a "bohemian chapel," had been packed away.

About all Djuna had left from her time with Thelma, besides her memories and the pain, was the doll Thelma had given her. It was a symbol of the child their lesbian relationship could not produce. Thelma had battered and broken it in a fit of jealous rage. Djuna kept it with her for the rest of her life.

Her relationship with Charles Henri Ford, twenty years her junior, had turned out poorly also. Djuna dubbed him "Charles Impossible Ford," and said "she had never known another human being so careless of other people and their needs." He always needed to act as if he were unfettered; she quipped that he was as "loose as a cut jockstrap." Their affair had been shattered by the Russian émigré painter Pavel Tchelitchew, with whom Ford had the most "tempestuous" affair of the painter's life.

But in Paris, Djuna had worked hard, written well, become famous. Perhaps the best description of Djuna in her prime is provided by Peggy Bacon in *Off with Their Heads*:

> Djuna Barnes: An elegant head lifted on a slender neck and long aristocratic body. Peach-blonde hair with ripples in it. Sharply tilted, scornful nose. Light eyes in shadowy hollows with a firm, hard gaze like a Siamese cat. Mouth forms an immobile ellipse, a trifle Hapsburg. Gives the effect of a solitary wading-bird, indifferent, poised and insulated, arrested in a long pause.

She had come to Paris on assignment for *McCall's* in 1919 or 1920 (she could never remember the precise date), bearing letters of introduction to James Joyce and Ezra Pound. She propped herself up in bed in the mornings at the Hôtel Angleterre, wearing a negligee, holding a pad of paper on her knees, writing her articles. She wrote pieces on the expatriate life, on American wives and their titled husbands, on women who go abroad to forget their troubles, interviews with James Joyce, with Coco Chanel, with D. W. Griffith—sending them back to the United States for publication. She had become a close friend of James Joyce; she was the only person other than his wife who was allowed to call him "Jim." She was a frequent guest at Natalie Barney's famous lesbian salon, the Academy of Women, at 20 rue Jacob. She had had a brief affair with Barney, and had written and published a satiric portrait of the Paris lesbian community who gathered there, *Ladies Almanack*, which instantly became an underground classic.

An unflattering yet incisive portrait of her from this time appeared in *The Chicago Times*:

> A face whose high cheek-bones suggest veiled fists beneath the chloroformed pity of large eyes: a face that is as white as a signal of terror, save for the scarlet martyrdom of full lips that have never become accustomed to life.

Before she left Paris for good in 1939, Barnes had written her finest, her most savage and brutal short stories, "Aller et Retour," "Cassation," "The Grande Malade," "The Passion"—stories about "when what is dark and suppressed spills out into the deceptive world of daily events and rational motives." She had become famous for her novels, *Ryder*, a best-seller in 1928, and *Nightwood*, published in 1936, which many read as a "cult guide to the homosexual underground nightworld of Paris," which Barnes knew intimately.

Early in her Paris years, her friends had counted on Barnes's energetic presence and witty repartee to liven things up at the Rotonde, the Dôme, the Coupole, and other gathering places in Montparnasse and St.-Germain-des-Près, on the Boul' Mich', frequented by her fellow expatriates. They had admired her regal presence and her beauty as she strode toward them down the boulevards. She was always meticulously made up, wearing deep red lipstick and nail polish, a turban, and chandelierlike earrings, tossing her cape (a hand-me-down from a wealthy friend) over her shoulder, a signature gesture. She had been photographed by the great photographers of her time—Man Ray, Lee Miller, and Berenice Abbott. She had been interviewed by Wambly Bald and Henry Miller. In time, she would be written as a magnetic character into the books and memoirs of the people whose lives she crossed, into

Jimmy Charters's *This Must Be the Place*; Ernest Hemingway's *The Sun Also Rises*; John Glassco's *Memoirs of Montparnasse*; Sylvia Beach's *Shakespeare and Company*; Janet Flanner's memoirs; her lover Charles Henri Ford's *The Young and Evil*; Paul Bowles's *Without Stopping*; James Joyce's *Finnegans Wake*; Natalie Barney's *Aventures de l'Esprit*.

Next to James Joyce, critics and fellow writers had regarded her as the most important expatriate writer working in Paris. Critics claimed her work rivaled Virginia Woolf's in significance. *The Saturday Review* had called her novel *Ryder* "the most amazing book ever written by a woman." She had published her most celebrated novel, *Nightwood*, to enormous acclaim; *The Listener* had proclaimed it "an undeniable work of genius." Between the wars, her friends had been the luminaries of the Paris artistic community—Colette, Gertrude Stein, Alice B. Toklas, Mina Loy, Romaine Brooks, Janet Flanner, André Gide, James Joyce, Ezra Pound, Ernest Hemingway, F. Scott Fitzgerald, Natalie Barney, Bob McAlmon.

Since she had first come to Paris, almost twenty years before, Barnes had been drinking heavily. When she became involved with Thelma Wood, her drinking had increased, as she staggered from one bar to another in search of her errant lover. Since she had finished writing *Nightwood* in 1933, and since her father had died "prematurely senile" (probably from the effects of syphilis) the year after, she was drinking herself into a state of collapse.

Djuna Barnes was going home. But she was not going back to the United States willingly. She had no choice. She could not stay in Paris, sick as she was, with no way to support herself, with the advancing German army posing a threat to the city, with all her friends leaving for the United States or for the South of France. She knew trouble awaited her on the other side of the ocean in the form of her family. They would be there to greet her, and they had plans for dealing with the wreck she had become.

At forty-seven, Barnes was alcoholic, seriously ill, depressed, and impoverished. She had been living in a nursing home, unable to work, unable to care for herself since the beginning of the German Occupation.

Recently, she had suffered a trauma that paralleled the events in her childhood, which had, no doubt, contributed to her steadily declining condition. She had been staying in a little hotel on St.-

Sulpice. At five in the morning, a porter broke into her room and tried to rape her. Although she was "extremely weak and sobbing," she defended herself. She beat him off, "chased him out into the hall and woke everyone up." He argued that he hadn't done what she had claimed. As usual, he said, she had been drinking, and had "imagined" everything.

As the Occupation forces advanced, Djuna's friend Emily Coleman, the writer, searched the nursing homes of Paris until she found Djuna to get her out. Coleman had begged Peggy Guggenheim, their mutual friend and Djuna's sometime financial supporter to pay Djuna's fare back to the United States. Coleman knew Barnes would be forced to stay in Paris for the duration of the war unless she acted quickly. She feared what would become of Djuna, stuck in Paris without support, for many American expatriates were fleeing, and Coleman herself was leaving for Arizona.

Peggy Guggenheim came through with the fare. She went to the station to see Barnes off. She was worried about Djuna, afraid she might harm herself during the journey. Peggy had arranged for Djuna to travel with Peggy's lover, the painter Yves Tanguy. In the moments before departure, Peggy told Tanguy to watch out for Djuna, a request he ignored. For the duration of the trip, Djuna was alone.

Her voyage home was terrifying and dangerous. The Germans had begun a series of U-boat attacks on merchant and navy vessels. On September 3, a German U-boat had sunk the ocean liner *Athenia*. Throughout the six-day crossing, Barnes and her fellow passengers feared they would meet the same end. They "kept terrified watch for German submarines at the ship's rail."

Although they made the crossing without incident, another hazard awaited when they neared New York. The Germans had mined New York harbor. As the ship made its way slowly through dangerous waters, Djuna Barnes waited on deck, ready to evacuate the ship if ordered to do so, wondering whether she would be killed instantly if the ship hit a mine. When the ship docked, she was exhausted from fear and worry. She was in far worse shape than when her journey began.

East Fifty-fourth Street
New York City
October 1939

A private assault force awaited Djuna Barnes when her ship docked. Members of her family were waiting for her at the pier. They had no sympathy for her, no words of kindness for what she had endured and survived. Instead, as she wrote Emily Coleman, they ruthlessly took her straight from her "six day sea trip (and all of us in terror of submarines)" to her mother's tiny apartment on East Fifty-fourth Street. There, as she put it, they "dumped me, penniless, into one room with my mother."

The arrangement did not last very long, and it made Djuna even worse. Her mother, Elizabeth, was also ill. All night long, Djuna could hear her mother "coughing and choking for breath." Their beds were only ten feet apart, so Djuna "could not sleep with the noise and terror of her death."

Of all the members of her family, Djuna harbored the most complex, unnerving constellation of feelings for her mother. It was upsetting to see her mother, at seventy-seven, so ravaged by illness, "sitting waiting for death like a child anticipating a disappointment."

Being thrust unwillingly into such close proximity to this woman who had done nothing to stop her suffering when she was a child must have been painful to Barnes. Yet Barnes had written her own feelings into the words of her character Matthew O'Connor in *Nightwood*: "It is my mother without argument I want!"

The family ascribed Djuna's poor condition to her weak moral fiber. She described her brothers' attitude toward her illness in a letter to Coleman:

> I do not know what is the matter with my brothers (I do not refer to their refusal to help me) they seem to hate me, to have an idea that I am a monster of some sort, they will not allow my name to be mentioned in conversation if they can avoid it. . . . They have set their minds to it that I am one; insane, two; a dope fiend, three; an incurable drunk, four; a degenerate and five, the trouble that is the trouble with them!!!!

Her mother, too, believed it was time for Djuna to reform herself. She thought Djuna was sick because she had succumbed to the immoral atmosphere in that capital of decadence, Paris. She reminded her daughter that she, too, had been to Paris: "It's Paris! You needn't tell me. Don't I know what that place can do? I accepted your father under the Arc de Triomphe, and look at us now!" Elizabeth told Djuna it was time for her to cast off her evil ways; it was her responsibility to shape up, to pull herself together. The way she uttered this command, Djuna thought, had "the venom of Calvin in it."

Elizabeth had become a Christian Scientist, and when she wasn't racked with fits of coughing, she would read Djuna pertinent selections from the work of Mary Baker Eddy. Often, if she couldn't sleep, she would read aloud through the night. Though Djuna mocked her family's attitude, she agreed with them. She believed she was morally weak and responsible for her own breakdown: "I fear my mother is right (she is horribly hard on me). 'You'll lose all your friends . . . if you don't pull yourself [together]—they all loved you once, but none will soon if you keep being in *your condition*.' "

Djuna knew her mother could be venomous and cruel; she called Elizabeth her "mother monster." She "never in her life" showed "any or (little) affection" to her daughter. Elizabeth confessed she was afraid that if she showed affection, what she loved "would be taken away" from her.

But Elizabeth could also be kind and tender-hearted. And this confused Barnes most. As she wrote Coleman, "I feel like a skunk for saying anything about mother's venom without saying also she can be nicer and more trouble-taking (about me) than can be imagined—it's the awful combination perhaps that is so hurtful."

Emily Coleman understood that Djuna's bond with her mother was deadly. She had asked her friend, without knowing the peculiar nature of Djuna's childhood, why she still took her mother's criticism so seriously: "You should really be beyond that by now. You must have a fearful tie with her." Coleman realized that Barnes as an adult was still "half child, worrying and shouting at her, and half yourself, keeping your own life secret; yet never free from her inside. You ought not of course to be so near her, it's killing." Djuna was afraid that "not even death would free her" from her mother.

Soon after moving in with her mother, Djuna suffered yet another breakdown. This one occurred, as far as Djuna was concerned, because she had been mistreated by her brothers, because she had been shoved into too close quarters with her mother, because she couldn't get any rest.

When Djuna broke down this time, her brothers acted swiftly. They had her incarcerated in a mental institution. She believed they had set up the conditions to ensure that she would have a breakdown so that they could lock her away. She wrote Coleman: they "tried to railroad me to a sanatorium at Lake something-or-other."

They took her there against her will. She fought so fiercely that she was bruised "from head to foot."

"Lake Something-or-other" *New York State* *Winter 1939*

Djuna Barnes's brothers believed that the attending doctors would reform their sister and make her over into a respectable, self-supporting citizen instead of the unworldly artist she had become. They would use the techniques of psychiatry to control her.

The key to the cure her brothers planned lay in the attending psychiatrists convincing Barnes that she had to give up a belief in her own talent, in her own genius. Instead of writing what she wanted to write, she would have to learn how to write what editors wanted her to write. She had to become a journalist again, as she had been at the beginning of her career, before she had begun to use her art for self-expression. She had to embrace the goal of becoming normal, even ordinary. It was essential for her to do whatever had to be done to become a commercial success. This meant she would have to give up writing fiction and poetry. The letters from the period are evidence that her brothers "resented her artistic success," and "her independence," and "her desire to investigate the meaning of the family's past."

> "You'll lose your so-called talent, but you will be a self-supporting citizen, ordinary and healthy, and you'll make money," [my brother] said and the doctor—"Well, how do you intend to solve

your problem if you don't make money? You are undoubtedly a different case for you are evidently a brilliant woman, but you've got to forget that until you can get it into line commercially." And *the horror of it, it is true.* I've got to forget or I starve.

When she was institutionalized, Barnes had written *Ryder* and *Nightwood*, many short stories, much poetry, a series of one-act plays (which Eugene O'Neill viewed as more promising than his own early efforts). Much of her work had made reference, though often obliquely, to the strange, torturous history of her family.

It was her own family history, one riddled with incest, physical abuse, and perversion, that Barnes had re-created in her art. Although other people might have had problematic families, she told T. S. Eliot she couldn't "picture anyone['s family] quite as abominable as mine."

As a writer, she had not yet publicly divulged that the source of her art was her life. She had safeguarded her secret, her family history. She possessed that she called an "innate dislike of parading, or 'telling on' the innermost secret." She felt "it should only be exposed . . . by the best artist" and should not be done for money: "when it is done for money, it becomes (for me) a brothel of the spirit." Yet, as a survivor of incest, she also needed to tell her story, to have her readers bear witness to what she had survived. She believed that she had an obligation to share her experience with her readers, women and men who, like her, had experienced abuse. These people were her "special" audience, readers who would read between the lines and understand:

> In exposing it in art, it is lifted back into its own place again, given back to itself, tho also given to the reader, the eye. Only the best reader will understand it, like initiation, which is not for everyone.

Djuna had not told anyone directly what she had endured until recently; in 1937, she revealed the secret that she was a survivor of incest to Emily Coleman (who had begun to guess the truth). Even then, she did not tell Coleman the full extent of what she had endured. She couldn't. The truth was too horrible.

In her art, Djuna Barnes had written of a father's belief in and practice of polygamy; of a family organized in imitation of Sodom and Gomorrah; of a son's lust for his mother; of a father's instructing his son to have sex with his sister; of a father's intent to damage his offspring; of a mother's tolerance of a man's assault on their children, of his horsewhipping them; of a girl's sharing her father's bed after her mother has abandoned them. She had described an older woman who uses a young girl as a slave for her own pleasure; a mother who pimps her son to men and women; a man who believes it is his destiny to impregnate every woman in the world, and who tries to do so; women who have been tossed out like so much rubbish onto the streets of New York to fend for themselves; a father who watches with glee as his wife and his mistress beat one another; a man's use of a sexual tool shaped like a crown of thorns, deliberately designed to cut into a woman's genitals, to make her "sore"; a girl who has been raped and then blamed for it; a girl who becomes pregnant by her father.

The motives of Djuna's brothers for trying to prevent her from writing what she wanted to write, to turn their sister into a "normal" writer, were far from pure. Under the guise of reforming her, they wanted to silence her. They no doubt suspected that in time, if she became healthy, Djuna would return to her favorite subject— their family. And now after her years in Paris, she was very well known. A new work by Djuna Barnes would be sure to receive widespread critical attention. Djuna's mother lived in fear that her daughter would reveal even more of their family secrets. Djuna's family knew that though Djuna had written much, there was even more of their story to tell.

Djuna Barnes was incarcerated for the first time by her family for a two-week period. At first, she acceded, though somewhat reluctantly, to the wishes of her brothers and doctors, and she cooperated with the cure they had arranged for her. In truth, she had very little choice.

As part of her cure, a doctor ordered her to write down the events of her life. Describing the regimen forced upon her, she wrote Emily Coleman: "I must tap out a few thousand million pages of my past history every morning for the doctor."

Whether he realized it or not, the doctor had ordered Djuna to write the very story her family was trying to make her forget. Though she scoffed at this exercise, going back over her troubled past yet again was an important part of her eventual recuperation. This time, in writing the details of her life, and in rehashing them in letters to Emily Coleman after she was released, something in her changed. She got angry. And she understood that her writing could be both a cure and a weapon she could use against her persecutors.

When she had written her family history before, she had written in opaque and convoluted language; she had hinted and suggested; she had used the techniques of mockery and irony, so that many of her readers missed the tragedy and the horror of the lives she was describing. In time her tactics would change. As she wrote to Emily Coleman, she had decided that if she ever embarked upon another major work, she wanted it to be "unmitigated and cruel, as cruel as fact."

Shepherd's Bush Road, Cromwell Grove London 1889

Djuna Barnes's mother, Elizabeth Chappell, was born in Rutland, England. She grew up in a successful working-class household, a family of cabinetmakers and builders. If her daughter's account of her life is accurate, Elizabeth was a physically abused child. In the account in *Ryder* in which Elizabeth's father dies, next to him is a

> long horse-whip, his last partner in this world's work. . . . It had lain there twenty-four hours, for the day before he came to die he had chased his favourite daughter, Amelia, then seven, about the yard with it, because she, poor unwitting, had thrown the clothes-basket into the hencoop.

Elizabeth, we also know, was raped "in her youth by a fourteen-year-old lad."

Elizabeth saw Wald Barnes, her husband-to-be, for the first time one day in London. She had come to study violin at London's Conservatory of Music, her interest in music having been urged along by her father, who played the piano. Barnes was a short man, five foot seven, redheaded, with a full, curly beard. She was living in Shepherd's Bush with her sister when Wald Barnes moved into the garden flat next door in Cromwell Grove, with his mother, Zadel Gustafson, and her second husband, Axel Gustafson.

According to Djuna Barnes, when her mother saw her father for the first time, he was wearing pants patched in the seat with green cloth, and he was dangling a rat by its tail—it was his custom to surround himself with rats he had trained to follow him. In one version of their meeting, Wald was sitting on the wall that separated their gardens; Elizabeth was so captivated by him that she pulled him down onto her side of the wall. From that moment, Elizabeth was enthralled. At first, she had no idea that he intended her to lead a very unusual life, that she would become his captive in a tyrannical, abusive household—though, according to Djuna's account, Elizabeth's sister warned her that he would be trouble.

Before the year ended, they married and moved to the United States with his mother, Zadel. According to Djuna, Elizabeth brought a good deal of money into the marriage. That might have been the reason Wald chose to marry her; the "several sources of revenue" Zadel and Wald had been drawing upon had been used up when Wald met Elizabeth, and no member of the family was willing to engage in conventional work. Wald believed he was special, entitled to care, too good to work. He sponged off people his whole life.

Storm King Mountain
Cornwall-on-Hudson, New York
1892–1907

Djuna Barnes was born in 1892. By the time of her birth, her parents and Zadel had moved from England and had settled into a small cottage Wald had built with his own hands on the grounds of an estate owned by Wald's brother, Dr. Justin Budington. Zadel had taken Elizabeth and Wald there after her separation from Axel Gustafson.

Justin Budington was a wealthy and successful eye surgeon in New York City. He used the estate mainly as a trysting place for himself and his mistress. Wald became a kind of caretaker for the property, and Zadel became a permanent fixture in their household.

The family compound was on Storm King Mountain, overlooking the Hudson River. It was an isolated spot, far removed from the prying eyes and interference of neighbors. The household was entirely self-sufficient, though hardly well off; its members raised their own food, made their own clothing. Djuna Barnes lived here until she was sixteen. In 1907 the family was forced to move after Justin Budington's death.

Djuna was Wald and Elizabeth's second child, their only daughter. She was originally named Djalma after the Prince in Eugène Sue's novel *The Wandering Jew.* One of her brothers consistently mispronounced her name, calling her Djuna. And Djuna she became.

Name changes, identity changes, were not unusual in this family. By the time he was fifteen, Djuna's father had changed his name so often that he could not remember every alias he had used. One reason given in Djuna's fictional account of her father's life in *Ryder* was that he was wanted for murder.

His given name was originally Henry; his surname was originally Budington, the surname of his father, who was a "professional . . . spiritualist." He changed his surname to his mother's maiden name, Barnes, because he hated his father (whom his mother had married at sixteen and had divorced in 1879 after a twenty-year marriage), and probably because he wanted to bear his mother's name to show his deep emotional tie to her. He settled on Wald because it was unusual enough, and sounded important enough, for the man he believed himself to be. The name Barnes comes from the Norse Bjorne; the Barnes family had Nordic origins.

Unusual, pretentious names were the rule in the Barnes household, indicating that Wald and Elizabeth saw their brood as different from, grander than, other people's children. The names they chose for their sons were inventions, unusual combinations of names that resonated with mythical significance, as if like Zeus's children, they had sprung full-grown from their father's forehead. Apart from Djuna's elder brother, Thurn (he was born in 1890), there were Zendon (1990), Saxon (1902), and Shangar (1904).

Wald Barnes decreed that his children be educated at home by himself and his mother, Zadel. In part, he decided this because he distrusted the educational system and wanted his children to be taught those skills that he and his mother revered and practiced—music and a sensitivity to the archaic uses of language. He himself was a composer of operas. Zadel Gustafson was a prolific writer and published many books, both for children and for adults; she wrote a biography of the singer Genevieve Ward; she wrote a novel called *Can the Old Love?*; ironically, given the debauched life she led, she had joined the purity and temperance crusade, and published articles espousing these causes in *Harper's New Monthly Magazine*.

Keeping his children at home also assured Wald Barnes that no one would interfere. It enabled him to maintain his absolute rule over his brood, preventing his children from understanding that not every family behaved the way they did. For some time, one of Wald's regular mistresses and their children also lived on the Storm King estate. Elizabeth and this mistress, and the children, often flew into jealous rages and battered one another, much to Wald Barnes's amusement.

Wald Barnes had established a household in which, through cajolery, brainwashing, charm, threats of violence, and actual violence, he maintained total and absolute control over his wife, their children, his mistresses, and their children. He controlled every feature of the enclave's life—what they learned, how they dressed, what they ate. They endured what Judith Herman in *Trauma and Recovery* has described as a life lived in captivity.

Though Elizabeth might have complained about Wald behind his back, she allowed him to carry out his wishes, bizarre and brutal as they may have been. She permitted him to move his mistresses into the compound without complaint. (The most famous was the opera singer Marguerite Amelia d'Alvarez, whom Djuna hated.) He required that his children swallow gravel, like chickens, to aid their digestion. He beat them—Djuna recounted how Elizabeth held one of her infant brothers down while Wald whipped him. He enjoyed lassoing them with a rope and dragging them through the dirt.

Within the boundaries of his private enclave, Wald Barnes established himself as a kind of high priest, or god, of a new religion. He invented its tenets as he went along, but he eventually wrote them down in a document he called his "Credo," which, according to Djuna, he later burned. His "Credo" consisted mainly of aphorisms.

That freedom consists in keeping the wood cut, the fire lit and the animals productive. That women are monstrous and beautiful; man, active. That knowledge is knowing that the horse founders, the ship sinks, and women take comfort in what has no evidence. That time is a slut with whom one mates, and life is best faced backwards.

Wald Barnes seems to have enunciated his system of beliefs to justify his behavior. He was apparently a mad but magnetic personality, and compelled or convinced his weak-willed wife, Elizabeth, to go along with whatever he wanted after she gave her money over to him and joined his household. When they first met, he evidently kept from her his belief in polygamy. She perhaps learned of it on their journey to the United States, when, according to Djuna's account, he manipulated her into a shipboard *ménage à trois*.

He had learned his ways of behaving, it seems clear, at least in part from his mother, Zadel, to whom he was connected by seductive or overtly incestuous ties. Djuna believed that Zadel was the power in the family. She thought Zadel believed her son to be "weak," with "great gifts," but "like the criminal in a famous murder case, that had been forgotten."

Zadel was a magnetic, unforgettable personality. She specialized in theatrical and grand gestures. One of Djuna's earliest memories was of her grandmother's burying a pet canary, according it an "elaborate funeral," wrapping it in "her very best Liberty pink silk scarf." Her son ruled through charm and tyranny; Zadel ruled through charm alone.

Zadel was responsible for Djuna's education. She read aloud to her granddaughter from works like Thackeray's *The Rose and the Ring*, from Shakespeare and the Bible; she taught Djuna how to write. She taught Djuna that she was gifted and talented, that she was a genius. Zadel believed her training would enable her granddaughter to fulfill her thwarted "literary and feminist aspirations."

In Djuna's account, Zadel and Wald shared stories of their sexual exploits; they were compatriots in pursuing sexual pleasure. Wald learned the tenets of polygamy from Zadel. Djuna described

Wald as his mother's most earnest courtier. If Djuna's account of her father's history is accurate, Zadel offered her son to men and women; he became at her urging and by her example, a male prostitute. She established a "salon" in England, ostensibly a gathering place for reformers, which provided a screen for her life as a prostitute. Zadel, and not Wald Barnes, was, her granddaughter believed, "the law" behind this *ménage*.

Wald's father, Henry Budington, had been born of a family with roots in Connecticut and Massachusetts. He was the "son of Methodist parents 'of the quiet sort' who practiced strict temperance." Djuna's grandfather was the author of a work, *Man Makes His Body, or the Ascent of the Ego Through Matter*, which argued that "bad thinking" and "abnormal physical habits" had dire effects on the psyche:

> Right thinking builds good heads; bad thinking builds bad
> heads. . . . If anyone indulges in abnormal physical habits: the use
> of tobacco, alcohol, chloral, opium, . . . sex excess . . . the brain
> organ for that special passion is enlarged, . . . until the habit
> becomes . . . overpowering.

One view has it that Wald Barnes, sick of his father's conservatism, of his strict Methodism, began to live out his life "in precise reaction against everything that he [Henry Budington] was and stood for." Henry Budington, though, in a memoir, refers to the Methodist church where his grandfather worshiped as having been nicknamed "Sodom." One wonders whether, behind the pretense of religiosity, the Budington family, too, had adhered to sexual practices like those of Zadel and Wald.

Djuna's mother's family were strict Calvinists. This might have conditioned Elizabeth to accept the absolute rule of her husband, and to see the world as a place of suffering. For Djuna, her mother's family's Calvinism explained her behavior; it "accounts for *everything!*" Yet Djuna also described how Elizabeth's father had beaten her. Based upon what researchers have discovered about incest and violence as a family pattern, these explanations of Wald's and Elizabeth's behavior as a reaction to their rigid upbringings do not ring true.

According to Djuna's and her grandmother's own testimony,

Djuna and Zadel had a long-standing incestuous relationship. It is Zadel who is the key to the origin of this family's incestuous and destructive behavior, though Zadel's own initiation into sexuality remains a mystery.

Zadel Gustafson was born in Middletown, Connecticut, on March 8, 1841, the daughter of Duane Barnes. She was the fourth of the fourteen children her father had with two wives. Many of the children had unusual names—Marilla, Hinta, Reon, Gaybert, Culmer, Kilmeny, Justa, Urlan, Niar, Unade.

These names point to a family history steeped in the practice of spiritualism—spirit possession. Zadel's family, like her son's, occupied a marginal position in society. But according to Djuna's retelling, the spiritualism in Zadel's past seems linked (as it sometimes was) to sexual practices beyond conventional morality. In her novel *Ryder*, Djuna depicts her grandmother's report that she had conceived her son by the "figure of Beethoven passing mystically through her" body. Wald Barnes spent the greater part of his life writing symphonies and operas, acting as if he had, in fact, been sired by Beethoven's ghost.

Yet *Ryder* suggests that Zadel made use of another man's body to act as a conduit for Beethoven's spirit. In *Ryder,* Djuna describes how her grandmother begets her father in an illicit relationship; she describes her grandmother's belief in polygamy, the pornographic pictures on her wall, the huge number of sexual partners she has had.

After the collapse of her twenty-year marriage to a professional spiritualist, Henry Aaron Budington, Zadel married Axel Gustafson, moved to England, and, according to Djuna's report, established a literary salon in Grosvenor Square, which Oscar Wilde and his mother, Speranza, attended. (It was actually in Brunswick Square.) Djuna's account shows Oscar Wilde interested in Wald Barnes, lifting "his . . . auburn forelock, murmuring, 'Beautiful, beautiful!' "

Zadel maintained a friendship with Karl Marx's daughter, Eleanor, and numbered among her friends other radicals such as Elizabeth Cady Stanton, who mentions Zadel in her memoirs. Zadel and Axel collaborated on their "quasi-spiritualistic work, *The Foundation of Death,*" in 1888, the year before Wald Barnes met Elizabeth.

Given Zadel's incestuous behavior toward Djuna, and the primary position that she occupied in Wald's household, one wonders whether Zadel had violated her son as well, which, in turn, led him to violate his offspring.

Wald Barnes was a self-styled freethinker. The tenets of his religion were a blending of Mormonism, the Old Testament, and Greek mythology, with a bit of mesmerism thrown in for good measure. Its rituals remain a mystery. But his daughter described enough of them in her writing that it is possible to piece together Wald Barnes's practices and beliefs.

The chief tenet of this new faith decreed that Wald Barnes repopulate the earth with his offspring. He believed himself entitled, even obligated, to copulate with as many women as he could to father as many children as he could. He saw no difference between animals and people, and his daughter describes him adorning two cows who have become his "lovers."

Two constant features of his attire were a red cap, worn winter and summer as a sign of his virility, and a piece of sponge on his saddle, which he used to wipe himself after intercourse. He called the sponge his "nose-gay"; according to Djuna, he would smell it to get himself excited.

Djuna's drawing of Wald Barnes as "Ryder" on horseback, surrounded by women, dangling his sponge from a ribbon, appears in her novel about his exploits, *Ryder*. (The novel's first edition contained nine original illustrations by her.) A favorite fantasy, according to Djuna, which he repeatedly tried to enact, was to have two women in bed with him and to impregnate each of them within seconds, so that two of his offspring would be born simultaneously.

When Djuna was an adolescent, it seems as if producing a child by having intercourse with her began to preoccupy him. The testimony surrounding this is confused and unclear. But throughout her life, Djuna referred to her experiences in terms of the Adam and Eve story, to Adam's having sex with a woman who came from his body. She tells the story in *The Antiphon*.

In 1937, Emily Coleman shared with Barnes her realization that Barnes was a survivor of incest. "O Djuna," Emily wrote, "I understand so much in you which was hitherto not revealed to me: your great secrecy about the thing of your spirit." And, in empathy for what her friend had endured: "Is not anyone with a childhood like yours justified in being bitter? . . . Family means *sex*. I suddenly knew it. The original 'family.' The Garden of Eden. Eve created out of Adam's rib. . . . Something wrong."

Coleman's realization helped Djuna. She was relieved to know that, for the first time in her life, she could reveal her secret to someone:

> I am very happy that you have come into a knowledge of what home, family, blood ties mean. It's startling that it just struck you. . . . I've said nothing to anyone: what a victory that you know now, why I am so "secret."

Djuna Barnes wrote overtly of incest in an early version of *Nightwood*. She also alludes to a daughter's giving birth to her father's child in *Ryder:* "What Infant gives Birth to its Parent, what Child crawls out of the Cradle, that its Mother may have where to lay her Head?" Producing a child who was the result of an incestuous liaison with his daughter would, given his beliefs, be an act of great significance for Wald Barnes.

From the hints in Djuna Barnes's writings, and from her letters and private papers, it can be assumed that the Barnes *ménage* practiced spirit possession, incest (probably between Wald and his mother, almost surely between Wald and his children, among the children themselves, and certainly between Zadel and Djuna), ritual rape, voyeurism (children compelled to watch sexual acts or to witness rape disguised as religious ritual), group sex (involving Wald and his wife and one or another of his many mistresses and perhaps their children), sadistic behavior (beatings, the torture and killing of animals, the use of sexual tools to inflict pain), bestiality.

Wald Barnes considered it beneath his dignity to work for a living. He "fished, grew mushrooms in his cellar and kept poultry and a few animals." Throughout his life, he sponged off relatives, sent his women out to scavenge money, perhaps even to prostitute themselves, and lived off the earnings or the labor of his children. Djuna sewed and baked for the household; she minded her siblings and her father's mistress's children; she planted and plowed the fields, milled flour, killed chickens, cooked food.

Wald Barnes was a megalomaniac, answerable for his behavior to no one but himself. Whenever he got into trouble with the law, his mother bailed him out, he used his charm to disarm his critics, or he moved his household.

Rethinking her childhood, recalling her grandmother Zadel's place in her past, Djuna Barnes wrote Emily Coleman: "Suffering for love is how I have learned practically everything I know, love of grandmother up and on." In *Ryder*, the father figure, representing Wald Barnes, says of his daughter, who represents Djuna:

> My daughter is simple and great, like a Greek horror, her large pale head, with its wideset uncalculating eyes, is that of a child begotten in a massacre and nursed on the guillotine.

Huntington, New York
1909–1910

During 1909 and 1910, Djuna Barnes experienced a series of events that were, for her, the ultimate betrayal by her family. She would re-create these events in gruesome detail in her play *The Antiphon;* they would be reenacted on the stage for her audience to witness.

Wald Barnes had decided that Djuna, who was eighteen years old, should "marry" the brother of one of his mistresses, a fifty-two-year-old man by the name of Percy Faulkner. Wald conceived of Djuna's "betrothal" and the mating and marriage of his daughter to his lover's brother as a religious ritual justified by his personal credo. In effect, he planned his daughter's rape by a man old enough to be her father: she was to be " 'given' sexually" by her father and grandmother to Faulkner "like an Old Testament slave or daughter." To compound the insult, Wald Barnes insisted upon a "bride price" for Djuna—he sold his daughter into sexual slavery.

In the months preceding the "wedding," Djuna was "plainly unhappy yet unwilling to reveal the cause." Zadel Barnes, who, it seems, helped her son conceive the plan, acted as go-between. She urged Percy Faulkner to reassure Djuna. She wanted the old man to give her an "outward sign" of his concern for her, which would, in turn, give Djuna "inward assurance" that all would be well.

Djuna, though, wanted nothing to do with this rite. She would not acquiesce to the future her father and grandmother had planned for her. For eighteen years, she had known no life beyond the Barnes enclave. She had attended no school, visited no other family, had no friends, no contact with the outside world, knew nothing of the way other families behaved. For the years she spent on the Long Island farm, some of the family's "most prominent visitors" were the " 'Eaches' or spirits, who used Zadel's body" to manifest themselves—"Jack London, Franz Liszt, Ludwig von Beethoven, and Chopin were among the more noteworthy."

Though she had been sequestered, something within her at first resisted submitting to her father's will, to his insistence that she become a sexual sacrifice to his cause.

When Djuna was "betrothed" to Percy Faulkner, she was involved in a long-standing incestuous relationship with her grandmother Zadel that had inflicted its own special damage. As an adult, Djuna admitted that she couldn't tell where her grandmother left off and where she herself began. This incestuous relationship had led to a merging of their identities: "I always thought I *was* my grandmother," Djuna wrote.

Though Zadel claimed that she had loved Djuna and taught her that she was special—"I was always blissfully sure that anything I wanted, I would have, and I was right"—Djuna was torn apart by jealousy at her grandmother's special relationship with her father. In *Nightwood* she describes a dream in which her father reunites with his dead mother in a coffin: they will be forever joined in death. A disconsolate Djuna figure is forever shut out of this dyad, left to mourn the loss of her grandmother, a part of herself, someone who has become an extension of her own body:

> There in my sleep was my grandmother, whom I loved more than anyone, tangled in the grave grass . . . , and flying low, my father who is still living; low going and into the grave beside her, his head thrown back and his curls lying out, . . . and me, stepping about its edges, walking and wailing without a sound. . . . There they were in the grave grass, and the grave water and the grave flowers and the grave time, one living and one dead and one asleep.

Zadel's incest with her granddaughter was an act of betrayal. But she had tried to convince Djuna that her actions were prompted by love and care, that Djuna and she shared a special relationship, that Djuna was her favorite grandchild. In a tale called "Where is the Child?" Zadel wrote that a woman can do no wrong; she has "the divine unfailing impulse of a heart as warm and true and trustful as a child." Behind the shield of this delusion, Zadel committed incest with her granddaughter, and probably convinced herself that what she was doing was for Djuna's own good.

In 1909, Zadel betrayed Djuna in still another way, and Djuna would be left to sort out her conflicting emotions about her grandmother for the rest of her life. Zadel joined Wald in the scheme to "marry" Djuna. This meant that Zadel, too, wanted to have Djuna raped. She was not protecting Djuna; she was allowing her to be assaulted. Zadel's collusion in the scheme also meant that Wald's will was supreme, that Djuna was not "special" to her grandmother at all.

How far back in Djuna's life her incestuous relations with her grandmother went is unclear. But by 1909, their sexual relationship had become such a commonplace that Zadel wrote of it openly in her letters to Djuna whenever Zadel's business affairs took her away from the Long Island farm where the Barnes *ménage* was living.

In the code words Zadel used in her letters, Djuna and she were "Starbits" and "Flitch." The letters were openly sexual, referring with pet names to Djuna's bodily parts, to her "pink pebblums." They often included drawings illustrating Zadel's physical desire for her granddaughter and the sexual acts the two of them would engage in when Zadel returned home.

Zadel called herself Djuna's "ownest lishous grandmother"; she exclaimed how "eager" she was "to get home to the bed" she and her granddaughter shared.

I'm huggin' you close to the Pinknesses, and they is chortlin' tremendous. [Zadel draws two laughing breasts, which she calls "Pink Tops."] Wot yer think of them little wed mouths open? [She refers to her nipples.]

Oh, Misriss! When I sees your sweet hands a huggin your own P.T.'s [Zadel draws Djuna's breasts]—I is just crazy and I jumps on oo. Like dis. Wiv this wesult. [Zadel draws herself and Djuna in bed, breast to breast, herself overpowering Djuna. In another drawing, her own and her granddaughter's breasts reach to meet, "nipple to nipple."]

Djuna's relationship with Zadel was characterized, according to Zadel's own admission (and as in every act of incest), by her dominance and her granddaughter's submission: Zadel liked to overpower Djuna and she liked to draw pictures in which she pounced on her granddaughter's body. Djuna had learned by her grandmother's behavior that she had no choice where sex was concerned; her body was a plaything for the adults in the family to use.

Although "Starbits" seems an invention, the word "Flitch" has a long history, and, given Zadel's interest in archaic usage, we can be sure she knew what it meant. In its older uses, "flitch" meant male genitalia; the word could also mean a piece of fish.

Djuna used both meanings of the word in her accounts of her relationship with her grandmother and of her nightmares. In *Nightwood*, she described how her grandmother dressed herself up as a man and strutted around, "wearing a billycock and a corked moustache, ridiculous and plump in tight trousers and a red waistcoat, her arms spread saying with a leer of love, 'My little sweetheart!' "

In a letter, she told Emily Coleman about a recurrent nightmare: a giant seal woman or a fish overwhelms her; other creatures attack her; she realizes they are members of her family:

Melancholia, melancholia, it rides me like a bucking mare—a seal woman came up out of my sleep and told me to feel her, she was almost like a human, but prickly when you touched her, and she had legs and a pelvis, but nothing else, and she said she could not talk much because she was fish, she smelled like a fish, briny, and her brothers were ferocious puppy sea animals with puppy hair, and they came out of a lake to fight me, and one of them ate my only weapon, a long brush, and my cain [sic], head and all . . .—how is that for a dream? Animals, always animals, it's sickening, and those babies of my mother's and now it's fish.

The seal woman/fish dream also enacts Djuna's merging with her grandmother; it enacts the sexual practices she was forced to perform, and the attacks on her by her brothers, "ferocious puppy seal animals." But the dream also reveals that Djuna had a weapon, a long brush, which she would use to tell her story. She understands, though, that her "weapon," her art, is at risk. One of her brothers will try to destroy it.

She had this dream in 1938, a year before her family put her into the asylum. She knew throughout her life that her family would try to silence her.

In 1910, Djuna Barnes could fight her family no more. She capitulated to her father's and grandmother's wishes. They gave her to Percy Faulkner as his "bride," and he took her to Bridgeport.

Djuna Barnes described the event in an early, deleted passage of her novel *Nightwood*:

> "And then I had a lover and a doll, and because he was a man who had held me on his knee when I was a child, and because I had a doll and ate caramels, and looked up at him and said 'yes,' he couldn't bear it. He thought, perhaps, that he was bored, but it was something else; he was an old man then and he wanted something simpler and older, so he took me away to a transients' hotel in Bridgeport, if you know what kind of a hotel that is—"
>
> "I should hope to say I do! Men going upstairs panting, and women going up slowly, saying, 'For the love of God, can't you wait.' "

Whether the ritual rape was first enacted at the family farm before the couple left for Bridgeport is unclear, but it seems so. The earlier version of *Nightwood* describes the entire family's participation in the event, which occurred around Christmas. The narrator is describing how the "old man" is frightened because his young "bride" won't cry despite what she has endured. It seems unnatural to him.

> "... and it frightened him still further, beyond endurance, because I wouldn't cry, and he said, 'Go back home and don't tell anyone, because after all I never did intend to marry you!' "

Years later, before Djuna returned from Europe, her brother Saxon sought psychiatric help to recover from his traumatic past in the Barnes family. One experience stood out: "he had witnessed his father's abuse of Barnes during their childhood."

In Djuna's telling, Wald Barnes had wanted a witness to testify that the deed had taken place; perhaps that witness was Saxon Barnes. Djuna wrote Emily Coleman about Saxon: "He is my favourite brother, and there is a tie between us that is very strange and strong."

In one of Djuna's tellings of the event, Elizabeth refused to allow Wald to be the witness of the rape. She spread flour in front of the door so that she could tell whether her husband had entered the room. Elizabeth knew her husband well. Though she had agreed to Faulkner's raping Djuna, she was afraid that if Wald was a witness, he would rape their daughter, too.

In another retelling of the scene, though, the Djuna figure is raped yet again. But this time, it is her father.

And I picked up the carving knife then, seeing that night back on the hill, my brother playing the trombone somewhere so that it came softly up to the trees and I had said, "No, I will marry you in my heart but I will not marry you in church." Because this was a big new ideal my father had in his head. Then I remembered the ceremony beside the Christmas tree, when my father and my grandmother stood by, and my mother by the door in her apron, crying and thinking God knows what; and he put a ring on my finger and I kissed him. Before that, it must have been two hours, I had gone down on the floor and hugged my grandmother by her knees, dropping my head down, saying "Don't let it happen!" and she said, "It had to happen."

And I was in bed that first night, and he said, "Christ! You don't bleed much." And I said, "It is all the blood it has." And all before the door my mother had strewn flour—to give herself hope, hoping there would be no foot-mark in it going my way.

So I took the carving knife and leaned across the table, strong and blind with something coming up in me out of what my father had in his head for women and love, and for the Christmas tree and the flour on the floor, and he jumped out of the window backward into the garden. And then I came back home and I wasn't crying. And then I got thin, and fell when I walked, and my grandmother came to me and said: "What is it that he has done that you are sent back home?" And I told her. And that too was my childhood.

From the family farm on Long Island, in the year 1910, Elizabeth Barnes wrote a letter to Djuna, who was in Bridgeport with Percy Faulkner: "I miss you—don't feel guilty tell me everything, but not that your [sic] forlorn." Djuna could tell her mother what had happened to her. But she was not allowed to complain.

Huntington, New York
1910–1912

Djuna Barnes's "marriage" to Percy Faulkner blew the Barnes *ménage* apart.

When she returned to the family compound from her time with Percy Faulkner, she became anorexic. She lost so much weight that she nearly died. She entered a protective state of dissociation. She could not feel: "I did not cry."

Finally, Elizabeth had had enough. After her daughter's near-death, she divorced Wald Barnes. But she always blamed Djuna for what happened, for the breakup of the family. On February 22, 1912, Elizabeth "issued a summons to Wald, forcing him to respond within twenty days." Divorce papers were filed on August 2, 1912. The marriage was terminated three months later, on November 6, 1912. Wald married his mistress, Fanny Faulkner, soon after.

When Djuna recuperated sufficiently, she and Elizabeth moved out.

Wald Barnes recanted his beliefs, which proved to Djuna beyond a doubt that her father was a charlatan and that her suffering had occurred for no real reason but to satisfy his perverted libidinous wishes. If he really had believed that he was the founder of a new kind of religion, her pain would have been justified. His saying he had been mistaken infuriated her. He became dependent upon the two children from his liaison with Fanny Faulkner, Duane and Muriel, Djuna's half brother and half sister, who stayed with him.

After she and her mother left the family, it became Djuna's responsibility "to earn a living for me and some for them [the members of her family]."

Queens, New York
Bronx, New York
1911–1915

Djuna Barnes left the family farm on Long Island and came to New York City to patch together a new life when she was nineteen years old. She already had a "marriage" behind her. Though she had gone to Bridgeport with Percy Faulkner, she had never before interacted with the world beyond her family.

While she was still on Long Island, she began to plan her career as a writer: she "started sending poems off to magazines before she was 18." In 1911, when she was nineteen, she had her first work published, a poem called "The Dreamer." It was an auspicious debut; the work was published in *Harper's*; Zadel had contacted the editors for her granddaughter. The editor, Frank Davis, praised the "fine imaginative work" of the poem. As a gift, he sent along a book by Ambrose Bierce, urging her to pay attention to its "very harsh and brutal" style.

At first, she lived in Queens. Then she and her mother set up an apartment in the Bronx. She lived there until 1915, when she moved to Greenwich Village and began the first phase of her independent life.

Displaying the resourcefulness, blind trust, and sense of entitlement sometimes exhibited by survivors of incest, Djuna Barnes had walked into the "offices of *The Brooklyn Daily Eagle*, . . . straight from the Long Island farm." She was wearing "braids and wooden clogs, fortified by grandmother Zadel's sand cookies (good for digestion)," but still suffering the effects of her past. She asked for a job, and she got one. She published her work before she was twenty years old.

She became a "newspaperman"—her word—a freelance journalist with the *Eagle,* and, later, with *The Morning Telegraph* and *The New York Herald*. She attended art classes at Pratt Institute and at the Art Students' League, and developed her signature Beardsleyesque drawing style. She ignored her Uncle Reon's admonition that she would serve herself far better by taking gym. Her ability to illustrate her articles with line drawings made her work more salable. Before she left for Europe, she had an exhibition of her drawings—"many with strong social commentary against war and poverty."

It was her investigative journalism and her writing that helped her figure out how the world worked for other people. Her writing helped her recuperate. It earned her a living that allowed her to loosen the bonds that had tied her to her family; she frequently made as much as fifteen dollars an article—she could write several in a day—and as much as five thousand dollars a year. It was her writing, her ability to tell her story, that ultimately saved her life.

From the first, Barnes interviewed people who, like her, were outsiders: street people, working people, people with strange occupations, people who were trying to break free from the restrictions their lives had imposed upon them. She pioneered a participatory journalism; according to her biographer, Andrew Field, "no other woman journalist was doing the sort of things [Barnes] was prior to World War I." She learned how it felt to be rescued from a burning building by jumping into a net; she hugged a gorilla. For her most famous article, "How It Feels to Be Forcibly Fed," she underwent the kind of force-feeding imposed upon the Industrial Workers of the World agitator Becky Edelson and hundreds of militant British suffragists on hunger strike. Her arms were bound to her sides so that she couldn't resist; she had to swallow or she would choke to death. She wrote of this experience:

> I saw in my hysteria a vision of a hundred women in grim prison hospitals, bound and shrouded . . . in the rough grip of callous warders, while white-robed doctors thrust rubber tubing into the delicate interstices of their nostrils and forced into their helpless bodies the crude fuel to sustain the life they longed to sacrifice.

In her work, she exhibited a deep respect for victims and survivors of abuse and misfortune. She became a self-styled debunker of the fraudulent. Having lived her life with Wald Barnes, she could detect a phony at forty paces. But she also developed a taste for interviewing the famous: Broadway celebrities, actors, dancers. She wrote nearly two hundred articles during this period. They bore such headlines as "The Tingling, Tangling Tango as 'Tis Tripped at Coney Isle," "Sad Scenes on Sentence Day in the Kings County Court; The Strangest Part of This Drama of Life Is the Audience, Made Up of Shiftless Men Who Never Seem to Tire of Listening to the Tales of the Fallen and Vicious," "Woman Police Deputy Writer of Poetry; Mrs. Ellen O'Grady Not so Keen about Freud, but Believes in the Psychological Movement; Ardently Interested in Her Special Task of Preventing Sex Crime and Confident of Eventual Success!"

Among the scores of people she interviewed were Lillian Russell, Diamond Jim Brady, Flo Ziegfeld, Mother Jones, Billy Jones, Alfred Stieglitz, Jack Dempsey, and David Belasco. Each of her pieces exhibited an eye for the telling detail and an ability to describe the difference between the public persona and the private self. One example, from her interview with Lillian Russell in 1914:

> I could just make her out in the dim room, sitting over there in the corner upon a wide chair like a throne, just make out the high-piled drift of gold that is her hair, the still beautiful eyes, only half-claimed from youth, the smiling mouth that has expressed all that can live within a black satin gown.

In her interview with Stieglitz, she departed from the predictable format and inserted a meditation on the role of the artist as she perceived it and as she practiced it:

> And I thought: From the place I have been standing eternally, looking out toward the world with my eyes and seeing men pass and look back at me, and I cold and lonesome and increasing steadily in mine own sorrow, which is caught like the plague of other men, until I am full and my mouth will hold no more, and my eyes will see no more, and my ears can stand nothing further, then do I begin the steady, slow discharge which is called "wisdom," but which is only that too much the eyes cannot see, the ears cannot hear, the mouth cannot hold.

Barnes gave up journalism because of an ethical dispute with a newspaper. She was asked to cover "a rape case in which a girl in her teens had been raped six times." Her editor at the *Journal American* wanted the victim interviewed. Barnes concocted a story to gain entry to the girl's hospital room. She interviewed the girl, but "felt guilty" about exploiting her, about turning someone else's tragedy into copy. "When she told her editor she would never cover another rape case and would not write a story about this one or give the information to anyone else, he fired her on the spot."

When she left for Europe in 1919 or 1920, when she was twenty-eight, she had become one of the most highly regarded members of the Greenwich Village set, an important and respected columnist, illustrator, playwright, poet, and short-story writer. She published her early works, which concerned dissolution and despair, "the spectacle of human wreckage," in *All-Story Weekly, Munsey's Magazine, Playboy, Vanity Fair, Smart Set, The Dial,* and *The Little Review.* From the first, she wrote works that dealt with incest: "Mother," "Oscar," and "Indian Summer" all appeared in her first collection, *A Book.*

She had traded in her clogs and braids and had become one of the most stylish, elegant, handsome women in Greenwich Village, though her clothes, even her lingerie, were more often than not mended cast-offs from wealthy friends. A memoir of the period records her wearing "a tailored black broadcloth suit with a white ruffled shirtwaist, a tight-fitting black hat, and high-heeled black shoes; and I rarely saw her without a long shepherd's crook which she carried like a Watteau figure in a fête galante." As elegant an appearance as she made, all her living quarters in the Village were modest: she lived in walk-ups whose floors were covered in linoleum, with defective toilets, leaking bathtubs. One of her residences was 42 Washington Square South. John Reed memorialized it in a poem: he caviled about the frigid water, the single bathtub, the dust, the smell, but he concluded that life lived there was "a joy."

Greenwich Village became for Djuna Barnes a place of possibility, a place that stimulated her imagination, a place where she could reinvent herself. She lived there in its heyday of bohemianism and radicalism, when writers, painters, and dramatists flocked there to take advantage of the low rents. Hers was the Greenwich Village of Edna St. Vincent Millay, Floyd Dell, Emma Goldman, Isadora Duncan, Max Eastman, John Reed, Eugene O'Neill, Mabel Dodge Luhan, Margaret Anderson, Jane Heap. It was a place where sensuality was prized, sexual freedom encouraged, middle-class conventions discarded, equality between the sexes tested, the profession of letters respected, life lived for the moment, traditional politics scorned, anarchism and socialism preached, new institutions formed—magazines, clubs, little theaters, experimental schools, picture galleries, poetry societies. "Everywhere was a sense of . . . comradeship and immense potentialities for change."

Djuna loved the Cafe Lafayette, the Brevoort, the bench-sitters in Washington Square Park, the polyglot quality of the Village, where no one was a typical American—its dark-eyed Italian children, Jewish girls, Norwegian immigrants, Japanese servants, artists, vendors, undertakers, scrubwomen, and poets.

The Village provided her with a publisher for her first artistic endeavor, *A Book of Repulsive Women*. The eccentric Bruno Guido issued her work as one of a series of chapbooks. Her poems were about women as victims whose bodies were strewn about the city—prostitutes and suicides, walking zombies whose innocence had been traduced, whose bodies were altars of vice, whose potential had been obliterated by suffering, who were "destroyed from within by unspecified 'crimes.'" These were poems about what might easily have been her story. One, called "Suicide," describes two corpses:

> Corpse A
> They brought her in, a shattered small
>   Cocoon,
> With a little bruised body like
> A startled moon;
> And all the subtle symphonies of her
> A twilight rune.
>
> Corpse B
> They gave her hurried shoves this way
>   And that.
> Her body shock-abbreviated
> As a city cat.
> She lay out listlessly like some small mug
> Of beer gone flat.

She illustrated these poems with macabre, frightening drawings. One was of a "demonic, malformed, naked woman with pointed ears and a lewd smile"; another, "a woman, nude to the waist and grasping the tail of a serpent."

When Guido Bruno asked her why her work was so morbid, she rebutted:

> Morbid? . . . You make me laugh. This life I write and draw and portray is life as it is, and therefore you call it morbid. Look at my life. Look at the life around me. Where is this beauty that I am supposed to miss? . . . Joy? I have had none.

In the Village, she made friends: Mabel Dodge Luhan, whose salon she attended; Eugene O'Neill, when he was just starting out; Margaret Anderson, founder of *The Little Review;* Jane Heap, Anderson's lover; the eccentric Dadaist poet Baroness Elsa von Freytag von Loringhoven, famous for her shaved and vermilion-lacquered head, for wearing canceled postage stamps plastered to her cheeks, for painting her lips black, and powdering her face a bright yellow, for wearing a coal scuttle on her head.

Barnes had a brief career as an actress. She appeared as a nun in Paul Claudel's *The Tidings Brought to Mary* and in Leo Tolstoy's *The Power of Darkness.* But she was "terrified" of being onstage, and gave up acting in favor of writing her own plays.

Her "exciting and baffling" plays—*Three from the Earth, An Irish Triangle, Kurzy of the Sea* (starring Ida Rauh)—were performed by the Provincetown Players. One was on the same bill with *The Dreamy Kid* by Eugene O'Neill. She learned that she could command an audience. This was where she tried to put her past behind her by using it in her art.

In later years, she recalled how the plays she saw in New York originated in the lives of their authors. It was through the Provincetown Playhouse that she learned how to mine her life for her art. Members of the Playhouse, she remembered,

> used to sit in groups and recall our earlier and divergent histories. One would say, "I was well smacked by my mother for chewing the paint off the gate post." . . . So we talked, and so we went our separate ways home, there to write out of that confusion which is biography when it is wedded to fact. . . . Of such things were our plays made. Eugene O'Neill wrote out of a dark suspicion that there was injustice in fatherly love. . . . I wrote out of a certitude that I was my father's daughter.

From the time of this first foray into living in the world, though she could be a superb conversationalist, especially known for her barbed and sardonic repartee, she was also reserved and withdrawn, a legacy from her life in the Barnes enclave. Margaret Anderson remarked that "Djuna would never talk. She never allowed herself to be talked to. She said it was because she was reserved about herself. . . . It embarrassed her to approach impersonal talk about the personal element."

During the Greenwich Village years, she had many lovers, always playing the role of the "ferocious but loving martyr." Having been reared in an abusive atmosphere, it was difficult for her not to re-create the patterns of childhood. Her taste ran to alcoholic, abusive partners.

She once reported that she had had nineteen male lovers before "giving up" on men and "taking a female lover." Among the male lovers were Lawrence Vail (who eventually married Peggy Guggenheim), Putzi Hanfstaengl (who became Hitler's official pianist and helped hide him after the Munich Beer Hall Putsch), Jimmy Light (an actor who eventually became codirector of the Provincetown Players), Marsden Hartley (a painter, a "pale, hawk-faced man, whose appearance was as abstract as some of his paintings"), and Horace Liveright, the up-and-coming publisher. She was attracted to men who drank, who were wild, who were homosexual or bisexual, or who were indifferent to her.

One of the most important loves of her Village life was the poet Mary Pyne. She was married to the hobo poet, Harry Kemp; she worked for the Provincetown Players, acting in Eugene O'Neill's *Before Breakfast*. She had "Titian red hair, gray-blue eyes and creamy skin and red lips"; she "combined the charm of Mimi in *La Bohème* with the spiritual beauty of a Della Robbia Madonna."

Djuna nursed Mary Pyne during her terminal illness and believed she would never recover from Mary's death. Mary Pyne was Djuna's first serious lesbian relationship. To Mary, she dedicated her elegy "Six Songs of Khalidine." One reads, in part:

> The flame of your red hair does crawl and creep
> Upon your body that denies the gloom
> And feeds upon your flesh as 't would consume
> The cold precision of your austere sleep—
> And all night long I beat it back, and weep.
>
> It is not gentleness but mad despair
> That sets us kissing mouths, O Khalidine.
> Your mouth and mine, and one sweet mouth unseen
> We call our soul. Yet thick within our hair
> The dusty ashes that our days prepare.

After Mary Pyne's death, she lived with Courtenay Lemon for two years and married him. For a time, they lived in a room in a seventeen-room apartment at 86 Greenwich Avenue, let by James and Susan Light (associated with the Provincetown Players). The apartment at 86 Greenwich Avenue was the center of Village artistic life, but the accommodations were modest. She was in awe of Lemon's intellect, and, at first, she was devoted to him:

> My husband was a scholar, he really had a fine mind. . . . He works on the *American* to earn a living—and uses his money to buy books. . . . He's writing a book on the philosophy of criticism—but it'll never be finished. He's been working on it seven years. . . . He had me absolutely stunned so that I didn't know whether I was coming or going. . . . Oh, you couldn't pry me away from him.

Eventually, she grew to dislike the restrictions he placed on her behavior: "he thought earrings were very foolish. . . . I couldn't stand it any longer." But something more serious than his dislike of her earrings forced the relationship apart. In 1919, she wrote him, telling him to leave her alone:

> Dear Courtenay,
> You promised that you would not trouble me again—I have nothing to say & nothing which I want to listen to.
> I know this sounds unkind—but it is final—I can't be tortured any more.
> Djuna

When she left for Paris, he stayed behind, and their relationship dissolved.

East Fifty-fourth Street
New York City
April 1940

After Djuna Barnes's first stay in the asylum, she came out, moved back in with her mother, and "crack[ed] up" yet again. A key feature of this breakdown was that Barnes lost her sense of self. "I *have* forgotten who I am; my family have completed the estrangement," she wrote Emily Coleman.

This time, one of Djuna's brothers admitted the family's motives:

[What] my brothers were trying to force me to do . . .—[was] "to crack up and crawl to me for help, when I'll give her another dose of the Sanatorium."

Saxon knew that living with Elizabeth would be pernicious for Djuna. He himself had had a "nervous breakdown and underwent psychiatric treatment" soon before Djuna returned from Paris; his doctor told him "he must no longer live with his mother."

Another dose of the sanatorium is just what the family gave Djuna. The second time, though, she resisted treatment. She realized her family had "betrayed her." Undaunted, Djuna "vowed to write a book about them." This book would be nonfiction. She vowed to "write about them all in a biography—there is no reason any longer why I should feel for them in any way but hate."

That work of nonfiction in time became transmuted into the play *The Antiphon*. Knowing she would write this work, knowing that she would explode the Barnes family's secrets, kept her sane. In the forty-two years remaining in her life, she never again lost control. She never again entered an asylum.

After her second stay in the asylum, she was returned to her mother's apartment. This time, though, she was not acquiescent. Her attitude toward her mother had undergone a major transformation. She could no longer keep her rage bottled up, keep her resentment and anger under control. She had discovered that in her absence her family had gone through her papers and burned the manuscript of a book she had begun to write.

She and her mother quarreled: Djuna "said things to her mother she had tried for months not to say." She called her mother "Mrs. King Lear."

Elizabeth Barnes threw Djuna out of her apartment, out onto the streets of New York City. Barnes had no money, no place to live, nowhere to go. Her brothers, who could have given her money, chose not to. Elizabeth and the family knew that, given her condition, she might die, but she was put out anyway.

For five days, she lived on the streets of New York City, wandering about. For five days, she had nothing to eat. She was transformed into one of the desperate street creatures she had written about many years ago in *A Book of Repulsive Women*, a street-dweller she had feared she might become:

> Barriers and heart both broken—dust
>   Beneath her feet.
> You've passed her forty times and sneered
>   Out in the street.
>
> A thousand jibes had driven her
>   To this at last. . . .

The ordeal hardened her against her family. No longer able to find excuses for Elizabeth and for her brothers, she understood that her life was in danger, that her family was vicious. She compared her mother to Hitler. She now knew that her mother was responsible for the torture she had suffered. She knew that her mother could kill her.

Barnes wrote Emily Coleman about what she had endured: "I have been put out by my mother—so I've not eaten for five days—I'm very weak—excuse—I can hardly write." She realized that her mother wanted her dead: "she hates me (as you say) for not being her—with a most deadly hatred—she'd love to see me dead, and yet she'd cry." This view of her mother as a sinister killer, hiding behind the guise of a muddle-headed fool, was new. Barnes had always understood her father's lethal potential. But she had not realized that her mother, too, could be deadly. From this time on, her health was not good, and she suffered increasingly from asthma and other ailments.

In those five days on the streets, Djuna Barnes learned something she would never forget. It became the controversial cornerstone of her play *The Antiphon*: a mother can collaborate with a father in a daughter's abuse and then want her dead because of what she suffered. Barnes rewrote the myth of mother as nurturer. In *The Antiphon*, Elizabeth Barnes, as Augusta, becomes the Hitlerian mother who watches her daughter being tortured, who wants her to die, who kills her.

5 Patchin Place
Greenwich Village
September 1940

In September 1940, with some assistance from her friends (Helen Westley, Eleanor Fitzgerald, Arlie Lewin, Janet Flanner, and others whom she routinely asked for help), Djuna Barnes was able to move into an inexpensive, tiny room-and-a-half apartment in Patchin Place on a cul-de-sac in Greenwich Village, near the Jefferson Market Courthouse and Women's Prison.

Around the small courtyard were ten little brick houses with Georgian cornices, divided into more than fifty apartments. At the end of the courtyard was a stout iron gate that shut Patchin Place off from the bustle of Greenwich Village.

From her windows, she could look into the courtyard; in the spring, she could see the ailanthus trees in bloom. She called Patchin Place her "own little prison courtyard." This place held fond memories for her. In her early Greenwich Village years, she had attended a dramatic performance of Yeats's *The King's Threshold* staged there one heavenly summer night. Her lover, Mary Pyne, had "played the princess, dressed all in blue with her long red and gold hair hanging down her back."

The apartment cost Djuna $49.50 a month. The neighborhood had every amenity—restaurants (a Chinese restaurant became a favorite), the Jefferson Market, which delivered groceries. It could take her four hours to write and revise her shopping list. She typed the list of groceries she needed—a quart of milk, a half pound of smelts. It would become interspersed with lines of poetry that came to her—". . . that balanced beast, the unicorn./Abused by too much love."

Before she decided to live alone, Djuna thought she might stay awhile, perhaps even live, with Emily Coleman and her new husband in Arizona. Emily had, after all, been the recipient of the most important of Barnes's secrets; Emily had saved her once before, in Paris.

After Emily returned from Europe, she went to Arizona and married a cowboy named Jake. He had never seen a lesbian before, and when Djuna climbed off the train after an interminable three-day ride, he hated her at once. Djuna sat on the dusty veranda of their ranchhouse in Concho, which she called "the shithouse-on-a-distant-hill," and watched her friend's marriage disintegrate before it had even begun. Emily herself was partly responsible; she was in one of her berserk phases; she became verbally and physically abusive. She taunted and infuriated Djuna, comparing her work to that of Henry Miller, a writer whom Djuna detested. After the visit ended, Barnes told a friend that "nothing in her life compared with the horror of her visit" to Coleman. It marked a turning point in their relationship; it proved to Barnes that it was time for her to try to go it alone.

Barnes would live in Patchin Place for the rest of her life. She was now entering what she called her "Trappist" period. In the early years, before she gave up drinking, she would meet Peter Jack, an English journalist, at the White Horse, a landmark Village watering hole. Her supporter in her Paris years, Peggy Guggenheim, provided Barnes with a stipend of $40 a month. It was "regularly late," though it could be counted upon. She upped the stipend to $100 a month in 1942, and later raised it to $300 a month, quipping that Barnes didn't need much money to live on because she was an artist and had "an inner life."

Barnes devoted herself to the quiescent solitude she now required to do her work. She devoted herself to connecting with the pain of what she had lived through.

At Patchin Place, she created a haven where she could feel protected. Her work, which dredged up all the pain she had endured in her life, required her to keep herself free from other upset, from other crises. She had had far too many of those in her life. No more striding along boulevards arm in arm with a lover. No more going to parties. No more staggering from one bar to another. No more slipping and falling on dance floors. No more being punched in the face by spurned suitors. No more razzle-dazzle. No more chasing notoriety. No more lovers.

Here, in this very small place, Djuna Barnes tried to heal herself. She gave up drinking; she gave up smoking. She saw people regularly but on a carefully controlled schedule. Her physical wants were few and easily satisfied by the small amounts of money she received from her publications and from generous friends.

She gave up close personal relationships, though she corresponded, through the years, with many old friends. Her most im-

portant correspondent in this period was T. S. Eliot. He urged her
to work; he called her "the greatest living genius." She feared she
was succumbing to "laziness and inertia," but his praise and promise to help in the publication of her work surely gave her courage
to face the greatest challenge of her writing career.

In the past, she had survived by "the lack of ability to hold the
memory too close." In writing *The Antiphon,* she would set herself
the task of remembering, of turning memory into testimony, and of
turning testimony into art. In the forty years she spent in Patchin
Place, in the last half of her life, she "released but five new works
for publication: a short article (1941); one story (1942); . . . two
poems (1969, 1971)," and *The Antiphon* (1958). It was the most important work of the last half of her life, the work that cost her the
most effort.

A few years before Elizabeth Barnes died, Djuna had asked her
to help her with her project, to recall their shared past. She had
given her mother one last chance to show that she was sorry for the
part she had played in her daughter's abuse. Elizabeth had refused:

> No! I do not have any wish to go back into the past to recover any
> of the memories I have and am trying [to] put behind me. And
> even if I did do so, the best facts are enof. Uppermost I have
> forgotten so much. What I do remember is not worth the trouble to
> put on paper and then too, I do not feel after Ryder, that I want
> anymore of me exploited.

After she finished reading *Ryder,* Elizabeth had thrown her
daughter's book out the window. For Elizabeth, the great evil
of her life was not what had been done to Djuna, but that Djuna
had written about it. Elizabeth had once remarked that "it was like
a coil of snakes around her neck having her children still alive."

5 Patchin Place
Greenwich Village
1945–1956

Djuna Barnes had conceived of *The Antiphon*, and had begun taking notes for it, as early as 1936, after a visit to Oakham, her mother's ancestral home in England. Barnes transformed a dilapidated manor house she had visited near her mother's far more modest home into Burley Hall, the setting for her play. It became the derelict home of the Hobbs family, where a daughter confronts her mother with their shared past.

But it was not until after her mother's death in 1945 that Barnes felt free to seriously begin *The Antiphon*, to unleash her torrent of rage at Elizabeth. Now that Barnes's mother was dead and Barnes lived in her own private space, she believed she could work without fearing that her efforts would be destroyed, as they had been when she had been incarcerated in 1939 and 1940 and the family had gone through all her papers and had burned her manuscript. On a small piece of cardboard, she typed the words "Do Not Disturb!" She tacked the sign up on her door. This was a warning to potential intruders that she would tolerate no abuse of her privacy; this was her domain, her protected world.

The Antiphon marked the first work in which Barnes excoriated her mother overtly. In writing it, she transformed Elizabeth into Augusta Hobbs, whom she called a "Carrion Eve."

In the drama, Barnes reveals everything about the life she has lived. She enacts every horrifying secret the Barnes clan tried so desperately to prevent her from revealing. In the person of the aging Miranda, an obvious self-portrait, she describes how, throughout her life, she was kept in domestic captivity within the religious cult her father created; how he tried to exert total control over her by seducing her into becoming a willing victim (like his wife), into allowing him to rape her. When she would not, he sold her into sexual slavery, and paid someone else to rape her before her brother as witness. She describes how her father's relentless abuse, and her mother's compliance, wore her down so that she agreed to the rape because the family willed it.

The Antiphon is set in 1939, within a world at war, amid the wreckage of Burley Hall. Barnes intended it as "an allegory for the collapse of western civilization"; but in her view, its "disintegration" is rooted in "child sacrifice."

The play recounts the strange saga of the Barnes clan, and Djuna's life within it. It tells how Victoria Hobbs (Zadel) moves to London with her son Titus (Wald) to use their wits, wiles, and sexuality to better their station; how Victoria establishes a popular salon, attracting the titled and the wealthy; how she "milk[s]" people of their money and finds lovers for her son, a sometime composer. Titus is magnetic, charismatic, and dangerous—a "magic flute player, like Orpheus or the Pied Piper, able to gather and wind women around him as quickly as he wound his lip around a reed."

The Antiphon tells how Victoria and Titus ingratiate themselves with the inhabitants of Burley Hall because they smell money they can acquire with little effort. It chronicles how Victoria promises maternal protection; how Hobbs shocks the Burley household with his liberal views but seduces them with his energy, spontaneity, and lack of inhibition; how Victoria woos a sister, Augusta (Elizabeth), for her son, suggesting that the family is titled, promising a life of excitement and privilege in London, lived among royalty, people of prominence and power, to this naive, unworldly, unsuspecting girl of seventeen, whom Titus marries and impregnates almost immediately.

At first, all is well. Soon Augusta realizes that Titus is sleeping with a woman musician who has come to perform her husband's compositions. In time, more and more mistresses are added. When Augusta complains to her mother-in-law, she is assured that Titus's behavior is necessary. The women are adding money to their coffers, and they are in desperate need of money. When Augusta complains to Titus, he insists that he is ridding the world of whores; he tells her he realizes he is a Mormon and has a right to as many wives as he wants.

Augusta's and Titus's second child is Miranda (Djuna). When her mother sees she has given birth to a girl, she bursts into tears. In time, the other women reproduce also. Titus fills the house with women and babies; all fight, none is happy. Escape from the captivity imposed by Titus is difficult—he has taken any money these women brought with them.

Titus decrees that he and his mother will raise the children. He begins to enunciate his creed, which insists upon his right to polygamy. He writes his philosophy into a formal credo. He starts his own religion, attracting a motley band of neighboring farmers who enjoy hearing that they have the right to fornicate at will, without regard to consequences. He preaches peace and a respect for animals, but he engages in orgies of wanton violence—wringing the necks of roosters; forcing his children to watch as he shoots a homeless dog that shows him some affection, using a shotgun stuffed with his wife's love letters to him; beating his children.

Miranda proves to be gifted. She will not bow to Titus's every whim. She will not become his willing victim, which infuriates him. Augusta does not protect Miranda from her father. She prefers her sons to her daughter, and scolds and punishes Miranda unrelentingly—she wants her "to suffer as she was suffering."

In time, in response to an inquiry by public officials, Titus recants his philosophy and burns his credo. He abandons Augusta and their children and marries another of his concubines. He becomes prematurely senile.

Augusta becomes embittered; she wants vindication for what she has given up, for what she has suffered. She insists that her sons seek out Titus and challenge him, but they ignore her. She holds to her fantasy that Titus is titled, and that she, and not his concubine, deserves every right and privilege.

Aging and alone, she is now without support, but her sons ignore her. Miranda, alone of all her children, responds to her mother's needs and offers help—money she earns by her writing; but Miranda will not follow her mother's suggestion that she prostitute herself to make money to support them.

Soon, the family begins to fear what Miranda will write about them. They find and destroy a work she has been composing about the family. Together, Augusta and her sons plot to institutionalize Miranda; Miranda discovers the plot and flees to Europe.

Djuna Barnes devoted more than twenty years of her artistic life to thinking about and writing and shaping *The Antiphon*, the most significantly autobiographical of her works. When interviewed about the sources of her art, she remarked that both the character Ryder in her novel of that name and Titus in *The Antiphon* were based upon her father:

Yes, Ryder and Titus, they are my father. Where did the basic story come from? From my life. Every writer writes out of his life. Ryder is my father. And Titus.

She told a friend, "if there was anything I wanted to know about her family, I should simply read her books."

At Patchin Place, she created the conditions under which she felt safe so that she could do her work. She lived in her austere apartment, writing in bed, sometimes from as early as five in the morning. Through these years, she carefully controlled her wants and her needs. While writing the play, she had many accidents. In 1949, she fell over a dictionary on the floor and broke some ribs. In 1951, she fell again, and fractured her spine. In 1952, she fell and broke her arm. It was as if writing a work about how she had been persecuted compromised, in part, her ability to care for herself.

Djuna Barnes was working in earnest on *The Antiphon* by 1949, but it took her until 1956 to complete a draft that satisfied her. She finished the play under the threat of a "doctor's death sentence."

He told her that she had cancer and would have to enter [the] hospital immediately, otherwise she would not live more than six months. She told him not to be ridiculous, that she had no intention of doing any such thing until she completed the play on which she was working.

In all, she produced twenty-nine drafts—four different versions—of the play before she was happy enough with it to send it out to readers.

For Barnes, writing was not a matter of invention: it was a "reconstruction" of events that had taken place in the writer's life. On the cover of her own copy of one of her drafts of the work, she wrote: "This is my story, its crying of a woman and a dog."

Working and reworking the story of her life gave her a certain mastery over her trauma. Her work would be performed in public, before an audience witnessing what had been done to her; this would enable her to reconnect with a community. This was a necessary stage for her healing. *The Antiphon* is the single most important, most powerful work in which she bore witness to the life she had been forced to live: T. S. Eliot called it a "cosmic explosion."

She wrote lines as they came to her, on the backs of envelopes, in the margins of shopping lists. She made revisions along the edges of her typed pages in pencil or in different-colored inks. Sometimes there were so many changes on a sheet that they obliterated the typed lines, and eventually she would make further changes to these inked or penciled revisions.

Over the years, she changed her characters' names; rewrote her prose as blank verse; deepened her imagery; deleted a Greek-like chorus; took notes on Dante's *Inferno*, another journey into hell, and incorporated imagery from that work in hers. Most importantly, she changed the tone of the work from sardonic, brutal comedy to high tragedy. In time, she dropped the jollity that was inappropriate to her story. In time, she could render the events of her life with the appropriate emotional density, with the appropriate emotional affect.

In time, she incorporated in her work her knowledge that victims of family violence, of crimes against children, suffered the same agonies as victims of Nazi concentration camps. They became the same people. They became the "living dead," unless they could tell their stories, unless others bore witness to their pain, unless they could mourn their suffering. She came to see that her life was the subject for high tragedy. The only appropriate language for rendering it was iambic pentameter, the language of Shakespeare.

The theme of *The Antiphon* became the damnation wreaked upon helpless, trusting children by their parents, and the torment inflicted by women whose responsibility was to nurture and protect their children. As Barnes phrased it in an early version of the play: "How is it that women who love children/So often damn the children that they have[?]"

The title (which means "The Response") shows that Barnes intended her work as a corrective answer to the perverted version of her personal history encoded in Barnes family lore. She wanted it known that she was not perverse from birth; her life had become blighted because of the way she had been treated. When Augusta harshly judges her daughter in the work, her son Jonathan answers:

> Your daughter is yourself,
> But only more offended.
> She's not you alone; she's also what you called for;
> She is response.

Barnes saw the work's implications reaching far beyond the exposure and relief of her own personal pain. In an early version of the play, she wrote, "Look at any nursery, it is the world!" Her "antiphon" answers and corrects romanticized distortions of childhood experience for those countless children, those "prisoners of childhood" (to use Alice Miller's phrase), whose lives have been compromised and damaged by captivity, neglect, and abuse.

The Antiphon portrays a world in which the "souls" of children, rather than being born into love and possibility, are "hanged upon umbilical [cords]." The father exists as a demonic force, to be sure. But the emotional core of this play is the daughter's rage at her betrayal by a mother who will not protect her, a mother who allows her husband to do anything he chooses.

The central theatrical event in *The Antiphon* became attempted rape by her father, and the rape that Djuna herself had experienced. But in her play, the mother is forced to witness what she had protected herself from seeing. And Barnes suggests that Miranda is raped twice, once by her father, once by his disciple. It is a brutal, shocking, powerful scene without parallel in the history of the theater. In comparison, the famous battle between Martha and George in Edward Albee's *Who's Afraid of Virginia Woolf?* seems tame.

Rather than taking responsibility for her part in the tragedy, rather than acknowledging her daughter's pain or helping her heal from the ravages of her past, the mother actively becomes her daughter's persecutor. As a child, the daughter had realized that her mother would not love her unless she allowed her mother to hurt her. One day Miranda comes into the house with a switch she has cut from a hedge and asks her mother to whip her for a crime she suspects she has committed but can't remember, so that she can become the child her mother desires, a child her mother can love. In the concluding scene of *The Antiphon*, mother and daughter are locked together in combat that takes the lives of both.

Barnes had created a tragic drama in three acts. It was a chilling, realistic portrayal of the pathology within a family headed by a tyrant, and organized so that each child (but especially Miranda) would be available for sexual abuse disguised as religious ceremony. Barnes showed the cracked cosmology of a woman raped by her father and his disciple. When she was sixteen, "he tried to make her mutton," a piece of meat, to be used sexually by any man he allows to have access to her, including her brothers. The audience witnesses Miranda's terror and self-loathing, her extraordinary bravery in simply continuing to live. As her brother Dudley puts it, "She's afraid of life."

Because Miranda has been ripped open, wherever she goes she sees "a rip in nature": "The world is cracked—and in the breach/My fathers mew." All time for Miranda is rape-time, "this lichen bridled face of time." Rape, the ultimate act of ownership, has imprinted her perpetrator's image on her consciousness for every moment of her life. She can never be free of him; she is his eternal prisoner.

Miranda's brothers are violent and barbarous, true sons of Titus Higby Hobbs; they are their "father's blasphemy." Dudley announces, "When I don't understand a thing—/I kick it!" Referring to Miranda, he says, "We loved the lamb/—Till she turned mutton." He describes her as "our deadly beloved vixen, in the flesh," and asks, "What more could two good brothers want?" This is a family fixated on sex, the males preoccupied with using their phalluses as sexual weapons of power and violence to force the status of victim upon women. Yet their father has violated them, too. Their favorite form of abuse is sodomy—they can dominate her without even seeing her face. When he sees Miranda and Augusta, Miranda's brother Elisha says, "Turn them to the wall"; Elisha "walks behind his love, to kick her down"; he gouges his "chin into the shoulder bone,/And whiz[es his] thumb into the buttock joint."

Jeremy fears Miranda. He understands that because she has been abused, she has a story to tell, and she is potentially deadly. She is a "Manless, childless, safeless document." He describes her leaving Paris "As the leopard . . . forsaking covert for some prowl." Her mother believes that she has been ennobled by suffering even as it has degraded her: "She's one of awful virtue," says Augusta, "and the Devil." Until she is safely dead, she might tell her story. It would defame each of them, and unmask the fraud of Titus Higby Hobbs: "If we take her home and loose her on our ledgers,/She'll blot us up." Because she can bear witness to the atrocities she had suffered, Miranda is a threat. She must be killed.

Act II is a terrifying litany of the perverse, sadistic behavior of Titus Hobbs and the complicity of Augusta. Titus beat his children and perhaps murdered a "bastard child." Dudley recalls how Augusta conspired: "Even as a baby in your arms/You let him lash me with his carriage whip"; "I have against my father that he whipped me/*Before I knew him.*" Augusta can only respond: "That puzzles children—" She is completely brainwashed; she is in his thrall. As Elisha says, "You also did exactly what he told you,/And let him get away with anything." They all lived the lie that they were leading a good Christian life, with Augusta "Knitting 'little things' for the Swahili."

Titus is no religious prophet, no hero, no saint. He is a clever, sadistic monster who has destroyed his children, made perverts of his sons and a prostitute out of his daughter. When confronted with her complicity, Augusta remarks, "I was a victim"; she says, "In my day we did not leave our husbands." Titus exerts his control by making his wife totally dependent upon him; he allows her no friends, permits her no means of self-support, completely erodes her sense of self. When Titus abandons his family, Augusta pushes Miranda into prostitution—it is the only skill Miranda has learned.

The whole family perceives Miranda's incestuous relationship with Titus as privileged; Elisha refers to Titus as Miranda's "first cadet." Yet they see that she alone has offered resistance: "Titus overwhelmed all but Miranda." Augusta feels enormous rivalry with her daughter. She wants to be told "How I was handsomer than she"; she tells Miranda that Titus's "acts to me/Were never gentle, fond nor kind;/Nor he never held nor stroked me anywhere." But she sees her daughter's resistance to her father's will as bringing the family to ruin: "I pushed four children from my list," Augusta says, "One stayed in the web to pull it down—"

Toward the end of the second act, the brothers attack Miranda. They don masks: Dudley a pig's, Elisha an ass's. Elisha tells Miranda she'll be "crawling in my gutters yet": he calls her an "abominable slug of vengeance": he mauls her and calls her "dog." Dudley cheers Elisha on, urging sodomy: "Slap her rump, and stand her on four feet! That's her best position!" Augusta stands by, gleefully chortling, "A game! A game!" When Miranda begs her mother's help to stop the abuse, Augusta replies: "I've seen my daughter die before, and make it."

The brothers drag a model of Hobbs Ark, a "doll's house," onto the stage. In the house are puppets representing members of the family, which Miranda employs to enact her rape. These are the props that will be used to turn Augusta's envy of Miranda into murderous rage.

The brothers thrust the Titus doll into Miranda's hand; Jack alludes to his sister's "marriage" to their father: "You have an husband in the hand,/A slave, a fit of pine to do your bidding./Was this the inch that set you out at hack?/Then 'tis a kissing splinter for a catch,/And you can game again!"

Augusta is pushed against the attic window of the doll's house; she is asked what she sees. She replies, "A bedroom no bigger than my hand." Miranda asks her mother whether she remembers what has happened in that attic room. Augusta replies, "I don't care what you've done, I forgive me." Miranda counters, telling her that what she sees is "Miranda damned, . . ./Dragging rape-blood behind her, like the snail—"

Jack accuses Augusta of turning Miranda into a prostitute by allowing the event to occur: "You made yourself a *madam* by submission/With, no doubt, your apron over head": "between you both, you made/Of that slaughter house a babe's bordel." Augusta admits, "I liked her most when she looked wanted." A brother suggests that Miranda had become pregnant from the rape: "There towered an infant on her face!"

To protect the family's reputation, Titus gives or sells Miranda to an old man who agrees to marry her: "A girl who'd barely walked away sixteen—/Tipped to a travelling cockney thrice that age,/. . . Why?/Titus had him handy—" Miranda has been so worn down by captivity in her father's household, so seduced by her father's claims to being an instrument of God's will, that she submits: "Though Miranda cried at first, like the ewe,/'Do not let him—but if it will atone—'/Offering up her silly throat for slashing."

It pains Miranda to know that her mother has betrayed her: "To think I had a mother should betray me!/Tax me guilty both of audit and default/Tot me up, as idiots their droppings,/And as indifferently, tick off the count." Augusta wants Miranda to forgive her: "Do not stamp me down for tally in the earth," she says. "Be merciful." But Miranda is beyond forgiveness; the most victimized member of the family is expected to pardon those who have degraded her. When Miranda refuses to forgive, refuses to forget, her mother responds by picking up a bell and beating her daughter to death: "You are to blame, to blame, you are to blame—"

* * *

Through the years when her play was in progress, Barnes worked and reworked the rape scene many times. In the fourth draft, the rape scene is more explicit. It describes how Miranda and her father have become locked in mortal combat, and its result:

> She's been knocked into the stubborn ever since
> The hour she drove between our father and the gate,
> Where he tried to make her mutton at sixteen—
> Initiated vestal to his "cause"!
> Self-anointed Titus, Little Corporal,
> Horn mad after false gods; madder still
> For her wild teeth and even wilder kicking.
> And having failed in that, what did he then?
> Hauled her, in an hay-hook, to the barn;
> Left her dangling; while in the field below
> He offered to exchange her for a goat
> With that old farm-hand, Jacobson.

An early draft recounted how Augusta sprinkled salt on the steps to ensure that her husband did not participate in the rape:

> You made you, madame, . . . by submission
> With apron over head, yet strewing salt
>   All up the stairs, and down the hall,
> Did you think to catch your villainy and his
> Counting in the salt, how many feet were whose or hers
> Walked that last mile? . . .
> Thrown in with a cockney, thrice her age
> . . . And left to it, tho she cried out . . .
> "Do not let it be, but if he will it—!"
> Showing what a hash her mind was made of.
> . . . [A]n abbatoir where like reindeer stretch out the throat for
>   slashing
> So I say, both you and your husband Titus
> In the setting, and denying of her,
> Made of that doll's room a babe's *bordel*.

The Antiphon, then, reenacted the most significant outrage perpetrated upon Djuna Barnes in a childhood filled with abuse. When she was sixteen, Titus/Wald Barnes had tried to rape his daughter; he wanted to possess her as a high priest or godhead. He had become preoccupied with sexual ceremonies in various religions. He forced her up against the pasture gate. But she struggled, biting and kicking him, fighting him off. Titus/Wald dragged her to the barn, where he threaded a hay-hook through her clothing and hoisted her up in the barn like a heifer. He gathered witnesses around, told them she was the first virginal sacrifice to his new religion. To complete the ceremony, he exchanged her for a goat, choosing an older man to perform the next phase of the sacrifice.

She was dragged into the house and up to a top-floor bedroom, the brothers watching, the mother not stopping it, and locked in with this older man. Miranda/Djuna, in a state of shock and dissociation, acquiesced to save her life. While the older man raped her, Miranda/Djuna cried out, "Do not let him, but if it will atone." Titus, hearing his daughter's cries, happily rubbed his hands together; Augusta put her apron over her head and threw salt on the stairs. Miranda crawled across the floor, leaving a stream of blood behind her, crying, "My mother, O my mother." Her brother Jeremy, forced to watch, was utterly terrorized and never forgot what he had seen.

T. S. Eliot had been an enormous support to Barnes through the years when she was creating *The Antiphon*. When she sent it to him for criticism, though, he lodged serious objections to Act II. He urged a "drastic cutting" of material in the middle of the act, where the rape scene occurs. He reminded her that in drama, it was necessary not "to overstep the limits of the essential."

Although Eliot did not directly object to the sexual violence at the center of this act, he made his meaning clear. This was the second time Eliot helped Barnes edit her work. The first time, he worked with her on *Nightwood*. Then, too, he urged her to expunge a telling of the very same event from her novel—a daughter's being sold into sexual slavery because she would not submit to rape by her father.

Barnes responded by slashing nearly three hundred lines. She deleted the entire hay-hook scene. The most overt explication of her father's bestiality and her mother's collusion never made it into the final version of the play. It was an ill-considered decision, though she capitulated to ensure the play's publication.

Removing the scene rendered Miranda's character far less understandable than it had been. When the play was published, critics lodged complaints about the characters' inscrutability, objections they might not have made had Barnes insisted on retaining this scene.

Cambridge, Massachusetts
May 21, 1956

Barnes had hopes that her play might be staged and become popular. The arcane *Ryder*, after all, had become a best-seller. She trusted that the experience she had portrayed in *The Antiphon* was common enough that her play would attract a wide audience.

Apart from a staged reading for her and some friends, *The Antiphon* received but one public dramatic performance during her lifetime. She reluctantly admitted that the work she had labored over for so many years would be performed rarely and for a limited audience. "In my lifetime," she wrote, "I'll probably not know what fate the play is to have. But the point is I really shouldn't care. If ever a thing were truly written for the writer this is it. This may be what is objectionable. If so it has to be so."

The Antiphon was performed for the first time on May 21, 1956, by the Poets' Theatre Company in the Phillips Brooks House in Cambridge, Massachusetts. Edwin Muir had arranged the event to coincide with a trip T. S. Eliot was making to the United States so that Eliot could attend the performance.

The reading was a disaster. When the actress who was to read the part of Miranda was presented to Barnes, the playwright screamed in shock at her inappropriateness. When a second actress was proposed, Barnes complained. This one was too fat; all the actresses were too fat; didn't they realize that Miranda and Augusta were thin, thin, thin? The players had not rehearsed, and so were unable to render the complex verse tragedy in any meaningful way. In places where Barnes "wanted quiet taut conflict, they thumped, scolded, and bickered." They stopped the reading to ask the dramaturge what she meant by this line or that one. With each new question, Barnes grew "more and more savage" in her responses to the actors. The small, select audience—Edwin and Willa Muir, T. S. Eliot, I. A. Richards—grew increasingly disquieted, and squirmed in their seats. Barnes began to clench her teeth. She whispered her disgust with the performance to Eliot, who sat at her side.

She had chosen to wear a white turban, tilted to one side. By the end of the performance, it had unravelled somewhat, taking on the appearance of "a loose combat bandage."

Of this event, Barnes wrote, "a more wretched reading than that of the Cambridge occasion I can't imagine." But like the professional she was, she remained undaunted. She turned to work immediately afterward, trying to make the drama more intelligible, shortening and simplifying the more elaborate speeches, revising, this time, with the needs of actors in mind. The changes she made after the Cambridge fiasco resulted in a play more amenable to public performance. The next time the play was performed, it met with great critical success.

1958

The Antiphon was first published in London by Faber and Faber in January 1958. Shortly after that, an American edition was published in New York by Farrar, Cudahy and Straus. The work received twenty-five reviews. Most critics remarked upon the difficulty of the play's language. An unnamed reviewer (James Burns Singer), writing in the *Times Literary Supplement*, complained:

> Not even Bertolt Brecht has gone to such lengths to alienate his audience. . . . And it is not only her potential audience that Miss Barnes has alienated but producers and actors as well. Her chief weapon in this process of alienation is not her plot or her setting but something more fundamental, her language.

But he also said, "Djuna Barnes not only possesses the style of her period, she helped form it."

After reading review after review lambasting her for her language, Barnes realized that the fundamental difficulty lay not in her style, but in her subject matter: "Is it so blasted difficult indeed." No, she concluded. The critical response was a warning that she had written "not only quite enough, but too much." She had published her work for people who did not want to hear about such matters. She had written the unspeakable. Her work made her readers uncomfortable. They would rather pretend these events could not exist.

Her work had too graphically, too violently enacted a taboo act onstage. Though readers might accept a child's rape, presenting that rape on the stage made viewers participants—either victims or perpetrators of violence, uncomfortable roles for theatergoers. Peggy Guggenheim had warned her friend that *The Antiphon* would present a problem for its audience: "It will terrify a lot of people—It says too much they are afraid to know."

But Barnes wondered, too, whether the highly personal nature of her drama had rendered it too difficult for others to follow. In further revisions she made to the text after reading the critics' responses, she tried to clarify the lines they had singled out as especially objectionable; she continued to do everything she could to make the work accessible, but she insisted that the elevated language of verse drama was the only one appropriate to describe Miranda's tragedy.

Stockholm
February 1961

The Cambridge performance led to a triumphant full-fledged production in Stockholm.

While Edwin Muir and Dag Hammarskjöld, U.N. secretary-general, were being awarded honorary degrees at Cambridge University, the two conversed, and Muir praised Barnes and *The Antiphon* so effusively that Hammarskjöld read the play.

He thought it an important work, and contacted Karl Ragnow Gierow, director of the Royal Dramaten Theatre in Stockholm. Hammarskjöld and Gierow asked Barnes for permission to translate *The Antiphon* and to produce it in Sweden. She knew translating the work would be difficult; she cautioned Gierow that there were "layers of meaning one within another." But they were undaunted, and Hammarskjöld became a champion of Barnes's work and a cotranslator of her novel *Nightwood*.

The Antiphon opened in Stockholm in February 1961. A dramatic headline in a Swedish newspaper proclaimed: "Controversial Genius: Exclusive U.S. Authoress in World Premiere at Dramatic Theatre: 'I Wrote Because I Was to Die.' "

On the day of the opening, Hammarskjöld sent roses to Barnes in Patchin Place. The leading Swedish critic Ebbe Linde reviewed it, calling it "an Imagist caviar party." A review by Ivar Harries in the Stockholm *Expressen,* under the headline "The Victorious Antiphon," read:

> —Yes, the audience really caught on, gradually. After the first act people were very awed and a little afraid of showing how lost they felt. The second act had a bewildering but inescapably exciting effect. The third act, which contains the real antiphon, the antiphon between a mother and daughter, broke down all resistance: there was no alternative but to surrender to the dramatic poem. It was one of Dramaten's great performances.

Djuna Barnes had had her triumph. Her work had been understood.

5 *Patchin Place*
Greenwich Village
1962–1982

After completing *The Antiphon,* Djuna Barnes became what she called a *"very* retiring lady." She spent much of her time "trying to keep disorder at bay." She had given up reading newspapers and knew very little about what was going on in the world. She saw friends and acquaintances relatively often, though her increasingly severe asthma and her arthritis severely restricted her mobility. She often required oxygen.

Among those with whom she felt comfortable, there was still the "wonderful little roar of Barnes' laughter." She could still deliver good lines: "Most of them had a good kick of the gutter in them, rendered in exalted but salty language." When praised about her appearance, about the beauty of her eyes, she retorted: "I *used* to be absolutely gorgeous *dear.*"

The Antiphon was the last major work Djuna Barnes completed and published in her lifetime. After she finished the final revisions to that work for its publication, she spent the next twenty years of her life working on one project after another. She wondered whether any of them would ever suit her enough to finish it: "I no longer have any idea when, or if, the poems will please me enough to go on re-writing and endlessly tearing up, a thing I have noticed in the old." She completed a play after *The Antiphon,* but she tore it up because it was too similar to her earlier work.

Except for a few poems and *Creatures in an Alphabet,* she never completed or published another work. She told her friend Hank O'Neal that on any given day she didn't know whether she should try to finish her poetry, burn all her papers, or lie in bed and scream. With *The Antiphon* behind her, Barnes could not imagine writing another major work. "How do writers keep on writing?" she asked a friend:

> Professional ones do, I don't see how my kind can—the "passion spent," and even the fury—the passion made into Nightwood the fury (nearly) exhausted in The Antiphon . . . what is left? "The horror," as Conrad put it.

She embarked upon, but never completed, a long prose poem. She called it by many different names: *The Book of Dan, Laughing Lamentations, Virgin Spring, Derelictions, Phantom Spring.* She described it as a "calm retrospective vision of life by a tired and wise old man." Her biographer Andrew Field, who has read the work, believes it is even more powerful than *The Antiphon.* He describes it as a work written by "an Emily Dickinson in Hell." Its theme? The "old family story." As she wrote in a late poem, "Rite of Spring": "Man cannot purge his body of its theme."

Djuna Barnes was still not finished with the theme that had preoccupied her from the time she began writing—the suffering Wald Barnes had inflicted upon her. But she found it difficult to work: "she seemed to lack the ability to begin where she had left off the day before; she would date a page and start again from the beginning." This resulted in "hundreds of versions of the same poem in various states of completion."

What she hoped for more than anything was to write "even a line of really brilliant verse." Her wish was granted "every now and then," but she could write "just a line or two, and nothing to hook them up." It could take her three or four eight-hour days to produce two or three lines of verse.

She would wake at five, make herself some breakfast, and get to work. Through the day, she fortified herself with drinks of Vegemato and small meals of oatmeal or bread with tea, resting whenever the arthritis in her back rendered further work too difficult. Among her shorter works-in-progress late in life were poems titled "Rakehill" and "The Ponder Rose." She was writing poems about castration and poems about "the famine of a kiss from an old man's mouth."

The work, for the most part, was gruesome and full of pain, as these representative lines show. From "Death and the Wood": "The maggots fasten on her breastbone's meat. . . . Death doth make her sing." From "Lament for Women": "a hood of blood we wear, a shirt of skin." From "Discant": "He lays her carcass on the butt . . . and howls aloud and licks the hand that . . . reeks of blood."

The one long work she completed was the verse alphabet, *Creatures in an Alphabet*, which she dedicated to Emily Coleman. It was published in 1982, after her death. In it, an animal represents each letter of the alphabet. Compared with *The Antiphon* and her other published oeuvre, the work is slight, trivial, even foolish. She herself was "convinced that only two or three of the animal verses [were] worthwhile." For the letter "E," she wrote: "The reason that the Elephant/Is both detained and yet at ease,/Is because it is four trees/that the Lord forgot to plant." Even so, each line had taken her "hundreds of versions in various untouchable piles of paper."

The reason for Djuna Barnes's incapacity to complete another monumental work in her lifetime was that her work had begun to frighten her. Whatever pleasure she had garnered in writing had been intermixed with "terror." To Willa Muir, she wrote:

> I can't (I think) write anymore of my writing . . . frankly I'm afraid of it, physically, I mean, it's like facing old age and death . . . I don't think I have the power now, to do both. The inspiration is

one metamorphosis, the writing is the second, preparation for death the third ... how many bodies can one fight through?

Writing *The Antiphon* had taken too much out of her. She no longer had the fight required to wrestle a long work to completion.

But she did have the courage, with her neighbors, to face down a developer intent on razing her Patchin Place home. Though shy and retiring at this stage of her life, she stood in front of a microphone and proclaimed she would "die if she were forced to move uptown." Then, in a typical Barnesian swerve of meaning, she said that this quiet cul-de-sac must be preserved "so that the young people had a suitable place to practice their mugging." Her notoriety helped the cause; the plan was abandoned.

In her later years, she was far from well. She had emphysema; her heart was weakening; hardening of the arteries was a problem; she had cataracts in both eyes and was almost blind in one; she had problems eating because she had lost so many teeth; she could not control her bowels—a legacy from her grandmother, who regulated her bodily functions in childhood with enemas ("proper ladies always made use of a warm water enema to empty their bowels"), a practice Barnes continued; she also had arthritis of the spine. She took a half dozen or so drugs a day. Among them was Darvon, the primary remedy she relied on for pain. It caused irritability, confusion, irrational behavior. She was afraid that if her health deteriorated further, one of her "family members might put her in a 'snake pit.' "

When contemplating what had happened to her body, she told a friend, "Don't think for a minute this is the real Djuna Barnes. The real Djuna Barnes is dead." In 1966, she wrote Natalie Barney, her old friend and sometime lover from her Paris days, describing what had become of her life:

> What am I doing with my time? But I thought I had gone into all that! Certainly *no* "little friend" and if I saw one I would jump into the river. . . . I live in complete isolation. I have no door-bell, and at one time had no telephone. I have bars at the window, and a police-lock on the front door . . . and all of this not from any additional ferocity to my nature, but merely as means to enduring.

Living? no, enduring yes. Physically I was too ill (my emphysema etc etc better) and entirely too fed up with the horror of what people turn out to be, to be pleased to see or talk with anyone. So I swept my doorstep clear. It is, at times ridiculous, because one would like to talk to someone, now and again, but *not* unless they are "one of ones people." How often do such go by? And then I write, or try to, and of all good things, at the point in life when poetry is *not* written, I write poetry. It pleases me not very often, but you can't just sit and read all day and all night . . . and then after that, I go out and spend of bit of your charming money. Thank you, it is a pleasure to have a little longer rope.

In her seventies, she described herself to a friend as looking like Holbein's portrait of Erasmus. Soon after she turned seventy, she reflected upon her life as an artist. She wrote: "An artist is of course murderer and murdered, a gizzard, which in the end digests itself; the dragon swallowing his tail; the wrestling of transfiguration." She understood that her revenge, her writing *The Antiphon*, was a hostile act. As author, she was a symbolic "murderer." Yet she understood as well that this was a regenerative act, a moment of "transfiguration."

Nonetheless, writing such a work had severe consequences. Just as she was a murderer, so, too, had she "murdered" herself; she had become "the dragon swallowing his tail." In writing the end of her play, in which her mother murders her alter ego, Djuna Barnes reexperienced her mother's murderous rage. She died two deaths of the spirit: the first through living her life, the second in writing about it. The only reason to endure the pain of creation, she believed, was to share the truth of her experience with others. Then they, too, might severely judge those who had injured them, rather than taking on the burden of guilt for crimes committed against them during the better part of a lifetime, as she herself had done. "A great artist," she believed, "gives something to everyone who hears, reads, or looks upon him."

5 Patchin Place
Greenwich Village
1982

In the last months before her death, Djuna Barnes decreed that she wanted "everything in her apartment destroyed, including all the drafts of the long poem" she had been working on for years. Her Patchin Place neighbors were alarmed because "for at least six months, they had smelled smoke coming from her apartment"; Barnes was "destroying her correspondence."

Recognition, which she believed had eluded her for many years, came as she was dying. She was awarded a senior fellowship by the National Endowment for the Arts. Her work had been an acknowledged influence on some of the finest writers of the twentieth century: Anaïs Nin, Carson McCullers, Dylan Thomas, T. S. Eliot, Lawrence Durrell, Malcolm Lowry, Hart Crane, William Faulkner, John Hawkes. Yet she persisted in referring to herself as the most famous unknown writer in the world.

She often overlooked the fact that she had always had her fierce and ardent admirers. Some were so touched by her work that they made pilgrimage to Patchin Place. One was Anaïs Nin, who infuriated Barnes by naming a character after her; Nin said of Barnes's work: "She sees too much, she knows too much, it is intolerable." Another was Carson McCullers, who tried to storm her apartment. McCullers camped out on her stoop, weeping, moaning, and ringing Barnes's bell. Annoyed, Barnes called out her window, "Whoever is ringing this bell, please go the hell away."

In the days before her death, she was in great pain, eased by the opiates administered by a doctor. As she neared her ninetieth birthday, it became a milestone that she awaited. She endured her suffering with the same stoic calm that had seen her through so many of her life's tragic moments.

It wasn't that she didn't want to die. She just wanted to reach ninety. Death in one sense would be a release from suffering. Near the end of her life, she asked her friend Hank O'Neal: "What if this isn't all there is? What if there's a hereafter? What if I die, then wake up and I'm sitting on a cloud? . . . What if I have to put up with this misery forever?"

Djuna Barnes died on June 18, 1982, six days after her ninetieth birthday. One of her last entries in her notebook was the following:

Blaspheme not God. For we are only what we've thought we are.

Not satisfied with this sentiment, she took her pen, filled with green ink. She crossed out the final word—"are"—and replaced it with the word "were."

She wanted her poem "The Walking-mort" to stand as her epitaph. Its lines suggest her need to rectify the sins of the past with her pen and the murderous, vengeful rage that was the most important impetus to her art.

> Call her walking-mort; say where she goes
> She squalls her brush with blood. I slam a gate.
> Report her axis bone it gigs the rose.
> What say of mine? It turns a grinning grate.
> Impugn her that she baits time with an awl.
> What do my seasons then? They task a grave.
> So, shall we stand, or shall we tread and wait
> The mantled lumber of the buzzard's fall
> (That maiden resurrection and the freight)
> Or shall we freeze and wrangle by the wall?

According to her wishes, Djuna Barnes's body was cremated, her ashes scattered in a dogwood grove on Storm King Mountain, where she was born. It was her first home, where she had grown, and where she had suffered so much agony and pain. It was the place from which she sought emotional release. Yet it was to this place that she wanted her final remains returned.

Djuna Barnes had gone home.

In the days before she died, Djuna Barnes's "little room was jammed with flowers and friends" who came to say farewell.

On her ninetieth birthday, Djuna Barnes received the greatest gift a writer can receive. On that day, according to Fran McCullough, her editor, patron, and friend, "something amazing happened."

A fan of hers, from Germany, "a beautiful young man with

golden curls who loved her work passionately, flew in for her birthday." He came without invitation; he came without knowing whether she would see him; he came because he needed to tell her something that he believed she needed to hear about the importance of her work to him:

> She lay sleeping deep into her pillows, helped by her pain drugs, but she roused herself for this young man and as he tenderly stroked her face and spoke to her about her work and her meaning in life, she grew completely radiant.

On one of the last days of her life, Djuna Barnes met her audience in the person of this young man. His pilgrimage, his message to her, and his love for her work eased her passing.

5

"A DESPERADO OF LOVE":

Henry Miller, June Miller, and *Crazy Cock*

It's true, I will admit in passing, that
hatred and vengeance were the mainspring
[of my writing]. But beyond that . . . there was
the idea of separation. I had to break with the
past, my own past particularly. Having
accomplished this I no longer felt the need
of hatred and vengeance.

—HENRY MILLER
Henry Miller's Hamlet Letters

Office of the Parks Commission
Queens, New York
May 21–22, 1927

Henry Miller sat at the typewriter in his office at the Parks Commission in Queens, writing. It was well after midnight. He had been at it for more than seven hours. He was exhausted, but he had eleven or so more hours of work ahead of him.

At five o'clock the evening before, after the office had emptied, he had taken a blank sheet of paper and rolled it into his typewriter. He already had put in a solid day's work performing "nonsensical labors" as a county park employee, another dead-end job. His friend Jimmy Pasta had gotten Miller this job after bumping into Miller when he was in trouble, wearing ragged clothes, without a penny in his pocket.

In a mood of "utter despair," he had begun to outline the novel he told himself he would have to write someday. It would be about his life with his second wife, June, a life that had begun with such hope and promise, which he now felt sure was ending. He called it "My Doomsday Book." He believed he was writing his epitaph.

Though Henry was married when he met June for the first time, he knew immediately that he would throw over his old life for her. He wrote her wild, intoxicated letters. He wanted to tell her that, in falling in love with her, he had become "a desperado of love."

Now those idyllic days were far behind. No longer love's bold and reckless outlaw, he had instead been subjected to a "veritable

pogrom of love." He had become a victim of love; he had been crucified on the cross of his own desire.

A month or so before, on a Saturday morning in April, while he
was out working, June had left home without telling him she was
going. She had "fled the coop" and sailed for Paris with her lesbian
lover, known as Jean Kronski. When his friends asked where June
was, he would lie, say she was "on vacation" in Europe. Since she
had abandoned him, he had been living "the life of a full-blooded
schizerino."

He had a few postcards from June—of the Eiffel Tower, the Arc
de Triomphe, and Notre Dame—which he propped on the mantel
in his parents' home, where he was living. They made him dream
of being in Paris himself. And though she had kept in touch with
him by cable, her cables were really only demands for money. She
had been gone barely a week when the first one came, and he had
sent her a draft for fifteen dollars. He believed he owed it to her;
for most of their marriage, she had supported him.

June hadn't responded to his desperate, pleading letters asking
when she would return, and what the food was like, and whether
she had sampled any fine wines, or seen any famous artists. Although she hadn't told him she would never come back, Miller
feared that their marriage would never be the same, that one day
it would end.

But just that day he had received a letter from June that gave
him some hope. She wrote him that Jean Kronski had skipped off
to Algiers with a crazy Austrian writer by the name of Alfred
Perles. June herself was on her way to Vienna with friends. Perhaps
there was some hope. Perhaps she and Jean had separated.

The afternoon before he sat down to outline his book, Miller
had heard the news that Charles Lindbergh had landed at Le
Bourget in Paris, successfully completing his historic solo Atlantic
crossing. The contrast between Lindbergh's spectacular achievement and sudden glory and his own thwarted efforts to become a
successful writer had made him feel even more despondent, even
more isolated and alone than before.

Lindbergh had flown solo across the Atlantic Ocean, and he
himself couldn't afford the fare to go and seek out June. He had
tried to raise the money, and had gone as far as soliciting some

from a man he had only just met. When the man put his hand on Miller's knee, he realized he couldn't go through with it.

He was thirty-six years old, yet he had to move back in with his parents because he couldn't afford to live alone *and* send June the money she required. He had skulked out of their old apartment in the middle of the night, carrying only a few manuscripts, his old Funk & Wagnalls dictionary, and a pair of her silk stockings. These he kept close to him, in the pocket of his overcoat, where he could touch them.

The last time he had moved back in with his parents, when he and June had run out of money, his mother had been so embarrassed that whenever someone had come to the door, she had made him put his typewriter away and hide in his clothes closet. "Writing," he remarked, "was like a crime I was committing." He would stay in that closet sometimes for more than an hour, the smell of camphor balls choking him—all so that his mother wouldn't have to admit that her son was a writer, so that she could pretend he wasn't there.

His mother was right. He would never amount to anything. He *was* a failure; he had even begun signing his letters "The Failure," and he had started a literary self-portrait using that as a title. It had been June's idea that he could become a writer. The truth was, he was "afraid"; he didn't think he had the ability. He would remember saying to himself, "Who was I to say *I am a writer?*"

He sat in his office in Queens, on that afternoon of Lindbergh's success, not far from Lindbergh's departure point, wondering where June was and what she was doing. He wondered whether she might have been in the crowd that greeted Lindbergh, whether she might have thrown him kisses. Throwing Lindbergh kisses would have been June's style.

Unable to control his despondency, he wrote her a letter. This one was even more desperate, more pleading, than any he had written before.

He warned her that if he didn't hear from her soon, he would kill himself. She "must reply by cable" if she wanted to stop him. He had no reason *not* to kill himself, he realized; he had become "the saddest fool of all." To prove to her how fixed he was on death, he wrote her a work called "Cemetery Idyll" to mail with his letter.

He hoped this letter would have an effect on June, make her

change her mind and come home. It probably wouldn't. He couldn't control her. He would have to realize that she could live without him. Thinking about her "gallivanting about" in Paris "like a bird of paradise," and receiving only the most meager replies to his "heartrending letters," finally made him angry. Too often, with June, he felt helpless, not angry.

On that night in May in the quiet office of the Parks Department, Henry Miller began to type out his notes for what would become a lifelong autobiographical project.

The book would start with the day he met June; it would end with her departure for France with Jean. He would call it *Lovely Lesbians*. It would be a "colossal tale of great love and great betrayal." He would tell the tale of the crucial four years of his life with June in eight chapters. The entire work came to him as a "sort of manic vision, hallucinatory in its hyperreality."

"Chapter I," he typed. "*Roses of Picardy*. Wilson's Dance Hall." His first glimpse of June. The time he had gotten tickets to the Palace to hear Thomas Burke sing. Every person had "one book in him, the book of his own life." This would be his one book: "the Book of My Life—my life with Her."

There would be a chapter called "Alimony," about leaving his first wife, Beatrice, about his divorce. Others would be titled "Cabaret," "The Failure." "Sidewalks of New York" would be about their trying to make a living by selling candy and by selling broadsides of his work "Mezzotints" on the city's streets. "Speak Easy" would detail his and June's abortive attempt to set themselves up in business. There would be a chapter called "Double Hegira," about June and Jean's flight. And "The Captive." This title he borrowed from Proust. He had become June's captive; June had become his Albertine. By writing, he could free himself from her and become a "working-class Proust," the Proust of Brooklyn. Writing this story would also be his way of torturing June with the truth.

The notes that came "*without effort*" that night and into the morning were not complete. He would continue to add to them in the weeks to come, but he had written out the chain of events between their first meeting and the present. He turned out page after page, and still there was more to the story.

He knew he would deal with their "battles royal, debauches," June's lies. He made up fictional names for his friends; he wrote out a catalog of "events and crises" they had endured, and another one listing June's lovers. He listed the manuscripts in his possession that he could cannibalize, letters he had written to friends about June that he could mine for details. He made a note to himself not to forget a suicide letter he had written her soon after they met. Everything he had written until now, he would use in this, his *magnum opus*.

At one point, he became hungry and went out to get a bite to eat. When he returned to the office, he resumed his task. As he typed, he "laughed and wept." Though he was only making notes, he felt as if he were writing the book, conjuring it, bringing it into being. He was reliving "the whole tragedy over again step by step, day by day."

He had written to June telling her he had decided to begin a book about her which would "immortalize her." He realized now that the book he planned was something else. It was not, as he had initially thought, a memorial to June. Nor was it, as he had first imagined, his epitaph. It was his *and* June's epitaph. "The book I was planning," he wrote, "was nothing more than a tomb in which to bury her—and the me which had belonged to her."

His book would be a substitute for his death. It would also be his way of getting back at her for all the pain to which she had subjected him. It would be his way of taking leave of her, but also his way of keeping her close to him in the time to come.

When he finished, there was a stack of thirty-two closely typed pages piled next to his typewriter. "*June*," he labeled it.

It was by now well after midnight. Exhausted by his effort, but "no longer racked by emotion, he was strangely calm." In outlining his book, he had "achieved some peace."

He lay down on the floor of his office to try to get some sleep. He would cable June in the morning, to tell her to disregard his suicide letter. He *wouldn't* kill himself. "He had work to do."

Henry Miller had no way of knowing, when he awakened, on that May morning in 1927, that he was in the midst of planning his life's work. In the preceding hours, he had sketched the basis for all his autobiographical works. *Crazy Cock, Tropic of Capricorn, The Rosy Crucifixion* (the collective title for *Sexus, Plexus,* and *Nexus,* his last published June novel, completed in 1959)—all were conceived, planned, and plotted during this one exhausting, painful, exhilarating, triumphant night and morning of work. He had outlined a body of work that, like Lindbergh's feat, would bring him great fame and notoriety.

He was ready for a hearty breakfast.

Wilson's Dance Hall
Broadway and Forty-sixth Street, New York City
Thursday Night, Late Summer 1923

On the Thursday night when he passed through the revolving door and staggered up the steep, ramshackle wooden steps to Wilson's Dance Hall, on the corner of Broadway and Forty-sixth Street in New York City, where he would meet June Mansfield for the first time, Henry Miller had "75 bucks"—a week's pay—in his pocket from the job he hated at Western Union, and he wanted to spend it all. He was in his early thirties, and his seven-year marriage was a fiasco. He had a wife waiting for him at home in Brooklyn who would only let him fuck her in the middle of the night when she was half asleep and could pretend it wasn't really happening, and a score of unwritten novels about his life as a Brooklyn boy rattling around in his brain. His life, he believed, was nothing but "diluted crap," but he was "too paralyzed to do anything about it."

He had walked out the door of his office in the Flatiron Building, where he worked for Western Union, which he would call the "Cosmodemonic Cocksucking Corporation." He was hungry for some female companionship, looking to bury himself in the body of a woman, looking for a woman who could liberate him from "a living death," if only for a short time.

In New York City, the place to find such a woman, Miller knew, was on Broadway, the "Gay White Way." He called it that "cuntlike cleft ... [running] through the dead and wormy center of Manhattan ... intended to dazzle and awe the savage, the yokel, the alien."

The string of red lanterns in the windows of Wilson's Dance Hall beckoned. "30 Lovely Ladies," the sign promised. "Dime a Dance." Henry Miller often used to find himself opposite the dance hall, staring up at it, on the afternoons when his wife sent him out looking for work. If he listened carefully, despite the traffic noises, he could pick out strains of music wafting into the street through the dance hall's spinning ventilators.

For the price of a dance, the hapless romantics and lonely sailors who frequented Wilson's could buy a few minutes of female companionship and conversation and the right to embrace a taxi-dancer, an elusive, not quite respectable woman, for the duration of a foxtrot or a waltz.

Most of the young women who worked in dives like Wilson's were "aspiring showgirls" or prostitutes, either taking some time off or looking for new tricks. Some were looking for a "dream man" who would rescue them from poverty. They worked seventeen hours a day, seven days a week. Most of them could be persuaded to spend some time after hours, for the right price, although the dance halls forbade the practice, just as they forbade over-ardent embraces on the dance floor. "No Improper Dancing Allowed," read the signs at each end of the hall.

In the past, on nights when he felt like this, Henry Miller went looking for "some low-down, filthy cunt who hadn't a spark of decency in her," the kind of woman he could fuck and forget. Or he would fuck one of his wife's friends, or the wife of one of his friends, or Camilla Fedrant, his mulatto secretary, or Gladys Miller, a waitress who read Nietzsche and Homer, who always smelled of grease. For a time, he even thought he might leave his wife for Gladys. Since his marriage had gone sour, he had been spending a lot of time in the "Land of Fuck," which was becoming a very lonely place. He had begun having imaginary conversations with the woman of his dreams, "some wonderful, new, completely satisfying woman," who would come along to liberate him, to make him whole. He was willing to wait for her, even if it took twenty years.

Upstairs, he went to the booth where Nick, the Greek, passed out tickets. Nick's enormous, hairy, ogrelike hands always reminded Henry of the hands of the "hairy monster" in the nightmares that had terrorized him regularly in his childhood.

Standing on the sidelines, Miller surveyed the dance floor. A friend described his appearance at the time as "neat and tidy, always bathed and sparkling with health and good humor." Outdoors, he always wore a battered felt hat, "cocked at a rakish angle." Inside, with his hat off, wearing his steel spectacles, he looked bookish, even monkish, without a trace of the wanton about him. He was probably wearing a well-tailored suit of imported cloth made for him by his father, a tailor. His expensive clothing often tricked people into thinking he was a wealthy man.

Even in repose, he commanded attention. He had an athlete's body, although when he took his clothes off, women were always startled at how thin he was. He ran up and down stairs; his gait was "springy, jaunty, alive." His eyes, "though a cold blue, more often suggested the warmth of quick interest, of lively response— until his gaze followed his thoughts outside the room. . . . These trances came upon him now and then. . . . Suddenly he was 'gone.' "

On this night, Miller was feeling detached and reckless. He was filled with desire, ready to take a chance, ready to walk out on his old, respectable, settled, responsible, unhappy life into a new one. "Adventure," he had said to himself, "—at all cost."

This is how he remembered seeing her for the first time.

I notice her coming toward me; she is coming with sails spread, the large full face beautifully balanced on the long, columnar neck. I see a woman perhaps eighteen, perhaps thirty, with blue-black hair and . . . a full white face in which the eyes shine brilliantly. She has on a tailored blue suit of duveteen. I remember distinctly now the fullness of her body, and that her hair was fine and straight, parted on the side, like a man's. I remember the smile she gave me— knowing, mysterious, fugitive . . . like a puff of wind.

. . . There was an illumination which came from some unknown source, from a center hidden deep in the earth. I could think of nothing but the face, the strange, womblike quality of the smile, the engulfing immediacy of it. The smile was so painfully swift and fleeting that it was like the flash of a knife. [She had] . . . a long white neck, the sturdy, swanlike neck of the medium—and of the lost and the damned.

She went by the name June Mansfield. She had sought him out because she had overheard him and another girl talking about Pirandello as they danced, and that had made her curious about him. Around the dance hall, she said she was educated, a Wellesley graduate, which wasn't true, and she had cultivated a British accent. She didn't want to be taken for an "uneducated pushover"; she wanted to "better herself."

He looked sedate, like an "ordinary businessman" or a teacher, and she had a taste for books. He was no teacher, no businessman, "just a Brooklyn boy," and had lived in a household filled with "brutality, discipline." He had helped his father in his tailor's shop, and he had also been, among other things, a "dishwasher, newsboy, garbage-collector, street-car conductor, hotel bellhop, typist, bartender, adding-machine operator, dock-worker."

She was, she said, sixteen years old at the time, although she had made herself up to look much older. In fact, she was twenty or twenty-one. She asked him whether he wanted to dance, and though he was "embarrassed and confused," he said, "Yes, yes, oh yes. I'll be right back." He returned with a "long string of tickets" in his hand.

They danced together for most of the evening, talking about gods, perversions, her friends—whores, addicts, drunkards, and gangsters—and about writers and books. Though he had graduated second in his class from Eastern District High School in Brooklyn, he had attended college only briefly, and had fled from City College in his first semester after beginning to read Spenser's *Faerie Queene*. He had told himself, "if I had to read stuff like that I give up." But he loved books, and they talked about Knut Hamsun, one of his favorite writers, and Strindberg and his character Henriette in *There Are Crimes and Crimes*.

June impressed him with her knowledge of literature. She spoke knowingly about Henriette, and told Miller "the wicked Henriette" was "the incarnation of evil." "Henriette is me, my real self, she seemed to be saying."

At two o'clock in the morning, standing on the sidewalk outside Wilson's, with a flower pulled into his buttonhole, Miller waited for June to get off work. As she strode toward him, her soft fur slipping off her shoulder, he noticed for the first time her long legs, her splendid carriage. He realized that she was taller than he was, and "he felt awkward."

"What a walk!" he thought. "It's not a walk, it's a glide." She came down Broadway, cutting "through the smoke and jazz and red-light glow like the queen mother of all the slippery Babylonian whores." Broadway, he realized, was "her realm." She was 100 percent American, "America on foot, winged and sexed." She was "Fate itself . . . cutting me through and through."

She took him by the hand and held it tightly and guided him "carelessly, recklessly," through Broadway traffic, to Chin Lee's China Garden. Seated in a booth across from her, watching her talk and smoke, he realized she was the woman in his dreams. Her voice was low, throaty, a voice he found "intensely erotic." Her talk was hallucinatory, mesmerizing. Coke talk, probably.

She talked only about herself in talk that was "formless as a dream." She told him about her father and her life with him at the edge of Sherwood Forest, and about her Gypsy blood, and how her parents were circus performers, and how her father raised horses. She told Miller how a man had defiled her by reaching under her dress. She told him about someone she had loved madly; about how she had been brutally raped; and about a man she had driven crazy who had killed himself. She talked about an old man who paid her $1,000 to deflower her, and how it had taken him ten days, and that she had done it to save her family's home.

He asked her whether there were any men in her life now. "None," she replied. Except "a rich lawyer who showered her with gifts, and a certain married man. And one man whom she loved without his knowledge."

One story segued into another, and Miller couldn't keep them straight or figure out who the players were. He couldn't tell what was true and what wasn't, and he didn't think whether she told the truth mattered. Whatever she told him, she told him as if it were true.

Her talk was as compelling as "the fierce torrents" of his "fiery, glowing talk." She held him spellbound; she noticed how "absorbed" he was by what she said, and she realized the she could seduce him with her stories. She, too, created herself through language. It was a familiar, intoxicating realm, this talk of June's, a combination of his gifts, his mother's and his sister Lauretta's crazy talk, and his father's alcoholic "boozy jabber." June, too, had private, shameful secrets. With her, as with his mother and sister, he never knew where truth ended and falsehood began. He wanted to penetrate her secrets, to get at the truth behind the smokescreen of her talk.

He told her that "more than anything," he wanted to be a writer, but he was disgusted and disillusioned. He had written a novel, *Clipped Wings*, about a dozen of the most pathetic, tragic Western Union messengers he had known—Gupte, the Hindu, whose throat had been slashed by a lover's husband; Charles Candles, "the Moral Moron," who blackjacked his children to death. His aim was to debunk the American Dream, the Horatio Alger myth. He had tried, once, but failed to get it published, though a chunk of it appeared in W.E.B. DuBois's magazine, *The Crisis*.

June encouraged him. Her father had wanted to be a writer too, only now it was too late for him. It wasn't too late for Henry.

He took her home in a taxi to the house she shared with her parents on Fifteenth Avenue in the Bensonhurst section of Brooklyn. She "put her head on his shoulder," and stunned him with her "passionate kisses," but she wasn't willing to make a date. Most women pursued him; June was elusive.

When he got home, it was early morning, and he could only catch a few hours' sleep before getting up to go to work.

Friday. He managed, somehow, to get through the day's work. He annoyed his wife by playing a recording of "Liebestraum" very loudly, then falling asleep early that evening, fully dressed, on the couch.

Saturday. He had promised to send June Sherwood Anderson's *Winesburg, Ohio,* and he wondered what kind of flowers she liked; he wanted to send some with the book. He realized that courting a woman like June would cost money, so he borrowed money on his life insurance, and from his friends.

He spent most of his half day of work composing a long letter to send with his gifts. He hired a special messenger to deliver everything to June. At noon, he returned home, but he was unsettled, and he soon became wildly excited, so he left Beatrice and spent the afternoon "walking fiercely" in Prospect Park.

June had given him her telephone number, but when he called her at five, as he had said he would in his letter, she wasn't home. She hadn't left him any message, nor could the "sad, foreign voice" on the other end say when she would come back.

Already, he was captured, obsessed with a single idea: "to have her at any cost." He had nothing to lose, he believed, because he had nothing to risk. He was "at the bottom rung of the ladder, a failure in every sense of the word," and he knew that entering

June's world would be "a sultry, passionate rebellion," a walk on the wild side. "I loved her," he explained, "because when I met her I was already a desperate, hungry soul. I had nothing to lose. I hated my wife. I wanted tenderness, love, joy, expansion, life, ecstasy, illusion."

He fell in love the same way he played chess, by "exposing himself constantly," by leaving himself "unguarded" and ready for sacrifice. In love, as in chess, "victory or defeat meant nothing to him"; it was how you played that counted. Henry's love play was "reckless"; often it became a "war of attrition." In June Mansfield, he had met his match.

He was playing a game he must have realized he could never win. In their first meeting, June had provided him with clues about her heartlessness and ruthlessness and her life in New York's underworld. But he had always wanted to love a *femme fatale*, a woman of immense sexual power, a woman "surrounded by death, bolstered by crime, nourished by evil." He knew there were two kinds of pain. There was the pain that came from not getting what you wanted. He had had *that* pain as a very young man when he had been too shy to declare his love for his first love, Cora Seward, and in his marriage. And there was the pain that came from getting what you wanted. With June, he would experience that pain.

Saturday night. Lovesick, like a somnambulist, he wandered around town, then boarded a passing trolley and rode it aimlessly for a few hours. He had to see her again, so he returned to Wilson's to look for her, but she wasn't there. She might have been in bed reading, or in bed with a prizefighter, or in trouble; he had no way of knowing. Without her, though, he was in "complete darkness." "Her absence," he thought, "blots me out."

Sunday morning. He decided the best strategy was to go "directly to her home" and beg for her love. "Here I am," he would say to her, "take me—or stab me to death." Or he would play the thug and tell her, "You are doomed—doomed to be mine, forever. I'm a desperado of love, a scalper, a slayer."

He camped on her doorstep for three days and nights, but she never came home. Once, a family member answered his ring, "brusquely parried his questions," then slammed the door in his face. At some point, he managed to talk to June's mother and asked her to tell him about June. Her stories "did not coincide" with what June had told him about herself at their first meeting. And no, they weren't Gypsies.

He decided he would wear her down with his persistence. He wrote her long, crazy, pleading letters. He figured that if a man "saturate[s]" a woman with his "need and longing, besiege[s] her everlastingly, she cannot possibly refuse him. . . . No woman can hold out against the gift of absolute love." She answered none of his letters; his "wild passion puzzled and even alarmed her," though she was flattered by his attention. She wondered whether he was a "dope-fiend."

At last, she "took pity on him," and left a note for him at Wilson's. She said she would meet him after work, at midnight, on Times Square, in front of the drugstore, and she asked him to stop writing her at home.

They climbed into a cab and went to Jimmy Kelly's in Greenwich Village, "a haunt of criminals" and writers. They spent money Miller didn't have. He was afraid he would be shot if he didn't pay the bill. June said that, at this place, they *would* "plug you full of holes for trying to pull a fast one." Terrified, Henry wired the night manager at Western Union to dip into the till and send him fifty dollars by messenger; he borrowed another twenty-five dollars from the messenger. He paid the bill. Then he took June home.

He told several stories, all different, about the first time they made love. Near the end of his life, he remembered that it was on the night they met, in the taxi on the way home. June was an animal, ready to make love anywhere, and he was "embarrassed and yet thrilled." In another account, written in his fifties, it was in the taxi after their second meeting, when they went to Jimmy Kelly's. June climbed on top of him and had "several orgasms before slumping back exhausted into the seat." After, while she was putting on her makeup, she became agitated, urging the driver to speed up—they were tailed by gangsters and had to get away. Another of his stories records that June was reluctant to engage in lovemaking, and that they had a "terrific battle" in a taxi, during which she fought off his advances.

She maintained that it had taken a while for them to become lovers. In time, though, she began to "take his declarations of grand passion seriously." She had been reluctant because she knew he was a writer, and she was afraid he was slumming and was "experimenting" with her "for the sake of writing a story." But she was intrigued, and imagined what it would be like to have the story of her life recorded.

One night, at Manhattan Beach, after June told him she liked his work, Henry was encouraged and tried to make love to her. He "wrestled with her on the sand." He said it was "attempted rape." June's version differed; "it was a pity he hadn't forced her" to have sex with him, she thought.

Though early in their relationship she made grand promises about their future as lovers and told him about her sexual history, they became lovers for the first time "weeks after their first meeting." They couldn't go to his brownstone in Brooklyn, so she took him to the Manhattan apartment of a man named Marder, whom she described as one of her "castoffs." It was in the bed of her supposed former lover that she finally "surrender[ed]" to Henry. Here was that rarity, he thought, a wanton woman, bold, open, and daring in her sexual behavior, who "satisfied him sexually."

What happened after, though, while they were washing themselves, did not augur well for their relationship. Marder returned home and let himself in with his own key. Obviously jealous of Henry, Marder nonetheless had "a big feast sent in, and the three got thoroughly drunk." June perched on Marder's lap, "kissing and petting him while she sang German songs." Henry realized that June and Marder were still lovers, and that they would continue to be lovers. His and June's lovemaking would not bind her to him in any special way, nor would his love for June keep her faithful to him.

When he questioned her, she admitted this was so, but made excuses. She said she didn't love Marder; she couldn't promise Henry that she wouldn't see him, but she only stayed with him to "cure him of his drunkenness." Henry persuaded himself that, despite her words and actions, June loved him in a special way; he began a pattern he would repeat in his years with her. In time, he thought, the power of his love would change her, and she would be faithful to him. Whether he intended fidelity to her is an open question. In some accounts, he insisted he was faithful to her throughout their years together; in others, he slept with other women, including his first wife, from the beginning.

After Henry and June made love that first time, June disappeared from New York. She and two female friends went to New England as the guests of "some backwoodsman" and two other men. It was probably sex for hire. Henry was "wracked with jealousy." He wooed her with a steady stream of letters and telegrams in which he impersonated Knut Hamsun's character Glahn the Hunter, in pursuit of "the remote and enigmatic Edvarda."

While away, June sent him letters pledging her devotion despite her behavior, and she joined him in his game and signed herself "Edvarda." He had captured her, she wrote: "I want to be your wife." Though Miller was thrilled with her capitulation, he was disappointed with the quality of her writing, which he found "childlike." It was so unlike her "extraordinary and chaotic verbal talent," and he wondered whether she was as educated as she made herself out to be.

She had become interested because she recognized his special qualities even as he himself did not recognize them. Here was a man she could mold and shape into her vision of what he should become.

They had begun to act the roles of characters from their favorite novels, heroes and heroines in the works of Strindberg, Hamsun, Dostoyevsky. People who knew them wondered whether any of their feelings were authentic, whether all of their behavior was in imitation of literature. Henry and June, it seemed, were "literary ghosts" without "souls of their own."

When June returned to New York, Henry met her at the train station in Rockaway Beach. He was thrilled to see her, and she was passionate. She showed him she was "naked under her raincoat" and she begged him to sleep with her right away.

He took her to a hotel, and they spent the night together. On August 16, 1923, Miller wrote his friend Emil Schnellock, "I had a wonderful night and day with June at the Rockaways. . . . See her again tonight. . . . We are getting on famously and fatuously." He was lying to Schnellock, as he was lying to himself. He and June had tried to have sex, but she complained that she was sore and that he was hurting her. She couldn't have an orgasm, and he wondered what that meant.

During the night, Henry dreamed that "he was hurtling in a dizzying tumble from a precipice, falling, falling until he slipped into the warm waters of the Caribbean . . . swirling downward in great spiral curves that had no beginning and promised to end in eternity."

Before he fell in love with June, he had been a frequent visitor to burlesque halls, houses of prostitution, and dance halls. He was fascinated by "perversion, insanity, crime . . . , vice." In falling in love with June, he entered the underworld of his own psyche. "The author had found his character"; yet "the character herself had been in search of an author."

244 Sixth Avenue
Brooklyn, New York
August 25, 1923

Henry Miller was standing at the stove in the kitchen of the brownstone apartment in Brooklyn he shared with his wife and daughter, frying bacon and eggs. He was cooking breakfast for himself and June, with whom he had spent the night. June was particular about her bacon, and he was paying careful attention so that it would be cooked the way she liked it, not too crisp.

The day before, on August 24, 1923, he had put his wife, Beatrice, and their daughter, Barbara, on a train to the country to visit one of Beatrice's old friends. Beatrice was taking this journey, she told Henry, because she needed to spend time away from him, to rethink their marriage.

To satisfy himself that their trip was real and not a ploy on Beatrice's part to entrap him into getting caught with June, Henry had traveled with his wife and child for a few stops. When it was time for him to change trains, to return to the city, Beatrice told Barbara to give her father a big kiss—she wouldn't be seeing him for "several weeks." Henry was convinced that Beatrice wasn't pulling a fast one, and he was euphoric that he had a good, long stretch of freedom ahead of him to spend with June.

Not that having Beatrice at home had prevented him from seeing June. Beatrice knew all about June. One evening, when he and

Beatrice were near Wilson's, he had even suggested that they go upstairs so that Beatrice could meet June and size up her rival. Beatrice had refused.

When he dressed himself up of an evening to go to Wilson's to find June, Beatrice would try to keep him home by appealing to his sense of guilt. "Getting ready to meet your sweetheart?" she would ask.

"Yes," he would answer. "I'm going to meet my little whore."

He and Beatrice had separated once before when his whoring had become too much for her. She thought of herself as "a grotesque written upon an old oak leaf vomited by a storm in late winter"—words she had found in Knut Hamsun's *Victoria* and had written on the flyleaf of a copy of the novel she had given Henry as a gift.

"Bea," he had told his wife one day, "I want to be free." She had "shouted, then wept." In despair, she took him to bed to try to win him back. Afterward, he told her, "I'll do anything you like except give you the illusion that I am going to live the rest of my life with you." As his friend Emil Schnellock knew, Miller was capable of "viciousness" and "monstrous cruelty."

But he wasn't yet ready to move out. Bea's resistance to his erotic advances, and his drive to wear her down, was "a spice that still excited him." He believed it was possible for a man "to take care of more than one woman"; at one point, he had proposed to Bea that they invite his former lover Pauline Chouteau to live with them. Though he needed June, he also wanted Bea. June, though she had told him she wanted to be his wife, hadn't changed her ways. He had recently started writing her "desperate letters . . . , including one in which he spoke of committing suicide if the situation were not resolved soon." But he had proposed no plan of action to her, had given her no ultimatum. He was paralyzed, "unwilling or unable to act." He wanted June to take the decisive first step. Love, he believed, was as Knut Hamsun described it; it "turns the heart of man into a garden of fungus . . . wherein mysterious and immodest toadstools raise their heads."

His predicament had become a constant topic of conversation among his friends, most of whom believed that, though charming, he was incapable of intimacy. On an outing to Prospect Park, Henry had begged his oldest friend Stanley Borowski to tell him "how to get untied." Henry half hoped that one of his friends would fuck

Bea and take her off his hands. Bea had asked Emil Schnellock to help her. Henry's father had also asked Emil to try to get Henry to "take a more sensible attitude."

His friend Conason warned him of leaving his wife; he told Henry he was "congenitally incapable of fidelity," and he shouldn't think June was the answer to his problems. Henry said that until now, he had been unfaithful because until June he had never met "a *real* woman." Most of his friends did not believe he would make any changes; if things were to change, either Beatrice or June would have to act. All agreed that sooner or later, his affair with June would become as much of a problem as his marriage to Beatrice. Disaster, his friend Emil thought, always seemed to follow in Henry's wake, and Henry always seemed perplexed about the mess his life had become.

June had become a compelling need in Henry's life, but even at the start of their relationship, his love for her was giving him far more pain than pleasure. She seldom returned to her parents' home in Bensonhurst, which drove him "mad with speculation"; the only place he could be sure of finding her was at Wilson's, in the arms of another man. His notes for this period read "Great despair, jealousy, torment."

He invited his own pain. He would ask June to tell him, in minute detail, about her other lovers. What did they do to her? Did she like it? Were they better than he was? "What had pleased her more? Excited her more?" She would answer honestly, nonchalant, because he had asked, because it seemed that he wanted to know, and because she knew her stories acted as "an aphrodisiac" to him. She always told him what he wanted to hear, not what he wanted to know. Her recitations to him were ceremonies of mutual "self-abasement." He liked her stories best when what had happened to her was "shameful and humiliating." This game they played would exact a terrible toll from them both.

Jealousy was what bound him to her, and this fact did not escape her. When his jealousy spilled over and he told her he couldn't take it anymore, she told him he was special: "because so many others had loved her, in loving him" she had bestowed upon him a special honor.

When it suited her, she could play the slut, the tramp, the prostitute. But she could play innocent too: "drenched in sex though she was, she made herself out as virginal and inviolable."

She was wildly erratic in her behavior toward him. Once, on a street in Bensonhurst, she threw herself down on her knees in front of him and wrapped her arms around him. She told him she was "in love with the strangest man on earth. You frighten me," she said, "you're so gentle. Hold me tight . . . believe in me always." She "clung to him passionately and cried out: . . . 'You're like a god to me. I could do anything for you.' "

Another time, he had gotten a $350 bonus, and, rather than taking the money home, he had treated his friends to a night on the town. At the end of the evening, he took all his pals to Wilson's to show her off; he was "tremendously proud" of being involved with her. He was so drunk that "he almost fell off the balcony watching her dance." Later, she came over to him, in front of his friends, and honored him by slipping a red rose another admirer had given her into his buttonhole. "You must be a great writer—for me!" she whispered. Those moments of special attention inflamed him, and when he was in despair, he replayed them for solace.

Nonetheless, despite her protestations of love, he wasn't sure of her—she made certain of that. She flirted shamelessly with his best friends, going so far as to make "overtures" to them. She had stood him up the night he had bought two tickets to hear Thomas Burke sing "Roses of Picardy" at the Palace.

Once, she had pulled him into an empty lot opposite her home in Bensonhurst, "to make love on the grass." When they were finished, she "seized him with astonishing force and pulled him down to her. 'You're wonderful. I love you, I love you,' she whispered in a broken voice." She broke the spell when "her voice hardened, and she said . . . , 'And now for the dirt.' And then, 'Lend me fifty dollars. My mother has to meet a mortgage on the house.' " Just like a common prostitute. But he had given her "the money she needed and resolved to protect her from such self-abasement even at the expense of his own self-respect."

When he met June, Henry Miller was outwardly conforming and living a middle-class life. Though burlesque queens and prostitutes fascinated him, he believed he was a hard-core romantic, thinking there was one "blindingly satisfying" woman for him, and that when he found her, she would change his life and undo his feelings of worthlessness.

June really inhabited the New York underworld into which Henry had been making frequent sorties. Her world was one of bisexuality, polygamy, prostitution, gangsters, guns, confidence schemes, extortion, blackmail, gold-digging, group sex, rape, drugs, incest, sadism, perversion, necrophilia, and suicide. With June, he was living life at "a fevered pitch." Their life together replicated the emotional maelstrom of his life with his crazy, violent mother, his alcoholic father, and his disturbed sister.

June was the woman of his dreams. She was a woman no man could ever possess, and Miller knew that from the start. He imagined her coming to him, her body always clotted with another man's sperm. She was a woman who used sex for pleasure, for profit, and to get what she wanted. But she was also a woman who withheld sex to get what she wanted. She seemed tough, hardboiled, manipulative. But she was fragile, and deeply disturbed. Henry told himself that her psychosis was "consistent with the insanity of New York." She was a pathological liar, a junkie, anorectic, suicidal, and perhaps even a paranoid schizophrenic—as incapable of commitment as Miller himself.

In wanting her, he was inviting betrayal. In fantasy, he thought he could make her faithful. In loving a woman who preferred multiple sexual partners, a woman who performed sexual acts rather than a woman who made love, he was reliving his earliest sexual experiences. They had taught him that sex was a matter of losing control. His romantic ideal was now, and would always be, the unattainable woman, the woman who made him suffer. June became his tormentor.

When Henry Miller took June to his home on the day Beatrice went away, June was curious about his way of life. She wanted to be shown where he worked, and he showed her the big rolltop desk he had taken from his father's tailor shop and moved into the center of his "huge lugubrious parlor." Though he often put his feet up on the desk and dreamed of what he could write if he could write, the desk was empty, without a thing on it but "a sheet of white paper." Nothing he had attempted was very good.

Poking about in his and Beatrice's closets, June examined their clothing and pulled out one of Bea's kimonos. She took her clothes off and wrapped herself in it. *She* was really Henry's wife, she told him. Not Beatrice.

Instead of using Henry and Beatrice's bed upstairs, the lovers slept "on a couch in the downstairs kitchen." June hadn't wanted to make love in his "marital bed."

The next morning, he left her, naked, in bed and went out to buy supplies for their breakfast. When he returned a few minutes later, June, wearing a bathrobe, let him into the apartment, and he began to prepare breakfast.

Unexpectedly, the "double doors to the kitchen rolled open and there stood Beatrice." She had caught him in the act. And she had witnesses. Behind her stood the landlord and the landlord's daughter. The bed was in disarray and had obviously been used. There were "used condoms lying out."

Miller told several versions of the event. In one, when his wife arrived, he was in bed "stark naked, with June"; he was so surprised, he jumped out of bed, and June, ashamed, "pulled the sheet up to her chin." In another, he was arranging the platter of bacon and eggs. In a third, he and June were cooking the bacon together.

Beatrice ordered Henry to get "that woman" out of her house, and she went upstairs. Henry and June left twenty minutes later; "the marriage was over," and his life with June had begun. He said "his only regret" was that he hadn't had time to finish eating his bacon and eggs. In a more macho recounting, he recalled that, undaunted and unhurried, he had finished cooking and sat down to enjoy his breakfast. Then he packed a small valise and left, with June, for his friend Emil Schnellock's. Regrettably, the bacon was ruined; it was far too crisp for his taste.

The next day Beatrice called him at Western Union and told him to clear his things out of the apartment; "she would be filing for divorce." At first, he was in a "state of shock." But he believed he would get through this; he said he had "always been able to detach myself from a strong attachment without the least emotion. . . . I have slipped out of a relationship whenever I had acquired what I needed." Soon, though, he would want Bea again, desiring what he no longer could have.

The day after he left home, he wrote Emil a letter to memorialize the breakup of his marriage and the beginning of his new life with June. "We have had our fling, you and I," he told his friend, referring to their womanizing. Now he wanted nothing more than "great steady reaches of tranquility and peace."

With June, he would have anything but tranquility and peace. His life with her was one of exquisite torture, of supreme suffering. It would take him the rest of his life to try to understand it. It would deal him the terrible "bloody wound of love" he believed artists required to do their most important work—the wound that would kill him, but out of which he would be "born anew."

91 Remsen Street
Columbia Heights, Brooklyn
Winter 1924–Spring 1925

Henry Miller sat at his "far too costly" desk in his far too costly apartment in a wealthy neighborhood in the Columbia Heights section of Brooklyn, trying to work. Both the typewriter and the desk were presents from his second wife, June. He had been divorced from Bea for a year, having "by his immoral behavior . . . forfeited the rights of parenthood." He would stare at a blank piece of paper for hours and then "slowly and painfully tap out a sentence or two."

The first few months of his and June's life together had been a disaster. Unwilling or unable to strike out on their own, they had stayed in a few of his friends' apartments.

Their first home was a room in an abortionist's apartment in the Bronx that smelled of medicine and dried blood. They dubbed it Cockroach Hall, after the column of roaches that climbed up and down the walls behind their bed. June was still working at Wilson's, and she and Henry only had an hour together when he got off work before she had to leave for the dance hall. She expected him to come and pick her up after work, and he refused, telling her that by midnight he was too tired from working all day long. One night, she came home with a story that she had been picked up in a car outside Wilson's "and raped by three men in a field." He could not decide whether it had happened or whether she was lying to pay him back for not meeting her after work. But he was, as she had already discovered, "intrigued by women who are devious, who lie, who play games, who baffle me, who keep me on the fence all the time."

June nagged him to marry her, yet she tortured him with the stories of the sex she had with "many, many men." He wasn't ready to remarry. He wasn't sure he had done the right thing in leaving Bea. Within a week of abandoning her, he wanted to go back home. Something she had said to him preyed on his mind: "I feel truly sorry for you. You don't know what you are walking into." She was right.

When he went to see Bea on Sundays, they would make love on the sofa, on the kitchen table, standing up, from behind—locations and positions she had never before permitted. Bea found ways to make him linger and he always stayed later than he should. Since they had separated, she couldn't get enough of him.

Once, June got so upset waiting for him that she tried to kill herself. She almost died, and was saved only because a Western Union pal of his stopped in and found her unconscious, near death. Henry was beginning to see just how unbalanced June was. The romanticism of her strange behavior lost some of its appeal when he had to contend with it daily.

In their nightly conversations in Cockroach Hall, he had determined that she had lied to him about her life. Her name was not Mansfield but Smith, an anglicized version of Smerth, her family name, which meant "death." Mansfield was a name she had taken when she started to work in dance halls; she said she had chosen it because it was the closest English equivalent to the word "cemetery." Her parents had emigrated from Romania because of poverty; in Romania, her father was a farmer and a lumberjack, not a raiser of horses; in the United States, unable to get other work, he had become a ragpicker. Her father, who she said adored her, had beaten her mercilessly and thrown her out of the house, "calling her a worthless slut." Like many other abused children, she had become a denizen of the streets at an early age. She had never been to college, and her English accent was phony. The money she got from the old man who deflowered her she hadn't used to help her family, but had "squandered . . . on a Macy's stenographer named Maureen."

After Cockroach Hall, they had stayed in Emil Schnellock's studio in Manhattan. Then they stayed with another friend, Harold Hickerson, head piano teacher at the New York Conservatory of

Musical Art, in a tiny room at 524 Riverside Drive. June had started to call Henry "Val," short for "Valentine," his middle name, which he detested.

On Riverside Drive, Henry could never get a good night's sleep, and he was always exhausted. June would talk from the time she came home from work until five o'clock in the morning. The only way he could get her to stop talking was to make love to her.

One night, while they were living on Riverside Drive, he "found sores on his penis." June had given him a venereal disease, and he was terrified it was syphilis. She dismissed the possibility and told him he couldn't have caught anything from her. Although she helped her admirers have orgasms, she never slept with them— they were all "too old" for intercourse.

Though Henry resented June's followers, she hated the way he was treating her. She accused him of preferring his male friends to her, of ignoring her and favoring them. The long intellectual conversations of their earlier days together were over; June realized that if there was a man around, Henry would prefer to talk to him. Once, infuriated, she took all her possessions, made up "a parcel wrapped with paper and twine," and left him, though she soon came back.

But their strong mutual sexual desire, and their sexual pleasure, were powerful bonds. Henry always admitted that June was the woman with whom he had the best sexual relationship. When they were apart, it was the sex he missed and wanted again. And he couldn't have sex with June without having June. Her one fail-safe weapon with him was withholding and granting sex. He discovered that if she made him suffer and he complained bitterly enough, she would mollify him by giving him what he needed and wanted most from her.

June learned that she could control Henry by leaving him: he was driven to love not by being sure of it, but by longing. If she left him for a time, his interest in her reawakened and his complaints vanished. When her father died, Henry and June were not getting along, and she disappeared for ten days. This drove Henry into a panic. She reappeared at his Western Union office, wearing black, and he was "stabbed to the heart by her great beauty."

Though she wouldn't give up her street life, June was "determined to win him." Their friends thought she realized he was her only chance for a "life of Art." Being near "people who were alive and vibrant" was very important to her, and Henry could be an extremely magnetic personality. Though she had many men in her life who might pay her for her services, none had made her any promises or offered to live with her. She saw, too, that Henry was insecure enough and malleable enough to be willing to become her creation. Years later, she boasted, with reason, "It was I who first discovered Henry as a saint. It was I who invented his qualities."

Henry and June had married in what he called a "filthy ceremony" in Hoboken, New Jersey, before a civil magistrate on June 1, 1924. They had to borrow money for the wedding. He was thirty-two; June was twenty-one. On the subway ride to New Jersey, they had quarreled violently. She protested that he didn't love her and didn't want to marry her. He told her she was right, and she bolted from the train, determined to end the charade. He chased her, caught her, and "put his arms around her, saying he was sorry." He had an "infatuation for the marriage state," and believed that marriage would calm her.

They had grabbed two bums off the street to act as witnesses in the civil ceremony. Miller and June did not exchange rings. After the ceremony, they couldn't figure out what to do with themselves. They wandered around until they found Emil Schnellock's brother Ned and his wife, and went with them to a burlesque on Houston Street to watch the performer Cleo do a striptease. During the show, that she was now married became clear to June. She had a "hysterical fit," and started "laughing madly." Henry became frightened at her irrational behavior, and begged Ned to try to quiet her by telling her that if she became a mother, *that* would straighten her out. It was not an auspicious beginning.

Whatever June's shortcomings, she believed Henry had the makings of a writer. With her encouragement, he had quit his job at Western Union in September 1924. His work had become so inept that in time he probably would have been fired. For the first time, he had an unbroken stretch of time in front of him in which to write. As he walked away from his office, he looked with pity at the "poor buggers with briefcases under their arms" walking down Broadway. "From now on," he told himself, "I'm going to be a writer, and I'll live or die by it." As he walked down the street, he repeated to himself, "My own master absolute."

June had given him the courage to quit. "She really buoyed me up, really helped me. She believed in me," he said. "If I hadn't met her I should probably never have become a writer." On the way home, he bought a recording of a Beethoven quartet, some flowers, and a bottle of wine to celebrate.

June was "deliriously happy" at the news, and she told him she would do whatever was needed to earn money. By now, Henry knew what that meant. The beginning of his career as a writer meant that June would use her talent for "golddigging" to support them. Her prostitution would support his writing. He entered into the arrangement knowingly. "I knew all along that I was being fucked," he explained to his friend Emil, "I was not so naive as you may have imagined."

"If you'll just work seriously," June promised, "I'll do anything for you." He started calling himself a pimp, though there is no evidence that he helped her find her tricks. She managed very well without his help, if he stayed out of her way. A note of his from the period reads, "Misery over June's golddigging which constantly preys on my mind."

It was under these conditions in the early days at Remsen Street that Henry Miller was trying very hard to become a writer. The elegant Remsen Street apartment had been June's idea. They needed their own place if their marriage was going to survive. Nothing this extravagant, he thought. She had dressed herself up in a tight red Persian dress and dragged him around to find a suitable apartment. She was at her most striking, "at her very best" during this time, galvanized by the image of their home and the notoriety he would bestow upon her. Their former passion, which had suffered in the apartments of his friends, had reemerged with even greater intensity. As they went from one apartment to another, searching for a suitable home, they made love in hallways, in vestibules, in stairwells.

The apartment they found, with two large front rooms, a kitchenette, and a private bath, was beyond their means, but June insisted they take it. The rent was ninety dollars a month. What with his alimony and her monthly allotment to her mother, they knew they would struggle. They only had ten dollars between them, and June had gotten the money for part of the ninety-dollar deposit from "an admirer," a clerk at the Hotel Bossert. But she had high expectations for the money Miller would make when he got down to work.

He loved the apartment. It was the most beautiful place he had ever lived in. It had inlaid wood floors, wood-paneled walls, silk-tapestried wallpaper, and stained-glass windows. June decided they would live a pampered life. She brought home presents—a desk and typewriter for Henry, "silk dressing gowns, books, pipes, phonograph records, Moroccan slippers, a chess set." He wasn't used to such luxury. But he admired how "clean, polished, and simple" the apartment was. He and June had so few possessions that the apartment was uncluttered and airy. They had set up their daybed in the middle of a big open room, and during the day, the light streamed in through the high windows. He called it his "Japanese love nest" because it was so austere.

As he and June were walking in Brooklyn one day, they heard cantorial music, and he asked her whether she was Jewish. She replied that she was, and he was "oddly moved and even expressed an interest in converting." He vacillated from being virulently anti-Semitic in his speech and his behavior to fantasizing that he himself was Jewish.

From the time when he was a teenager, Henry Miller had "wanted nothing more of God than the power to write." In his twenties, he was confined to his father's tailor shop, "a slave to the most idiotic kind of routine imaginable." He broke away by imagining what he would write when he had the time. "Inwardly," he said, "I was a perpetual volcano." In daily walks from Delancey Street to his father's shop at Fifth Avenue and Thirty-first Street, Miller imagined writing volumes as vengeance against his mother's devouring, rapacious love. One he envisioned calling "The House of Incest." He invented the "tremendous dialogues," characters, and scenes he would portray. Other than one abortive attempt to write with "a little broken pencil," he never put "a line of any of this . . . to paper." He understood that it was difficult to know where to "begin if you were a smothered volcano."

On Remsen Street, when he first tried to write, he discovered that he had nothing to say, "nothing about which he really burned to write." His friend Emil had told him that he should write as he talked; Henry thought it good advice, but he couldn't see how to put it into practice.

In the early part of the year, he had tried revising his novel *Clipped Wings*. He imagined he could write something that would sell, and could prove to himself that he had the makings of a writer. He imagined the work on the best-seller lists, imagined himself saying to his friends with pride, "There is my name signed to it, you see. Proof." In reworking the book, he had written a new character and a "rags-to-riches" story. Instead of proving, like the other stories in the novel, that Horatio Alger was unequivocally wrong, this new story proved Alger might be right. The novel was a mess. His work only made it worse, not better. Even as he feared he couldn't complete a work, he decided to give it up.

He was very good, he realized, at pretending he was a writer, but he had "*absolutely* no confidence" in himself. Now that he was "free, spoon-fed," with "leisure, paper, everything," he couldn't do it. During the day, he wandered the streets of Brooklyn and Manhattan to collect material. Or he took a solitary walk on the Heights "to think an idea through." He sat at his desk, read some books, made lists of words he wanted to use someday in his work from his Funk & Wagnalls dictionary—"gallipots, neumes, rath, fortalice, verjuice, dingle, thurible, mullioned, spume, and whorls." Or he manufactured plots, made lists of people he wanted to write about, fashioned wall charts, and wrote very long letters to his friends. On a really bad day, he pretended to work, waiting for June to leave; then he escaped "his desk and typewriter."

At night, when June was working, he made himself a meal, or ate out at the French-Italian restaurant on the corner. Or he read in the Montague Street branch of the public library. Or he stayed home and played a recording of a piece by Scriabin, his favorite composer. But he didn't write.

He figured he could start modestly, "with exercises." But he had written only one sketch—"Rhapsody in Blue"—in a month's time and he believed it was all June's fault that he wasn't writing well. When she wasn't home, he wondered and worried about what she was doing; he imagined her in intimate conversation with her admirers, or worse. He would wait for her to come home. Sometimes he waited for her at the subway station. Since he never knew when she was coming home, his days and nights were filled with longing. June maintained he wasn't working well because he wasn't working. He was sleeping all day long, then meeting his cronies for lengthy conversations about "chess, books, behaviorism, architecture, Bertrand Russell, Shaw, the institution of marriage and sex," or an "absinthe orgy," which often lasted half the night.

When June was home, Henry claimed he couldn't work because she wouldn't leave him alone. She came up behind him and told him "how good it was for her to see him at work." She picked up his pages and read them. Or she walked through the room, her silk dressing gown unfastened, so that he could glimpse her lush naked body, and they wound up in bed. If he tried to get up too soon after they made love to get back to his desk, she became "furious." Did he think she was "just a little piece of tail to be knocked off quickly?"

June talked a good line about her "Val" and how he had to become a great writer for her, but she wouldn't give him time to do his work. When he told her he needed a few hours to himself, she would "fly into a rage of desperation," telling him that he was "a fanatic for work." He was more interested in it "than in her despite all her sacrifices"; "he didn't love her; he only wanted to use her." After an hour of fighting, she would tell him, "Go to work. I won't bother you any more today."

51 Remsen Street
Brooklyn
Spring 1925

By the spring of 1925, Henry Miller had spent six months living "the true life of an artist . . . on nothing but nerve." He had begun his apprenticeship as a full-time writer, producing some work that sold, but it would take him "ten years of misery" to become successful.

Though June had told him to leave money matters to her, they were desperately poor, consistently behind on their rent, and behind on his alimony payments to Bea. He vacillated between trying to earn his own keep, devising a way for them to work together so that he could keep his eye on her, and living off her "golddigging" and trying to write. For a time, he unsuccessfully tried journalism, diligently sending out "long, fatuous" inquiry letters listing possible topics, and samples of his work. This involved "fruitless errands to editorial offices, ... rage, despair, ennui. *And postage stamps!"* In response to one submission, an editor wrote, "It is obvious, young man, that you will never be a writer."

During the coldest months of the winter of 1924, to scrape some money together, Henry and June sold imported candy, door to door, sixteen hours a day, near Borough Hall, on the East Side of Manhattan, and in Greenwich Village. Henry was so ashamed that he often took out his rage on June and mistreated her. He refused to go into office buildings to sell, claiming that June was far better at it. Waiting for her outside, in the cold, his overcoat pockets stuffed with boxes of candy, he clung to railings in pain, suffering from the piles that afflicted him every time he was under stress. Once, June was nearly raped, and soon after, they gave up the candy business.

To help with the rent, against June's wishes, Henry moved a buddy of his, Joe O'Regan, into the apartment. But O'Regan was a womanizer and betrayed Henry's friendship by his "infatuation with June," and Henry made him move out. Henry and June tried a few schemes to extort money from her admirers, but it was too risky a business to rely on.

Finally, June resorted to doing what she did best. She became a hostess and waitress in a succession of Greenwich Village speakeasies, tea shops, and restaurants—Raymos, the Peroquet, the Roman Tavern, and the Pepper Pot—so that she could meet men. She collected a new group of admirers to torment Henry: Moreau, a professor from the Sorbonne; Nat Pendleton, a wrestler; Hans Stengl, an illustrator; the Cuban chess champion Roberto de Silvor. In a good week, she earned $150 to $200 in "tips," but they still never had enough money; in all likelihood, her drug use was escalating. During the months when Miller was beginning to write, their major support came from her admirers.

In describing his writing at this time, Miller said: "Oh yes, I do write, but how painfully, and how poorly, how imitatively." At Joe O'Regan's suggestion, he produced a series of "Mezzotints," short prose pieces, printed in editions of 500 on colored cardboard, which could be sold directly to readers. Henry's model was his idol Walt Whitman, who had also sold his own work.

By the spring of 1925, Henry had written thirty-five pieces. Some, like "Make Beer for Man," took up social issues such as Prohibition in a lighthearted way, using what Miller called a "purposeful, literary buffoonery." "Keep your libraries. Keep your penal institutions. Keep your insane asylums. . . . GIVE ME BEER."

By far the most interesting Mezzotints described June and Henry's feelings about her, which he was unable to express directly. Desperate for material, he ransacked his old letters, scrapbooks, and notebooks.

A number of the Mezzotints, "Free Fantasia," "Pursuit," and "Cynara," were taken directly from his letters to June. One, "Suicide Letter," reproduced excerpts from the letter in which he threatened to kill himself if June didn't act decisively to help him end his marriage.

"June the Peripatetic" used metaphor to suggest that she was a streetwalker. "The Art of Peddling" described their candy-selling. "Dawn Travelers" described the people he saw in the early morning when he was waiting for her to come home, "who clean and sweep out places, who open and close shops." Like him, they were "monsters of despair."

"Dance Hall" recounted June's taxi-dancing at Wilson's. It played on Shakespeare's metaphor for sexual intercourse (making the beast with two backs) to relate that women like June used dance halls to find tricks:

Hire an instructress. . . . Music . . . moans piteously. Glistening fiends . . . press hot bodies together until they fuse into one shameless, molten quadruped . . . under signs reading: "No improper dancing." Can a girl retain her virtue? At a nickel a dance?

Miller had stumbled upon the value of using his life with June as a subject, and it was an important breakthrough for him. Living off June, inwardly infuriated by her countless betrayals, powerless to stop them but outwardly exhibiting no jealousy, he used the Mezzotints to broadcast her abuses. None was overtly vicious, but anyone who knew their history could read the implications in his words.

Taken together, the Mezzotints portrayed Miller as a man betrayed, as a cuckold, as a failure, as self-destructive, and as suicidal. He described himself as a man who loved immoderately, who suffered for love, whose lover was untrue. He had begun his lifelong habit of literary exhibitionism—making public his most private experiences, especially those concerning love and sex. If he felt abused or powerless, writing the Mezzotints taught him he could use his art to strike back. Like much of his later work, though they exhibited a surface bravado, these prose pieces were born of suffering and despair.

Though Henry and June tried to sell the Mezzotints door to door, she decided she was the perfect salesperson, that she could see to her established clientele. She decreed that it made sense to sign *her* name, June E. Mansfield, to Henry's work and pass it off as hers. Ironically, Henry Miller, celebrated as a macho writer, began his literary career as a female impersonator, a literary crossdresser, writing and selling his work under his wife's name.

The plan worked all too well. June stayed out until two a.m. selling the Mezzotints. When she returned home, she told Henry stories of how some men "bought the whole series," how others paid her "triple and quintuple" the asking price. She described the new and interesting men she met, like Alan Cromwell, an FBI agent, who promised to pay her seventy-five or eighty dollars for a pile of Mezzos if she talked to him or accompanied him to a concert.

Miller suspected that as his wife sold his work, she was also selling herself. Even so, for a time, he created more for her to peddle.

June E. Mansfield created a small reputation for herself as a writer in Greenwich Village, and a few men became her literary patrons, providing her with an allowance to continue writing. Others provided her with contacts so that she started getting commissions to write pieces for magazines like *Snappy Stories*, which, of course, Henry wrote.

Why he permitted her to pass off his work as hers is hard to say. He admitted being "a passive sort of man, weak in a way"; "women of strength and character" attracted him, and he liked the "battle of wits" that such a relationship entailed. In this battle, he would increasingly use his pen as a weapon.

Miller hoarded a store of resentment against June. He called her actions, which he didn't challenge, her "crimes" against him. His "Dance Hall" and "June the Peripatetic" were his first, timid sallies against her. In time, he became bolder, and deadlier. He told Emil writers had to sacrifice the people in their lives to create their art. Paraphrasing G. B. Shaw, he wrote, "The true artist will sacrifice everything, let his mother starve, his wife and children go hungry, rather than forsake his vision."

Miller said about writing the Mezzotints, "Now my business is after my own heart. I sell myself—my work." His subject *was* his heart, and he had turned the exploration of his feelings into a business. Though the Mezzotints were bringing in a small, steady income, he gave up the scheme. He said he was unable to stick to a project; probably, he wearied of being June's accomplice. What she was doing was starting to drive him crazy.

In the spring of 1925, the landlord evicted Henry and June from their Remsen Street apartment. They hadn't paid the rent for several months, and they had allowed the place to become a mess. "The glories of Remsen Street," which had lasted all too briefly, were over. The landlord said they could forget the back rent if they vacated "in a reasonable time."

They again stayed at a few of their friends' apartments. Again, they were dependent on others' goodwill. They soon wore out their welcome when they didn't help with the rent, and their friends asked them to move on.

Later in the spring, Henry raised some money from his relatives, and he and June tried, and failed, to run a speakeasy at 106 Perry Street in the West Village. Henry took on the jobs of "manager, waiter, sandwich-maker, short order cook, bartender, runner of errands, purchaser of supplies, bookkeeper, housecleaner and head of the garbage detail." June entertained her male friends in a room set aside for her exclusive use.

At Perry Street, the effect of Henry's compromises for June began to show. He began to drink very heavily, to harass her customers, and to explode into furious, violent rages. He wondered whether he was going crazy.

He ran off to Florida for a time, with two of his friends. Ostensibly, it was to cash in on the land boom and make some fast money, but also, it was to escape June and their creditors and the charade his life with her had become. The trip was a disaster, and he soon ran out of money and had to ask his father for the fare home.

The honeymoon with June was over.

Remsen Street
Brooklyn
Fall 1926

Henry and June had come down in the world since the days of their Japanese love nest. For a time, they were so poor that Henry (who was now thirty-five) moved in with his parents and June lived with her mother. His notes for the period read, "No more hopes. . . . Complete failure and submission—absolutely licked." During the summer, they had gone to North Carolina with Joe O'Regan to try to make money in real estate, but had failed. While there, June had conceived a plan to sell silk stockings to rich matrons, but that didn't work. She missed the Village and wanted to return.

When they got back to New York, Henry was determined to make money honestly, "to extricate self from life of extortion and golddigging," as he put it. His notes show he was far from enthusiastic. "Disgust with N.Y. Trapped again," he wrote.

For a time, he tried to make some money by selling encyclopedias door to door; then by hawking newspapers on street corners. He discovered that his voice would disappear if he tried to use it to command attention. He wrote the first of his "begging letters," addressed to "Friends and Givers of Alms," mimeographing fifty copies, which he sent to friends.

As always, June commanded him to "stop this nonsense and get down to work," which meant he should stop looking for work and begin writing. He tried to write his way out of poverty and reliance on her. He had written his friend Emil Conason, "the only means of subsistence for yours truly seems to be the cheap magazines. God knows whether I have talent enough to make them or not. . . . Hell, I'm not sure that I can do anything any more."

While he was living at his parents', Miller's hopes for a writing career were raised by two incidents. One of his Mezzotints, comparing the Bowery Savings Bank to the beauties of a cathedral, was published in *Pearson's*, under the name June E. Mansfield. An editor at *Liberty* commissioned him to write an article about words for $250, based upon an interview with the editor of his beloved Funk & Wagnalls dictionary, Dr. Vizetelly.

Miller was happy to meet the manly Vizetelly, glad of an example of a virile man of letters. When Miller told Vizetelly the number of words he knew, Vizetelly told Miller that he knew more words than Shakespeare. This Miller was thrilled to discover.

The piece was turned down, but Miller was permitted to keep the money. These modest successes did not meet June's expectations. She believed that by now, because she had put her faith and effort into Henry, he should have been on his way to becoming the next Dostoyevsky.

She had found steady work at the Pepper Pot in Greenwich Village, then hostessing work at the Catacomb. Finally, they could rent a room on Remsen Street, but their new place was a considerable comedown from their old digs.

They had grown apart. June had become notorious, known as the "Queen of Greenwich Village." She had started frequenting Village homosexual and lesbian hangouts. A homosexual poet had described her in a poem as "that magnificent half-woman June." She kept her marriage a secret from her new friends, many of whom were lesbians. She changed her looks. She plucked her eyebrows into a thin arch, coated her face with white liquid, rubbed blue shadow under her eyes, rouged her lips a bright red, then dusted her entire face with "a ghoulish green powder" until it took on "a cadaverous glow."

She cut circles out of her brassieres so that her nipples showed through her sheer black or purple dresses. She wore no hat or stockings. Instead of underwear, "she wore a strip of black velvet saturated with perfume." When she was ready to leave the apartment, she wrapped herself in "a long, flowing black theatrical cape."

"Don't you see what you look like?" Henry said to her as she left for work.

"Like a whore, I suppose," she answered, which made him feel so guilty that he apologized and told her "she looked truly dazzling."

He had become terribly bourgeois, she thought. Not only did he despise the way she dressed, he disapproved of "the way she exploited herself sexually." He wanted a clean, airy space to live in. He even wanted to have his wife at home, where she belonged, enough money to "fix the house up pretty," with pretty pictures hanging on the walls!

June assumed he had become "indifferent" to her because he

wouldn't fight for her. She was jealous of his male friends. Henry, she realized, was a man's man; she suspected that his preference for male camaraderie was based on his unacknowledged homosexuality.

Henry was tired of her elusiveness. Paradoxically, he also believed she was hemming him in. She believed they should be so close that they were "molded into one being." He felt she was no better than his mother. She wanted to "make him smaller and smaller until she could put him in her suffocating womb."

She insisted upon a new set of rules and that he shouldn't interfere with her doing "the dirty work" that paid the rent. He wasn't allowed to answer the door; when he came home, he had to ask her whether all the customers were gone; when she brought home an admirer, he wasn't allowed to stay.

Though he couldn't live without her, his dreams during that period reveal that he began to see her as lethal. In one, June hovered over him, "the ghoul queen of a million dead souls . . . [;] maggots were in his armpits and hair, and slugs feasted on his heart." Another of his dreams shows his terror of anal rape at the hands of unknown assailants. In it, he tried to hitchhike somewhere, but some people captured him and pushed him into a dirty enclosure. They "reached inside his rectum with dirty paws and slashed his guts and privates into ribbons with a rusty jack-knife," then dumped his mutilated body in front of his parents' home.

At times, at night, Henry wandered into the Village to find June. In the past, she had begged him to meet her; now she didn't want him near her. He stood outside the Catacomb, where she worked, watching her through the plate-glass window. He saw how, when she met someone new, she would lead him to a quiet corner. With "her elbows squarely on the table," she would "sit and talk and gaze admiringly into his eyes," just as she had with him when they first met.

She had a new string of admirers, "millionaires," she boasted, and she often wouldn't come home until four in the morning. She had developed an alarming tic, which he believed was a sign of how dependent on drugs she had become.

Sometimes, he would wait for her at the subway station. Once, while standing on the platform, he looked into a mirror and forgot who he was. "*What is your name?*" he asked himself. "*Who are you?*"

* * *

Many years later, in writing to Emil Schnellock, Miller described this time in his life, admitting that he was as responsible as June for the debacle their life had become.

When I think of how I pushed her in the streets, cold bitter nights when we were selling the leaflets, or selling the candy, pushed her with love and vengeance and God knows what. I was mad, crazy. I loved her, and I was hungry. I was desperate. Nobody understood what I was. . . . I wanted to be somebody. I thought I was an artist, a poet. I was a dreamer. . . . I pushed her into everything. I see it all too clearly. I pushed her away from me. . . . I was a coward because I loved her, and didn't love her enough. . . . I was glad that she sacrificed herself for me. . . . It was all twisted, tortured, all crazy, wrong, from start to finish.

The Iron Cauldron, Greenwich Village, and Remsen Street, Brooklyn Autumn and Winter 1926–1927

In the autumn of 1926 and the winter of 1926–1927, after June met Jean Kronski, Henry Miller hit bottom, entering the worst period of his life, his "Season in Hell." It was, he said, the "very lowest point of my whole career, my morale was completely shattered." But it was also "the Janus period, the turning-point" of his life, when he began to understand his past and to chart a meaningful future.

When June met Jean, she had already become ambivalent toward Henry. All she had to show for their years together while "she was working her heart out" were his pieces of ephemera. He was no genius; at best, he was "a charming nobody." She was searching for a new artist, one with *real* talent, whom she could support and inspire.

June was working at the Iron Cauldron, a gathering place for "freaks, eccentrics, . . . homosexuals, lesbians, nuts on leave of absence from asylums." One day, she looked up and saw "the most beautiful girl I had ever seen in my life." She had "long black hair which she wore like a mane, high cheek bones, violet blue eyes, beautiful strong hands"; she was wearing run-down shoes and overalls; she was penniless, and she was looking for work. June saw her head hanging down, as if she were in trouble, and decided instantly that this girl needed her help.

She was seventeen years old, and had just come to Greenwich Village from the West Coast. She looked like an artist, so June decided she was one. As June later described, "I went over and spoke to her, told her I wouldn't think of letting a person of her beauty and artistic talents work at such menial chores as washing dishes or waiting on tables, that I would wait on the tables and look after her." Soon the two were inseparable, and, as the Millers' friend Ceil Conason said, "nothing so upset Henry's life as much as did this girl's association with his wife, June."

June had found her bohemian artist. She probably also saw in the girl the lonely outcast she had been when, at sixteen, she had been thrown out of her house by her father. The girl's name was Marion, and she was an orphan who had lived in two foster homes. June didn't think the name Marion suited her, so "I named her Jean." Because she claimed to be Russian, June gave her the last name "Kronski" from a character in her husband's novel, and a lineage. She was, June decided, "a bastard, and a descendant of the Romanoffs."

According to June, "Jean was literally half mad. . . . She was a drug addict." She walked through the streets of the Village "carrying a douchebag, with *Alice in Wonderland* in one pocket of her overalls and the *Tao Te Ching* in the other." Yet June believed "she was on the way to becoming a brilliant sculptress." Jean also wrote expressionistic poetry, painted surreal pictures, made puppets, danced, and read several languages. She had patterned her life after Arthur Rimbaud's, and her quest for destabilizing experiences, which she could turn into art, made June's life look staid. When she met June, Jean had already been institutionalized.

Before long, Jean had moved to Pierrepont Street in Brooklyn, just north of Remsen Street, to be closer to June, and Henry was hearing the name "Jean Kronski" more than he liked. He suspected that the change in his wife's appearance, and her increasing drug use, might be due to her new friend. Their place became littered with presents from Jean: "Japanese prints, a Russian ikon, barbaric bracelets, amulets, embroidered moccasins, perfume."

One day, June carried home "a grotesque puppet" Jean had made, called "Count Bruga." It had "violet hair and violet eyes, . . .

a Pulcinella nose, a loose, depraved mouth, consumptive cheeks, a mean, aggressive chin, murderer's hands, wooden legs, a Spanish sombrero, a black velvet jacket." June gave it a place of honor on the dresser and told Henry, "There's genius in it, positive genius." She had finally found a "real" artist in Jean.

Jean had taken the name "Count Bruga" from a character in Ben Hecht's latest novel, in which Hecht "crucified" his former friend Maxwell Bodenheim, portraying his "legendary decadence." Hecht's use of a work of literature as revenge sparked Miller's interest. Soon Miller started his own revenge piece—a play about Jean and June that he hoped would "torture" them.

June started staying out with Jean all night long. Sometimes, they wandered Greenwich Village, frequenting speakeasies. Other times, June stayed at Jean's place. When Henry asked why, she said Jean needed her. Once, she sat next to Jean in an all-night cafeteria, watching her compose her poetry. Another time, Jean had visions of being visited by ghosts, and June couldn't leave her alone, she said, because she kept running into the street. Once a drunkard had tried to rape Jean, and June had to stay with her and comfort her.

Not long after they met, the police took Jean into custody and confined her to Bellevue mental hospital. June told Henry that Jean would be released only if she agreed to take care of her. Though he believed this was a ruse, he "hopelessly agreed" to allow Jean to move in with them.

When Henry met Jean, he "detested her." He saw June according her "the same almost religious awe" she had formerly reserved for him. Once he even saw June washing Jean's feet.

He knew Jean was a lesbian, and he suspected that Jean and his wife had become lovers, especially because June demanded that Jean not be told of their marriage. Henry was ignorant about same-sex love. He started to read explorations of lesbianism and homosexuality—Krafft-Ebing, the Satyricon, Auguste Forel's The Sexual Question, Otto Weininger, the Psychopathia Sexualis, littering the margins with June's and Jean's names. He insisted that his doctor friend Emil Conason examine Jean, which he did, finding her "sexual organs normal." But Conason also told Henry that June "had always been a lesbian."

Henry believed there had to be something wrong with any man like him whose wife was "violently attracted to another woman." Though he had told June to find a friend, in part so that he could have time to be with his own friends, he hadn't imagined anything like this happening. "You forced me to seek someone else," June claimed. He tried to woo her away from Jean. Failing that, he resolved to "torture Jean and drive her back to the asylum."

In reprisal, Jean wrote poetry about him. One, an imitation of Rimbaud called "To HVM," she wrote to show that Henry had lost the poetry in his soul:

> His pupils upheld his eyelids
>   with
>   spherical
>   blue
>   columns
> Where he placed the gift of a
> TARANTULA
> (with a tiny pink bow
> around its neck and spectacles resting on its nose)
>   This he pushed
>   with
> a
>   pin
> From his sardonic heights
> . . . Such a being has forgotten the fast-fading
>   stars

Before long, when he came home, he found June and Jean in bed, sleeping together. He tried kicking them out, but they returned. He ran away a few times, to Emil's, to the home of friends in Pennsylvania. At one point, he suggested a "rota system" to June as the only fair way for him and Jean to divide her time, but Jean's need for June prevailed. "Now I know I'm licked," he wrote. "Impossible to combat the two of them." His notes from the period read, "Commence to go really nuts now."

He began to stage dramatic scenes, hoping they would make an impact. He propped the puppet, Count Bruga, against a pillow on their bed. He stuck his and June's marriage license in one of the puppet's hands, his divorce papers from Beatrice in the other. He gathered his old love letters to June, old photos, manuscripts, and Mezzotints, including "June the Peripatetic," and wrote "desperate love messages" on them. Then he threw them around the bedroom. When June came home and saw what he had done, all she said was, "Is this another one of your gestures, Val?" She didn't even bother reading what he had scribbled. She said it was the work of "Val the nut."

He had written June a note, once, about his continuing belief in himself, in their marriage, despite all they had lived through. "Don't worry, kiddo, we're coming through," he wrote. He found it in her handbag. *"Five years!"* she had scrawled across the back. "It was eloquent, those FIVE YEARS," Miller wrote. "Nothing to show on the credit side. . . . No books published, no name, no money earned, no slightest recognition."

Even she admitted she had been "a slut" for him so that he could write, so that he could "be somebody." And she had nothing to show for it.

Henry Street
Brooklyn
Winter 1926–1927

In the midst of a raging snowstorm, Jean, June, and Henry dragged their few belongings from Remsen Street and Pierrepont Street to a cold, dank "sunken basement" apartment in "a dingy house" on Henry Street. There, in a destructive *ménage à trois,* the three of them led what Henry called an "underground life."

Jean took the best room. She hung puppets and death masks on the walls, and painted bizarre murals. She painted a portrait of Henry surrounded by skulls and serpents. The ceiling she painted lavender, the color for lesbian love. Henry hung a picture of his daughter, Barbara, on one wall in the apartment and a portrait of himself by Emil Schnellock in the bathroom. On the back of the toilet, Jean painted her version of a line from Virgil: *Et forsan haec olim meminisse iuvabit*—"Perhaps someday it will help to have remembered these things."

By now, Henry and Jean were locked into a state of mutual loathing, though he was often transfixed by her, and spent time combing her hair and paring her toenails. When he tried to tell her how much he was suffering, she told him it was good for him, that it would give him something to write about, that he should study the life of Rimbaud.

The three of them were going crazy. June was using more drugs than ever before, and she spent days vomiting. Henry was drinking heavily, panhandling for money, and trying to sell his blood. He had sunk so low that he had lost most of his friends, except Schnellock, who tried to save him from June. Once they were so cold that they broke up their furniture and used it for firewood, then scavenged for packing cases to use for furniture. To raise money, Jean offered herself to doctors for medical experiments. She routinely stole money from June, but June forgave her.

When June and Jean locked themselves into Jean's room, Henry drove himself crazy imagining what they were doing. Sometimes, Jean locked herself in her room, writing poetry, with a homosexual friend of hers named Shelley, who masturbated her, she said, to inspire her. After a time, June got disgusted and threw him out. When June brought her tricks home to earn money, Henry sat in the shed behind the house, listening through the walls, trying to hear what his wife was doing. "More golddigging on a grand scale," he wrote, "—only now it's a burlesque." When he couldn't stand the sight of the two women, he tried to beat them with a stick, and he once threw a knife into Jean's door.

The place looked like a coke joint, the "atmosphere sepulchral." The beds were unmade, the "sheets a mess." There were never any clean towels, so they used their dirty clothes to wipe themselves. The sinks were perpetually clogged with food, so they washed dishes in the filthy bathtub. The shades were drawn, the windows black with filth. The floor was littered with the detritus of Jean's artwork, with cigarette butts, dirty dishes, books.

Drunk, stoned, out of their minds, the three of them sat around the table in the kitchen. They called it the "gut table." There they had "endless lacerating discussions" about what was perverted and what wasn't. Jean cited the example of Rimbaud's life to defend herself. She described how she had been paid for staging exhibitions of lesbian sex.

They flung accusations at each another for hours. The women claimed that Henry was insensitive, a megalomaniac. He tried to pressure June into admitting that she and Jean were lovers. The most he ever got from June was a statement that Jean was "a platonic lesbian," whatever that meant. Henry was a homosexual, lazy, a baby, a failed artist, they retorted. June was a prostitute, he shouted, a lesbian, and Jean was crazy. No, June screamed back. *He* was the crazy one.

When June and Jean went out, he often followed them, trailing them to the "hangouts of the Village homosexuals," the Pepper Pot, the Caravan, the Vagabondia, the Mad Hatter. Or he would stay behind and rifle their belongings to find evidence that they were lovers.

He became obsessed with the thought that his wife preferred a woman to him. When he overheard June telling Jean, "my love for Val is only like that of a mother's for a child, that's all," he realized he would have to fight for his wife's affections. He believed that if only he could find definite proof that June was a lesbian, he would have a powerful weapon to use against her. He seemed to think that having proof would make June give Jean up. He found love letters to Jean from "David," "Lovely Jo," "Michael darling"—her lesbian admirers. Once he found a note from Jean signed "desperate, my lover," and a letter from Jean to June that read: "You would be a rare, delicate pervert (pardon!) if all this chaos which surrounds you were removed. Please, don't you see what you contain?"

June and Jean had begun to talk about going to Paris together. In the past, when he had begun to hope that he might become a writer, Henry had spent hours at Schnellock's apartment, poring over a map of Paris. He spread it out on Schnellock's huge maple desk, imagining himself there. Now June and Jean were appropriating his dream. Their talk was of "Paris. Goddamned Paris. Eternally Paris," he complained.

He couldn't imagine where they would get the money for the trip. But they began making puppets and selling them in the Village, and the sound of their hammering and sawing kept him awake all night long. When it became obvious that they were serious, he vacillated between begging June to let him come, asking her, "what's going to happen to me without you here?" and telling June, "Alright, go for a little while. But let me know where you are." At times, June would tell him that he could come with them, but though he hoped it was true, he didn't believe her.

Henry was penniless, rudderless, and he felt powerless to fight June's will. "When it comes to an open quarrel," he confessed, "I fail to administer the timely slap in the face. Instead, I act the injured and humiliated one. More, when things go downhill I never apply the brakes: I have what amounts to a perverse desire to see just how far out of hand a situation can get." He believed he was "afraid to get angry" because he had a "great violence" within him; he knew that if he lost his temper, he would go "completely haywire," that he could kill.

In describing his childhood, Miller declared that he had gotten into an argument with a boy and they had fought so viciously that he had killed him. "I never went to the police, naturally." When Henry introduced June to his mother, she told June, "he's no good, he's a murderer." If Miller had killed a boy, as he claimed, his extreme passivity in the face of June's provocation is understandable—he was afraid he would murder her. In the days at Henry Street, he discovered another form of vengeance—the written word—when he began to sketch the story of his life with June and Jean.

But Henry Miller had been the victim of sexual abuse in childhood. This helps to account for his self-destructive passivity in his damaging relationship with June (and also his homophobia and his compensatory machismo).

He described what had happened to him in print just once, in his *Book of Friends, Volume I* (1976), without naming his abuser—one of Miller's biographers, Mary V. Dearborn, has subsequently identified Henry's abuser as a man named Tillotson. Miller told how, as a grammar-school boy, he had belonged to a Boys' Brigade sponsored by the Presbyterian church he attended.

> The man who organized this brigade, Major ——, was a queer. He loved boys—and all the parents referred to him as a "lovely man." He loved us a little too much for his own good. Every night, when we reported for duty, he ushered us into his little office, made us sit on his lap, then hugged, squeezed and kissed us as much as he could. We all dreaded these sessions but none of us had the courage to tell on him. No one would have believed us anyway, because he didn't look the part. . . . One day, however, someone did tell on him, and he was expelled from the church in disgrace. To tell the truth, we felt sorry for him.

With June, Henry was reenacting his childhood abuse and sense of powerlessness, and his addiction to sexual excitement and overstimulation. In watching June and listening to her stories, he was reliving the voyeurism of his early experience. The sight of Jean's closed door, and the sounds of his wife and Jean behind it, fascinated and enraged him. Probably, this reawakened feelings triggered by his abuser's closed door, but he couldn't act. He was obsessed by wanting to know what lesbians did when they had sex, just as he had probably imagined what his abuser was doing to his next victim.

His life with June made him feel powerless, just as he had felt as a boy when he was molested, and as he felt in the face of his mother's mad incestuous longing. That longing had erupted into murderous rage when she tried to kill him with a kitchen knife after he told her about a love affair he was having.

With June and Jean out on the town one night, Henry Miller began having flashbacks to Tillotson's abusive caresses, to his mother's suffocating love. He wanted to die. He swallowed a bottle of pills. After, he opened the window in his bedroom to the "shivering blasts" to weaken himself.

It was winter, and everything in the yard was dead. Soon, he, too, would be dead. He threw himself onto the bed, naked. He would lapse into a "deep, painless sleep." It was the only answer.

His doctor friend, Conason, who had provided the pills, had substituted an opiate for the deadlier drug Miller had requested. So Miller did not die, though he had fully intended to kill himself.

He had written June a suicide note, telling her she was his vulture. She hadn't taken him seriously. When she saw him on the bed, drugged and lethargic, she held him and caressed him. For a time, he thought he had frightened her into caring for him again. Then Jean came and took her away. June left him in bed, promising to come back soon. Instead, she took her time and had dinner.

On this jaunt, she carried with her the suicide note he had tucked into her pocketbook. When she and Jean finally returned, he found it sticking out of the purse.

It was crumpled and food-stained and had a cigarette hole burned into it. He imagined that in the seedy joint they frequented, June had taken it out to read to her lover while waiting for their dinner to come. He could see June blowing smoke rings across the table at Jean, his suicide note in her hand. They had read it together, he suspected, but hadn't taken it seriously. They had lingered over dinner, while he might have died, and they had returned home radiant. He couldn't be sure that June had even bothered to read it all the way through to the end. But she hadn't rushed home to save him.

Miller sat "by the light of a flickering candle" at the gut table in the "cold dank basement" of the Henry Street apartment. With a broken pencil, he was "trying to write a play depicting my own tragedy," as he put it. He had been trying for some time to sketch the story of his life with June, and how she had wronged him, and his obsessive jealousy of Jean. "To be obsessed," he later understood, "means to long to be free."

Though he wanted to write "a play in three acts," he "never succeeded in getting beyond the first act." But the play he sketched became the basis for his presentation of all his subsequent work about their *ménage à trois*—*Crazy Cock*, the *Tropics*, *The Rosy Crucifixion*—novels composed as a series of dramatic scenes.

From time to time, he showed the work to June and Jean, asking them how it should end. Jean "insisted upon the death of all three," adding parenthetically that the husband was responsible for the tragedy because he hadn't provided his wife with "any romantic thrills." June thought the three of them would "depart for Paris and live forever after in a contented haze of Pernod." Henry challenged this ending: how was that possible, he asked June, since the wife "was also cheating on the husband with countless men." June became hysterical; she called him "a puritanical martinet, a teutonic pedant, bourgeois, . . . a foul fool." For good measure, Jean added her insult, that he was "impotent as a writer and as a man."

In February, Miller went to bed and stayed there for ten days. "He had sunk into a deep, murderous depression." At times, "he spoke only in monosyllables, if at all; at other times he would rant for hours." He leaned "against a wall like a statue, only his eyes moving."

While in bed, unwilling, unable to get up, he spent his time reading the book June had given him for Christmas. It was a volume by Marcel Proust. He realized that he could tell the story of his life as Proust had told the story of his. Proust's obsession with Albertine, he recognized, was no different from his for June. Proust provided him with a form he hadn't yet considered, that of the autobiographical novel.

He had come to the "edge of madness," he said. But "sobered by the folly and waste of mere experience of life, I halted and converted my energies to creation. I plunged into writing with the same fervor and zest that I had plunged into life." He saw that he had another choice, another way of dealing with his pain, besides killing himself. He could write about it. He could incorporate his personal pain into a work of art that would be "something greater than the frame of personal misfortune."

In the moments when he decided to tell his story, he entered another realm, "a realm of tougher, more elastic fiber." Writing, he had realized, could save him. Writing, he knew, could show the world how cruelly she had wronged him.

He had toyed with using writing to retaliate against abuse since he was a young man. On his walks to and from his father's tailor shop, he had imagined writing volumes about incest as vengeance against his mother's devouring love.

It took him several years to develop the courage to write his story about June and Jean in the first person, with himself as both participant and observer. In his first attempts to tell this story, he adopted a third-person narration that probably allowed him to put some distance between himself and the painful events he recounted.

He carried his notebook for the work about June and Jean with him "like a loaded gun," copying down any "revealing thing the two women said, threatening to expose them through art."

At some point, he began to keep a "June notebook," sometimes expanding his cursory notes and typing them into lengthy entries. He referred to them as he composed his work. These notes suggest how much out of his element Miller was in living June's underworld life.

Under the heading *"Destructiveness"*:

clothes, towels, shoes, socks, hats, expensive gowns, worn to shreds in no time, or ruined by cigarette holes, by spilt wine or gravy, or paint. Habit of doing what she likes regardless of what she has on—because it would cramp her style. Allowing others to wear her things and ruin them for her: fur coat, beautiful slippers, evening wraps, mantillas, scarves, etc. Mislaying, losing, having things stolen: purses, bracelets, pendants, costly kerchiefs, gloves, money. Finding 50 dollar bills floating around on the floor, staircase, in clothes closet, etc. where they had fallen out of bag in which they are usually carried all crumpled up, like used toilet paper. Hence super-cautiousness on my part in guarding own personal belongings which have a special personal value for me. Dictionary, for instance, watching it each time [June] uses it so that it will not be dropped on floor, or leaves wrinkled, or pages cut out or torn. (Giving as excuse, sometimes, the fact that it is still unpaid for.)

Money matters:

always, everywhere, no matter under what circumstances we live, an accumulation of debts with tradespeople, friends, etc. Living always into the future, big plans for big coups, with only ridicule for saving, caution, solid effort, etc. (All this petty, narrow, bourgeois, futile.) In order to liquidate small annoying debts gets involved in larger ones because of some scheme.

Forbidden fruits:

enchantment which drugs, vice, eccentricity, anti-social acts (murder, thievery, incest, etc.) have for both [Jean] and [June]. Always a contempt for the normal, the sane, the thorough-going, the respectable. (Also Richard, the homo following her like a puppy.) Mother & daughter in love with each other, then falling in love with June and having jealous scenes. As witnessed by the degenerate Italian dope fiend.

To pay them back for how badly they were treating him, Henry made June and Jean read what he was writing about them. He even forced Jean to take dictation from him, to write down as they came to him the words he would use to indict her. He wanted to torture them with the truth, even as he hoped that seeing his version of their story would make June and Jean change their ways. He naively believed that if only he could convince June that Jean was a pervert, June would leave her, and their marriage would be saved; he forgot the wreck their marriage had become even before Jean came on the scene.

Henry Street
Brooklyn
Spring 1927

It was nighttime. The basement apartment was dark and empty. The shades were drawn. Someone had pulled all the bureau drawers open. There was clothing strewn about everywhere. All the trunks and suitcases were gone. It looked as if the place had been ransacked by burglars. Then again, their place usually was a mess.

Miller had come home to his ravaged Henry Street apartment from his new job as gardener with the Parks Department. June and Jean had celebrated his hiring by "decking the table with flowers and providing French wine." He suspected they were planning something because of the glances that passed between them at the table and some signs that they had begun packing.

It was a Saturday. On Saturdays he only had to work a half day. So he had time, on his way home, for socializing, and to run some errands. He bought June the two pairs of stockings and brassiere she had told him she needed. He also picked up a bouquet of violets, June's favorite flower, to surprise her, and a German cheesecake to treat himself after a long, hard week.

It took him a while to figure out what had happened. He found the note from June under a life mask Jean had made of him that functioned as a paperweight. She had left it on the gut table near the filthy window. He lighted a match to read it. "Dear Val," he read. She told him she and Jean had sailed that morning for Paris, that she didn't have the heart to tell him because she loved him too much to say good-bye, and that he should write her care of American Express, Paris. "Love," she signed it.

So. She had really done it, as he had known she would—after vowing to him that she still wanted and needed him and wouldn't give him up, though she wanted and needed Jean, too, and wouldn't give her up; after treating him to hothouse strawberries with heavy cream for breakfast that morning, and "waving to him until he had turned the corner" on his way to work. That was when he should have suspected something was up.

He went on a rampage. All the rage he had been holding in for months exploded.

He started to break things. First he took down every picture on the wall and smashed them; even his own portrait he removed from the bathroom wall and tore into shreds. He pulled the curtains from the windows and spit and pissed on them. He ground his life-mask into powder under foot. He hurled the floor's litter, dirty glasses, sardine tins, soiled shirts, and torn magazines, at the frescoes on the wall.

In a corner, he spotted a pair of June's silk stockings, rolled into a ball. He picked them up, used them to wipe the tears from his eyes, smelled them, and kissed them. He put them in his pocket, where he would keep them, so that he could touch them, all the time she was gone.

180 Clinton Avenue
Brooklyn
July 1927–July 1928

A month after June's flight to Paris with Jean Kronski, Henry Miller planned his life's work about June, the "colossal tale of great love and great betrayal." He didn't begin to write seriously at his grand plan for two more years; he lacked the courage, he later said.

In July 1927, June returned to the United States, with Count Bruga under her arm but without Jean, and resumed her life with Henry for the next two and a half years or so. June and Jean had had a huge fight in Paris which precipitated their separation; Jean had become disgusted with June's passing herself off as a writer. In June's absence, Henry had lived with his parents on Decatur Street, worked for the Parks Department, hung out with his friend Emil Schnellock, and frequented the taxi-dance halls, patronizing in particular one young woman from Texas, with whom he discussed literature.

June arrived in New York singing the praises of Paris, telling Henry that the two of them would have to go there together. She had brought back with her souvenirs of "the exotic, the curious, the artistic, the decadent" Paris she had sought out: "George Grosz's *Ecce Homo*, her paperbacked copy of the *Kama Sutra*, stubs from the Cirque d'Hiver, autographed manuscripts of poems, a poster peeled from a pissoir on the Rue Blondel, handwritten menus, a Zadkine sculpture." To hear her tell it, she had become the darling of Paris overnight: she claimed to have met Oskar Kokoschka and Augustus John at the Dôme, to have charmed Ossip Zadkine, and to have had Cocteau and Picasso chasing her. Her tales no doubt made Henry jealous, but he would soon be using his work-in-progress to launch a few volleys in her direction.

After the briefest "honeymoon" period, during which a repentant June fixed elegant French meals and poured out glasses of exotic liqueurs for after-dinner drinks, their marriage returned to business as usual for her. She began to bring home all manner of luxuries, at first without saying where she was getting the money to pay for them: thick woolen blankets, soft rugs, bags full of groceries, phonograph records, bottles of Napoleon's favorite wine, Gevrey-Chambertin.

She had found herself a reliable "sugar daddy," a man she called "Pop," in the fur trade, who she claimed was "ugly as a toad" but loved literature. She told Pop she was unmarried and living with an invalid mother, which enabled her to protect her privacy, but also to lead him on. Pop became the Millers' major means of support for the next two years. Though she initially told her husband she and Pop never slept together, and though she and Henry would laugh together over Pop's love letters, later, in the midst of an argument, she told him she had slept with Pop "too many times for me to remember."

June convinced Pop that she was a writer by showing him some of the Mezzotints and passing them off as hers, and Pop paid June to write a novel for him. It was Miller, of course, who sat at his desk regularly throughout the year and produced the work, which he called *Moloch*. Though he learned discipline, and though writing under her name gave him fluency and broke the writing block that had tortured him for years, with "reams" spilling out "pell-mell," knowing the uses to which she was putting the work infuriated him, and he often had "bughouse reveries mixed with choking fits."

In what became a lifelong habit, he recirculated the material he had used in *Clipped Wings*, but he wrote it in a different way, and he added new material: the novel was about his job at Western Union, his anti-Semitism, and his marriage to Beatrice. Describing what it felt like to transform himself into a female persona to write this work, which June was supposed to be writing, he said: "Every time I sat down to write a page for [Pop], I readjusted my skirt, primped my hairdo, and powdered my nose." June showed Pop the novel in installments, and when he approved the first fifty pages and committed to the payout, she and Henry "celebrated with a bottle of Chartreuse."

"Remarkable," Pop commented upon reading the work. "You sound like a man. You have great promise."

Reading of her husband's anti-Semitism must have pained June. That he chose to write about his first marriage annoyed her, but what upset her even more was that at the novel's conclusion, the Henry character (called Dion Moloch in the novel) decides to return to his first wife (called Paula), and not to divorce her after all. With a few strokes of the pen, Henry had obliterated his marriage to June, suggesting that his life would have been much better if he hadn't chosen to leave Beatrice, if he hadn't married June.

At the end of the novel, Dion Moloch contemplates a renewal of his love for Paula:

> All the lies, the counterfeits, the baseness of his past was
> transmuted by her love into the gospel of devotion. The parched
> infidelities, like a barren soil in which they had struggled and
> starved together, promised to blossom and flower under the
> rivulets of this reawakened passion. Deep down in the rich subsoil
> of love hope took root.

He had reduced their titanic love to but one of many of his "parched infidelities."

Until he wrote *Moloch*, Henry hadn't discovered any defense he could use against June. His leaving her, his rages, violence—even a suicide attempt—nothing had seemed to affect her before. When he had planned his life's work in the Parks Department Office, he knew he would be writing about her, and he believed that his writing would ease his pain and help him get back at her. But when she showed him so clearly that his writing had the power to affect her, he learned that he could use his project—the rewriting of their life together into his work—as a powerful weapon against her in any future "battle royal" they had.

Paris
and Various Destinations in Europe
July 1928–January 1929

As reward for producing the work, and to enable her to develop her writing potential, Pop gave June $2,000, treating her to a trip to Europe, and Henry accompanied her, but to get the money, she probably made some kind of commitment to Pop.

The Millers sailed in July, and after a brief stay in London, a Channel crossing, and a train ride, they arrived at the Gare St.-Lazare in Paris. Even the train station excited Henry, with its "glassed-in roof" and the poetically named "big waiting room" called *La Salle de Pas Perdus*, "The Hall of Lost Footsteps."

They set themselves up in the Hôtel de Paris at 24 rue Bonaparte. After unpacking, they threw open the windows and stepped out onto the balcony. In the courtyard below, Henry saw a young man repairing a bicycle. "Bon jour," he shouted merrily, testing his French, "ça va?" He was thrilled to hear in return, "Ça va!" Hearing the bells from St.-Germain and watching the lights of Paris coming on, he knew he wanted to explore every street.

The trip changed the balance of power and marked a turning point in the Millers' marriage. Though June had been in Paris before, and though she had met many artists and writers, it was Henry who felt familiar with the place. He took in everything hungrily: "the fleshy beauty, almost enough to produce an erection, of the statues in the Tuileries; the pornographic photos displayed in the window of a shop near the Folies Bergère; the Seine at night, . . . ; an old woman sleeping on a newspaper beside Notre-Dame; the beggars working the streets and cafes on the Boulevard Sebastopol." June introduced him to Marcel Duchamp and the sculptor Ossip Zadkine. Henry spent hours sitting in cafés, drinking coffee, daydreaming, talking about his current literary interests—Dostoyevsky, D. H. Lawrence, Spengler—only here, these were considered not idle pastimes, but important pursuits.

They took a bicycle trip from Paris to Marseilles; it was not a success because June so often refused to see the literary sights that interested Henry, and glumly and doggedly wanted to pedal on to the next destination. At one point, in a café in Monte Carlo, he "watched June quake with silent tears"; she seemed "very young and a little pitiful." He realized how desperately she needed her throngs of adoring admirers to survive, and that he felt better away from the old pals who knew him only as a failure.

They took a train tour around Europe, through Belgium and Germany to Vienna and Budapest, into Romania, Poland, and Czechoslovakia, coming back to Paris for a while before departing for the United States.

June introduced him to Alfred Perles, the man who would later become his "bosom companion" in Paris; their meeting was an important moment for Henry. On a warm day in May, the three of them got together a picnic of bread, cheese, ham, bananas, and wine, and took it to the Jardin de Luxembourg. Perles didn't like June, thought she was a *poseuse,* that she was bad for Henry, and his attitude showed it. Henry, he liked immediately, thinking him "simple and genuine."

They talked about Henry's writing—he had carried an early version of his June book with him to Europe, but hadn't worked on it—and Henry told Perles he knew he hadn't yet found his own voice, and that he needed "an entirely new departure which could only come about with an entirely new mode of life." The new mode of life, he intimated, and Perles agreed, was life without June. Paris, Henry realized, would provide the climate and the stimulus he had lacked in the United States.

In Paris, writers, even unpublished ones, were respected, and Henry had completed two novels, had already published some shorter work, and had a third novel—his June novel—completely planned. In Paris, he had the status he had longed for in the United States. The farther he got from Brooklyn, the firmer and surer he became. The farther June got from Greenwich Village, the more powerless and pathetic she seemed.

Lovely Lesbians/Crazy Cock
Brooklyn and Paris
Winter 1929–1930

When June and Henry returned to New York after their nine-month absence, her cocaine and alcohol abuse escalated, perhaps because they learned that while they were away, Jean Kronski had killed herself after being committed to an asylum. June took up her life where she had left off before they left for Europe; Henry began to wander the streets "aimlessly." June alternated between abusing him and adoring him; she became "desperate" in her insistence that he make use of her to become a great writer. To him, it seemed like Henry Street all over again, but without Jean.

With June becoming dangerously unstable, Miller continued to work on his novel about her while living with her in an apartment in the Fort Greene section of Brooklyn, though June was away, up to her old tricks, much of the time. What he accomplished by the spring of 1929 was a careful plot of his work. It would have four parts: the early days of his relationship with June; Jean's arrival, her relationship with June, and his attempted suicide; his jealousy of Jean, June's lies, and their departure for Paris; their reconciliation. He noted that he wanted the central section to provide a "tremendous wealth of incidents and characters, piled up crescendo, at lightning pace, allegro fortissimo, con furioso." The last scene he wanted to write was June's arrival in New York, without Jean, and "the sight of her leaning over the rail, . . . the sublime mystery of that face as it turned toward me, searching for me in the crowd."

But while he was living with June, it was impossible to write what he wanted. She tried to take over his work, to make him write it the way she wanted, as an elegy for her dead lover Jean and an idealization of herself, and she temporarily succeeded. She insisted that he drop the first scenes, arguing that the novel's true beginning was Jean's arrival. He hadn't yet decided on a title for the novel. Should he call the work *Lovely Lesbians*? Or *Crazy Cock*?

By the end of ten months' work, with June looking over his shoulder, he had "only his notes, notes on notes, notes on how to rearrange his notes, notes made of passages saved from his manuscript, notes on how to reemploy these, and four hundred pages of typed manuscript which pretended to constitute a fictive narrative but really consisted of one long note on a novel he had not meant to write." Telling his version of his life would prove impossible until he and June lived apart.

Because of the circumstances under which he wrote, and his need to protect his image of his marriage, this early version of the work was not as vicious an assault against June as it would become in its later versions. Miller did everything he could to protect the image of June as blameless and worthy of his love. In the early drafts, he "portrayed himself as fighting Jean for his wife's love, with June herself an unwitting pawn." While he was living with her, it was impossible to unleash his fury against her. At first he created a portrait of June that idealized her, and it is the Jean character whom Miller assassinates in print—in one version murdering her with a bread knife.

But Miller could only delude himself about June's innocence for so long. As he rewrote the novel and showed it to her, and she corrected what she thought he had gotten wrong, he began to get still other versions from her about what had *really* happened. This further confused him, and reawakened his doubts about her truthfulness. Writing this work was like picking at a scab. Still, if he kept reliving those days as he rewrote them into fiction, it was just a matter of time before he would begin to blame her, too, for what had happened, and to strike out at her in his art.

In March 1930, Miller left for Paris without June, with a trunk and two suitcases containing good suits, tailored by his father, which could always be sold; a copy of Whitman's *Leaves of Grass;* carbon copies of his manuscripts *Moloch* and *Crazy Cock,* and ten dollars in his pocket that he had borrowed from his friend Schnellock, which would have to last until June wired money. On his passport application, in answer to the question "Why do you want to visit France?" he had answered, *"for pleasure!"*

It had been June's idea that he go, and she paid for his passage. The story she gave him was that she was sending him to Paris to "write a novel that would make him famous and establish her as one of the muses of the ages." More likely, "she had a [new] lover," Stratford Corbett, an insurance man (whom June married after she and Henry divorced), and Henry was in the way. He agreed to go because it had become impossible for him to work with June around, and he wanted to finish the book he had started about her. He still believed it would change his fortunes.

Their marriage had reached a stalemate. In the months since their return from Europe, he realized June wasn't changing her ways. She didn't see him making any real progress in his work. In sending him away, she couldn't lose: if he produced something publishable, she could share in the glory, but while he was away, she could cement her relationships with men who might turn out to be better long-term prospects.

In Paris, before he made friends, Miller lived a marginal life, sleeping in cinemas, in cheap hotels (with tattered wallpaper, patched carpets, and broken windows), or even outside, on the street, or under bridges, with the *clochards,* using his bundle of manuscripts as a pillow, sustaining himself on "luck, charm, and nerve." An acquaintance said he lived in "poverty that was hungrier than anything I ever heard of outside a concentration camp." Still, a few days after arriving, he wrote, "I will write here. I will live quietly and quite alone. And each day I will see a little more of Paris, study it, learn it as I would a book."

He soon found a modest little restaurant, off the Place St.-Sulpice, the Restaurant des Gourmets. There he could get a meal for forty-eight cents, "including wine, butter, bread, serviette and pourboire," and credit besides. He learned he could count on the generosity of Parisians, who didn't regard poverty as a sign of moral turpitude, and the companionship of others who were as down and out as he. When Alfred Perles ran into him, Miller was sitting in a café without a centime in his pocket, hoping someone he knew would come by to pay his bill.

He missed June terribly, and was unbearably lonely. In time, he learned "I had to nourish myself *from within.*" He sustained himself by going to the cinema, wandering the streets of Paris as he had in New York, seeking out the streets "consecrated to the memory of writers—Balzac, Eugène Sue, Rousseau, Baudelaire, Cervantes, Villon, Victor Hugo." He learned the difference between one *arrondissement* and another—the "animated elegance of the champs Élysées, 'sterilized, cauterized, and polished like a piece of old silver'; the working-class pigments of the vegetable market at Les Halles with its aromas of leek, cheese and fish; the Italian girls with smoldering eyes set in enameled faces near the Place d'Italie." Almost immediately, he began to write his friend Schnellock encyclopedic letters describing his adventures, and to record his impressions in a notebook—"The Legend of the Pissoirs . . . Flea Market, Clignancourt . . . Kandinsky . . . Surrealism . . . Abbatoir Hippophagique . . . Grand Guignol . . . Toilets on the right bank and toilets on the left/The Lesbians at the Jockey Club and the fairies at Rue de Lapp." He would use both when he began to write sketches about Paris and *Tropic of Cancer.* Of special interest were the Parisian prostitutes and their pimps, objects of his endless, almost obsessive fascination, for here they conducted their business in public and without shame. These women and their men were the Parisian equivalents of himself and June, and in watching the prostitutes, he was learning by proxy of his wife's secret life.

While continuing to work on his novel, Miller began to write a series of sketches about Paris, among them "Mademoiselle Claude," an exploration of the relationship between a prostitute and her pimp. He had developed a passion for this Parisian prostitute, who became a substitute for June, and in the sketch, he casts himself in the role of Mademoiselle Claude's pimp. Writing this work enabled him to see his relationship with June more clearly, though he substituted another woman for his wife. A central issue in the piece is the threat of the prostitute's giving her partner a deadly disease. Miller was "mortally afraid" of venereal disease, and, given June's preferred mode of making a living, with good reason. It was, as he described it, "The one great horror—to me! Unclean!" When June read "Mademoiselle Claude," she was furious because it broadcast the fact that he had been unfaithful to her. He registered her response, and in the future portrayed himself as a sexual adventurer. Though his biographers have taken his self-portrait as literal truth, it is more likely that he created this "cocksman" persona to infuriate June and also to balance the image he was creating of himself in *Crazy Cock* as a cuckold.

From his first days in Paris, Miller went to the American Express Office on the rue Scribe on the Rive Droite every day to see whether June had sent him a letter or some money. Within a month of his arrival, though, he had made friends among the expatriate community by hanging out on the *terrasses* of Montparnasse cafés. Many offered some money, a meal, or a bed for the night. When he ran into Alfred Perles at a café in Montparnasse in April 1930, his fortunes turned, for Perles became his "guardian angel" and best friend. He paid Miller's hotel bill, introduced him to other expatriates who might have a room or a couch to spare, read his work-in-progress, offered him a place to stay whenever he needed it, and, most importantly, treated him as a fellow writer.

No. 2 Rue Auguste Bartholdi
and Hôtel Central, Rue du Maine
Paris
Winter 1930–Autumn 1931

In August 1930, Miller had become excited: on June's departure after a three-week visit, he had begun to work again; he felt like his "old swashbuckling self." He had received a critique of his work from a "knowing young man" of "this novel that I've been dragging about from one hotel to another, across the ocean twice, thru bordellos and carnivals, a pillow at night in the movies, and under the bridge at the Seine."

Though his reader had commented favorably upon his originality and vitality and the work's "epic sweep," Miller had already decided to revise it radically. He was trying to find his voice, trying to adopt a tougher stance, more in keeping with the person he had become in Paris. He had determined that his style was inappropriate for the story he was telling. He thought this book signaled the end of his writing "realistic literature"; it wasn't first-rate, he knew, and it was "perhaps all too egoistic, too vain, too presumptuous." "Who am I," he wrote Emil Schnellock, "that I should think to make literature of my life?" He realized that "sentimentality" was a weakness, and that he had to toughen up his prose. He knew the direction his revision had to take:

> Out with the balderdash, out with the slush and drivel, out with the apostrophes, the mythologic mythies, the sly innuendoes, the vast and pompous learning (which I haven't got!). Out—out— damned fly-spots. . . . What I must do, before blowing out my brains, is to write a few simple confessions in plain Milleresque language. No flapdoodle. . . . No entomological inquests, no moonlight and flowers.

In the winter of 1930–1931, Miller revised his novel in an apartment he shared with Richard Osborn, an American lawyer who worked for the Paris branch of an American bank. He was encouraged when two of his Paris sketches, "Mademoiselle Claude" and an essay about the film *L'Age d'Or,* by Luis Buñuel and Salvador Dalí, were accepted for publication. These writings established him as a member of the avant-garde. Meantime, his revision of *Crazy Cock* pushed the work in a new direction: he incorporated surrealist flights and made it tougher, bolder, meaner. He had come to believe that "the book is good," and likely to "create a sensation." In an antic frame of mind, he began to inscribe on the backs of the envelopes mailed to New York, "Return to: Henry V. Miller, Man of Letters, c/o American Express, 11 Rue Scribe, Vive la France! Liberté, Égalité, Fraternité, Pax Vobiscum."

Wearing corduroy trousers and a threadbare light gray jacket, Miller, now forty years old, sat at his typewriter in Osborn's seventh-floor atelier, his desk in order, his notes about him. He was sleeping on Osborn's divan, earning his keep by cleaning, cooking, stoking the wood-burning stove, and having "everything nice and ready for him when he came home from work." The apartment, overlooking the École Militaire, with the Champs de Mars and Eiffel Tower in the background, was the grandest place Miller had stayed.

Miller was working at times feverishly, "into the early hours of the morning." His bald head was "outlined by the strong light pouring through the immense expanse of glass." If he stopped work, he could watch the soldiers at the École Militaire, sloshing in the mud at their sword and bayonet practice. He was writing out as much hostility against June, as much aggression against Jean, as the soldiers were exhibiting toward one another on the drilling field below, and he had begun to see his marriage to June as a titanic battle for his own survival. He was, his friend Osborn had discovered, an angry man, "capable of homicide, literary homicide at least." Miller himself admitted, "With every line it is either murder in the first degree or suicide. . . . [T]here's a lot of slaughtering to be done." In Paris, he had found the peace to work. But he had also discovered his anger; now he was capable of work as violent as "a shrapnel shell in the bowels."

He had finally decided on *Crazy Cock* as the title of the novel. From time to time, he would consult his "omnivorous" June notebook, containing "a Proustian minutiae of details and observations," or the large sheet of brown wrapping paper tacked on the wall, listing words he wanted to use: "crapulous words, insulting words, explosive words, garnered from the weirdest sources."

By February, though, he was dejected. With the winter wind "whistling around the shuddering window-panes, the fire sizzling and crackling in the stove," he was "still muddling along with the book," unable to finish it. He wrote Schnellock that he was "sick and sore about it . . . disgusted . . . hate it . . . think it the vilest crap that ever was." The problem was "the form I have chosen"; he felt "cramped, walled in, suffocated." His spirits matched the "raw, mean rain."

Disgusted with himself, with his work, tired of June's wires— "Hold on, money soon"—and of "living on the edge of disaster," he had grown a beard, which, surprisingly was "dark red, but peppered with gray and white." Osborn thought it made him "look like something between a *clochard* and a Tyrolian Christ."

He had begun an affair with a married woman by the name of Bertha Shrank during the spring of 1931, which he used in his writing of *Tropic of Cancer*. This relationship might have relieved some of the loneliness he felt. Since sexual prowess was connected in Miller's mind with creativity ("The sap is running again. I wake up with semen in my hand. . . . Good sign," he wrote Schnellock), his affair might have helped him to continue working.

Despite his disgust with *Crazy Cock*, his fear of finishing it, and his sense that in revising it he had "ruined" it, he persisted and completed the work, his first novel about June, in August 1931, two and a half years after he had begun. He had learned discipline, if nothing else, and this was the story he wanted to write.

He was now living with Alfred Perles at the Hôtel Central on the rue du Maine and finishing the job of sweating the manuscript to 300 pages, half its original length. He liked his room, and the fact that he had someone to talk to. Perles was good for him; his motto was "Easy does it," so different from June's and the Miller family's code. From his window, Miller could see the "real Paris," the cheap prostitutes on the lookout for customers and the workmen eating their bread-and-cheese lunches. He had already begun talking about his "Paris book," another portrayal of his relationship with June, but with himself at the center. He looked like a bum; when he finished *Crazy Cock* and began his next book, he would take on the persona of the outsider; he would become a literary *clochard*.

Henry Miller's *Crazy Cock* was his first full-length revenge piece against June, and though it was not published in his lifetime, it served as a template for his future work, as well as a weapon in his ongoing struggle with her. During its composition and revision, he succeeded in working out, in rudimentary form, a coherent set of image patterns that he would return to and embellish in the *Tropics* and *Rosy Crucifixion*, and he established the fundamental logic of the universe he had inhabited and would describe in all his work.

Most importantly, he began to explore the significance of the life he had lived with June, and he began to understand the necessity of fighting her and what their life together represented. Not to fight it, not to strike out against it, meant nothing less than his own death. Miller wrote *Crazy Cock* as if his life depended upon it. In telling his story, he was trying to understand the cause of what he called his "suicidal manias." He blamed June, but in the process of writing, he started also to look at the causes rooted in his childhood.

He proceeded from autobiography, retelling the actual events in his life from the vantage point of his alter ego in the novel, Tony Bring, a name June suggested. He wrote of the anguish of his life with Hildred (June) before Vanya (Jean), Hildred's bringing the puppet Count Bruga home, Vanya's arrival, and Vanya's rape; his own nightmare visions, and his flashbacks to early, disturbing experiences. He told of his life in their *ménage à trois* in their basement apartment on Henry Street, of Hildred's mysterious trips into Greenwich Village and his journeys into the Village in search of her. He described his incapacity to control Hildred's/June's behavior, which, he believed, was deeply injurious to him, and the effect of the affair between Hildred/June and Vanya/Jean—his profound depression, his suicide attempt.

But he also wrote of the passion and pain of his and Hildred's/June's sex life, of the first night they met, the promise that they would all travel to Paris together. He explored his revulsion at Vanya's lesbian life, his discovery of love letters to Vanya written by other women, his finding Hildred and Vanya in bed together, his finding Vanya's letter to Hildred, and the scenes at the gut table. He described the increasing chaos of their household, his selling newspapers, their trying to sell their blood, Hildred's and Vanya's preparations for Paris. And he wrote of his abortive attempts to write, but also of his retreat to bed to read Proust and think about how he could turn the story of his life into art. He wrote of his beginning to tell his story.

In *Crazy Cock*, Miller imbues even the most mundane of these events with symbolic significance. They are outward signs of the hero's titanic struggle to wrest himself from a powerful, pleasurable, spellbinding, yet deadly obsession with carnality; to establish his autonomy and reclaim his soul by breaking free of the allure of surrendering to the power of a woman; to resist the pull toward self-extinction through writing a story that will expose his pain and strike out at his abusers. His life in the novel is one of continual emotional overstimulation, never-ending frustration, of passionate, potentially murderous rages, or aggression turned upon himself— resulting in a suicide attempt.

In *Crazy Cock*, Miller established a pattern of images in describing Hildred/June as both an abuser and a symbolic stand-in for all those who had harmed him. She (and Vanya/Jean) become the safer figures whom he can attack, upon whom he can vent his rage. At one point, in an alcoholic frenzy, he punches Hildred in the stomach. Elsewhere, Tony Bring shouts:

> I think if I had any sense I ought to strap you down and beat the piss out of you. I think I'm crazy, too, for tolerating all that I have. I swear to Christ if that woman [Vanya] appears again I'll mutilate her. And I'll fix you, too, mark my words. . . . I hope she's stuck in a sewer and her body full of rats.

The images he develops, his fantasies of retaliation, provide a vision of the world as seen by a survivor of abuse. Here is, perhaps, the most disturbing such image in *Crazy Cock*:

> So obsessed did he become by the thought of his helplessness that at last he closed his eyes and surrendered himself to a flight of fantastic, wanton cruelty. Like a cold, searching vivisectionist, he saw himself bending over her with a scalpel, stripping away the flesh from the brain, sawing through the bone with steady hand to expose the soft, dull-gray convolutions, the delicate, palatable tangle of mystery which no one could unravel.

Hildred/June's persona, first and foremost, represents the "vision of the great whore, mother of harlots and abominations of the earth"; she is a rapacious, diseased sexual vulture who preys upon men, and she must be destroyed if civilization is to survive, if art is to be created, and if men are to be free. She is both mother and whore: Hildred refers to Tony as her child; he sits on her lap to be petted when he feels poorly; he submits to her as "an invalid submits to the attentions of a nurse." As the lover of Vanya/Jean, she perverts what Tony Bring sees as the natural order of things, making the world a Sodom and Gomorrah by indulging her lesbian proclivities.

Subsidiary images buttress the central image of Hildred/June as a persecuting harlot and mother, a demon-destroyer who rules over the kingdom of death. Hildred's face has a "beautiful cadaverous glow"; she examines her body like "an undertaker who perceives suddenly what a beautiful corpse he has under his hand"; her laughter expresses "slaughterhouse mirth"; when Tony Bring watches her, sleeping, he has a vision of "her face . . . decomposing." She kills through disease: "her body [harbors] the active germs of all the venereal woes." She is "the creator of traps . . . snares"; "his vulture"; a devouring bird of prey, "tearing the red mouth back to the ears." But she is also a powerful "queen advancing to her throne," an "angel/demon," filling Tony Bring with both "terror and joy." His universe is a "field of blind energy . . . moved according to the caprice of a demented monarch."

The struggle he portrays is between man, the potential maker of civilization and art, and woman, the narcotic seducer and subverter, dissembler, and creator of chaos, who lures men into underground dens of torture and pleasure from which escape or release is well nigh impossible. Hildred/June is "the carnal, vital essence, the propulsive, elemental force" who "invaded his senses like a narcotic." In making love, Hildred/June unleashes a "veritable pogrom of love." Embracing her is embracing death: the two of them are "skeletons articulated with love." To become free, Miller writes, men must *"hate the whore and shall make her desolate and naked, and shall eat her flesh, and burn her with fire."*

As Hildred/June is the vulture, Miller describes himself as her prey, her eternal victim, who because of his overwhelming love for her has lost everything—his self-respect, his courage, his ability to distinguish truth from falsity, his desire to keep on living. He becomes a stand-in for Dostoyevsky's Underground Man, ineluctably bound to his abuser, living an "underground life" in a cloacal world of filth and vice. Living this life has contaminated him: he feels coated with "a thin, nauseous slime. Sewer gas. His brains stank. The whole world stank."

He characterizes himself as living a life of "final, uninterrupted isolation." He is a supreme masochist, who has learned to love his pain and the woman who inflicts it, but who is collecting insults so that he can lash out and become a sadist himself, harming those who have harmed him—as he sees it, because he has been provoked.

Tony Bring grovels before Hildred's far greater power. When he sees her with another of her lovers, he waits for her to notice him: as she approaches him, he is "engulfed by a wave of gratitude and abasement. He wanted to fling himself on his knees." He waits for her to harm him: in his imagination, he sees himself "at the head of a long flight of stairs and she had pushed him with all her might, left him stunned and helpless."

Throughout the novel, Tony Bring has fantasies and dreams of persecution, powerlessness, and dismemberment: in one, his feet are sticking out a window; a man comes along with an ax, chops them off, and buries the stumps; in another, he is pursued by a "mob armed with scythes and shotguns," but he is unable to protect himself, and so surrenders because he is "paralyzed, rooted to the spot."

In one of the most powerful images in the novel, he sees himself as a man suspended upside down, hanging by his feet, inside a cage, which hangs inside a freight car that is conveying him and other men to an asylum. When asked if he's balanced or unbalanced, Tony Bring won't respond, so he is "carried off . . . and placed in a refrigerator to cool off. . . . It was chilly in the refrigerator and the cages swung like pendulums. . . . It was ice-cold time, without divisions and without arrest. A circular, prenatal time, without . . . pulse, or flux." Because of what he has endured, he has become inert.

In the "tangled dream" which accompanies his suicide attempt, Tony Bring has a flashback to early experiences of abuse inflicted by an older man, and then an old woman. First:

An odor of bay rum filled his nostrils and he felt again a wiry mustache pressed against his lips. A voice, honeyed and ingratiating, whispered to him, but he would not look, for the sight of the old man's throat was like an open sepulcher.

Then, the most horrific image of his own sexual violation Miller ever created:

> Over the frozen rim of the void there rose a fiery ball raining rivers of scarlet. He knew now that the end had come, that from this livid, smoldering circle of doom there was no retreat. He was on his knees, his head buried in the black scum. Suddenly a hand seized him by the nape of the neck and flung him backward into the mire. His arms were pinioned. Above him, digging her bony knees into his chest, was a naked hag. She kissed him with her soiled lips and her breath was hot as a bride's. He felt her bony arms tightening about him, pressing him to her loins. Her loins grew big and soft, her belly white and full. . . . Suddenly, in her clawlike grip, there glittered a bright blade; the blade descended and the blood spurted over his neck and into his eyes. . . . Gory, she raised her face, and again the blade descended . . . plunged into his throat and laid the gullet open. . . . The sky was one great river of scarlet.

Who are these abusers whom Tony Bring/Henry remembers as he tries to kill himself? Is the man Tillotson, the scout leader who abused him? Another older man? Perhaps Miller's father? Miller's father sported a mustache; he was alcoholic; and Miller has described both his homoerotic experience and his finding a packet of pornographic playing cards in his father's safe. And who is the old woman? His mother, who was physically abusive and violent? One of his older female relatives? Whomever they may represent, Tony Bring's nightmare visions link his suicidal mania with what he has survived, just as, perhaps, Miller's own "suicidal manias" were the result of what he had survived. In one scene, Tony Bring describes his suffering from hemorrhoids as a consequence of anal assault: he sees himself as "A man who's being strangled in the rectum."

Miller had described wanting to write a book about incest ever since he wanted to write. Whoever these abusers are, Miller has, through his use of imagery—the sepulcher in the male abuse dream and the soft loins and clawlike grip in the female abuse dream—associated them both with Hildred/June, who has taken on their function. The real subject of Crazy Cock, and of many of Miller's other works, is Miller's compulsive reenactment in adulthood, with June, of the overstimulation, torture, abuse, humiliation, soul-murder, and degradation he had experienced as a child with whomever these figures represent, and his attempt to rescue himself from the effect of that abuse, and to avenge himself, through writing. All the major work of his lifetime was propelled by violence; the most obvious target was June, but, as *Crazy Cock* suggests, she was only the emblem of every victimization he had endured. In describing what the act of writing was for Tony Bring, Henry Miller suggests something of what the act of writing *Crazy Cock* must have been.

> Late one afternoon, as if electrified, he sprang out of bed, consumed a hearty meal . . . , and began to write. . . . The words rose up inside him like tombstones and danced without feet; he piled them up like an acropolis of flesh, rained on them with vengeful hate until they dangled like corpses slung from a lamppost. . . . And he had his words copulate with one another to bring forth empires, scarabs, holy water, the lice of dreams and dream of wounds. He sat the words down and laced them to a chair . . . and then he fell on them and lashed them, lashed them until the blood ran black and the eyes broke their veils. What he remembered of his life were the shocks, the seismographic orgasms. . . . Abasement not reaching just to the earth, but through the earth. . . . Everything that was loved being hated fiercely.

When Miller showed *Crazy Cock* to Alfred Perles, Perles thought it was "worse than no good, it was beyond repair. There was no form, no discipline, no story discernible in his wild ramblings— only violence, repressed fury, a purposeful purposelessness, anarchy at its most futile"; Perles "disliked the book so much . . . he had quite literally taken sheafs of it and torn them apart." Most of Miller's other friends agreed. Osborn thought the style of the book was "old-fashioned." Walter Lowenfels thought it "corny and purple writing, trash, pulpy"; Michael Fraenkel thought it "inexorably flat, sterile, insipid" and told Miller to "tear it up," to write as he talked, to write as he lived, to write as he felt and thought.

Anaïs Nin, who later became Miller's lover, did not agree. When he showed her the work, she thought it "a ferocious and resplendent book," though not without faults: "I couldn't find you," she told him, "I would only see a man who was telling a story." She thought the portrait of June one-sided, that Miller had only written "the hate, the violence."

This criticism, with his own analysis, prepared Miller to rewrite the June saga, but in the first person, in his own voice. Near the end of his work on *Crazy Cock*, he felt hemmed in by the form he had chosen, by the notes he had taken, by the careful plan he had made. He decided that in his next work, he would "explode," he would get himself "across . . . direct as a knife thrust." He decided, too, that he would never again use the third person: "Hereafter, in referring to myself, nothing but the first person singular, a capital I, and no grimaces behind it. Be a man, as my father always counselled. Out with it!"

Despite the majority opinion against the work, and his knowledge that he would tell the story again, Miller tried for years to have it published. He submitted it in 1932 to Covici-Friede, Inc., but they rejected it in 1933. He later told a literary agent that he couldn't represent *Tropic of Cancer* unless he also took *Crazy Cock*, the story Miller really wanted to tell. *Crazy Cock* never saw print in Miller's lifetime; it was published posthumously by Grove Weidenfeld in 1991.

The novel he had completed, if he had allowed it to be edited to remove some heavily overwritten passages, was publishable, despite his friends' objections. Though less restrained than his later work, it was a remarkable piece of writing, with much to recommend it. Had it been published, it could not have been ignored. It was far bolder than many novels of its day, with some extraordinary writing, keen psychological insights about a powerful, abusive sexual entanglement with its roots in the players' pasts, sophisticated imagery, and marvelous flights of surrealism. One scene, in which Miller describes Vanya's being gang-raped, is in my judgment the most powerful, sympathetic description from the victim's point of view ever written by a man.

In 1932, June came to Paris. At some point, she had read the work. She was horrified that while he was writing her love letters, he was also savaging her in his novel. They had a furious fight about his using her as a literary subject, and she told him:

You are the greatest enemy I have in the world. I'm going to kill you. I read your letters as if God had written them, and all the while you were defaming me with your low filthy mind, your disgusting words.

She warned him not to publish the novel, or any work which mentioned her, or she would sue him. Then she changed her mind:

No, I want it published just as it is so the whole world can see what sort of person you are. When I read *Crazy Cock* it nearly killed me, but this is too funny, it's so distorted. . . . All you prove is that your own mind is petty and small. Now you'll expose yourself to everyone.

In July 1934, while he was hard at work on *Tropic of Capricorn*, his third novel about June, Henry Miller wrote his friend Richard Osborn that, in writing his work, he intended to erect "a tomb of June that will live for several centuries to come. That's what comes of injury and insult. The Jewish cunt will twitter!"

Miller intended that his life's work would be a reprisal against June for the harm she had done him. And he recognized that in writing about her, he had precipitated their divorce. When June joined him in Paris in the winter of 1932, she learned of his affair with Anaïs Nin. By that time, she had read her portrait in *Crazy Cock*, and during this last visit she read *Tropic of Cancer*, in which she is depicted as crawling with bugs and is associated with the central image of the fucked-out cunt of a whore from whom all evil in the universe emanates. She learned that he intended to publish both books, and she was furious.

Before she left him, she warned that if he published his cruel portraits of her, she would strike back by telling Anaïs Nin's husband about their affair.

"Big blowup—everything over at last," Miller wrote to Emil Schnellock on November 28, 1932. June's last message to Miller was a piece of toilet tissue with the scrawled words, "Please get a divorce immediately." He took it and pasted it carefully into his "June Notebook." In the mess that she had left behind, he found a single silk stocking. He kept it to shine his shoes.

A few months later, he wrote Schnellock about June. Richard Osborn had written that he had seen June in Greenwich Village, on the arm of a young man, and had tried unsuccessfully to talk to her about Henry: "June is very bitter and will hear nothing about me—except to know if the book has been published."

Miller thought he had pried her out of his mind; but when he heard she was with another man, he realized his feelings were still strong: "there is this June," he wrote Schnellock, "this damned Jewish vulture gnawing into my vitals whether I want it or not—first with her passivity, her jealousy, her overwhelming sex and clawing beak, and now with hatred and malice and vindictiveness."

In the midst of a drunken fury, he admitted that what he really wanted was for June to "get down on her knees and *beg me to forgive her*. I want her to weep until her heart breaks." He had her number: he knew who "June Smith-Smerth-Mansfield-Miller-Cunt-Balls-Whore" was "down to the roots of her insatiable cunt," but he had loved her anyway, and that had been his misfortune. He was a "victim of love."

But he could see, too, that he had pushed her away from him. He knew June had loved him in her own way, "no doubt about it," and that they might still be together were it not for what he had written:

> Had I not been a fool artist I might have held her. I might today have been happy. But I could love her and at the same time I could ridicule her. I had to tell her the truth about herself, and she could not stand that.

He told Schnellock he couldn't "bear to have her hate me." He was even willing to commit suicide if he knew it would stop June's hatred: "if killing myself will soothe her conscience, if putting this miserable Henry Miller who loved her so much out of the way, will help any, I will do it."

"What does she want me to do?" he asked himself and Schnellock.

> Does she want me to stop writing about her? I can't do that. That is my life. Unfortunately. All too unfortunately.

Writing about June *was* Henry Miller's life. He wrote about her throughout the rest of his stay in Paris; he wrote about her when he returned to the United States, through all his years in California. He wrote about her through his affair with Anaïs Nin; his third marriage, to Janina Lepska; his fourth marriage, to Eve McClure (whom he described as a cross between Anaïs and June). He completed *Nexus*, his last published novel about June, in 1959, twenty-seven years later, when he was approaching his seventieth birthday, thirty-two years after he had written out his initial plan for his life's work about June in the Parks Department in Queens. In each of his works, he wrote out his rage. But he also wrote out his love. And, like Milton's Satan, Miller's Hildred/Mona/June was his most compelling creation: her portrait was imbued with the tremendous power and significance of an icon. Though he had wanted to erect a tomb of June that would live for centuries, what he erected as well was a monument to her memory.

Forest Hills, New York
September 1961

The only time Henry Miller saw June after her departure from Paris in 1932 was nearly thirty years later, in September 1961, when Henry was approaching his sixty-ninth birthday and June was fifty-eight. He was on his way back to his home in California after a trip to Europe. He was poor but at the height of his fame, with *Tropic of Cancer*, which had finally been published in the United States, the "blockbuster" of the year.

June had been looking forward to his visit, and had set a "sumptuous table" to welcome him, buying "good wine and plenty of food, remembering his enjoyment of them." When she saw him, she "gazed at him with admiration," telling him he looked "wonderfully well, rakish, handsome, dapper, full of energy and exhilaration."

When he saw her, he was shocked. Instead of the arresting character he had been writing about for years, the June who greeted him was a crippled old woman, though she struck him as courageous and full of spirit.

After leaving him in Paris and returning to New York, June had married Stratford Corbett, the lover she had left behind, but he abandoned her at the end of 1942. After World War II, she lived "miserably in a dump on Clinton Avenue, near many of their old haunts." Her weight had fallen to sixty-seven pounds. Throughout her life, she was always "broke and starving," subject to a number of physical ailments: she had lost her teeth, her eyes were bad, and she had become arthritic. She never had enough money for the medical care she required and the penicillin she needed. She had spent time in an asylum, and had undergone shock treatments; during her stay, she had suffered a crippling fall. Recently, she was trying to recover, and had been working at a civil service job for the City of New York. In recent years, Henry had received many letters from her, begging him for "money, food, his books, snapshots of himself and his family, his watercolors—anything."

One thing about June hadn't changed. Her voice, which had mesmerized him, was still as "striking" as he recalled. And she talked as compulsively as she had in the past, but he now saw through the sameness of her stories.

He was so disturbed by seeing her that he wanted to leave as quickly as possible, but she expected him to stay. "She pointed to the bed. He began to weep and left hurriedly."

In reviewing their final moments together, Miller felt he had "triumphed in her decline, winning his reputation by writing about June." He wondered whether he could write an account of this meeting to use it as "a marvellous pendant to his autobiographical romances. Its theme would be: June was stronger—but *he* had won."

After their final meeting, Henry Miller abandoned the writing of his lifelong autobiographical saga about her. He had completed *Nexus*, the third volume of *The Rosy Crucifixion*, and had planned another volume describing his and June's first trip to Europe. But seeing her put a "closure on his real-life 'rosy crucifixion,' and he no longer felt the need to write about it."

Henry Miller's major life's work about June was nearly complete.

Near the end of 1961, around the holidays, Miller tossed off a play in three days, *Just Wild About Harry*. He had spent Christmas, and his sixty-ninth birthday, depressed and alone. He was living by himself—he and Eve had separated, and his current lover, Renate Gerhardt, couldn't be with him.

For his Christmas dinner, he had fixed himself a bowl of spaghetti, making enough for leftovers he could reheat the next day, his birthday. To amuse himself, he spent some time painting watercolors. Then, on a whim, he began to write a play, a form he hadn't tried since his underground days in Henry Street with June and Jean.

The play he wrote was a reprise of his years with June. This time, he re-created himself not as June's victim, but as "the swaggering Harry, a womanizer and near-gangster." Writing about June, he was happy to discover, cured his depression.

Pacific Palisades, California
October 1977

Henry Miller wrote the final portrait of his life with June in October 1977 for his young inamorata, Brenda Venus. Unlike his earlier writings, this was not a revenge piece, but rather a work in which he admitted a few things he hadn't before. He still kept a "mysterious and haunting" picture of June where he could see it, hung on a wall near the entrance to his kitchen.

He was living in Pacific Palisades, in a house that looked "like the home of a movie star," and he was just as famous. Even though his home was grand and elegant and had a heated swimming pool for his daily exercise, inside he had re-created a more luxurious version of the bohemian basement apartment in Henry Street he had shared with June and Jean. He encouraged his guests to draw and write all over the walls; he pasted psychedelic posters on the ceilings; and he created a bathroom with a montage of photos, sayings ("Even nice people get Syphilis"), and pictures of "everything from . . . fakirs and sages . . . to houris and whores" on the walls.

Miller was living the life of a semi-invalid, though he had a constant stream of visitors. He "shuffled about the house leaning on a walker, usually clad in a blue terrycloth bathrobe and pajamas," wearing "slippers even on his infrequent trips out of the house," and had devised a scheme whereby friends cooked an evening meal for him. An order to his cooks, reading, "No health foods!", was posted in his kitchen.

In June 1976, at eighty-four years old, he had started a relationship with Brenda Venus, a young actress who had appeared with Clint Eastwood in the film *The Eiger Sanction*, which lasted until his death in 1980. He thought she looked like June. He told her that despite his reputation and what he had written, he had always been, and still was, an "incurable Romantic," that he really was old-fashioned in his views about sex—he didn't like to share "the woman [he was in love with] with other men," and that he liked his women passionate but pure.

Although he told her "sex was out of the question," he described his fantasies about making love to her: "You are insatiable. . . . You have lost your mind. You are totally sex and nothing else." He thought of her all day long, accompanying his reveries by singing himself old songs, like "Roses of Picardy," the song that was associated in his life and work with the despair of his love for June. He asked Brenda to describe to him in detail her sexual fantasies, and to help her he sent her Japanese erotic cards, books of Tantra yoga positions and erotic Indian temple sculpture. But he didn't neglect her intellectual edification, and sent along the names of books she should read (Knut Hamsun's *Mysteries*, the works of Dostoyevsky) and vocabulary words for her to learn—a list of "M's for Brenda, plucked from *the skull of a literary gent*—at random: menstrual/marsupial . . . metempsychosis/ metabolism/ . . . masturbation/ marijuana . . . monogamy."

Henry Miller often spoke to Brenda Venus of June. He told her in detail of their marriage—how June "was the most sought-after woman he had ever known," how she was "always ready to make love to Henry anywhere, time, or place," how she never wore underwear, how she always wore "an open kimono, keeping herself as exposed as possible."

One night, at dinner, Brenda asked him why, if he spoke of June with such obvious fondness, he had written of her "with such contempt."

"Why, why, why?" he shot back. "Don't ever ask me 'why?' There is no answer to why. People do what they want to do."

Brenda persisted.

You portrayed June like a streetwalker, a nickel-and-dime whore, which she wasn't. Or was she? You coaxed her into marrying you, not the other way around. She supported you and loved you. If she took money from a man and gave it to you, so you could be the literary giant you are today, then *you* are the hypocrite! You *killed* June in Paris with *Tropic of Cancer*!

For the first time, someone was challenging Miller about the way he had written of June, and he was so furious that he "dropped his fork and almost leaped out of his wheelchair." He told Brenda that she hadn't been there, didn't know what had happened, and couldn't understand.

The following day, Brenda received a "special delivery letter and telegram berating" her. But then he called, apologizing.

Sometime later, she asked him to explain what his "relationship with June *really* was," and to write a "short scene" as illustration.

In October 1977, fifty years after he had planned his life's work, on the eve of his eighty-sixth birthday, Henry Miller again picked up his pen to sketch a "Scene from Unfinished Play" for Brenda about his life with June. The physical act of writing was now very difficult for him, and he couldn't see very well, having lost the sight of one eye during a lengthy operation—"one-eyed Jack," he called himself. He wrote it, he told Brenda, "to answer a lot of questions" both for himself and for her. It was to be his last work about June. In it, he described their relationship in a way he hadn't before.

The scene takes place in a "modest flat in a big city—sparsely furnished but in good taste, *à la Japonaise*"—the love nest at Remsen Street—and describes the lives of a married couple: Hal, "a young aspiring writer who has had nothing accepted," and Stella, who "has sacrificed . . . in order to help her young husband become a famous writer" by whatever work she does when she goes out alone at night.

Hal has been trying to write about her, "reproducing *our* life as nearly as possible," but his stumbling block is how to describe what she does at night.

As a present to Miller, Brenda acted out the scene, taking both parts.

STELLA
(Quickly)

You didn't make me out to be a whore, I hope. . . .

HAL

To tell the truth, the first thing that came to mind was—a whore. But a very discreet, very intelligent one. . . .

STELLA

. . . You want me to be sexy, but no fucking, right? Is that just to save your face? You know it's an impossible situation. . . . I hope you made me attractive.

Henry Miller sat in his bathrobe, in his wheelchair, and watched Brenda reenacting the concluding moments of the last words he would ever write about his life with June. The right side of his face was smiling, but the left side was grimacing, an effect of his disability.

HAL

I made you "irresistible"—how do you like that? . . . So then you *are* whoring it?

STELLA

If you want to call it that!

HAL

Well, what else could you call it? It's all my fault. I should never have allowed you to play the man's part.

(Another pause—his face suddenly brightening)

You know something—it makes no difference at all! *I love you.* I'll always love you.

6

AFTERWORD

I n 1939, Henry Miller stayed in Greece with his good friend Lawrence Durrell. Miller regarded it as a time of rest owed him after the intense period of writing he had been through in Paris. He had finished *Crazy Cock* and *Tropic of Cancer*, and he now knew that he could call himself a writer.

Forever interested in the mystical, Miller decided to consult a soothsayer in the Armenian refugee quarter of Athens, teeming with the "destitute, homeless, penniless." It took him a long time to find the home of the soothsayer, Aram Hourabedian, for it was "buried in the heart of the labyrinth." But the encounter changed his life.

In the clean and orderly living room, speaking to Miller in French, the soothsayer told him that he was destined for greatness, but that he had "created many enemies (by what I had written) and caused much harm and suffering." Hearing this, Miller felt "chastened," but he also felt a "sense of responsibility." After, he decided to think about why he had used his writing to avenge himself.

In time, in response to his experience with Aram Hourabedian, Henry Miller developed a philosophy about the creative process in which he examined why writers like himself (and like Leonard Woolf, D. H. Lawrence, Djuna Barnes, and all the other writers I have referred to) created works of art that wounded others. He concluded that the most pressing motive was to prevent the self from fragmenting, and to heal the self.

I will close this excursion into the writing of literature as re-

venge with this observation by Henry Miller. It is the most eloquent expression I have found to explain why certain works of art
are conceived with malice. For what Miller observes is how,
through the alchemy of human suffering, our stories can be transformed into works of art, and how we, as creators, enrich the human landscape through giving voice to our pain.

> The therapeutic aspect of art is then, in this higher state of
> consciousness, seen to be the religious or metaphysical element.
> The work which was begun as a refuge and escape from the terrors
> of reality leads the author back into life, not *adapted* to the
> reality ... but *superior* to it, as one capable of recreating it in
> accordance with his own needs. He sees that it was not life but
> himself from which he had been fleeing, and that the life which
> had heretofore been insupportable was merely the projection of his
> own phantasies. It is true that the new life is also a projection of
> the individual's own phantasies but they are invested now with
> the sense of real power; they spring not from dissociation but from
> integration. The whole past life resumes its place in the balance
> and creates a vital, stable equilibrium which would never have
> resulted without the pain and the suffering. It is in this sense that
> the endless turning about in a cage which characterized the
> author's thinking, the endless fresco which seems never to be
> brought to a conclusion, the ceaseless fragmentation and analysis
> which goes on night and day, is like a gyration which through
> sheer centrifugal force lifts the sufferer out of his obsessions and
> frees him for the rhythm and movement of life by joining him to
> the great universal stream in which all of us have our being.

NOTES

INTRODUCTION:
Literature as Revenge

The phrases in bold type refer to the first words of the paragraph on the page given. References are provided, using the last names of authors, for page numbers for direct quotations and information within that paragraph. Complete citations are provided in the Sources.

PAGE

3   **In 1613, Overbury:** Bowers 25 ff.; McElwee.

4   **Overbury's weapons:** McElwee 41.

4   **In September:** Bowers 26.

4   **Sir Thomas Overbury:** Paglia xiii: "How and why does an artist create? The amorality, aggression, sadism, voyeurism, and pornography in great art have been ignored or glossed over by most academic critics."

5   **I conceived:** DeSalvo, *Virginia Woolf's First Voyage.*

5   **When I became interested:** DeSalvo, *Virginia Wolf;* Woolf *Letters* II 474; *Letters* IV 250–51; see Morgan.

6   **Woolf herself:** DeSalvo "Lighting the Cave," 195–214; in a letter to Sackville-West, Woolf wrote, "For Promiscuous you are, and that's all there is to be said of you" (Woolf *Letters* III 514); Woolf *Letters* III 474; DeSalvo and Leaska, eds., Sackville-West *Letters* 264.

6   **Beauvoir's *The Mandarins:*** Bair 422; my thanks to Deirdre Bair for providing this information before the publication of her biography of Beauvoir.

7   **Beauvoir had promised:** Bair 501.

7   **Elizabeth Harlan:** Elizabeth Harlan, personal communication; Cate 545; Sand, however, disclaimed this motive in *My Life* (234), where she writes, "It has been claimed that I portrayed his [Chopin's] character with great analytical accuracy in one of my novels. This is an error."

7   **Not content to use:** Cate 545; my thanks to Elizabeth Harlan for providing these references to Sand.

7   **Every biography:** Benstock 393; see Glendinning and Fromm; Nin *Henry and June* 20, 233, 236; Trefusis (I should like to thank Mindy Werner for providing information about *Broderie Anglaise*); Carpenter 160, 180, 192; Virginia Woolf *Diary* III 165; White *passim;* Land 33–48, 66–67, 76; Lottman; Susan Cheever *Treetops;* Angier; Storr *Solitude* 116; Belford; Battestin and Battestin, *Henry Fielding;* Dearborn; Nin *Diary* 307; Land, Wijsenbeek; Middlebrook 265–66; for information about Flaubert's revenge against Louise Colet, I should like to thank Francine du Plessix Gray, biographer of Louise Colet; Mellow *passim;* DeSalvo, *Nathaniel Hawthorne* 82–84.
8   **Otto Rank:** Nin *Diary* 307, 329.
9   **I have taken:** A. West uses the phrase in his Introduction to *Heritage;* Gardner 137.
9   **When I told:** Koestler "The Logic of Laughter" in *The Act of Creation.*
10   **It took me some time:** Two differing views on revenge are provided in *Wild Justice* by Susan Jacoby, who urges us to understand the human need for vengeance, and in *Anger* by Carol Tarvis, who observes that getting angry often makes us angrier.
10   **Incest is:** Herman; Shengold; Hawkins; Bass and Davis.
10   **The pain inflicted:** Middlebrook 100.
10   **But the pain:** Nin *Diary* 144.
10   **She should:** Nin *Henry and June* 86; 97; 270; Miller and Fowlie 60.
11   **The budding novelist:** Plath 133; Stevenson 214, 227.
11   **That "batch of stuff":** Plath 138.
11   **Plath published:** Stevenson 302.
11   **The character Nora:** Field 160.
12   **Djuna Barnes:** Field 149, 162, 163, 160.
12   **Thelma Wood:** Field 160, 196, 168.
12   **In Elizabethan life:** Bowers 21–23.
13   **Taking revenge:** Tarvis 203.
13   **A revenge piece:** Storr *Human Destructiveness* 10; Storr *Human Aggression* 14, 19; Miller in Perles and Durrell 59; Meyers *D. H. Lawrence* 406.
14   **When erotic relationships:** Storr *Human Aggression* 70.
14   **Just as in the animal:** Huffington; Angier 80; Land 13, 224–25.
14   **Nonetheless:** Middlebrook 52.
15   **When Lee Miller:** Baldwin.
15   **Instead, not too long:** Baldwin 168.
15   **In *This Quartet:*** Baldwin 168.
16   **Contemporary libel laws:** Lewis; Mayer.
16   **Sometimes victims:** Land 69; 46–47.
17   **The massive, ongoing study:** Rothenberg *Creativity and Madness* 69.
17   **Writing the work:** Rothenberg 46, 70, 41.
17   **Sigmund Freud:** Freud "Creative Writers and Day-Dreaming"; see also Storr's critique of Freud's position in *Solitude* 64.
17   **Freud also believed:** Freud "Creative Writers," 150, 152.
18   **The writer creates:** Freud 150.
18   **That internal turmoil:** Freud 151.

18   **And what of the reader:** Freud 153.
18   **In his monumental work:** Koestler 27, 188.
18   **Our act:** Koestler 303; Storr *Solitude;* Tytell; Miller *Stories* 111.
18   **The creation:** Storr *Human Aggression* 88.
18   **One should not:** Rothenberg 168; Miller *The Books in My Life* 97.
19   **Sir Francis Bacon:** Bacon 13.
19   **It is far better:** Bacon 14.
20   **Revenge ensures:** Bacon 14.
20   **Yet Thomas Moore's:** see Moore 291.

"THAT STRANGE PRELUDE":
Leonard Woolf, Virginia Woolf
and *The Wise Virgins*

The phrases in bold type refer to the first words of the paragraph on the page given. References are provided on a paragraph-by-paragraph basis for direct quotations and sources for information within that paragraph. In the case of Virginia Woolf's letters, if the number of the letter is referred to, it is preceded by the symbol "#." Complete citations are provided in the Sources.

Saragossa, Spain, September 4, 1912

PAGE

25   **Leonard Woolf sat:** V. Woolf [VW] *Letters* [L] II #645; Q. Bell *Virginia Woolf* I 4–5.
25   **During the morning:** VW *L* II #644.
25   **After dinner:** VW *L* II #644 #645.

Trinity College, Cambridge, 1900–1901

PAGE

26   **The first time:** There are several different accounts of their first meeting, giving different dates. They appear in VW *L* I #31; L. Woolf [LW] *Sowing* 183; VW *Moments of Being* [*Moments*] 186–87; LW *L* 50 fn 1.
26   **Leonard might have caught:** LW *Sowing* 128; Dunn 100.
27   **After a time:** VW *L* I 34; #37.
27   **These dances:** VW *L* I #35; see VW *Passionate Apprentice* [*Passionate*] 149.
27   **Leonard Woolf spent no time:** LW *Sowing* 183.
28   **Leonard Woolf was uncomfortable:** *Lytton Strachey by Himself* 110; LW *L* 108.
28   **Virginia believed she:** VW *L* I #71; LW *Sowing* 167–69.
28   **Leonard was nervous:** LW *Sowing* 184; LW *L* 29; LW *Sowing* 159.
28   **Never sure of himself:** see LW *Sowing* 184; see Deacon; LW *Sowing* 196; VW *L* I #222.
29   **In the long and awkward:** LW *Sowing* 184.
29   **Given his insecurities:** LW *Sowing* 180; VW *Passionate* 149.
29   **Leonard had already met:** LW *Sowing* 180.
29   **Leonard and Sir Leslie:** VW *Moments* 109; LW *Sowing* 42, 82, 100; Sir Leslie Stephen Letters, Berg.

30   **Virginia Stephen had heard:** VW *Moments* 164.
30   **The exploits:** VW *Moments* 165.
30   **One day:** VW *Moments* 166.

46 Gordon Square, Bloomsbury, November 17, 1904
PAGE
30   **The second time:** LW *L* 50; LW *Growing* 11.
31   **The dinner took place:** VW *L* I #237; LW *Beginning Again* [*Beginning*] 27.
31   **Before Leonard departed:** VW *Moments* 188–89.
31   **We do not have a record:** LW *Sowing* 160; VW *L* I #183; VW *Moments* 190; Dunn 97.
31   **Through his years:** LW *L* 116.
32   **To Virginia:** VW *Moments* 184.
32   **It was possible:** Dunn 91.
32   **It was essential:** VW *Passionate* 213.
32   **Until this time; the most important person:** VW *L* I #74; #89; 91.
32   **Violet had given:** VW *L* I #189.
33   **Each sister:** VW *L* I #202.
33   **She wanted:** VW *L* I #203.
33   **She began to write:** VW MH/A.26, Monks House Papers.
33   **It had been a very difficult year:** VW *L* I p. 141; #186; #181; #183.
34   **It had taken:** VW *L* I #152.
34   **During her father's illness:** VW *Moments* 182–83; VW *L* I #170.
34   **Vanessa dismantled:** VW *Moments;* DeSalvo *Virginia Woolf.*
34   **Leonard Woolf, like Virginia:** LW *L* 43, 35, 47–48.
35   **He was not going to Ceylon:** LW *Sowing* 193, 202; LW *L* 30, 45,47, 50.
35   **Before he decided:** LW *L* 30, 48, 35; Lytton Strachey [LS] to LW, 10 June 1907, Berg Collection.
35   **He did very poorly:** LW *L* 45, 48, 44, 51.
36   **In the weeks before his departure:** LW *L* 51; LW *Sowing* 202; LW *Growing* 37–38.
36   **Just a short time:** LW *L* 50–51.
36   **When he walked:** LW *Growing* 11; LW *L* 52.
36   **Leonard Woolf would celebrate:** LW *L* 51.

Jaffna, Ceylon, July 1905
PAGE
36   **Leonard was lonelier:** LW *L* 83, 73, 75, 76; LW *Growing* 92.
37   **But in the evenings:** LW *L* 72, 80.
37   **He lived in a bungalow:** LW *Growing* 64, 122.
37   **Leonard opened:** LS to LW November 26, 1906, Berg.
37   **The news was a shock:** LW *L* 97.
37   **Leonard had been in Vanessa's company:** LW *L* 24.
38   **Leonard did, finally, admit:** LW *L* 98.
38   **Thousands of miles:** LW *L* 43, 98.

Jaffna, Ceylon, Autumn 1905–Winter 1906

PAGE

38 **With Vanessa:** LW *L* 102; LW *Growing* 147; LW *Sowing* 81.

39 **He admitted:** LW *Sowing* 82, 66–67, 41–42.

39 **In his friendship:** see VW "Old Bloomsbury" in *Moments.*

39 **Vanessa was in a separate:** LW *L* 106, 116.

39 **Before his letter:** LW *L* 102, 107, 116.

39 **The madness:** LW *L* 113, 115, 118.

40 **Nor did Strachey's letters:** LW *L* 62, 119; see Deacon.

46 Gordon Square, Bloomsbury, Autumn 1905–Winter 1906

PAGE

40 **"Cambridge youths,":** VW *L* I #250.

40 **Contemplating these sorry:** VW *L* I #250.

40 **She had read:** Spielmann and Layard 188; VW *L* I #251.

40 **Her passionate friendship:** VW *L* I #250.

40 **Another source of conflict:** VW *Passionate* 232.

40 **Early in the year:** VW *Passionate* 222.

41 **The only morning:** VW *L* I passim.

41 **She was very busy:** Kirkpatrick 135–37; VW *Passionate* 243.

41 **She was earning:** VW *Passionate* 235.

Jaffna, Ceylon, December 1906

PAGE

41 **Leonard Woolf had received:** LW *L* 122.

41 **Leonard had received:** LW *L* 122.

42 **Before the news:** LW *L* 120, 122–123.

42 **Idealized by Leonard:** LW *L* 140, 124.

42 **"Please be ready:** LS to LW, November 26, 1906, Berg.

42 **Too worn out:** LW *L* 123.

29 Fitzroy Square, Bloomsbury, 1906–1907

PAGE

43 **After Thoby's death:** Gordon 26.

43 **She considered Thoby's doctor:** VW *L* I #330.

43 **At first:** VW *L* I #333, #325.

43 **After Vanessa was engaged:** VW *L* I #335; VW *Passionate* 382 ff.

44 **Virginia was furious:** VW *L* I #333, #355; Q. Bell *Virginia Woolf* I 118.

44 **She felt "desperate":** VW *L* I #347.

44 **At Fitzroy Square:** VW *L* I passim.

44 **Vanessa married:** VW *L* I #336; VW *Passionate* 374.

44 **In October:** VW *L* I #390.

44 **Living separately:** VW *L* #369.

Jaffna, Kandy, and Hambantota, Ceylon, 1907–1909

PAGE

45 **During the two years:** LW *Growing* 24.

45   **He became "almost:** LW *Growing* 27, 173.

45   **He had learned:** LW *Growing* 36, 120.

45   **Although he grew:** LW *Growing* 166: Meyerowitz; Wilson.

45   **He worked:** LW *Growing* 79, 59; LW *L* 59.

46   **Unlike many:** LW *L* 58; LW *Growing* 212.

46   **The first time:** LW *L* 64.

46   **His first platonic:** LW *Growing* 102.

46   **But if he was:** LW *Growing* 155–56.

47   **He knew:** LW *L* 134.

47   **Although he had fallen:** LW *L* 142.

47   **When he left:** LW *Growing* 156.

47   **On February 1:** LW *L* 144–45; the editor says Lytton's letter was about Leonard Woolf's marrying Virginia; it is likely that the two of them were discussing who should marry Virginia.

47   **Lytton's love life:** LS to LW February 5, 1909, Berg.

47   **Leonard wrote:** LW *L* 145.

48   **Even as he proposed:** Holroyd 405.

48   **On February 19:** LW *L* 147; VW and LS *L* 32.

49   **After his meeting:** LW *L* 147.

49   **Nothing came:** LW *L* 148.

49   **In the summer:** LW *L* 148–49.

49   **The strategy worked:** LW *L* 150; one wonders whether, if Strachey had not written in this way to Leonard, Leonard would have had the courage to pursue his suit when he returned to London.

29 Fitzroy Square, Bloomsbury and St. Ives, Cornwall, April 1908–1911

PAGE

50   **Clive Bell:** quoted in Dunn 101.

51   **She wrote him:** VW *L* I #406; Clive Bell [CB] to VW, April 18, 1908, Berg.

51   **Virginia joined Clive:** VW *L* I #412, #408; VW *L* I #410.

52   **Clive supported:** VW *L* I #357; Vanessa Bell [VB] to VW February 7 [1909], Berg; Spalding 51, 82.

52   **Clive and Virginia's affair:** Spalding 65.

52   **For Virginia:** see DeSalvo, *Virginia Woolf;* VW *L* I #409.

53   **After Virginia's affair:** Spalding 96.

53   **The affair became:** Trombley 9; VW *L* III #1542.

53   **By 1911:** VW *L* I #570.

London, Cambridge, and Dartmoor, June–December 1911

PAGE

53   **Leonard Woolf was thirty-one:** LW *Growing* 247; LW *Beginning* 15.

54   **The first person:** Holroyd 465.

54   **Leonard dined:** LW *Beginning* 18–20.

54   **He joined:** Holroyd 466.

54   **Leonard discovered:** LW *Beginning* 26.

55   **It was only:** Kirkpatrick 135–41.

55 **Lytton Strachey had:** Spater and Parsons [Spater] 54.
55 **Strachey was always:** LW *L* 99.
55 **Strachey's information:** Spater 53.
56 **Leonard and Virginia's:** Gordon 137.
56 **"Dear Mr Wolf,":** VW *L* I #571.
56 **He had returned:** LW *Beginning* 36–37.
57 **Shortly after:** LW *L* 166, 156.
57 **Leonard and Virginia:** LW *Beginning* 48; Spater 58.
57 **In November:** LW *Beginning* 75; LW *L* 167.
58 **Leonard moved:** Spater 59.
58 **Leonard had saved:** LW *Beginning* 75.
58 **Living together:** Alexander 65.

38 Brunswick Square, London, Asheham House, Sussex, January–February 1912
PAGE

58 **It was:** LW *L* 168–69.
58 **Unsure:** Spater 59.
59 **Immediately after:** LW *L* 169–70.
59 **She parried:** LW *L* 169.
59 **After Virginia:** LW *Beginning* 57–59.
60 **Leonard joined:** VW *L* I #602.
60 **Though Leonard:** VW *L* I #602.

Burley, Cambridge Park, Twickenham, 38 Brunswick Square, Bloomsbury, Asheham House, Sussex, March–May 1912
PAGE

61 **Jean Thomas's:** VW *L* I #531; VB *L* 94.
61 **Virginia described:** VW *L* I #606; #609.
62 **On March 21:** LW *Beginning* 82.
62 **While at Twickenham:** VW *L* I #608.
63 **Leonard envied:** LW *L* 31.
63 **After she was released:** LW *Beginning* 81–82.
63 **He had written:** Spater 61–62.
64 **She continued:** VW *L* I #612, #613, #618.
64 **He had read:** LW *L* 173.
65 **"There are moments":** VW *L* I #615.
65 **On May 29:** LW *L* 176; VW *L* I #620, #622, #623.
66 **Virginia's decision:** Holroyd 490.
66 **The engagement:** Q. Bell *Virginia Woolf* II 1.
66 **The only way:** VW *L* I #620.
66 **When she told:** VW *L* I #631.
67 **Her illness:** VW *L* I #625; Julia Stephen, *Notes from Sickrooms*.
67 **And he:** LW *Beginning* 69.

London, August 10, 1912
PAGE
67   Leonard and Virginia: VW L II #642; LW *Beginning* 70.
68   Attending the ceremony: VW L II #643, #642; L I #635.
68   Leonard had not: LW *Downhill All the Way* 254.
68   Marie Woolf: LW L 178.
68   In marrying: LW *Beginning* 75.
69   Virginia told: VW L II #640, L I #627; Meyerowitz 15; VW *Night and Day* quoted in Poole 39.

The Plough Inn, Holford, Somerset, Late August 1912
PAGE
70   Leonard told: LW L 162.
70   Leonard blamed: Q. Bell *Virginia Woolf* II 6.
70   Sexually demonstrative: LW L 116.
70   How did: see DeSalvo *Virginia Woolf*; Poole 51.
71   While the Woolfs: VB L 123–24; the letter is in response to a letter from VW that is not extant.
71   Leonard obliged: VB to VW September 2 [1912], Berg.
72   Just as Virginia: VB L 117–18.
72   Vanessa wanted: VB to LW August 29, 1912, quoted in Dunn 184; VB L 123–24.

The Wise Virgins, September 1912–June 1913
PAGE
73   Leonard began: LW L 183; VW L II #666, #655.
73   It was: VW L II #665, #666; LW L 183.
74   But there was: VB L 131–32.
74   And there was: VB to VW January 22 [January 26, 1913], Berg.
74   His fears: VB to VW September 14 [1912], Berg.
74   What had happened: VB to VW September 14 [1912], Berg.
75   Early in 1913: VB to VW January 22 [1913], Berg.
76   Before his honeymoon: LW *The Wise Virgins* [*Virgins*] 104.
76   It was a novel: *Virgins* 84.
77   One of the worst: *Virgins* 154.
77   He decides: *Virgins* 37, 36, 16, 39.
78   The Wise Virgins: *Virgins* 96, 97.
78   When Camilla: *Virgins* 145, 147, 155.
78   If this is how: *Virgins* 191, 201.
79   Though Gwen: *Virgins* 207–8, 213.
79   When Gwen: *Virgins* 218, 220, 221, 223, 222.
79   Gwen tells: *Virgins* 227.
80   Camilla appears: Paglia 128–29.
80   Until Virginia: It is difficult to ascertain the earliest date by which Virginia read the novel.

13, Cliffords Inn, Fleet Street and Burley, Cambridge Park, Twickenham, June–September 1913

PAGE

81 **"Marriage:** VW *L* IV #2157.

81 **The trouble:** LW *Beginning* 150.

81 **According to Thomas:** J. M. Thomas to Violet Dickinson September 14 [1913], Berg.

81 **When Leonard:** LW *L* 185.

81 **She was responding:** VB *L* 141–42.

82 **After his visit:** LW *L* 186–87.

82 **Unable to face:** LW *L* 187.

82 **At the beginning:** LW *L* 187–89.

82 **She said:** VW *L* II #679.

83 *The Wise Virgins:* LW *L,* letter from Bella Woolf, November 19, 1913, indicates that Leonard had shown the novel to Virginia.

83 **During this period:** LW *L* 195 fn 1 to letter from Bella Woolf dated November 19, 1913, states that the novel was finished three months earlier; this would date the completion of the work at about August 19, during their stay at Asheham.

83 **Her recuperation:** J. M. Thomas to Violet Dickinson September 14 [1913], Berg.

83 **The trip:** LW *Beginning* 151.

83 **With almost no:** Poole 138.

83 **Leonard, however worried:** LW *Beginning* 153–54.

84 **Virginia was now:** LW *Beginning* 154, Poole 100, VW *Diary* IV, entry for July 14, 1932.

84 **They made:** LW *Beginning* 155–56.

38 Brunswick Square, Bloomsbury, Tuesday, September 9, 1913

PAGE

84 **The next day:** Holroyd 546.

84 **On the morning:** LW *Beginning* 156.

85 **Leonard left:** LW *Beginning* 156.

85 **Leonard had another:** Spater 73 provides a translation of Leonard's diary entry for the day, kept in code.

85 **Virginia Woolf did not recover:** LW *L* 191; LW *Beginning* says she did not recover consciousness until Thursday; contemporary records indicate she did not recover until Friday.

85 **Although he was:** LW *Beginning* 157.

85 **In the months:** LW *L* 196–97, 195, 493; Bella Woolf's letter is quoted in Gordon 154.

86 **Leonard decided:** LW *L* 197.

86 **Lytton Strachey's:** Lytton Strachey to LW December 16, 1913, Berg; Holroyd 553.

86 **After soliciting:** LW *L* 197.

86 **Despite the majority:** LW *L* 199.

87 This decided: LW *L* 205.

87 How the Woolf: VW *Night and Day*, quoted in Poole 47.

87 Virginia's recovery: VW *Diary* I entry for September 15, 1915; VW *Diary* II 283.

87 In 1915: VW *Diary* I 55, 32: Poole believes "the amount of repression" in Woolf's remarks regarding the novel was "massive" 101; LW *Beginning* 161; Gordon 155.

88 Both Leonard: VB quoted in Poole 101.

88 In time, Virginia: Poole 72; Spater 81; Gordon 156.

88 Although he was: Spater 70.

88 Leonard Woolf: VW *Diary* II 283.

89 Publishing: LW *Beginning* 91.

89 After the debacle: LW *L* 568, 197, 283.

89 In 1933: VW *Diary* IV 193.

"LIKE A LION RAGING AFTER ITS PREY":
D. H. Lawrence, Ottoline Morrell,
and *Women in Love*

The phrases listed below refer to the first words of the paragraph on the page given. References are provided, using the last names of authors, a shortened form of the title (if there are two sources by the same author), and page numbers, on a paragraph-by-paragraph basis, for direct quotations and for sources for information within the paragraph. In the case of D. H. Lawrence's letters, the volume number is provided. If the note refers to the number of the letter, it is preceded by the symbol "#." Complete citations are provided in the Sources.

Greatham, Pulborough, Sussex; February 1915

PAGE

93 Lady Ottoline Morrell: Lawrence [DHL] *Letters* [*L*] II #860; *Collected Letters* [*CL*] II 1140; *L* II 271; Morrell *Memoirs* [*Memoirs*] 275.

93 She was: *Memoirs* 147; Morrell *Garsington* [*Garsington*] 26; Darroch 38; *L* II 296; Nehls I 273; *L* II #854; *Memoirs* 276; Seymour 75; *L* II #856.

93 At first: *Memoirs* 275; Nehls I 271.

94 They were house-proud: *Garsington* 33; *L* II #1227; #1245; #1213; #1240; #1245; *Memoirs* 202.

94 Her rooms: *L* II #847.

94 They liked to be: *L* II #1243; Woolf *Diary* I 78.

94 They liked beautiful: Nehls I 293; Garnett 111.

94 Each was: *L* II #899.

95 They went: *Memoirs* 275–76; Nehls I 272; *L* II #878; Darroch 61; *Memoirs* 275.

95 She looked: *Memoirs* 276.

95 **He was hard:** Nehls I 270; Worthen *Idea* 61 ff.; see Delavenay; Introduction to DHL *The Rainbow* ed. Kinkead-Weekes; DeSalvo Introduction to DHL *The Rainbow; Garsington* 35, 74; *Memoirs* 159; Seymour 75, 82, 224.
95 **D. H. Lawrence:** *L* II #905; Tytell 65.
96 **She might have:** Nehls I 71; see Feinstein 95; Nehls I 154.
96 **Lawrence told Ottoline:** *L* II 274, #838.

"The Daughter of a Thousand Earls"

1.

PAGE

96 **Ottoline remembered:** *Garsington* 244; Woolf *Diary* I 66; Darroch 15–16; see the account of Ottoline's childhood in Seymour; Morrell *Album,* Introduction by Cecil 3.
97 **Ottoline seemed born:** Darroch 15–16; see Seymour for an account of her childhood.
97 **The family:** Darroch 16; see Seymour.
97 **When she was four and a half:** *Memoirs* 3; Darroch 17; see Seymour.
97 **Ottoline became:** *Memoirs* 5, 49, 158; see Seymour.
98 **Ottoline's half brother:** Darroch 18.
98 **During her childhood:** *Memoirs* 158, 300.
98 **As a child:** Seymour 22.
99 **Paradoxically:** Darroch 19; see the account of Ottoline's childhood in Seymour.

2.

PAGE

99 **When Ottoline was sixteen:** Seymour 25–27; Darroch 22.
99 **Ottoline's mother:** Seymour 27–28, 67.
99 **After her mother died:** Darroch 26–29.
100 **In the summer of 1898:** *Memoirs* 50; Darroch 30–32.

3.

PAGE

100 **After a period:** Seymour 20, 39–40.
100 **Both were:** Darroch 39; *Memoirs* 74; Seymour 43.
100 **Philip had wanted:** Darroch 39–40; Seymour 42; *Memoirs* 74.

4.

PAGE

101 **As an adult:** *Memoirs* 49, 158; Seymour 25; Morrell *Album* Introduction by Cecil 3; Woolf *Diary* I 175.
101 **Ottoline spent much time:** Holroyd 597.
101 **Her first adulterous:** Seymour 62–63.
102 **She believed:** Seymour 33.
102 **When she met Lawrence:** Seymour 52–57.

5.

PAGE

102 **Ottoline Morrell was irresistibly:** *Memoirs* 121, 155; Sassoon 7, 20; *L* II #896.
103 **She had an eye:** *Memoirs* 121, 155; *Garsington* 91.
103 **It was impossible:** Carrington 32–35.
103 **That most astute:** *Garsington* 131.
103 **She was very, very tall:** Holroyd 596; Sassoon 8–9; Russell *Autobiography 1872–1914* 316; Woolf *Diary* I 61, 79 201, 246, 272.
104 **She needed to be:** *Memoirs* 184–85.
104 **No matter that she:** *Memoirs* 184.
104 **He had to be grateful:** Woolf *Diary* I 79.

"The Son of a Nottinghamshire Miner"

1.

PAGE

104 **David Herbert Richards Lawrence:** Darroch 21; DHL "Autobiographical Sketch" 300, 592; Moore 21–25; Nehls I 5, 7, 9, 10, 21–22.
105 **She was small and slight:** Nehls I 22; Chambers xxx, 20; Meyers 12.
105 **Soon after the Lawrences:** Nehls I 7, 21.
105 **D. H. Lawrence spent:** Nehls I 4–5, 143.
105 **Lawrence's mother:** Nehls I 8.
106 **When Lawrence was six:** DHL "Nottingham"; Nehls I 8.
106 **The Lawrence children:** Nehls I 23; DHL *Collected Poems* I 13.
106 **Lydia Lawrence always worried:** Nehls I 16–17; Chambers xv.
106 **Lydia Lawrence always saw:** Chambers xv; Nehls I 4, 9, 16; Moore 25, 27, 41; DHL "Autobiographical Sketch" 592.
106 **She had high:** Nehls I 17, 21; Chambers 185.
107 **From the first:** Nehls I 16, 17, 20, 21, 23, 32; Chambers 106.
107 **He was devoted:** Nehls I 23; DHL "She Looks Back" in *Look!* 33; see Murry *Son.*
107 **He saw his mother's:** DHL in Murry *Son;* see DHL *Fantasia.*
107 **Those who knew:** Chambers 235; Nehls I 23, 25, 28.
108 **His violence:** Nehls I 37, 48–50, 64; Chambers 160.
108 **But he could also be:** Nehls I 271; Asquith 357.

2.

PAGE

108 **At sixteen:** Feinstein 31; Murry *Son* 102.
109 **One important trauma:** Nehls I 26; see Herman.

3.

PAGE

109 **D. H. Lawrence did not endure:** Lucas 62; Nehls 106–9.
109 **When Ford met Lawrence:** Nehls I 116, 127, 152.
110 **Lawrence subsequently:** Nehls I 102–3; Meyers 74.

110   **He held a very high opinion:** Nehls I 86, 95, 283; Lucas 116.
110   **Lawrence believed:** Nehls 110, 115.
110   **Though working-class:** Nehls I 119, 137.

4.

111   **Lawrence put a copy:** Nehls I 137.
111   **Lawrence's mother:** Meyers 64.
111   **After Lydia Lawrence's death:** Nehls I 81; Chambers 184; Meyers 64.
111   **He could not bear:** Chambers 167; Nehls I 141.
111   **He used his early life:** Nehls I 148; see Chambers.

5.

111   **When Lawrence met:** Nehls I 240; F. Lawrence [FL] *Not I* 39.
112   **She felt stuck:** see FL *Not I.*
112   **She asked him:** Lucas 76.
112   **Frieda had:** Green 44–46.
112   **Gross had been:** Green 44–46, 351.
112   **Lawrence and Frieda:** Nehls I 161; FL *Memoirs* 176.
112   **Lawrence wooed her:** FL *Not I* 23.
113   **One belief:** FL *Memoirs* 190.
113   **The *Magna Mater:*** FL *Memoirs* 278.

6.

113   **It is said:** FL *Memoirs* 342; DHL *Look!;* Feinstein 128.
113   **They traveled:** Nehls 163; FL *Not I* 24.
114   **They went to Germany:** FL *Memoirs* 169.
114   **In Gargagno:** FL *Memoirs* 171–72; Nehls I 182.
114   **Four months after:** FL *Memoirs* 174; Green 10–11; see the account in
        Lucas.
114   **Her affair:** FL *Not I* 30–31; Feinstein 88; Green 133.
114   **His friend:** Murry *Son* 79 and "The Sexual Failure" in *Son;* Green 132.

7.

115   **Frieda said:** FL *Memoirs* 176, 184, 341; FL *Not I* 179; Lucas 182, 245.
115   **When Lawrence:** FL *Memoirs* 108, 184, 341.
116   **Frieda believed:** FL *Memoirs* 114, 133, 137, 144; FL *Not I* 73.

"Only One Ottoline"

1.

116   **Lawrence had heard:** *L* II #850.
116   **Lady Ottoline:** *Memoirs* 273; *L* II 2, note 4 253; *L* II #833.

116 Ottoline especially: Delany 45; *Memoirs* 273.
117 Lawrence's work: *Memoirs* 274; Meyers 6, 10.
117 As a young woman: *Memoirs* 274.
117 Even as a child: *Memoirs* 277.
117 Ottoline believed: *Memoirs* 274.
117 After reading: Delany 45; Nehls I 240; Meyers 159.
118 In January 1915: *Memoirs* 275.
118 He responded: *L* II #833.
118 He told Ottoline: *L* II #833, #838.

2.

PAGE

118 From the first: *Memoirs* 277.
119 When Ottoline met: Lucas 124; Darroch 88–90; see Seymour.
119 Ottoline was used: *Memoirs* 277.
119 Ottoline and Russell: The most complete account of their love affair is provided in Seymour; see also Russell *Selected Letters;* Russell *Autobiography 1872–1914* 314–15; *Memoirs* 155.
119 Russell's looks: *Memoirs* 273; Russell *Autobiography 1872–1914* 318.
120 When they went: *Garsington* 95; *Memoirs* 259.
120 She wanted to go: *Garsington* 45.
120 Still, she had an obligation: Russell *Autobiography 1914–1944* 11; *Garsington* 43, 260, 269; Seymour 214.

3.

PAGE

120 On January 21: *L* II #833.
120 Over the years: Darroch 54; see Seymour.
121 Those who walked: Darroch 49, 54.
121 On this day: Nehls I 266; *Memoirs* 217.
121 She seated Lawrence: *L* II #834, #865; *Memoirs* 283.
121 After dinner: Nehls I 265–66.

4.

PAGE

122 After tea: *L* II note 2 263.
122 "Ah," Frieda chortled: Nehls I 266–68.
122 A few days: *L* II #848; Nehls I 268.
123 Grant's work: *L* II #848, #888.

5.

PAGE

123 Introducing Lawrence: Nehls I 271; *Memoirs* 275, 276, 277, 284.
123 She wrote in: *Memoirs* 277.

"The Powers of Darkness"

1.

PAGE

124 **Lawrence was initially:** *L* II #838, #848, #855.
124 **The time they shared:** *L* II 4, #855.
124 **At first:** *L* II 13.
124 **Very soon after:** *L* II #868.
124 **Inadvertently:** *L* II #869; Delany 59.

2.

PAGE

125 **Soon after:** *L* II #855; *Memoirs* 276; Russell *Portraits* 111; *Garsington* 35.
125 **Russell was transfixed:** *Memoirs* 276; Russell *Portraits* 115.
125 **Soon after meeting:** FL *Memoirs* 196; Nehls I 281.
125 **As much as:** *L* II #855.
125 **In the autumn:** *L* II #854.
126 **All property:** *L* II #865.
126 **Though his ideas:** *L* II #854; Delany 62, 64.
126 **He expected:** *L* II #878.
127 **Though, at the beginning:** *L* II #869, #868, #870; FL *Memoirs* 196.
127 **By the beginning of March:** *L* II #878.
127 **Ottoline and Lawrence:** *Garsington* 78.
127 **Frieda, I think:** *L* II #899, #909.
128 **When Lawrence was creating:** *Garsington* 32–34.
128 **Lawrence believed:** *Garsington* 59; *L* II #878; see especially DHL Chapter 15 *Fantasia.*
128 **This was what:** *L* I 469.
129 **Lawrence thought:** *L* II #878.
129 **He wanted nothing:** *L* II #892, #899.

3.

PAGE

129 **In March:** Nehls I 275; Moore 279; Russell *Portraits* 111; Delany 74, 77; *L* II #878, #896.
129 **Russell gave:** Nehls I 287.
129 **The trip:** *L* II #892.
130 **What had prompted:** *L* II #901, #892; Delany 80.
130 **He wrote:** *L* II #890, #900.
130 **Ottoline tried:** *L* II #892; see the history of the Cambridge Apostles in Deacon.
130 **After his visit:** Delany 80–81.
131 **Even more than:** see the account in Murry *Son; L* II #901; Meyers 166; Meyers provides the most complete account of DHL's struggle with homosexuality.
131 **Lawrence's friendship:** *L* II #896.
131 **As for Russell:** *L* II #896.

An "Old, Tragic Queen"

1.

PAGE

132   **Maria Nys was a young:** Nance 7.
132   **Maria developed:** Darroch Chapter 10; *Garsington* 85.
132   **Just after:** *L* II footnote 1 325.
132   **When Lawrence found out:** *L* II #905.
133   **He believed:** *L* II #905.
133   **Lawrence held:** Green 114.
133   **Lawrence lashed out:** Green 114, quoting DHL's *Fantasia of the Uncon-scious.*
133   **Lawrence's outburst:** *L* II #894, #920.
134   **Like Maria:** *L* II #907.
134   **It was a living arrangement:** *L* II #903.
134   **Lawrence knew:** *Garsington* 43; *L* II #903, #902.
134   **The Lawrences now had:** *L* II #936.
135   **The purpose:** *L* II #907.
135   **Lawrence began to change:** *L* II #881; Nehls II 337; Asquith 37.

2.

PAGE

135   **The joy-filled:** *L* II #933, #909, #895, #909
135   **Lawrence had become:** *L* II #896, #909, #920.
136   **He was having:** *L* II #925, #922, #918.

3.

PAGE

136   **In late April:** *L* II #896.
136   **She was "shocked":** Seymour 219, *Memoirs* 289.
137   **At the heart:** see Meyers: Darroch 148.

4.

PAGE

137   **In June 1915:** *L* II #938.
137   **Although Lawrence:** *Garsington* 35.
137   **Frieda, as always:** *Garsington* 36.
137   **Ottoline thought:** *Garsington* 36–37.
137   **With Frieda around:** *Garsington* 37.
138   **But Ottoline recognized:** *Garsington* 37.
138   **On the last night:** Darroch 144; *Garsington* 37.
138   **"Poor Lawrence":** *Garsington* 41.
138   **The best times:** *Garsington* 69.
138   **Even Philip Morrell urged:** *Garsington* 36; Asquith 58.

5.

PAGE

139 **In the summer:** *L* II #946, #951, #986; Darroch 145.
140 **In the coming months:** *Garsington* 59.

6.

PAGE

140 **It was July:** *L* II #961.
140 **Throughout the summer:** *L* II #950.
140 **Lawrence now wanted:** *L* II #895; #953; #961; #894; #896; Lucas 126.
141 **Lawrence had begun:** *L* II #946, #919.
141 **In July:** *L* II #923, #933, #949, #951, #961; Meyers 167.
141 **Ottoline and Russell:** *L* II #955; *Garsington* 65.

7.

PAGE

141 **In August:** *L* II #970, #966.
142 **He wrote:** *L* II #966, #986.
142 **Lawrence wrote Ottoline:** *L* II #987.
143 **Lawrence had told:** *Garsington* 61.

8.

PAGE

143 **The autumn of 1915:** *L* II #1049, #1024, #1039; Holroyd 604.
143 **Lawrence's personal:** Holroyd 604; Seymour 247.
143 **The courts:** Seymour 246.
143 **The Obscene Publications:** see Meyers.
143 **Though his relationship:** Seymour 246.
144 **Philip Morrell:** Nehls I 335.
144 **Lawrence was grateful:** Meyers 193.
144 *The Rainbow* **seizure:** *Garsington* 39; Darroch 147; *L* II #1042.
144 **Throughout the autumn:** *L* II #983.
144 **Garsington, which:** *L* II #1045; #1054.
145 **Lawrence shared:** *L* II #1051, #1082.
145 **Ottoline, no doubt:** *L* II #1049.
145 **Still, his visits:** *L* II #1049; *Garsington* 69.
145 **He tried:** *L* II #1089.

9.

PAGE

145 **In the middle:** *L* II #1067; Darroch 149.
146 **Ottoline continued:** *L* II #1084; Seymour 247.
146 **At a farewell:** Nehls I 337–38.
146 **In December:** *Garsington* 75, 79.

10.

PAGE

146   **On a last visit:** Darroch 148; *Garsington* 70.
146   **Looking on:** *Garsington* 70.

"Shooting Them with Noiseless Bullets"

1.

PAGE

147   **At the end:** FL *Not I* 83.
147   **Frieda was very:** FL *Memoirs* 198.
147   **In his months:** *L* II 641, Ford 165; see Delany; see Meyers 197 ff.
147   **At first, Cornwall:** *L* II #1124; #1123; #1125, #1155; #1139.
148   **He had made:** Delany 199; *L* II #1133, #1136; Seymour 248.
148   **In Cornwall:** *L* II #1132.
148   **Predicting what:** *L* II #1179, #1174.

2.

PAGE

148   **It was a long winter:** *L* II #1139, #1135, #1151.
149   **Lawrence spent:** *L* II #1145.
149   **Frieda realized:** Delany 189, 190.
149   **Maitland Radford:** *L* II #1145, #1158.
149   **Nonetheless:** *L* II #1135, #1136.
149   **He hoped that:** *L* II #1145, #1143.
150   **But Ottoline:** see *L* II #1145; Delany 200.
150   **Lawrence hoped:** *L* II #1151.
150   **Ottoline, though:** *L* II #1151, #1145, #1163; #1174; Darroch 151.
150   **Frieda and Lawrence:** FL *Memoirs* 198; *L* II #1156, #1178.
151   **Lawrence ruined:** *L* II #1174.

3.

PAGE

151   **"To Ottoline Morrell:** *L* II #1156.
151   **Russell's break:** Seymour 251; Delany 208; *L* II #1174, #1204, #1179.
152   **Ottoline tried:** Delany 207; *L* II #1244.
152   **By February 25:** Ross *Composition* 101; *L* II #1189; *Garsington* 93.
152   **Ottoline wrote:** *Garsington* 93.
152   **Years later:** *Garsington* 93–94.
153   **Lawrence was beginning:** *L* II #1174.
153   **Lawrence never published:** Meyers 215.
153   **Ottoline saw:** *Garsington* 94.
153   **Lawrence, as he told:** *L* II #1163; Delany 250.
154   **Her affair with Russell:** Seymour 262.
154   **By September:** Seymour 272–77; Delany 252.
154   **Her "soul mush":** *L* II #1244.

"Like a Lion Raging After Its Prey"

1.

PAGE

154   **The Lawrences:** *L* II #1204; Delany 208, 215–16.
155   **Lawrence thought:** *L* II #1187, #1204; Delany 208.

2.

PAGE

155   **With the return:** *L* II #1204, #1212.
155   **He wanted to start:** DHL *Women* Introduction by Farmer xxvii [Farmer];
        L II #1213, 594.
155   **Before beginning:** *L* II 579, 563–64.
155   **Lawrence busied:** *L* II 566, 571, #1214, #1225.
156   **Upstairs:** FL *Not I* 84; *L* II #1227.
156   **When he worked:** *L* II 564, #1227, 599; *Garsington* 63.
156   **Mansfield and Murry:** Delany 217–23; Farmer xxvii.
156   **During this time:** FL *Not I* 80; Delany 223.
156   **Murry and Mansfield:** Delany 222; Seymour 263; see Carrington.
157   **Once, Murry reported:** Nehls I 376; Seymour 264.
157   **Lawrence had wanted:** Nehls I 375; 379; Delany 224.
157   **Katherine Mansfield:** Lucas 142; Delany 231.

3.

PAGE

157   **In early April:** Delany 220–21.
158   **Lawrence was beginning:** Delany 221; *L* II #1227.

4.

PAGE

158   **About April 19:** Davis 35; Delany 226.
158   **As he worked:** *L* II #1236.
158   **First, Lawrence:** Delany 216; DHL "Prologue" in Meyers 214.
159   **Birkin (Lawrence):** DHL "Prologue" 95.
159   **Birkin knows that guilt:** DHL "Prologue" 99.
159   **Hermione nauseates:** DHL "Prologue" 104–5.
160   **Frieda Lawrence:** Meyers 219.
160   **Lawrence's battle:** Meyers 221; DHL "Prologue" 107.
160   **The prologue:** DHL "Prologue" 102.
160   **On May 5:** *L* II #1237, #1227, #1239; Farmer Introduction to DHL *Women
        in Love* [Farmer] xxviii.
161   **On May 24:** *L* II #1242; Delany 228.
161   **Near the end:** Delany 224; Seymour 247.
161   **Frieda, in a fury:** Seymour 251–52: *L* II #1240.

5.

PAGE

162 **Within two months:** Davis 35; Ross *Composition* 101; Delany 240.

162 **Lawrence had been:** Ford 165; Davis 35.

6.

PAGE

162 **In the middle:** Delany 229–30.

162 **One night:** Delany 232–34; Nehls I 381.

162 **General conscription:** Delany 236–38.

163 **After Murry:** Meyers 199, 203.

7.

PAGE

163 **With a handwritten:** Davis 35; Farmer xxix; Ross *Composition* 101; *L* III 79.

163 **During the warm summer:** Lucas 143; Delany 239.

163 **Once, she went:** Delavenay 226; FL *Not I* 88; Meyers 198, 206.

164 **Lawrence typed:** Letters II 631.

164 **To relieve:** Letters II 645.

164 **On September 26:** *L* II #1286; Farmer xxx; Ford 181.

"A Terrible and Horrible and Wonderful Novel"

1.

PAGE

164 **As Lawrence was writing:** Delany 226; Delavenay 226; see Meyers 199 ff.; this discussion of the novel is based upon the typescript Lawrence sent to Ottoline Morrell; page numbers refer to those on the typescript (D. H. Lawrence *Women in Love* Xerox of Typescript [Toronto Typescript; TT]); Lawrence revised the novel before publication; see Ford 195, 168; Meyers 205.

165 **The novel's settings:** Davis 40; the blazer was later altered to black and brown; Nehls I 377.

165 **In *Women in Love*:** Ford 195.

165 **Richard Aldington:** Aldington 216.

2.

PAGE

166 **Frieda once smashed:** Nehls I 395; Delany 256; Hermione holds the paperweight in her left hand; Ottoline was right-handed; in her copy of the novel, in the margin, opposite this scene, Ottoline wrote: "Frida [sic] was left-handed!" [Moore 346].

166 **As Lawrence proceeded:** Nehls I 436.

167 **After Lawrence's breach:** Nehls I 436; TT 114, 119.

167 **At the end of April:** *L* II #1232.

3.

167 **But it was:** Davis 49, Lucas 141.
168 **Lawrence's most vicious:** TT 1.

4.

168 **Lawrence poured:** TT 162, 161, 167, 164, 140, 56, 193, 169, 365, 165, 366, 38, 140, 192–93.
169 **One of his cruelest:** TT 362–63.
169 **Lawrence turned:** TT 94, 114.

5.

169 **As the sisters:** TT 12.
169 **She is an ardent:** TT 12.
170 **Her most important:** TT 13.
170 **Hermione's/Ottoline's:** TT 13.
170 **She becomes:** TT 359.
170 **Hermione enters:** TT 21.
170 **Lawrence savagely describes:** TT passim.
170 **In a schoolroom:** TT 39.
171 **Birkin verbally:** TT 44, 48.

6.

171 **Like Garsington:** TT 95, 112.
171 **It is to Breadalby:** TT 114, 167.
171 **Through Ursula's:** TT 95, 96.
172 **The invited guests:** TT 96, 98, 101.
172 **Hermione is obsessed:** TT 102.
172 **She knows:** TT 102, 104.
172 **At dinner:** TT 104.
172 **After dinner:** TT 105, 106.
173 **At breakfast:** TT 114.
173 **After lunch:** TT 123, 124.
173 **She is electrified:** TT 125.
173 **Rupert fights:** TT 125, 124.

7.

174 **In the novel:** TT 376.
174 **When Ursula:** TT 357, 358.
174 **Ursula jeers:** TT 375–76, 378.
174 **Ursula warns:** TT 375, 210.

8.

"Daniel in the Lion's Den"

1.

2.

3.

4.

5.

"A Season in Hell"

1.

PAGE

179 **While Ottoline Morrell:** *Garsington* 166.
179 **Katherine Mansfield:** Seymour 278.
180 **It was a troubled:** *Garsington* 166.
180 **Throughout the festivities:** Seymour 281–82; Darroch 179–81; *Garsington* 154.

2.

PAGE

180 **Ottoline received:** Farmer xxxiii; Garsington 162.
180 **She sat down:** Darroch 172; Garsington 128.
181 **After she finished:** Darroch 175; Delany 273.
181 **She wrote Lawrence:** *Garsington* 128–29.
181 **She showed:** Delany 274.
181 **Huxley, who was living:** *Garsington* 128; Darroch 175.
182 **What Ottoline didn't:** Darroch 157–58, 172; Delany 276.
182 **By the end of February:** Darroch 183.

3.

PAGE

182 **After she saw:** *Garsington* 156; she used the term to refer to her state in October 1916, but it also applies to her mental state at this time.
182 **"Was I really:** *Garsington* 128, 151.
182 **Lawrence's contemptuous view:** *Garsington* 32.
183 **Ottoline now felt:** *Garsington* 228.

4.

PAGE

183 **Lawrence's portrait:** *Garsington* 233–34.
183 **The Bloomsbury:** *Garsington* 151.
183 **The Lawrences:** *Garsington* 190; Delany 277.

5.

PAGE

184 **Ottoline entered:** Seymour 282.
184 **While there:** Seymour 283.
184 **Even worse:** Seymour 284.
184 **In the wake:** *Garsington* 152.

6.

PAGE

185 **Her depression:** *Garsington* 233; 174.
185 **In time, Ottoline:** Garsington 232–33, 173.

7.

PAGE

185 **Ottoline did not:** *Garsington* 233.
185 **Lawrence's portrait:** *Garsington* 234.
186 **She believed:** Huxley 18; Seymour 323–24, 431–33; Darroch 228.
187 **After leaving:** Darroch 183–84; Seymour 269; *L* IV #3089.
187 **Though she had revered:** *Garsington* 234–36.
187 **Once so careful:** Holroyd 659; Asquith 300.
187 **Even Russell's:** Delany 276; Darroch 181.
187 **The only happy moments:** Darroch 184; Seymour 289.
188 **She invited Virginia Woolf:** Woolf *Letters* II #830; Seymour 287; Woolf *Diary* I 66.
188 **In time:** *Garsington* 234, 190; Seymour 432.

8.

PAGE

188 **Lawrence's portrait:** Delany 276; *Garsington* 129, 151; in her memoirs, she says she had nothing to do with him until 1929, but they were in contact earlier.

"Months and Years of Slow Execution"

1.

PAGE

188 **After Ottoline:** *L* III 87; Darroch 176; *Garsington* 129; Asquith 294.
189 **Replying to Ottoline:** *L* III 87; *Garsington* 129.
189 **Frieda Lawrence:** FL *Memoirs* 210, 327, 343.

2.

PAGE

189 **When Ottoline read:** Farmer xxxiii; *L* III 55.
189 **In mid-January:** Farmer xxxiv.

3.

PAGE

190 **After Ottoline:** *Garsington* 129.
190 **Ottoline's problem:** Seymour 283.
190 **Unknowingly, Lawrence:** Seymour 282.
190 **Philip Morrell:** Farmer fn 41, xxxv–xxxvi; *Garsington* 129. Ottoline refers to Philip's going to "Putnam's, Lawrence's agent." Pinker was Lawrence's agent; Asquith 294.
190 **After Morrell's visit:** see *Garsington* 129; *L* III 95.
191 **In March 1917:** *L* III 104; see the account in Farmer.
191 **Though Pinker:** Ross *Composition* 97.
191 **Through the war years:** Farmer xxxvii–xxviii.

4.

192 **Along with his publishing:** for an account of the Morrells' helping pacifists, see Seymour.
192 **Writing to Catherine:** *L* III 87, 90.
192 **Losing Ottoline's:** see Seymour 252.
192 **Lawrence persisted:** *L* III 216, 226.
192 **By alienating Ottoline:** Darroch 177–78.
192 **Lawrence acted:** *L* III 109.
193 **In time:** *L* III 112.
193 **Lawrence would have:** *L* III 318.

5.

193 **He had often expressed:** Nehls I 430; *L* III 6–7, 123.
193 **Lawrence and Frieda visited:** Moore 357; Lucas 149.
193 **The Lawrences' house:** Moore 358; *L* III 167, 169; Moore 358.
194 **He and Frieda:** Nehls I 425; Sagar 82.
194 **The Lawrences:** Ross *Composition* 122.
194 **Frieda remarked:** Nehls I 429.
194 **The Lawrences moved:** Darroch 177; Lucas 146.
194 **After London:** Moore 367–69.
194 **In February 1918:** *L* III 209.
195 **In July 1918:** *L* III 257.
195 **But he was not:** *L* III 267.

6.

195 **Lawrence's was:** Lucas 156–57.

7.

195 **In the summer:** Ross 119.
195 **In November 1919:** Delavenay 227.
196 **He was making:** Moore 388–89.
196 **Though he would return:** Moore 387, 389.

"A Book the Police Should Ban"

1.

196 *Women in Love:* *L* III 11; *L* IV #2255; Farmer xlviii.
196 **The dream:** Feinstein 171, *Garsington* 129; Darroch 174.
197 **Lawrence had heard:** *L* IV #2258.
197 **The *Times:*** Farmer lii.
197 **Virginia Woolf:** VW *Letters* II #1182, 476.

2.

PAGE

197   On September 23: Aldington 282.
197   Under the banner: Nehls II 89 ff.
198   Hermione was: Nehls II 89 ff.

3.

PAGE

198   When the novel: Nehls I 593; Nehls II 91; Aldington 218; Farmer 1, xlix;
      Ross *Composition* 130; the amount was fifty pounds in Nehls II 92, 94;
      Branda 316.
198   *Women in Love:* Aldington 283; Feinstein 171; Farmer liii–lv.
199   As a result: Aldington 283.
199   At the beginning: *L* IV #2597; Lucas 190; Farmer li.

4.

PAGE

199   Lawrence moved: *L* IV #2597.
199   Though in her memoirs: *L* IV #2670, #2703.

"A Time to Laugh Over Our Old Quarrels"

1.

PAGE

200   Frieda Lawrence: *L* V #3868; Seymour 360.
200   Lawrence and Frieda: *CL* II 1062.
200   Lawrence wrote: *CL* II 1061.
200   He responded: *CL* II 1063.
201   He hoped: *Garsington* 129; *CL* II 1139.
201   He told her: *CL* II 1064, 1113; Lucas 240.
201   Lawrence used: *CL* II 1111.
202   Throughout 1929: Seymour 362; *CL* 1140.
202   Lawrence and Frieda: *CL* II 1139.
202   In one: *CL* II 1140.

2.

PAGE

202   In the last: Darroch 247.
203   The exhibition: Lucas 245; FL *Not I* 198–99.
203   Among the paintings: For an account of the exhibit, and reproductions
      of the paintings, see Millett.
203   The authorities: Millett 17; Sagar 186.
203   After the seizure: Moore 595.

3.

PAGE

204   Her "entrance: Seymour 360; Darroch 247.

204 " 'He ought: Nehls III 383–84.
204 Though the catalog: Lucas 246.
204 Lawrence surely heard: Darroch 247.

4.
PAGE
204 In the last: CL II; *Garsington* 138.
204 In 1929: CL II 1235.
205 D. H. Lawrence: CL II 1235; Nehls III 437, 451, 463; *Garsington* 138; Seymour 363.

5.
PAGE
205 Ottoline Morrell's: Darroch 24, 178.
205 Her "Recollections: Darroch 249.
205 She wanted: All quotes appear in *Garsington* 139–46.

"JUSTICE, NOT REVENGE":
Djuna Barnes and the Making of *The Antiphon*

The phrases listed below refer to the first words of the paragraph on the page given. References are provided on a paragraph-by-paragraph basis for direct quotations and sources for information within that paragraph. Complete citations are provided in the Sources.

PAGE
210 "I wrote *The Antiphon*": DB to Willa Muir 7/23/61 in Curry 42.

5 Patchin Place, Greenwich Village, New York City, Early April 1958
PAGE
211 Djuna Barnes sat: O'Neal 10; O'Neal 7–8; Field 168.
211 I am reading: Thurn Buddington to DB 4/2/58 in Dalton 71.
212 Djuna Barnes saw things: Broe, Introduction to *Silence* 6; DB to Willa Muir 7/23/61 in Curry 42.

Gare d'Austerlitz, Paris, October 1939
PAGE
213 It was late: Guggenheim 205.
213 Djuna Barnes waited: Guggenheim 205; Field 216, 17, 211, 209.
213 Her dream: Blankley 207–8; see Benstock; Field 132; Jay *Amazon* 8.
213 In retrospect: Field 153, 155, 157, 152; O'Neal 30.
214 The only home: Field 151; Benstock 257.
214 Her relationship: Field 163, 167, 165.
214 But in Paris: Bacon in Broe Introduction to *Silence* 5.
214 She had come: see DB *Interviews*; Plumb 25; Jay *Amazon* 24; Lanser 165.
215 An unflattering: in Field 119.
215 Before she left: Plumb 62; Kannenstine 68; see Marcus; see Benstock.

Storm King Mountain, Cornwall-on-Hudson, 1892–1907

PAGE

224 **Justin Budington:** Dalton 53; Field 180.
225 **Djuna was Wald and Elizabeth's:** Field 25.
225 **His given name:** Field 25, 171, 173.
225 **Wald Barnes decreed:** Field 173; Dalton 56; Broe "My Art" 55.
226 **Though Elizabeth:** Flanner in Broe *Silence* 155.
226 **Within the boundaries:** Field 193; Field 182–83.
227 **He had learned:** DB *Ryder* in Field 179.
227 **Zadel was a magnetic:** Field 175.
227 **Zadel was responsible:** Field 179.
227 **In Djuna's account:** DB *Ryder* 16.
228 **Wald's father:** Field 170–77.
228 **One view:** Field 177–78.
228 **Djuna's mother's family:** DB to EC 2/19/40 in Dalton 80.
229 **Zadel Gustafson:** Field 170–71.
229 **These names:** Field 171.
229 **After the collapse:** Field 174; DB *Ryder* in Field 174.
229 **Zadel maintained:** Field 174; Stanton.
230 **The chief tenet:** Field 174; DB *Ryder* 56–57.
230 **Two constant features:** Field 181–82.
230 **In 1937:** EC to DB 10/30/37 in Dalton 90–91; EC in Broe "My Art" 43.
231 **Djuna Barnes wrote:** DB in *Ryder* in Dalton 201.
231 **Wald Barnes considered:** Field 181, 184.
232 **Rethinking her childhood:** DB to EC 2/2/34 in Broe "My Art" 51; DB *Ryder* in Wagstaff 24.

Huntington, New York, 1909–1910

PAGE

232 **Wald Barnes had decided:** Field 43; Broe "My Art" 53.
232 **In the months:** Field 43; Broe "My Art" 42.
233 **Djuna, though:** Broe "My Art" 53.
233 **When Djuna:** DB to EC 12/14/35 in Broe "My Art" 43.
233 **Though Zadel:** DB to EC 12/14/35 in Broe "My Art" 43; DB *Nightwood* 148–49.
234 **Zadel's incest:** in Dalton 57; see Broe "My Art."
234 **How far back:** Broe "My Art."
234 **In the code words:** Broe "My Art"
234 **Zadel called herself:** in Broe "My Art" 42.
235 **Djuna's relationship:** see Herman.
235 **Djuna used:** DB *Nightwood* 63.
235 **In a letter:** DB to EC 5/21/38 in Dalton 62; for a fine analysis of this dream, see Dalton.
236 **Djuna Barnes described:** in Dalton 37–40.
236 **Years later:** Dalton 423.
237 **In Djuna's telling:** DB to EC 7/25/38 in Dalton 424.

237 **In another retelling:** Field 43; in Dalton 39–40; 321; Field 193. Both T. S. Eliot and Emily Coleman had a hand in the published version of the text. Both influenced Barnes to "cut substantial portions of the manuscript." The editing "resulted in the pruning of the most radical material from the text, including several passages that deal more explicitly with the issue of molestation" (Dalton 321). According to her biographer (Field 193), Barnes cut the text from about 190,000 to 65,000 words.

238 **From the family farm:** Elizabeth Chappell Barnes to DB in Dalton 84.

Huntington, New York, 1910–1912

PAGE

238 **Finally, Elizabeth:** Broe "My Art" 77.
238 **Wald Barnes recanted:** Field 44, 192.
238 **After she:** in Dalton 39–40.

Queens, New York; Bronx, New York, 1911–1915

PAGE

239 **While she was still:** Hanscombe 88.
239 **At first, she lived:** Dalton 102–3; Field 43.
239 **Displaying the resourcefulness:** Broe "Gunga Duhl"; O'Neal xii.
239 **She became a "newspaperman":** Broe "My Art" 55, 80; see Levine; Broe Introduction in *Gender* 21.
240 **It was her investigative:** Broe Introduction in Gender 25.
240 **From the first:** Field 54; in Dalton 105.
240 **In her work:** Duncan 182; see DB *Interviews, New York*.
241 **Among the scores:** DB *Interviews* 49–50.
241 **In her interview with Stieglitz:** in Plumb 21.
241 **Barnes gave up:** O'Neal 52.
242 **When she left:** Kannenstine 17; Broe "Gunga Duhl" 2.
242 **She had traded:** Rascoe 135; in Churchhill 37.
242 **Greenwich Village:** DB *Greenwich Village;* Parry 266; Cowley *Genteel* 179.
242 **Djuna loved:** DB *Greenwich Village.*
243 **The Village provided:** Blankley 185; see Kannenstine 22–24; DB *Book of Repulsive Women* n.p.
243 **When Guido Bruno:** in DB *Interviews* 386.
244 **In the Village:** Parry 311.
244 **Barnes had a brief career:** O'Neal 56.
244 **Her "exciting:** Langner 110; Churchill 168–69; Provincetown Players, Playbill/Sixth Season; see Larabee and Retallack.
244 **In later years:** in Altman 274.
244 **From the time:** Anderson 181.
245 **During the Greenwich Village years:** Field 196.
245 **She once reported:** Wagstaff 72; Field 60, passim; O'Neal 41; Langner 71.
245 **One of the most important:** Langner 111.

245 **Djuna nursed:** Mayerson 155–56; Field 103; in Hanscombe.
245 **After Mary Pyne's death:** in Hanscombe 91–2; in Wilson 85–86.

East Fifty-fourth Street, New York City, April 1940
PAGE

246 **After Djuna Barnes's first stay:** DB to EC 3/30/40 in Broe "My Art" 41.
247 **This time:** DB to EC 4/25/40 in Dalton 69; Wagstaff 184.
247 **Another dose:** DB to EC 3/25/40 in Dalton 424; Wagstaff 185.
247 **After her second stay:** Wagstaff 8; Field 191.
247 **She and her mother:** DB to EC 4/18/40 in Wagstaff 169; Field 220.
247 **For five days:** DB *Book of Repulsive Women* n.p.
248 **Barnes wrote Emily:** DB to EC 4/18/40 in Dalton 100; DB to EC, undated posted 4/18/40 in Dalton 83.

5 Patchin Place, Greenwich Village, September 1940
PAGE

249 **In September 1940:** Broe "My Art" 60.
249 **Around the small courtyard:** Field 230.
249 **From her windows:** Field 218, 240, 231.
249 **The apartment cost:** O'Neal 76–77; Field 218; Wagstaff 169.
249 **After Emily returned:** Field 217.
250 **Barnes would live:** Broe "My Art" 60; O'Neal 134.
250 **Barnes devoted herself:** Herman; DB to EC in Broe "My Art" 41.
250 **At Patchin Place:** Herman; Field 132–33.
250 **She gave up:** Field 219.
251 **In the past:** DB to EC 9/20/35 in Broe "My Art" 51; O'Neal passim.
251 **A few years before:** Elizabeth Chappel Barnes to DB 4/30/41.
251 **After she finished:** Field 220.

5 Patchin Place, Greenwich Village, 1945–1956
PAGE

252 **Djuna Barnes had conceived:** Kannenstine fn 1 180; Curry 2.
252 **But it was not:** Field 191; O'Neal 5.
252 **In the drama:** Wagstaff 176; Herman.
252 *The Antiphon:* Wagstaff 170, 174.
253 **The play recounts:** Curry 192–200, 164.
254 **Miranda proves to be:** Curry 198.
254 **Soon, the family:** in Field 185; O'Neal 127.
255 **At Patchin Place:** Field 221.
255 **Djuna Barnes was working:** Field 229.
255 **For Barnes:** Foreword to *Ryder* in Curry 106–7.
255 **Working and reworking:** Herman; in Broe 269.
256 **In time, she incorporated:** Herman; see Curry.
256 **The title:** in Curry 130.
257 **Barnes saw the work's:** in Curry 69.
257 *The Antiphon:* in Curry 231.

257   **The central theatrical event:** Barnes disclaimed this reading, but numerous critics have argued that it evokes a daughter's rape by her father; see Field, Curry, Dalton, Wagstaff, DeSalvo.
257   **Barnes had created:** DB *Antiphon* 137, 82, 83, 84.
258   **Miranda's brothers:** DB *Antiphon* 98, 100, 147, 99, 139.
258   **Jeremy fears:** DB *Antiphon* 179, 104, 140, 180.
258   **Act II:** DB *Antiphon* 165, 143, 144.
259   **Titus is no:** DB *Antiphon* 159, 160, 169.
259   **The whole family:** DB *Antiphon* 147, 142, 212, 117.
259   **Toward the end:** DB *Antiphon* 178, 179, 176, 175, 180.
260   **The brothers drag:** DB *Antiphon* 181.
260   **The brothers thrust:** DB *Antiphon* 182.
260   **Augusta is pushed:** DB *Antiphon* 184, 185.
260   **Jack accuses:** DB *Antiphon* 185, 186, 164, 185.
260   **To protect:** DB *Antiphon* 186.
260   **It pains Miranda:** DB *Antiphon* 195, 204, 223.
261   **Through the years:** in Curry in Broe *Silence* 291–92.
262   **Barnes responded by slashing:** Curry 108, 122.

Cambridge, Massachusetts, May 21, 1956

PAGE

263   **Apart from a staged reading:** in Curry 142.
263   **The reading was a disaster:** Field 223.
264   **She had chosen:** Field 223; Curry 89 ff.
264   **Of this event:** in Curry 105–6.

1958

PAGE

264   *The Antiphon* **was first published:** in Curry 136; Field 224.
264   **After reading:** in Curry 136; see Herman.
265   **Her work had too graphically:** in Wagstaff 16.
265   **But Barnes wondered, too:** see Curry 134 ff.

Stockholm, February 1961

PAGE

265   **He thought it:** in Curry 138.
266   *The Antiphon* **opened:** in Plumb 103–4.

5 Patchin Place, Greenwich Village, 1962–1982

PAGE

266   **After completing** *The Antiphon:* DB to Saxon Barnes 6/26/67 in Dalton 100; in Broe *Silence* n.p.; Field 216.
266   **Among those with whom:** McCullough in Broe *Silence* 367.
267   *The Antiphon* **was:** O'Neal 50; in Broe *Silence* n.p.
267   **Except for a few poems:** O'Neal 83; in Broe *Silence* n.p.
267   **She embarked upon:** O'Neal 85; Field 242–43.
267   **Djuna Barnes was still:** O'Neal 13.

5 Patchin Place, Greenwich Village, 1982

"A DESPERADO OF LOVE":
Henry Miller, June Miller, and
Crazy Cock

The phrases listed below refer to the first words of the paragraph on the page given. References are provided on a paragraph-by-paragraph basis for direct quotations and sources for information within that paragraph. Complete citations are provided in the sources.

Office of the Parks Commission, Queens, New York, May 21–22, 1927

278 **A month:** according to Ferguson 133, the name of June's lover was Martha Andrews; all Miller's other biographers refer to her as Jean Kronski; HM *Nexus* 153; Dearborn 110; HM *Capricorn* 246.

278 **He had a few:** Martin 138; Dick 184; Dearborn 110.

278 **The afternoon:** Martin 138.

279 **He was thirty-six:** Martin 135–38.

279 **The last time:** HM *Life.*

279 **His mother:** Martin 129; Dearborn 100–1; HM *Life* 33.

279 **He sat:** Martin 138.

279 **Unable to control:** Martin 138.

279 **He warned:** Martin 138–39.

279 **He hoped:** HM *Nexus* 149.

280 **The book:** Martin 139; Dearborn 110–1.

280 **"Chapter I,":** Martin 139; HM *Books* 98.

280 **There would:** Martin 139; Ferguson 149; Dearborn 108.

280 **The notes:** HM *Nexus* 165; Dearborn 110.

280 **He knew:** Dearborn 110–1.

281 **At one point:** HM *Nexus* 165.

281 **He had written:** HM *Capricorn* 334.

281 **When he finished:** Dearborn 110; Ferguson 153.

281 **It was:** Dearborn 111.

281 **He lay down:** HM *Nexus* 165; Martin 139; Dearborn 111.

281 **Henry Miller had no way:** HM *Life* 50; Ferguson 77.

Wilson's Dance Hall, Broadway and Forty-sixth Street, New York City, Thursday Night, Late Summer 1923

PAGE

282 **On the Thursday night:** Dick 164, and June Miller say they met in the Orpheum Dance Palace; other biographers and Miller say it was Wilson's; HM *Capricorn* 208; HM *Aller* 12; Dick says Miller was thirty— Ferguson says he was thirty-two; Ferguson 76–77.

282 **He had walked:** Martin 60; HM *Capricorn* 64.

282 **In New York City:** HM *Capricorn* 98–99.

282 **The string:** Ferguson 70; HM *Capricorn* 339–40.

283 **Most of the young women:** Ferguson 76; Dick 164–65; HM *Capricorn* 105.

283 **In the past:** HM *Capricorn* 119, 197; Ferguson 74–75; Dearborn 75.

283 **Upstairs:** HM *Capricorn* 340.

283 **Standing on:** Porter 10.

284 **Even in repose:** Porter 9–10.

284 **On this night:** Martin 76.

284 **This is how:** HM *Capricorn* 340–41.

284 **She went:** Dick 166, 169.

285 **He looked:** Dick 165; HM *Just a Brooklyn Boy;* HM *This Is Henry* n.p.; Martin 79.

285 **She was:** Dick 165; there is a dispute about her age; June maintained she was sixteen when they met.

285 **They danced:** Martin 77; Jong 64; HM *Life* 185; HM *Capricorn* 341; Ferguson 82.
285 **June impressed:** Ferguson 82; HM *Capricorn* 341.
285 **At two o'clock:** HM *Dear, Dear Brenda* [*Brenda*] 112; HM *Capricorn* 342; Ferguson 77.
285 **"What a walk!":** HM *Capricorn* 342.
286 **She took:** Dearborn, 79, 81; Martin 77; Ferguson 82; Dick 167.
286 **She talked:** HM *Capricorn* 343; Martin 83.
286 **He asked her:** Dearborn 79.
286 **One story:** Dearborn 79; Ferguson 82; HM *Capricorn* 343–44.
286 **Her talk:** Porter 11–12; Dearborn 79–81; Martin 29, 77, 83.
286 **He told her:** Dick 167; Martin 70–73.
287 **He took her home:** Dearborn, 79; Ferguson 77; Dick 166; Martin 78.
287 **Friday:** Martin 80.
287 **Saturday:** Martin 80.
287 **He spent:** Ferguson 79.
287 **June had given:** HM *Sexus* 6.
287 **Already, he was:** Ferguson 79; HM *Sexus* 5–6; Porter 123.
288 **He was playing:** Dick 166; HM *Books* 97.
288 **Saturday night:** HM *Sexus,* 7.
288 **Sunday morning:** HM *Sexus* 9.
288 **He camped:** Dick 166; Ferguson 80.
289 **He decided:** HM *Sexus* 11; Ferguson 80.
289 **At last:** Ferguson 80–81.
289 **They climbed:** Ferguson 81; Dick 166; Martin 80.
289 **He told:** HM *Brenda* 112; Ferguson 81.
289 **She maintained:** Ferguson 80.
290 **One night:** Dearborn 80–81.
290 **Though early:** Ferguson 81.
290 **What happened after:** Martin 85.
290 **When he questioned:** Dearborn 82.
291 **After Henry:** Ferguson 82.
291 **While away:** Martin 85; Ferguson 85.
291 **They had begun:** Ferguson 82.
291 **When June returned:** Dearborn 82.
291 **He took her:** Ferguson 86; Martin 85.
292 **During the night:** Martin 85.
292 **Before he:** Dearborn 74; Ferguson 82.

244 Sixth Avenue, Brooklyn, New York, August 25, 1923
PAGE

292 **Henry Miller was standing:** Ferguson 86.
292 **The day:** Ferguson 86.
292 **To satisfy:** Martin 87.
292 **Not that having:** Ferguson 85.
293 **"Yes,":** Martin 81.
293 **"Bea,":** Martin 81; Dearborn 81; Porter 74.

293 **But he wasn't:** Martin 81: HM *Life* 193; Ferguson 85.
293 **His predicament:** Ferguson 83, 86; Dearborn 82.
294 **His friend:** Ferguson 83–84; see Porter.
294 **June had:** Dearborn 80.
294 **He invited:** Martin 83–84.
294 **Jealousy was:** Martin 82.
294 **When it suited:** Martin 82.
295 **She was wildly:** Ferguson 81; Martin 85.
295 **Another time:** Ferguson 84; Dearborn 80; Martin 80.
295 **Nonetheless:** Ferguson 84; Martin 81.
295 **Once, she had:** Martin 79; Dearborn 86.
295 **When he met:** Ferguson 84.
296 **June really:** Martin 83; Dearborn 80–81.
296 **June was:** Dearborn 81.
296 **When Henry Miller:** HM *This Is Henry* 37.
296 **Poking about:** Dearborn 83.
297 **Instead of using:** Dearborn 83.
297 **Unexpectedly:** Ferguson 86.
297 **Miller told:** Dearborn 83; Martin 83, 87; HM *Life* 199; Ferguson 86.
297 **Beatrice ordered:** Ferguson 86; Dearborn 83; Martin 88.
297 **The next day:** Ferguson 86–87.
297 **The day after:** Ferguson 86.
298 **With June:** HM *Capricorn* 230; HM *Aller* 12.

91 Remsen Street, Columbia Heights, Brooklyn, Winter 1924–Spring 1925

PAGE
298 **Henry Miller:** Martin 90, 94; Dearborn 93.
298 **Their first home:** Martin 89–90; Dearborn 86; HM *Life* 88.
299 **June nagged:** Dearborn 86; Martin 90, 93.
299 **When he went:** Martin 90.
299 **Once, June:** Dearborn 84.
299 **In their nightly:** Martin 92–93.
299 **After Cockroach:** Ferguson 93; Dearborn 84.
300 **One night:** Dearborn 83–84.
300 **Though Henry:** Martin 90.
300 **But their strong:** HM *Life* 199; Ferguson 94; Dearborn 85–86.
300 **June learned:** Dearborn 85.
300 **Though she:** Dearborn 86; Dick 161, 169.
301 **Henry and June:** Dick 167; Dearborn 87; Martin 93; Ferguson 96.
301 **They had grabbed:** Dick 167; Ferguson 96; Dearborn 87; Martin 94.
301 **Whatever June's:** Dearborn 89; HM *Life* 199; Ferguson 99.
302 **June had:** HM *Life* 199; Dick 173; HM *Colossus;* Ferguson 99.
302 **June was:** Dearborn 89; Porter 123.
302 **"If you'll:** Martin 97, 118; Ferguson 107.
302 **It was:** Dearborn 88.
302 **The apartment:** Dick 168; Dearborn 88.
303 **He loved:** Dearborn 88–89; Martin 94.

303 **As he and June:** Dearborn 91.
303 **From the time:** HM *Art and Outrage* 31; Martin 43; HM *Life* 187; HM *This Is Henry* 34.
303 **On Remsen Street:** Martin 96; Dearborn 92.
304 **In the early:** HM *Art and Outrage* 31; Martin 91.
304 **He was very:** HM *Life* 200; HM *Art and Outrage* 31; Martin 96–97; Tytell 160.
304 **At night:** Ferguson 97.
304 **He figured:** HM *Life* 200; Ferguson 102; Dick 168.
305 **When June:** Martin 97; Ferguson 97.
305 **June talked:** Martin 97.

51 Remsen Street, Brooklyn, Spring 1925
PAGE

305 **By the spring:** HM *Letters to Emil* [*Emil*]; HM *Life*.
305 **Though June:** Dearborn 92; Martin 110.
306 **During the coldest:** Ferguson 103.
306 **To help:** Ferguson 102.
306 **Finally, June:** Martin 98–99; Dick 163, 173; she maintained she never used drugs; Ferguson 120.
306 **In describing:** HM *Art and Outrage* 31.
306 **By the spring:** HM *Emil* 13; Ferguson 107–8; Martin 101–102.
307 **A number:** Martin 103–4.
307 **"June the:** Martin 103–4.
307 **"Dance Hall":** Martin 103–4.
308 **Though Henry:** Dearborn 94.
308 **The plan:** Dick 174.
308 **June E. Mansfield:** Martin 111.
308 **Why he:** Dick 169.
308 **Miller hoarded:** HM *Books* 96; HM *Emil* 13.
309 **Miller said:** Ferguson 105.
309 **In the spring:** HM *Emil* 13; HM *Life* 200.
309 **They again:** Ferguson 108–9.
309 **Later in the spring:** Dick 178.
309 **At Perry Street:** Martin 105.
309 **He ran:** Ferguson 146.

Remsen Street, Brooklyn, Fall 1926
PAGE

310 **Henry and June:** Martin 108–9, 113–4; Dearborn 99.
310 **When they:** Dearborn 101–2.
310 **For a time:** Dearborn 95, 102.
310 **As always:** Martin 118; Martin 115.
310 **While he:** Dearborn 100; Martin 111; Ferguson 123.
311 **She had found:** Dearborn 102.
311 **They had grown:** Ferguson 145; Martin 119–20; Dearborn 102.
311 **She cut:** Dearborn 102–3; Martin 121.

311   **"Like a whore:** Martin 121.
311   **He had become:** Ferguson 123; HM *Emil* 13–14.
311   **June assumed:** Ferguson 123.
312   **Henry was tired:** Dick 162; Martin 118.
312   **She insisted:** Martin 119–20.
312   **Though he couldn't:** Martin 119.
312   **At times:** Martin 121.
312   **She had:** Dearborn 100–3.
312   **Sometimes, he:** Martin 105–6.
313   **Many years:** HM *Emil* 124.

The Iron Cauldron, Greenwich Village, and Remsen Street, Brooklyn, Autumn and Winter 1926–1927

PAGE

313   **In the autumn:** HM *Time of the Assassins* [*Assassins*] 1–2; HM *Art and Outrage* 29.
313   **When June:** Ferguson 123; Martin 106.
313   **June was working:** Dick 180; others, like Ceil Conason, thought her "homely"; Ferguson 122.
314   **She was seventeen:** Dick 180–84; June said she was seventeen, but Martin says she was twenty-one.
314   **June had found:** Dick 181–82; Ferguson 133 claims she was really Martha Andrews, the daughter of wealthy parents, and that she was known as Mara.
314   **According to June:** Ferguson 135; Dick 180–1; Martin 124; HM *Assassins* 2; Dearborn Introduction to HM *Crazy Cock* [Dearborn Introduction] xx.
314   **Before long:** Dearborn Introduction xix; Dearborn 103; Ferguson 135; Dick 181.
314   **One day:** Nin *Henry and June* [*H and J*] 29; Martin 123; Ferguson 132.
315   **Jean had taken:** Ferguson 124.
315   **June started:** Ferguson 136; Dick 182.
315   **Not long:** Dearborn 104; Ferguson 135.
315   **When Henry:** Ferguson 135; Martin 125.
315   **He knew:** Martin 126; Ferguson 137; Dearborn 104–5; Martin 124.
315   **Henry believed:** Dearborn 104–5; Ferguson 133.
316   **In reprisal:** Ferguson 138.
316   **Before long:** Martin 130; Ferguson 137; Dearborn 104–5.
316   **He began:** Ferguson 136; Ferguson says the statement was Jean's; Martin 126; Dearborn 104.
317   **He had written:** HM *Emil* 138.
317   **Even she:** Dick 181; HM *Emil* 124; Martin 127.

Henry Street, Brooklyn, Winter 1926–1927

PAGE

317   **In the midst:** HM *Assassins* 2; Dearborn 106; HM *This Is Henry* n.p.
317   **Jean took:** Dearborn 107–9; Ferguson 139.

317 **By now:** Dearborn 107; HM *Assassins* 1.
318 **The three:** Dearborn 107–9; HM *Emil* 124.
318 **When June:** Ferguson 145; Dearborn 106–9.
318 **The place:** Dearborn Introduction xx; Nin *H and J* 46.
318 **Drunk:** HM *Assassins* 1–2; Ferguson 137, 143, 145.
319 **When June and Jean:** Ferguson 142.
319 **He became obsessed:** Ferguson 142, 147.
319 **June and Jean:** Ferguson 141, 151; Porter 12.
319 **He couldn't:** Ferguson 146, 151; Martin 132.
319 **Henry was penniless:** Dick 169; HM *This Is Henry* 31.
320 **In describing:** Her statement squares with Miller's account, though his biographers dismiss his admission as braggadocio.
320 **But Henry Miller had been:** see Shengold.
320 **He described:** HM *Book of Friends* 65.
320 **With June:** see Shengold.
321 **His life:** Dearborn 54.
321 **With June and Jean:** HM *Crazy Cock* 68.
321 **It was winter:** HM *Crazy Cock* 68.
321 **His doctor:** Porter 15; Dearborn 105 says it was "only a gesture," though his friend Emil thought it was a serious suicide attempt; for another account, see Ferguson 145.
321 **He had written:** HM *Crazy Cock* 72.
321 **It was crumpled:** accounts appear in HM *Crazy Cock;* Martin 126–27; Ferguson 145–46; Dearborn 105–6; Porter 15.
322 **Miller sat:** HM *Assassins* 2; HM *Hamlet* 90.
322 **Though he wanted:** Dearborn 108; HM *Assassins* 2.
322 **From time:** Martin 129.
322 **In February:** Ferguson 147; Dearborn 108.
323 **He had come:** HM *Assassins* 5.
323 **In the moments:** HM *Capricorn* 334.
323 **He had toyed:** Martin 43.
323 **He carried:** Ferguson 142; Dearborn 108.
323 **Under the heading:** HM *Life* 143; Dearborn 108; Ferguson 142.

Henry Street, Brooklyn, Spring 1927
PAGE

325 **It was nighttime:** Tytell 163.
325 **Miller had:** Ferguson 152.
325 **It took him:** Dearborn 110; Dick 184; see also Ferguson 152, Martin 132.
325 **So:** Martin 132; Ferguson 152.
325 **He went:** Martin 134.
326 **In a corner:** Martin 134.

335 **In the winter:** Tytell 172–73; Ferguson 176; Dearborn 137; Martin 181, 198, HM *Emil* 66; see Osborn in Porter.
336 **Wearing corduroy:** Nin *H and J* 64; HM *Life* 144.
336 **Miller was working:** Porter 28–34; HM *Stories* 74–75.
336 **He had finally:** Martin 218; Porter 28–29.
336 **By February:** Porter 30, 37; HM *Emil* 72.
337 **Disgusted:** HM *Emil* 71; Porter 31.
337 **He had begun:** HM *Emil* 67.
337 **Despite his disgust:** HM *Life* 75–76.
337 **He was now living:** Martin 231; HM *Life* 147, Perles 27.
339 **In *Crazy Cock,* Miller established:** HM *Crazy Cock* 52, 173; all page numbers through the end of the discussion of the novel refer to *Crazy Cock* unless otherwise indicated.
339 **Hildred/June's persona:** 9, 41.
340 **Subsidiary images:** 28, 30, 32, 45, 21–22, 72, 19, 18, 49.
340 **The struggle:** 98, 84, 178–79, 9.
340 **As Hildred/June:** see Shengold 120; 15, 35–36.
341 **He characterizes:** 8.
341 **Tony Bring:** 18, 21–22.
341 **Throughout the novel:** 158–59.
341 **In one of the:** 174.
341 **In the "tangled dream":** 68–69.
342 **Who are these:** 197.
342 **Miller had described:** 198–99.
343 **When Miller showed:** Perles 98; Martin 247, 218, 231, 250; Ferguson 186; Dearborn 133.
343 **Anaïs Nin:** Nin *H and J* 33, 86.
343 **This criticism:** Dearborn: 128.
344 **Despite the majority:** HM *Emil* 108, 115; Martin 262–63.
344 **In 1932:** Martin 273.
345 **She warned:** Martin 273.
345 **In July 1934:** Dearborn 161.
345 **Before she left:** HM *Emil* 112.
345 **"Big blowup:** HM *Emil* 110, 112; Dearborn 147.
345 **A few months:** HM *Emil* 120.
345 **Miller thought:** HM *Emil* 121.
346 **In the midst:** HM *Emil* 123.
346 **But he could see:** HM *Emil* 123.
346 **"What does she want:** HM *Emil* 124.

Forest Hills, New York, September 1961
PAGE
347 **The only time:** Martin 459, 464.
347 **June had been:** Nin *Diary* VI 314; Martin 459.
347 **When he saw:** Martin 459; Dearborn 280.
347 **After leaving:** Martin 458–59; Dearborn 280; Nin *Diary* VII 78; Nin *Diary* VI 372.

Pacific Palisades, California, October 1977

AFTERWORD
Notes

The phrases listed below refer to the first words of the paragraph on the page given; references are provided on a paragraph-by-paragraph basis for direct quotations and sources for information within that paragraph. Complete citations are provided in the Henry Miller section of the Sources.

SOURCES

INTRODUCTION:
Literature as Revenge

Aberbach, David. *Surviving Trauma: Loss, Literature and Psychoanalysis.* New Haven: Yale University Press, 1989.

Alvarez, A. *The Savage God: A Study of Suicide.* New York: Random House, 1972.

Angier, Carole. *Jean Rhys.* New York: Viking Penguin, 1985.

Bacon, Sir Francis. "Revenge," in *Essays.* New York: E. P. Dutton, 1947.

Bair, Deirdre. *Simone de Beauvoir: A Biography.* New York: Summit Books, 1990.

Baldwin, Neil. *Man Ray: American Artist.* New York: Clarkson N. Potter, 1988.

Barnes, Djuna. *Nightwood.* New York: New Directions, 1937.

Bartlett, Phyllis. *Poems in Process.* Oxford: Oxford University Press, 1951.

Bass, Ellen and Davis, Laura. *The Courage to Heal: A Guide for Woman Survivors of Child Sexual Abuse.* New York: Harper & Row, 1988.

Battestin, Martin C. with Battestin, Ruthe R. *Henry Fielding: A Life.* New York: Routledge, 1989.

Baumeister, Roy F. *Masochism and the Self.* Hillsdale, New Jersey: Lawrence Erlbaum Associates, 1989.

Belford, Barbara. *Violet: The Story of the Irrepressible Violet Hunt and Her Circle of Lovers and Friends—Ford Madox Ford, H. G. Wells, Somerset Maugham, and Henry James.* New York: Simon & Schuster, 1990.

Benstock, Shari. *Women of the Left Bank: Paris, 1900–1940.* Austin: University of Texas Press, 1986.

Bloom, Harold. *The Anxiety of Influence: A Theory of Poetry.* New York: Oxford University Press, 1973.

Boorstin, Daniel J. *The Creators: A History of Heroes of the Imagination.* New York: Random House, 1992.

Bowers, Fredson Thayer. *Elizabethan Revenge Tragedy, 1587–1642.* Gloucester, Massachusetts: Peter Smith, 1959.

Broe, Mary Lynn, ed. *Silence and Power: A Reevaluation of Djuna Barnes.* With an afterword by Catherine Stimpson. Carbondale: Southern Illinois University Press, 1991.

Brink, Andrew. *Creativity as Repair: Bipolarity and Its Closure.* Hamilton, Ontario: Cromlech Press, 1982.

————. *Loss and Symbolic Repair: A Psychological Study of Some English Poets.* Hamilton, Ontario: Cromlech Press, 1977.

Carpenter, Humphrey. *Geniuses Together: American Writers in Paris in the 1920s.* Boston: Houghton Mifflin, 1988.

Cate, Curtis. *George Sand.* Boston: Houghton Mifflin, 1975.

Chasseguet-Smirgel, Janine. *Creativity and Perversion.* New York: W. W. Norton, 1984.

Cheever, Mary. *The Need for Chocolate and Other Poems.* New York: Stein & Day, 1980.

Cheever, Susan. *Home Before Dark.* Boston: Houghton Mifflin, 1984.

————. *Treetops: A Family Memoir.* New York: Bantam Books, 1991.

Cody, Morrill. With Hugh Ford. *The Women of Montparnasse.* New York: Cornwall Books, 1984.

Dearborn, Mary V. *The Happiest Man Alive: A Biography of Henry Miller.* New York: Simon & Schuster, 1991.

DeSalvo, Louise. "Lighting the Cave: The Relationship between Vita Sackville-West and Virginia Woolf." *Signs* 8:2 (Winter 1982), pp. 195–214.

————. *Nathaniel Hawthorne.* Brighton, Sussex: Harvester Press, 1987.

————. " 'To Make Her Mutton at Sixteen': Rape, Incest, and Child Abuse in *The Antiphon*," in Mary Lynn Broe, ed., *Silence and Power*, pp. 300–15.

————. *Virginia Woolf's First Voyage: A Novel in the Making.* Totowa, New Jersey: Rowman & Littlefield, 1980.

————. *Virginia Woolf: The Impact of Childhood Sexual Abuse on Her Life and Work.* New York: Ballantine Books, 1989.

DeSalvo, Louise and Leaska, Mitchell A. *The Letters of Vita Sackville-West to Virginia Woolf.* New York: William Morrow, 1985.

Donaldson, Scott. *John Cheever: A Biography.* New York: Random House, 1988.

Drew, Bettina. *Nelson Algren: A Life on the Wild Side.* New York: Putnam, 1989.

Field, Andrew. *Djuna: The Formidable Miss Barnes.* Austin: University of Texas Press, 1983.

Freud, Sigmund. "Creative Writers and Day-Dreaming," in *The Standard Edition of the Complete Psychological Works of Sigmund Freud.* Trans. from the German under the general editorship of James Strachey. Volume IX. London: Hogarth Press, 1959, pp. 143–53.

————. "Dostoyevsky and Parricide," in *The Standard Edition of the Complete Psychological Works of Sigmund Freud.* Volume XV. London: Hogarth Press, 1961, pp. 175–98.

Fromm, Gloria G. "Rebecca West: The Fictions of Fact and the Facts of Fiction." *New Criterion*, January 1991, pp. 44–53.

Gardner, Howard. *Creating Minds: An Anatomy of Creativity Seen Through the Lives of Freud, Einstein, Picasso, Stravinsky, Eliot, Graham, and Ghandi.* New York: Basic Books, 1993.

Gardner, John. *On Becoming a Novelist.* New York: Harper & Row, 1983.

Gilmore, Thomas B. *Equivocal Spirits: Alcoholism and Drinking in Twentieth-Century Literature.* Chapel Hill: University of North Carolina Press, 1987.

Gilot, Françoise and Lake, Carlton. *Life with Picasso.* New York: McGraw-Hill, 1964.

Glendinning, Victoria. *Rebecca West: A Life.* New York: Fawcett Columbine, 1987.

Hawkins, Janet. "Rowers on the River Styx," *Harvard Magazine,* March–April 1991, pp. 43–52.

Herman, Judith Lewis. With Lisa Hirschman. *Father-Daughter Incest.* Cambridge: Harvard University Press, 1981.

Holmes, John. *The Selected Poems of John Holmes.* Introduction by John Ciardi. Boston: Beacon Press, 1965.

Huffington, Arianna Stassinopoulos. *Picasso: Creator and Destroyer.* New York: Simon & Schuster, 1988.

Jacoby, Susan. *Wild Justice: The Evolution of Revenge.* New York: Harper & Row, 1983.

Jamison, Kay Redfield. *Touched with Fire: Manic-Depressive Illness and the Artistic Temperament.* New York: Free Press, 1993.

Koestler, Arthur. *The Act of Creation.* New York: Macmillan, 1964.

Kofman, Sarah. *The Childhood of Art: An Interpretation of Freud's Aesthetics.* Trans. by Winifred Woodhull. New York: Columbia University Press, 1988.

Kris, Ernst. *Psychoanalytic Explorations in Art.* New York: International Universities Press, 1952.

Land, Myrick. *The Fine Art of Literary Mayhem: A Lively Account of Famous Writers and Their Feuds.* New York: Holt, Rinehart & Winston, 1962.

Langguth, A. J. *Saki: A Life of Hector Hugh Munro.* New York: Simon & Schuster, 1981.

Lehman, David. *Signs of the Times: Deconstruction and the Fall of Paul de Man.* New York: Poseidon Press, 1991.

Lewis, Anthony. *Make No Law: The Sullivan Case and the First Amendment.* New York: Random House, 1991.

Lottman, Herbert. *Colette: A Life.* Boston: Little, Brown, 1991.

Lowes, John Livingston. *The Road to Xanadu.* Boston: Houghton Mifflin, 1927.

Lynn, Kenneth S. *Hemingway.* New York: Simon & Schuster, 1987.

May, Rollo. *The Courage to Create.* New York: W. W Norton, 1975.

Mayer, Michael F. *What You Should Know About Libel and Slander.* New York: Arco, 1968.

McElwee, William. *The Murder of Sir Thomas Overbury.* London: Faber & Faber, 1952.

Mellow, James R. *Nathaniel Hawthorne in His Times.* Boston: Houghton Mifflin, 1980.

Meyers, Jeffrey. *D. H. Lawrence: A Biography.* New York: Alfred A. Knopf, 1990.

———. *Hemingway: A Biography.* New York: Harper & Row, 1985.

Middlebrook, Diane Wood. *Anne Sexton: A Biography.* Boston: Houghton Mifflin, 1991.

Miller, Alice. *For Your Own Good: Hidden Cruelty in Child-Rearing and the Roots of Violence.* New York: Farrar, Straus, & Giroux, 1983.

————. *The Untouched Key: Tracing Childhood Trauma in Creativity and Destructiveness*. Trans. from the German by Hildegarde and Hunter Hannum. New York: Doubleday, 1990.

Miller, Henry. *The Books in My Life*. New York: New Directions, 1969.

————. *Henry Miller's Hamlet Letters*. Ed. with a historical introduction by Michael Hargraves and an original preface by Henry Miller. Santa Barbara: Capra Press, 1981, 1988.

————. *Stories, Essays, Travel Sketches*. Ed. by Anthony Fine. New York: MJF Books, 1992.

Miller, Henry and Fowlie, Wallace. *Letters of Henry Miller and Wallace Fowlie (1943–1972)*. New York: Grove Press, 1975.

Mizener, Arthur. *The Saddest Story: A Biography of Ford Madox Ford*. New York: World, 1971.

Moore, Thomas. *Care of the Soul: A Guide for Cultivating Depth and Sacredness in Everyday Life*. New York: HarperCollins, 1992.

Morgan, Ted. *Maugham*. New York: Simon & Schuster, 1980.

Nin, Anaïs. *The Diary of Anaïs Nin, 1931–1934*. Ed. with an introduction by Gunther Stuhlmann. New York: Harcourt Brace Jovanovich, 1966.

————. *Henry and June: From the Unexpurgated Diary of Anaïs Nin*. New York: Harcourt Brace Jovanovich, 1986.

————. *Incest: From A Journal of Love; the Unexpurgated Diary of Anaïs Nin; 1932–1934*. With an introduction by Rupert Pole and biographical notes by Gunther Stuhlmann. New York: Harcourt Brace Jovanovich, 1992.

O'Hare, David, ed. *Psychology and the Arts*. Sussex, New Jersey: Harvester Press, 1981.

Paglia, Camille. *Sexual Personae: Art and Decadence from Nefertiti to Emily Dickinson*. New Haven: Yale University Press, 1990.

Pennebaker, James W., Ph.D. *Opening Up: The Healing Power of Confiding in Others*. New York: William Morrow, 1990.

Perles, Alfred and Durrell, Lawrence. *Art and Outrage: A Correspondence About Henry Miller Between Alfred Perles and Lawrence Durrell (With an Intermission by Henry Miller)*. London: Village Press, 1959, 1973.

Plath, Sylvia. *The Bell Jar*. New York: Harper & Row, 1971.

Richardson, John. With the collaboration of Marilyn McCully. *A Life of Picasso*. Volume I, 1881–1906. New York: Random House, 1991.

Rothenberg, Albert, M.D. *Creativity and Madness: New Findings and Old Stereotypes*. Baltimore: Johns Hopkins University Press, 1990.

————. *The Emerging Goddess: The Creative Process in Art, Science, and Other Fields*. Chicago: University of Chicago Press, 1979.

Ruitenbeck, Hendrik M., ed. *The Literary Imagination: Psychoanalysis and the Genius of the Writer*. Chicago: Quadrangle Books, 1965.

Sand, George. *My Life*. Trans. from the French and adapted by Dan Hofstadter. New York: Harper & Row, 1979.

Sarason, Bertram D. *Hemingway and the Sun Set*. Washington, D.C.: Microcard Editions, 1972.

Schank, Roger C. *Tell Me a Story: A New Look at Real and Artificial Memory*. New York: Charles Scribner's Sons, 1990.

Shengold, Leonard, M.D. *Soul Murder: The Effects of Childhood Sexual Abuse and Deprivation*. New Haven and London: Yale University Press, 1989.

Stevenson, Anne. *Bitter Fame: A Life of Sylvia Plath*. With additional material by Lucas Myers, Dido Merwin, and Richard Murphy. Boston: Houghton Mifflin, 1989.

Storr, Anthony. *Churchill's Black Dog, Kafka's Mice, and Other Phenomena of the Human Mind*. New York: Ballantine Books, 1988.

_____. *The Dynamics of Creation*. New York: Atheneum, 1985.

_____. *Human Aggression*. New York: Atheneum, 1968.

_____. *Human Destructiveness*. New York: Basic Books, 1972.

_____. *Solitude: A Return to the Self*. New York: Free Press, 1989.

Tarvis, Carol. *Anger: The Misunderstood Emotion*. New York: Simon & Schuster, 1982.

Trefusis, Violet. *Broderie Anglaise*. Trans. from the French by Barbara Bray. London: Methuen, 1987.

Tytell, John. *Passionate Lives: D. H. Lawrence, F. Scott Fitzgerald, Henry Miller, Dylan Thomas, Sylvia Plath—In Love*. New York: Carol, 1991.

White, Antonia. *Diaries 1926–1957; Volume I*. Ed. by Susan Chitty. New York: Viking, 1991.

Wijsenbeek, Carole. "Marcel Proust," in Hendrik M. Ruitenbeck, ed., *The Literary Imagination*.

Woolf, Virginia. *The Diary of Virginia Woolf*. Volume III, 1925–1930. Ed. by Anne Olivier Bell. Assisted by Andrew McNeillie. New York: Harcourt Brace Jovanovich, 1980.

_____. *The Question of Things Happening: The Letters of Virginia Woolf*. Volume II: 1912–1922. Ed. by Nigel Nicolson and Joanne Trautmann. London: Hogarth Press, 1976.

_____. *The Letters of Virginia Woolf*. Volume III: 1923–1928. Ed. by Nigel Nicolson and Joanne Trautmann. New York: Harcourt Brace Jovanovich, 1977.

_____. *The Letters of Virginia Woolf*. Volume IV: 1929–1931. Ed. by Nigel Nicolson and Joanne Trautmann. New York: Harcourt Brace Jovanovich, 1978.

_____. *Orlando*. New York: Harcourt Brace Jovanovich, 1928.

"THAT STRANGE PRELUDE":
Leonard Woolf, Virginia Woolf,
and *The Wise Virgins*

Alexander, Peter F. *Leonard and Virginia Woolf: A Literary Partnership*. New York: St. Martin's Press, 1992.

Annan, Noel. "Leonard Woolf," in *The Bloomsbury Group: A Collection of Memoirs, Commentary and Criticism*. Ed. by S. P. Rosenbaum. Toronto: University of Toronto Press, 1975, pp. 187–94.

_____. *Leslie Stephen: The Godless Victorian*. Chicago and London: University of Chicago Press, 1984.

────────. *Leslie Stephen: His Thought and Character in Relationship to His Time.* Cambridge: Harvard University Press, 1952.

Bell, Clive. Letters to Virginia Woolf. Monks House Papers. University of Sussex, England.

Bell, Quentin. *Virginia Woolf: A Biography.* New York: Harcourt Brace Jovanovich, 1972.

Bell, Vanessa. Letters to Virginia Woolf. Berg Collection, New York Public Library.

────────. *Selected Letters of Vanessa Bell.* Ed. by Regina Marler. New York: Pantheon, 1993.

Brenan, Gerald and Partridge, Ralph. *Best of Friends: The Brenan-Partridge Letters.* Ed. by Xan Fielding. London: Chatto & Windus, 1986.

────────. *Personal Record: 1920–1972.* New York: Alfred A. Knopf, 1975.

────────. *South from Grenada.* London: Readers Union, Hamish Hamilton, 1958.

Caramagno, Thomas C. *The Flight of the Mind: Virginia Woolf's Art and Manic-Depressive Illness.* Berkeley: University of California Press, 1991.

Caws, Mary Ann. *Women of Bloomsbury: Virginia, Vanessa and Carrington.* New York: Routledge, 1990.

Deacon, Richard. *The Cambridge Apostles: A History of Cambridge University's Elite Intellectual Secret Society.* New York: Farrar, Straus, & Giroux, 1985.

DeSalvo, Louise A. "Sorting, Sequencing, and Dating the Drafts of Virginia Woolf's *The Voyage Out.*" *Bulletin of Research in the Humanities* 82:3 (Autumn 1979), pp. 271–93.

────────. *Virginia Woolf's First Voyage: A Novel in the Making.* Totowa, New Jersey: Rowman & Littlefield, 1980.

────────. *Virginia Woolf: The Impact of Childhood Sexual Abuse on Her life and Work.* New York: Ballantine Books, 1989.

Dunn, Jane. *A Very Close Conspiracy: Vanessa Bell and Virginia Woolf.* Boston: Little, Brown, 1990.

Forster, E. M. *The Longest Day.* New York: Alfred A. Knopf, 1922, 1953.

Furbank, P. N. *E. M. Forster: A Life.* New York and London: Harcourt Brace Jovanovich, 1977, 1978.

Gordon, Lyndall. *Virginia Woolf: A Writer's Life.* New York: W. W. Norton, 1984.

Hawkins, Janet. "Rowers on the River Styx." *Harvard Magazine*, March–April 1991, pp. 43–52.

Heilbrun, Carolyn G. *Hamlet's Mother and Other Women.* New York: Columbia University Press, 1990.

Heine, Elizabeth, "The Earlier *Voyage Out:* Virginia Woolf's First Novel." *Bulletin of Research in the Humanities* 82:3 (Autumn 1979), pp. 294–316.

Holroyd, Michael. *Lytton Strachey: A Biography.* Reprinted with revisions. New York: Penguin, 1979.

Kelvin, Norman. *E. M. Forster.* With a preface by Harry T. Moore. Carbondale and Edwardsville: Southern Illinois University Press, 1967.

Kenney, Susan M. "Two Endings: Virginia Woolf's Suicide and *Between the Acts.*" *University of Toronto Quarterly* XLIV:4 (Summer 1975), pp. 265–89.

Kirkpatrick, B. J. *A Bibliography of Virginia Woolf.* 3rd ed. Oxford: Clarendon Press, 1980.

Lehmann, John. *Virginia Woolf and Her World.* London: Thames & Hudson, 1975.

Love, Jean O. *Virginia Woolf: Sources of Madness and Art.* Berkeley: University of California Press, 1977.

Macaulay, Rose. *The Writings of E. M. Forster.* New York: Barnes & Noble, 1970.

Meyerowitz, Selma S. *Leonard Woolf.* London: G. K. Hall, 1982.

Noble, Joan Russell, ed. *Recollections of Virginia Woolf.* New York: William Morrow, 1972.

Poole, Roger. *The Unknown Virginia Woolf.* Atlantic Highlands, New Jersey: Humanities Press, 1978.

Rose, Phyllis. *Woman of Letters: A Life of Virginia Woolf.* New York: Oxford University Press, 1978.

Spalding, Frances. *Vanessa Bell.* New York: Ticknor & Fields, 1983.

Spater, George and Parsons, Ian. *A Marriage of True Minds: An Intimate Portrait of Leonard and Virginia Woolf.* New York and London: Harcourt Brace Jovanovich, 1977.

Spielmann, M. H. and Layard, G. S. *The Life of Kate Greenaway.* London: Adam and Charles Black, 1905.

Strachey, Lytton. Letters to Leonard Woolf. Berg Collection, New York Public Library.

————. *Lytton Strachey by Himself: a Self-Portrait.* Ed. by Michael Holroyd. New York: Holt, Rinehart & Winston, 1971.

Stephen, Julia. *Notes from Sick Rooms.* Orono, Maine: Puckerbrush Press, 1980; reprint of London edition of 1883.

Stephen, Sir Leslie. Letters to Julia Stephen. Berg Collection, New York Public Library.

Thomas, J. M. Letters to Violet Dickinson. Berg Collection, New York Public Library.

Trombley, Stephen. *'All that Summer She was Mad': Virginia Woolf and Her Doctors.* London: Junction Books, 1981.

Wilson, Duncan. *Leonard Woolf: A Political Biography.* London: Hogarth Press, 1978.

Woolf, Leonard. *Beginning Again: An Autobiography of the Years 1911 to 1918.* New York: Harcourt Brace Jovanovich, 1964.

————. *Downhill All the Way: An Autobiography of the Years 1919 to 1939.* New York: Harcourt Brace Jovanovich, 1967.

————. *Growing: An Autobiography of the Years 1904 to 1911.* New York: Harcourt Brace Jovanovich, 1961.

————. *The Journey Not the Arrival Matters: An Autobiography of the Years 1939–1969.* New York: Harcourt, Brace & World, 1969.

————. *Letters of Leonard Woolf.* Ed. by Frederic Spotts. New York: Harcourt Brace Jovanovich, 1989.

————. *Sowing: An Autobiography of the Years 1880 to 1904.* New York: Harcourt Brace Jovanovich, 1960.

————. *The Wise Virgins: A Story of Words, Opinions and a Few Emotions.* New York: Harcourt Brace Jovanovich, 1914.

Woolf, Virginia. *Books and Portraits: Some further selections from the literary and biographical writings of Virginia Woolf.* Ed. with a preface by Mary Lyon. New York: Harcourt Brace Jovanovich, 1977.

————. *The Diary of Virginia Woolf.* Ed. by Anne Olivier Bell. Volume I, 1915–1919. London: Hogarth Press, 1977.

————. *The Diary of Virginia Woolf.* Ed. by Anne Olivier Bell. Assisted by Andrew McNeillie. Volume II, 1920–1924. New York: Harcourt Brace Jovanovich, 1978.

————. *The Diary of Virginia Woolf.* Ed. by Anne Olivier Bell. Assisted by Andrew McNeillie. Volume III, 1925–1930. New York: Harcourt Brace Jovanovich, 1980.

————. *The Diary of Virginia Woolf.* Ed. by Anne Olivier Bell. Assisted by Andrew McNeillie. Volume IV, 1931–1935. New York: Harcourt Brace Jovanovich, 1980.

————. *The Diary of Virginia Woolf.* Ed. by Anne Olivier Bell. Assisted by Andrew McNeillie. Volume V, 1936–1941. New York: Harcourt Brace Jovanovich, 1984.

————. [Early Writings]. [?1902], [1904]. Fragment of a bound exercise book which contains fragment of an unfinished novel. Monks House Papers, University of Sussex. MH/A.26.

————. *The Flight of the Mind: The Letters of Virginia Woolf.* Ed. by Nigel Nicolson and Joanne Trautmann. Volume I, 1888–1912. London: Hogarth Press, 1975.

————. "Haworth, November 1904," in *Books and Portraits,* pp. 166–69.

————. *A Haunted House and Other Short Stories.* New York: Harcourt, Brace & World, 1921.

————. *Moments of Being.* 2nd ed. Ed. by Jeanne Schulkind. New York: Harcourt Brace Jovanovich, 1985.

————. *A Passionate Apprentice: The Early Journals, 1897–1909.* Ed. by Mitchell A. Leaska. New York: Harcourt Brace Jovanovich, 1990.

————. *The Question of Things Happening: The Letters of Virginia Woolf.* Ed. by Nigel Nicolson and Joanne Trautmann. Volume II, 1912–1922. London: Hogarth Press, 1976.

————. *Virginia Woolf and Lytton Strachey: Letters.* Ed. by Leonard Woolf and James Strachey. London: Hogarth Press and Chatto & Windus, 1956.

"LIKE A LION RAGING AFTER ITS PREY":
D. H. Lawrence, Ottoline Morrell, and *Women in Love*

Aldington, Richard. *Portrait of a Genius But . . .* New York: Duell, Sloan & Pearce, 1950.

Asquith, Lady Cynthia. *Diaries: 1915–1918.* With an afterword by L. P. Hartley. London: Hutchinson, 1968.

Bedford, Sybille. *Aldous Huxley: A Biography.* London: Chatto & Windus, 1973.

Branda, Eldon S. "Textual Changes in *Women in Love,*" *Texas Studies in Literature & Language* VI: 3 (Autumn 1964), pp. 306–21.

Callow, Philip. *Son and Lover: The Young D. H. Lawrence*. Chicago: Ivan R. Dee, 1975, 1991.

Cannan, Gilbert. *Mendel: A Story of Youth*. New York: George H. Doran, 1916.

Carrington, Dora. *Carrington: Letters and Extracts from her Diaries*. Chosen with an introduction by David Garnett. With a biographical note by Noel Carrington. London: Jonathan Cape, 1970.

Carswell, Catherine. *The Savage Pilgrimage: A Narrative of D. H. Lawrence*. Rev. ed. London: Martin Secker, 1932; London: Secker & Warburg, 1951.

Chambers, Jessie, writing as "E.T." *D. H. Lawrence: A Personal Record*. 2nd ed. Ed. by J. D. Chambers. New York: Barnes & Noble, 1935, 1965.

Clarke, Colin, ed. *D. H. Lawrence: The Rainbow and Women in Love, A Casebook*. London: Macmillan, 1969.

Corke, Helen. *D. H. Lawrence: The Croydon Years*. Austin: University of Texas Press, 1965.

Cowan, James C., ed. *D. H. Lawrence: An Annotated Bibliography of Writings About Him*. Volumes I and II. DeKalb: Northern Illinois University Press, 1982, 1985.

Daleski, H. M. *The Forked Flame: A Study of D. H. Lawrence*. Evanston, Illinois: Northwestern University Press, 1965.

Darroch, Sandra Jobson. *Ottoline: The Life of Lady Ottoline Morrell*. New York: Coward, McCann & Geoghegan, 1975.

Davis, Herbert. *"Women in Love*: A Corrected Typescript," *University of Toronto Quarterly*, October 27, 1957, pp. 34–53.

Deacon, Richard. *The Cambridge Apostles: A History of Cambridge University's Elite Intellectual Secret Society*. New York: Farrar, Straus, & Giroux, 1985.

Delany, Paul. *D. H. Lawrence's Nightmare: The Writer and His Circle in the Years of the Great War*. New York: Basic Books, 1978.

Delavenay, Emile. *D. H. Lawrence: The Man and His Work. The Formative Years: 1885–1919*. Trans. from the French by Katherine M. Delavenay. London: Heinemann, 1972.

Dostoyevsky, Fyodor. *The Possessed*. Trans. by Andrew R. MacAndrew. With an afterword by Marc Slonim. New York: New American Library, 1962.

Feinstein, Elaine. *Lawrence and the Women: The Intimate Life of D. H. Lawrence*. New York: HarperCollins, 1993.

Ford, George. *Double Measure*. New York: Holt, Rinehart & Winston, 1965.

French, Marilyn. *Shakespeare's Division of Experience*. New York: Summit Books, 1981.

Garnett, David. *The Golden Echo. Volume 2, The Flowers of the Forest*. London: Chatto & Windus, 1955.

Green, Martin. *The von Richthofen Sisters: The Triumphant and the Tragic Modes of Love, Else and Frieda von Richthofen, Otto Gross, Max Weber, and D. H. Lawrence in the Years 1870–1970*. New York: Basic Books, 1974.

Hardy, George and Harris, Nathaniel. *A D. H. Lawrence Album*. New York: Franklin Watts, 1985.

Herman, Judith Lewis, M. D. *Trauma and Recovery*. New York: Basic Books, 1992.

Holroyd, Michael. *Lytton Strachey: A Biography.* Reprinted with revisions. New York: Penguin, 1979.

Jamison, Kay Redfield. *Touched with Fire: Manic-Depressive Illness and the Artistic Temperament.* New York: Free Press, 1993.

Kalnins, Mara, ed. *D. H. Lawrence: Century Essays.* Bristol: Bristol Classical Press, 1986.

Kinkead-Weekes, Mark, ed. *Twentieth Century Interpretations of The Rainbow.* Englewood Cliffs, New Jersey: Prentice-Hall, 1971.

Lawlor, Sheila. *Britain and Ireland: 1914–23.* Totowa, New Jersey: Barnes & Noble, 1983.

Lawrence, Ada and Gelder, G. Stuart. *Early Life of D. H. Lawrence: Together with Hitherto Unpublished Letters and Articles.* London: Martin Secker, 1932.

————. *Young Lorenzo. Early Life of D. H. Lawrence, Containing Hitherto Unpublished Letters, Articles and Reproductions of Pictures.* Florence: G. Orioli, 1931.

Lawrence, D. H. *Amores.* London: Duckworth, 1925.

————. "Aristocracy," in *Phoenix II: Uncollected, and Other Prose Works by D. H. Lawrence.* Collected by Warren Roberts and Harry T. Moore. New York: Viking, 1968, pp. 475–84.

————. "Autobiographical Sketch," in *Phoenix II,* pp. 300–2.

————. "Autobiographical Sketch," in *Phoenix II,* pp. 592–96.

————. "Cocksure Women and Hensure Men," in *Phoenix II,* pp. 553–55.

————. *The Collected Letters of D. H. Lawrence. Volume II.* Ed. with an introduction by Harry T. Moore. New York: Viking, 1962.

————. *Collected Poems. Volume I. Rhyming Poems.* New York: Jonathan Cape & Harrison Smith, 1929.

————. *Collected Poems. Volume II. Unrhyming Poems.* New York: Jonathan Cape & Harrison Smith, 1929.

————. *The Complete Plays of D. H. Lawrence.* New York: Viking, 1965.

————. *The Complete Stories. Volume II.* New York: Penguin, 1976.

————. *The Complete Stories. Volume III.* New York: Penguin, 1977.

————. *Fantasia of the Unconscious and Psychoanalysis and the Unconscious.* London: Penguin, 1977.

————. "Foreword to *Women in Love,*" in *Phoenix II,* pp. 275–76.

————. *The Letters of D. H. Lawrence. Volume I, September 1901–May 1913.* Ed. by James T. Boulton. Cambridge: Cambridge University Press, 1979.

————. *The Letters of D. H. Lawrence. Volume II, June 1913–October 1916.* Ed. by George J. Zytaruk, James T. Boulton, and Andrew Robertson. Cambridge: Cambridge University Press, 1981.

————. *The Letters of D. H. Lawrence. Volume III, October 1916–June 1921.* Ed. by James T. Boulton and Andrew Robertson. Cambridge: Cambridge University Press, 1984.

————. *The Letters of D. H. Lawrence. Volume IV, June 1921–March 1924.* Ed. by Warren Roberts, James T. Boulton, and Elizabeth Mansfield. Cambridge: Cambridge University Press, 1987.

————. *The Letters of D. H. Lawrence. Volume V, March 1924–March 1927.* Ed. by James T. Boulton and Lindeth Vasey. Cambridge: Cambridge University Press, 1989.

————. *Look! We Have Come Through!* With an introduction by Frieda Lawrence, illustrations by Michael Adam, and foreword by Warren Roberts. Out of the Ark Press, Cornwall, for the Rare Books Collection of the University of Texas, 1958, 1959.

————. *Love Poems and Others.* London: Duckworth, 1913.

————. "Matriarchy," in *Phoenix II*, pp. 549–52.

————. *New Poems.* New York: B. W. Huebsch, 1920.

————. "Nottingham and the Mining Countryside," in *Phoenix: The Posthumous Papers of D. H. Lawrence.* Ed. with an introduction by Edward D. McDonald. New York: Viking, 1936, pp. 133–40.

————. "On Being a Man," in *Phoenix II*, pp. 616–22.

————. *Phoenix: The Posthumous Papers of D. H. Lawrence.* Ed. with an introduction by Edward D. McDonald. New York: Viking, 1936.

————. *Phoenix II: Uncollected, Unpublished, and Other Prose Works by D. H. Lawrence.* Collected and ed. with an introduction and notes by Warren Roberts and Harry T. Moore. New York: Viking, 1968.

————. "Prologue to *Women in Love*," in *Phoenix II*, pp. 92–108.

————. *The Prussian Officer and Other Stories.* Ed. by John Worthen. Cambridge: Cambridge University Press, 1983.

————. *The Rainbow.* Ed. by Mark Kinkead-Weeks. Cambridge: Cambridge University Press, 1989.

————. *The Rainbow.* With an introduction by Louise DeSalvo. New York: Signet, 1991.

————. "The Reality of Peace," in *Phoenix*, pp 669–94. First published in *England Review*, June-July-August 1917.

————. "Sex versus Loneliness," in *Phoenix II*, pp. 549–52.

————. *Studies in Classic American Literature.* Garden City, New York: Doubleday, 1923.

————. *Study of Thomas Hardy and Other Essays.* Ed. by Bruce Steele. Cambridge: Cambridge University Press, 1985.

————. *Twilight in Italy.* New York: Viking, 1958; originally published by B. W. Huebsch, 1916.

————. *Women in Love.* Ed. by David Farmer, Lindeth Vasey, and John Worthen. Cambridge: Cambridge University Press, 1987.

————. *Women in Love.* Ed. with an introduction and notes by Charles L. Ross. New York: Penguin, 1982; reprint of edition published privately in the U.S. by Thomas Seltzer in 1920.

————. *Women in Love.* Photocopy of typescript. 666 pages. Thomas Fisher Rare Book Library, Douglas Duncan Collection, University of Toronto.

Lawrence, Frieda. *The Memoirs and Correspondence.* Ed. by E. W. Tedlock, Jr. New York: Alfred A. Knopf, 1964.

————. *"Not I, But the Wind . . ."* New York: Viking, 1934.

Leavis, F. R. *D. H. Lawrence: Novelist.* New York: Alfred A. Knopf, 1956.

Lucas, Robert. *Frieda Lawrence: The Story of Frieda von Richthofen and D. H. Lawrence.* Trans. from the German by Geoffrey Skelton. New York: Viking, 1973.

Mansfield, Katherine. *Katherine Mansfield's Letters to John Middleton Murry*

1913–1922. Ed. by John Middleton Murry. New York: Alfred A. Knopf, 1951.

McDonald, Edward D., ed. *A Bibliography of the Writings of D. H. Lawrence.* With a foreword by D. H. Lawrence. Philadelphia: Centaur Book Shop, 1925.

Meyers, Jeffrey. *D. H. Lawrence: A Biography.* New York: Alfred A. Knopf, 1990.

Millett, Robert W. *The Vultures and the Phoenix: Paintings of D. H. Lawrence.* London and Toronto: Associated University Presses, 1983.

Moore, Harry T. *The Priest of Love: A Life of D. H. Lawrence.* Rev. ed. Carbondale and Edwardsville: Southern Illinois University Press, 1974; New York: Penguin, 1974.

Moorehead, Caroline. *Bertrand Russell: A Life.* New York: Viking, 1992.

Morrell, Lady Ottoline. *Lady Ottoline's Album: Snapshots and Portraits of Her Famous Contemporaries (and of herself), Photographed for the Most Part by Lady Ottoline Morrell.* Ed. by Carolyn G. Heilbrun. From the collection of her daughter, Julian Vinogradoff, with an introduction by Lord David Cecil. New York: Alfred A. Knopf, 1976.

―――. *Memoirs of Lady Ottoline Morrell: A Study in Friendship, 1873–1915.* Ed. by Robert Gathorne-Hardy. New York: Alfred A. Knopf, 1964.

―――. *Ottoline at Garsington: Memoirs of Lady Ottoline Morrell, 1915–1918.* Ed. with an introduction by Robert Gathorne-Hardy. New York: Alfred A. Knopf, 1975.

Murry, John Middleton. *The Autobiography of John Middleton Murry: Between Two Worlds.* New York: Julian Messner, 1936.

―――. *Fyodor Dostoyevsky: A Critical Study.* Boston: Small, Maynard, 1924.

―――. *The Letters of John Middleton Murry to Katherine Mansfield.* Selected and ed. by C. A. Hankin. London: Constable, 1983.

―――. *Son of Woman: The Story of D. H. Lawrence.* New York: Jonathan Cape & Harrison Smith, 1931.

Nance, Guinevera A. *Aldous Huxley.* New York: Continuum, 1988.

Nehls, Edward, ed. *D. H. Lawrence: A Composite Biography.* Volume I, 1885–1919. Madison: University of Wisconsin Press, 1957. Volume II, 1919–1925. Madison: University of Wisconsin Press, 1958. Volume III, 1925–1930. Madison: University of Wisconsin Press, 1959.

Nin, Anaïs. *D. H. Lawrence, An Unprofessional Study.* Denver: Alan Swallow, 1964.

Oates, Joyce Carol. "Lawrence's Götterdämmerung: The Tragic Vision of *Women in Love.*" *Critical Inquiry* 4:3 (Spring 1978), pp. 559–78.

Roberts, Warren. *A Bibliography of D. H. Lawrence.* London: Rupert Hart-Davis, 1963.

Ross, Charles L. *The Composition of The Rainbow and Women in Love: A History.* Charlottesville: published for the Bibliographical Society of the University Press of Virginia, 1979.

―――. "The Composition of *Women in Love*: A History, 1913–1919." *D. H. Lawrence Review* VIII: 2 (Summer 1975), pp. 198–212.

Ross, Charles L. and Zytaruk, George J. "*Goats and Compasses* and/or *Women in Love*: An Exchange." *D. H. Lawrence Review* VI:1 (Spring 1973), pp. 33–46.

Russell, Bertrand. *The Autobiography of Bertrand Russell: 1872–1914*. Boston: Little, Brown, 1967.

———. *The Autobiography of Bertrand Russell: 1914–1944*. Boston: Little, Brown, 1968.

———. *Portraits from Memory and Other Essays*. New York: Simon & Schuster, 1956.

———. *The Selected Letters of Bertrand Russell: Volume I, The Private Years, 1884–1914*. Ed. by Nicholas Griffin. Boston: Houghton Mifflin, 1992.

Sagar, Keith. *D. H. Lawrence: A Calendar of His Works*. With a checklist of the manuscripts of D. H. Lawrence by Lindeth Vasey. Austin: University of Texas Press, 1979.

———. *D. H. Lawrence: Life Into Art*. Harmondsworth, Middlesex, England: Penguin, 1985.

———. "*Goats and Compasses* and *Women in Love* Again." *D. H. Lawrence Review* VI:3 (Fall 1973), pp. 303–8.

Santayana, George. *My Host, The World. Volume 3, Persons and Places*. New York: Charles Scribner's Sons, 1953.

Sassoon, Siegfried. *Siegfried's Journey, 1916–1920*. London: Faber & Faber, 1945.

Seymour, Miranda. *Ottoline Morrell: Life on the Grand Scale*. New York: Farrar, Straus, & Giroux, 1992.

Sitwell, Osbert. *Left Hand, Right Hand. Volume IV: Laughter in the Next Room*. London: Macmillan, 1949.

Smith, Anne. *Lawrence and Women*. Plymouth and London: Vision Press, 1978.

Spender, Stephen. *World Within World*. New York: Harcourt Brace, 1951.

Tytell, John. *Passionate Lives*. New York: Birch Lane Press, 1991.

Ward, Alan J. *The Easter Rising: Revolution and Irish Nationalism*. Arlington Heights, Illinois: Harlan Davidson, n.d.

Woolf, Virginia. *The Diary of Virginia Woolf. Volume I: 1915–1919*. Introduced by Quentin Bell. Ed. by Anne Olivier Bell. London: Hogarth Press, 1977.

———. *The Question of Things Happening. The Letters of Virginia Woolf. Volume II: 1912–1922*. Ed. by Nigel Nicolson and Joanne Trautmann. London: Hogarth Press, 1976.

Worthen, John. *D. H. Lawrence: The Early Years 1885–1912*. Cambridge: Cambridge University Press, 1991.

———. *D. H. Lawrence and the Idea of the Novel*. Totowa, New Jersey: Rowman & Littlefield, 1979.

Zytaruk, George J. "What Happened to D. H. Lawrence's *Goats and Compasses*?" *D. H. Lawrence Review* IV:3 (Fall 1971), pp. 280–86.

"JUSTICE, NOT REVENGE":
Djuna Barnes and the Making of *The Antiphon*

Allen, Carolyn. "Writing toward *Nightwood*: Djuna Barnes' Seduction Stories," in Mary Lynn Broe, ed., *Silence and Power*, pp. 54–65.

Altman, Meryl. "*The Antiphon*: 'No Audience at All'?" In Mary Lynn Broe, ed., *Silence and Power*, pp. 271–84.

Anderson, Margaret. *My Thirty Years' War: The Autobiography, Beginnings and Battles to 1930.* New York: Horizon Press, 1969.

Barnes, Djuna. *The Antiphon* in *Selected Works of Djuna Barnes: Spillway, The Antiphon, Nightwood.* New York: Farrar, Straus, & Giroux, 1962.

—————. *The Book of Repulsive Women: 3 Rhythms and 5 Drawings.* Yonkers, New York: Alicat Bookshop Press, 1948.

—————. *Creatures in an Alphabet.* New York: Dial Press, 1982.

—————. *Greenwich Village As It Is.* New York: Phoenix Bookshop, 1978.

—————. *Interviews.* Ed. by Alyce Barry. Foreword and commentary by Douglas Messerli. Washington, D.C.: Sun & Moon Press, 1985.

—————. *Ladies Almanack showing their Signs and their tides; their Moons and their Changes; the Season as it is with them; their Eclipses and Equinoxes; as well as a full Record of diurnal and nocturnal Distempers,* Written & illustrated by a Lady of Fashion. Paris: Printed for the author and sold by Edward W. Titus, 4 rue Delambre, at the sign of the Black Manikin, 1928. Wilson Library, Rare Book Collection, University of North Carolina, Chapel Hill.

—————. "Mother," in Bonnie Kime Scott, ed., *The Gender of Modernism,* pp. 30–33.

—————. *Nightwood.* New York: New Directions, 1937.

—————. *New York.* Ed. with commentary by Alyce Barry. Drawings by Djuna Barnes. Foreword by Douglas Messerli. Los Angeles: Sun & Moon Press, 1989.

—————. "Rape and Repining." *Transition,* December 1927, pp. 20–28.

—————. *Ryder.* New York: H. Liveright, 1928; Elmwood Park, Illinois: Dalkey Archive Press, 1990.

—————. *Selected Works of Djuna Barnes: Spillway, The Antiphon, Nightwood.* New York: Farrar, Straus, & Giroux, 1962.

—————. "To the Dogs," in Bonnie Kime Scott, ed., *The Gender of Modernism,* pp. 33–39.

—————. *Smoke and Other Early Stories.* Ed. with an introduction by Douglas Messerli. College Park, Maryland: Sun & Moon Press, 1982.

Beach, Sylvia. *Shakespeare and Company.* New York: Harcourt, Brace, 1959.

Benstock, Shari. *Women of the Left Bank: Paris: 1900–1940.* Austin: University of Texas Press, 1986.

Blankley, Elyse Marie. "Daughters' Exile: Renee Vivien, Gertrude Stein, and Djuna Barnes in Paris." Ph.D. diss., University of California, Davis, 1984.

—————. "Return to Mytilene: Renee Vivien and the City of Women," in Susan Merrill Squier, ed., *Women Writers and the City,* pp. 45–67.

Bowles, Paul. *Without Stopping: an Autobiography.* New York: G. P. Putnam's Sons, 1972.

Broe, Mary Lynn, "Djuna Barnes," in Bonnie Kime Scott, ed., *The Gender of Modernism,* pp. 19–29.

—————. "My Art Belongs to Daddy: Incest as Exile, The Textual Economics of Hayford Hall," in Mary Lynn Broe and Angela Ingram, eds. *Women's Writing in Exile.* Chapel Hill: University of North Carolina Press, 1989.

—————. "Gunga Duhl, the Pen Performer." Review of *Djuna Barnes Interviews.*

Ed. by Alyce Barry. Foreword and commentary by Douglas Messerli. *Belles Lettres* I (September–October 1985), pp. 2–3.

_____, ed. *Silence and Power: A Reevaluation of Djuna Barnes.* Carbondale and Edwardsville: Southern Illinois University Press, 1991.

Broyard, Anatole. "Aged Unconventionality," Review of *Selected Works of Djuna Barnes. New York Times,* June 28, 1980, p. 19.

Burke, Carolyn, " 'Accidental Aloofness': Barnes, Loy, and Modernism," in Mary Lynn Broe, ed., *Silence and Power,* pp. 67–79.

Carpenter, Humphrey. *Geniuses Together: American Writers in Paris in the 1920s.* Boston: Houghton Mifflin, 1988.

Churchill, Allen. *The Improper Bohemians: A Re-creation of Greenwich Village in Its Heyday.* New York: E. P. Dutton, 1959.

Cody, Morrill. With Hugh Ford. *The Women of Montparnasse.* New York: Cornwall Books, 1984.

Conover, Roger L., ed. With a note by Jonathan Williams. *The Last Lunar Baedeker: Mina Loy.* Highlands, North Carolina: Jargon Society, 1982.

Cowley, Malcolm, ed. *After the Genteel Tradition: American Writers 1910–1930.* Carbondale and Edwardsville: Southern Illinois University Press, 1964.

_____. *—And I Worked at the Writer's Trade: Chapters of Literary History, 1918–1978.* New York: Viking, 1978.

_____. *Exile's Return: A Literary Odyssey of the 1920s.* New York: Viking, 1934, 1951.

_____. *A Second Flowering: Works and Days of the Lost Generation.* New York: Viking, 1973.

Curry, Lynda Catherine. "The Second Metamorphosis: A Study of the Development of 'The Antiphon' by Djuna Barnes." Ph.D. diss., Miami University, 1978.

_____. " 'Tom, Take Mercy': Djuna Barnes' Drafts of *The Antiphon,*" in Mary Lynn Broe, ed., *Silence and Power,* pp. 286–98.

Daley, Suzanne. "Djuna Barnes Dies: Poet and Novelist." *New York Times,* June 20, 1982, section 1, p. 32.

Dalton, Anne Beatrice. *The Book of Repulsive Women: Father-Daughter Incest in the Works of Djuna Barnes.* Ph.D. diss., University of California, Davis, 1989.

DeSalvo, Louise A., " 'To Make Her Mutton at Sixteen': Rape, Incest, and Child Abuse in *The Antiphon,*" in Mary Lynn Broe, ed., *Silence and Power,* pp. 300–15.

Doughty, Frances M. "Gilt on Cardboard: Djuna Barnes as Illustrator of Her Life and Work," in Mary Lynn Broe, ed., *Silence and Power,* pp. 137–54.

Duncan, Erika. *Unless Soul Clap Its Hands.* New York: Schocken Books, 1984.

Ebeling-Koning, Blanche T. "Famous, Unknown Djuna Barnes." *New York Times Book Review,* January 5, 1986, p. 4.

Field, Andrew. *Djuna: The Formidable Miss Barnes.* Austin: University of Texas Press, 1985.

_____. "Reminiscences," in Mary Lynn Broe, ed., *Silence and Power,* pp. 364–65.

Fitch, Noel Riley. *Sylvia Beach and the Lost Generation: A History of Literary Paris in the Twenties and Thirties.* New York: W. W. Norton, 1983.

Ford, Hugh. *Four Lives in Paris*. San Francisco: North Point Press, 1987.

Ford, Ruth. "Reminiscences," in Mary Lynn Broe, ed., *Silence and Power*, pp. 340–41.

Geddes, Minna Besser. "Emily Holmes Coleman," in Karen Lee Rood, ed., *American Writers in Paris, 1920–1939, Dictionary of Literary Biography*, Volume IV. Detroit: Gale Research Company, 1980, pp. 71–72.

Gildzen, Alex. "Reminiscences," in Mary Lynn Broe, ed., *Silence and Power*, pp. 345–48.

Giroux, Robert. " 'The Most Famous Unknown in the World'—Remembering Djuna Barnes." *New York Times Book Review*, October 8, 1983, p. 45.

Glassco, John. *Memoirs of Montparnasse*. With an introduction by Leon Edel. New York: Oxford University Press, 1970.

Guggenheim, Peggy. *Confessions of an Art Addict*. New York: Macmillan, 1960.

———. *Out of This Century: Confessions of an Art Addict*. Foreword by Gore Vidal. Introduction by Alfred H. Barr, Jr. New York: Universe Books, 1979.

Hanscombe, Gillian and Smyers, Virginia L. *Writing for Their Lives: The Modernist Women, 1910–1940*. Boston: Northeastern University Press, 1987.

Herman, Judith Lewis, M. D. *Trauma and Recovery*. New York: Basic Books, 1992.

Jay, Karla. *The Amazon and the Page: Natalie Clifford Barney and Renee Vivien*. Bloomington: Indiana University Press, 1988.

———. "The Outsider among the Expatriates: Djuna Barnes' Satire on the Ladies of the *Almanack*," in Mary Lynn Broe, ed., *Silence and Power*, pp. 184–93.

Kannenstine, Louis F. "Djuna Barnes," in Karen Lee Rood, ed., *American Writers in Paris, 1920–1939, Dictionary of Literary Biography*, Volume IV. Detroit, Michigan: Gale Research Company, 1980, pp. 18–22.

———. *The Art of Djuna Barnes: Duality and Damnation*. New York: New York University Press, 1977.

Kaviola, Karen. *All Contraries Confounded: The Lyrical Fiction of Virginia Woolf, Djuna Barnes, and Marguerite Duras*. Iowa City: University of Iowa Press, 1991.

Kennedy, J. Gerald. *Imagining Paris: Exile, Writing, and American Identity*. New Haven: Yale University Press, 1993.

Kessler-Harris, Alice and William McBrien, eds. *Faith of a (Woman) Writer*. New York: Greenwood Press, 1988.

Langner, Lawrence. *The Magic Curtain: The Story of a Life in Two Fields, Theatre and Invention by the Founder of the Theatre Guild*. New York: E. P. Dutton, 1951.

Lanser, Susan Sniader. "Speaking in Tongues: *Ladies Almanack* and the Discourse of Desire," in Mary Lynn Broe, ed., *Silence and Power*, pp. 156–68.

Larabee, Ann. "The Early Attic Stage of Djuna Barnes," in Mary Lynn Broe, ed., *Silence and Power*, pp. 37–44.

Levine, Nancy J. " 'Bringing Milkshakes to Bulldogs': The Early Journalism of Djuna Barnes," in Mary Lynn Broe, ed., *Silence and Power*, pp. 27–34.

Marcus, Jane. "Laughing at Leviticus: *Nightwood* as Woman's Circus Epic," in Mary Lynn Broe, ed., *Silence and Power*, pp. 221–50.

_____. "Mousemeat: Contemporary Reviews of *Nightwood*," in Mary Lynn Broe, ed., *Silence and Power*, pp. 195–204.

Mayerson, Charlotte Leon, ed. *Shadow and Light: The Life, Friends and Opinions of Maurice Sterne*. Introduction by George Biddle. New York: Harcourt, Brace & World, 1965.

McAlmon, Robert. *Being Geniuses Together: 1920–1930*. Revised with supplementary chapters by Kay Boyle. New York: Doubleday, 1968.

_____. *McAlmon and the Lost Generation: A Self-Portrait*. Ed. with a commentary by Robert E. Knoll. Lincoln: University of Nebraska Press, 1962.

McCullough, Frances. "Djuna Barnes." *New York Times Book Review*, July 17, 1983, p. 23.

_____. "Reminiscences," in Mary Lynn Broe, ed., *Silence and Power*, pp. 365–68.

O'Neal, Hank. *"Life is Painful, Nasty & Short . . . In My Case It Has Only Been Painful & Nasty." Djuna Barnes 1978–1981: An Informal Memoir*. New York: Paragon House, 1990.

_____. "Reminiscences," in Mary Lynn Broe, ed., *Silence and Power*, pp. 348–61.

Page, Chester. "Reminiscences," in Mary Lynn Broe, ed., *Silence and Power*, pp. 361–64.

Parry, Albert. *Garrets and Pretenders: A History of Bohemianism in America*. New York: Dover, 1933, 1960.

Plumb, Cheryl J. *Fancy's Craft: Art and Identity in the Early Works of Djuna Barnes*. Selinsgrove, Pennsylvania: Susquehanna University Press, 1986.

Ponsot, Marie. "A Reader's *Ryder*," in Mary Lynn Broe, ed., *Silence and Power*, pp. 94–112.

Provincetown Players. Circular, Season of 1916–1917. Berg Collection, New York Public Library.

_____. Circular, Season of 1917–1918. Berg Collection, New York Public Library.

_____. Playbill, Sixth Season, 1919–1920. Berg Collection, New York Public Library.

Rascoe, Burton, *We Were Interrupted*. Garden City, New York: Doubleday, 1947.

Raymont, Henry. "From the Avant-Garde of the Thirties, Djuna Barnes." *New York Times*, May 24, 1971, p. 24.

Retallack, Joan. "One Acts: Early Plays of Djuna Barnes," in Mary Lynn Broe, ed., *Silence and Power*, pp. 46–52.

Rieke, Alison. "Two Women: The Transformations," in Alice Kessler-Harris and William McBrien, eds., *Faith of a (Woman) Writer*, pp. 71–81.

Rose, Phyllis. "The Stature of an Eccentric." Review of *The Life and Times of Djuna Barnes* by Andrew Field. *New York Times Book Review*, June 26, 1983, pp. 9, 22–23.

Scott, Bonnie Kime, ed. *The Gender of Modernism: A Critical Anthology*. Bloomington: Indiana University Press, 1990.

Scott, James B. *Djuna Barnes*. Boston: Twayne Publishers, 1976.

_____. "Reminiscences," in Mary Lynn Broe, ed., *Silence and Power*, pp. 341–45.

Shields, Douglas Dix. "The Text as War Machine: Writing to Destroy." Ph.D. diss., University of Washington, 1988.

Smith-Rosenberg, Caroll. *Disorderly Conduct: Visions of Gender in Victorian America*. New York: Alfred A. Knopf, 1985.

Squier, Susan Merrill, ed. *Women Writers and the City: Essays in Feminist Literary Criticism*. Knoxville: University of Tennessee Press, 1984.

Stanton, Elizabeth Cady. *Eighty Years and More: Reminiscences 1815–1898*. With a new introduction by Gail Parker. New York: Schocken Books, 1971; reprinted from T. Fisher Unwin edition of 1898.

Stevenson, Sheryl. "Writing the Grotesque Body: Djuna Barnes' Carnival Parody," in Mary Lynn Broe, ed., *Silence and Power*, pp. 81–91.

Stimpson, Catherine. "Afterword," in Mary Lynn Broe, ed., *Silence and Power*, pp. 370–73.

Wagstaff, Ann Marie. "The Backward-Looking Prophet: An Examination of the Consequences of Childhood Exploitation in the Work of Djuna Barnes." Ph.D. diss., University of California, Davis, 1987.

White, Antonia. *Antonia White: Diaries 1926–1957*. Ed. by Susan Chitty. New York: Viking, 1991.

Wilson, Edmund. *The Twenties: From Notebooks and Diaries of the Period*. Ed. with an introduction by Leon Edel. New York: Farrar, Straus, & Giroux, 1975.

"A DESPERADO OF LOVE":
Henry Miller, June Miller, and *Crazy Cock*

Bald, Wambly. *On the Left Bank, 1929–1933*. Ed. by Benjamin V. Franklin. Athens: Ohio University Press, 1987.

Chatwick, Whitney and de Courtivron, Isabelle, eds. *Significant Others: Creativity and Intimate Partnership*. New York: Thames & Hudson, 1993.

Dearborn, Mary V. *Henry Miller: A Biography*. New York: Simon & Schuster, 1991.

Dick, Kenneth C. *Henry Miller: Colossus of One*. Netherlands: Alberts Sittard, 1967.

Durrell, Lawrence and Miller, Henry. *The Durrell-Miller Letters, 1935–1980*. Ed. by Ian S. MacNiven. New York: New Directions, 1988.

Ferguson, Robert. *Henry Miller: A Life*. New York: W. W. Norton, 1991.

Fitch, Noel Riley. *Anaïs: The Erotic Life of Anaïs Nin*. New York: Little, Brown, 1993.

Ford, Hugh, ed., *The Left Bank Revisited: Selections from the Paris Tribune 1917–1934*. Foreword by Matthew Josephson. University Park: Pennsylvania State University Press, 1972.

Franklin, Benjamin V. and Schneider, Duane. *Anaïs Nin: An Introduction*. Athens: Ohio University Press, 1979.

Gordon, William A. *The Mind and Art of Henry Miller*. Foreword by Lawrence Durrell. Baton Rouge: Louisiana State University Press, 1967.

Jong, Erica. *The Devil at Large: Erica Jong on Henry Miller*. New York: Turtle Bay Books, 1993.

Kennedy, J. Gerald. *Imagining Paris: Exile, Writing, and American Identity*. New Haven: Yale University Press, 1993.

Knapp, Bettina L. *Anaïs Nin*. New York: Frederick Ungar, 1978.

Lewis, Leon. *Henry Miller: The Major Writings*. New York: Schocken Books, 1986.

Mailer, Norman. *The Prisoner of Sex*. New York: New American Library, 1971.

Martin, Jay. *Always Merry and Bright: The Life of Henry Miller; An Unauthorized Biography*. Santa Barbara: Capra Press, 1978.

Miller, Henry. *The Air-Conditioned Nightmare*, Volume One. New York: New Directions, 1945.

_____. *Aller Retour New York*. Introduction by George Wickes. New York: New Directions, 1991.

_____. *Black Spring*. New York: Grove Press, 1963.

_____. *The Books in My Life*. New York: New Directions, 1969.

_____. *The Colossus of Maroussi*. New York: New Directions, 1941.

_____. *Crazy Cock*. Foreword by Erica Jong. Introduction by Mary V. Dearborn. New York: Grove Press, 1991.

_____. *From Your Capricorn Friend: Henry Miller and the* Stroker, *1978–1980*. New York: New Directions, 1984.

_____. *Henry Miller's Book of Friends: A Trilogy*. Santa Barbara: Capra Press, 1987.

_____. *Henry Miller's Hamlet Letters*. Ed. and with a historical introduction by Michael Hargraves and an original preface by Henry Miller. Santa Barbara: Capra Press, 1988.

_____. *Letters to Anaïs Nin*. Ed. and introduced by Gunther Stuhlmann. New York: Paragon House, 1965, 1988.

_____. *Letters to Emil*. Ed. by George Wickes. New York: New Directions, 1989.

_____. *Letters from Henry Miller to Hoki Tokuda Miller*. Ed. by Joyce Howard. New York: Freundlich Books, 1986.

_____. *My Life and Times*. New York: Playboy Press, n.d.

_____. *The Paintings of Henry Miller: Paint as You Like and Die Happy*. With collected essays by Henry Miller on the art of watercolor. Foreword by Lawrence Durrell. Ed. by Noel Young. San Francisco: Chronicle Books, 1982.

_____. *Quiet Days in Clichy*. New York: Grove Press, 1956, 1965.

_____. *Reflections*. Ed. by Twinka Thiebaud. Santa Barbara: Capra Press, 1981.

_____. *The Rosy Crucifixion: Book One; Sexus*. New York: Grove Press, 1965.

_____. *The Rosy Crucifixion: Book Two; Plexus*. New York: Grove Press, 1965.

_____. *The Rosy Crucifixion: Book Three; Nexus*. New York: Grove Press, 1965.

_____. *Stories, Essays, Travel Sketches*. Ed. by Anthony Fine. New York: MJF Books, 1992.

_____. *The Time of the Assassins: A Study of Rimbaud*. New York: New Directions, 1946, 1956.

_____. *Tropic of Cancer*. Introduction by Karl Shapiro. Preface by Anaïs Nin. New York: Grove Press, 1961.

_____. *Tropic of Capricorn*. New York: Grove Press, 1961.

————. *The Wisdom of the Heart.* New York: New Directions, 1941.

Miller, Henry and Fowlie, Wallace. *Letters of Henry Miller and Wallace Fowlie (1943–1972).* With an introduction by Wallace Fowlie. New York: Grove Press, 1975.

Miller, Henry and Venus, Brenda. *Dear, Dear Brenda: The Love Letters of Henry Miller to Brenda Venus.* Ed. by Gerald Seth Sindell. New York: William Morrow, 1986.

Nin, Anaïs. *The Diary of Anaïs Nin: 1931–1934,* Volume I. Ed. and with an introduction by Gunther Stuhlmann. New York: Harcourt Brace Jovanovich, 1966.

————. *The Diary of Anaïs Nin: 1934–1939,* Volume II. Ed. and with a preface by Gunther Stuhlmann. New York: Harcourt Brace Jovanovich, 1967

————. *The Diary of Anaïs Nin: 1939–1944,* Volume III. Ed. and with a preface by Gunther Stuhlmann. New York: Harcourt Brace Jovanovich, 1969.

————. *The Diary of Anaïs Nin: 1944–1947,* Volume IV. Ed. and with a preface by Gunther Stuhlmann. New York: Harcourt Brace Jovanovich, 1974.

————. *The Diary of Anaïs Nin: 1947–1955,* Volume V. Ed. and with a preface by Gunther Stuhlmann. New York: Harcourt Brace Jovanovich, 1974.

————. *The Diary of Anaïs Nin: 1955–1966,* Volume VI. Ed. and with a preface by Gunther Stuhlmann. New York: Harcourt Brace Jovanovich, 1976.

————. *The Diary of Anaïs Nin: 1955–1966,* Volume VII. Ed. and with a preface by Gunther Stuhlmann. New York: Harcourt Brace Jovanovich, 1980.

————. *Henry and June: From the Unexpurgated Diary of Anaïs Nin.* New York: Harcourt Brace Jovanovich, 1986.

————. *Incest: From a Journal of Love; The Unexpurgated Diary of Anaïs Nin, 1932–1934.* With an introduction by Rupert Pole and biographical notes by Gunther Stuhlmann. New York: Harcourt Brace Jovanovich, 1992.

————. *The Novel of the Future.* New York: Macmillan, 1968.

————. *A Photographic Supplement to The Diary of Anaïs Nin.* New York: Harcourt Brace Jovanovich, 1974.

Nin, Anaïs and Miller, Henry. *A Literate Passion: Letters of Anaïs Nin and Henry Miller, 1932–1953.* Ed. and with an introduction by Gunther Stuhlmann. New York: Harcourt Brace Jovanovich, 1987.

Osborne, Lawrence. *Paris Dreambook: An Unconventional Guide to the Splendor and Squalor of the City.* New York: Vintage Books, 1992.

Perles, Alfred. *My Friend Henry Miller: An Intimate Biography.* New York: John Day, 1956.

Perles, Alfred and Durrell, Lawrence. *Art and Outrage: A Correspondence About Henry Miller Between Alfred Perles and Lawrence Durrell (With an intermission by Henry Miller).* London: Village Press, 1973.

Pierpont, Claudia Roth. "Sex, Lies, and Thirty-Five Thousand Pages," *New Yorker,* March 1, 1993, pp. 74–80, 82–90.

Porter, Bern, ed. *The Happy Rock: A Book About Henry Miller.* Berkeley: Packard Press, 1945.

Schank, Roger C. *Tell Me A Story: A New Look at Real and Artificial Memory.* New York: Charles Scribner's Sons, 1990.

Schiller, Tom. *Henry Miller Asleep and Awake: A Visit with the Writer*, Los Angeles, 1973, film, 35 minutes.

Scholar, Nancy. *Anaïs Nin*. Boston: Twayne, 1984.

Shengold, Leonard, M.D. *Soul Murder: The Effects of Childhood Abuse and Deprivation*. New Haven: Yale University Press, 1989.

Snyder, Robert. *This is Henry Miller from Brooklyn*. Los Angeles: Nash Publishing, 1974.

Tytell, John. *Passionate Lives: D. H. Lawrence, F. Scott Fitzgerald, Henry Miller, Dylan Thomas, Sylvia Plath—In Love*. New York: Carol, 1991.

Wickes, George. *Americans in Paris*. New York: Doubleday, 1969.

Wickes, George, ed. *Henry Miller and the Critics*. With a preface by Harry T. Moore. Carbondale: Southern Illinois University Press, 1963.

Widmer, Kingsley. *Henry Miller*. Rev. ed. Boston: Twayne, 1990.

ACKNOWLEDGMENTS

Writing acknowledgments is one of the last tasks, and surely the most pleasant, that a writer undertakes in ushering a book into print. In the case of this book, my greatest debts are to those writers and scholars, living and dead, who have edited the private papers of my subjects, written their biographies, and interpreted their works. I owe a debt of gratitude to every work to which I have referred in my notes and sources. But, here, I would like to especially thank the following.

For the Woolfs and their circle—to those scholars whose work has enabled mine, and to those whose friendship has been sustaining: Peter F. Alexander, Lord Noel Annan, Joanne Trautmann Banks, Quentin Bell, Anne Olivier Bell, Louise Bernikow, Thomas C. Caramagno, Mary Ann Caws, Blanche Wiesen Cook, Beth Rigel Daugherty, Richard Deacon, Jane Dunn, Angelica Garnett, Diane F. Gillespie, Lyndall Gordon, Jean Guiguet, James M. Haule, Carolyn G. Heilbrun, Elizabeth Heine, K. C. Hill-Miller, Michael Holroyd, Mark F. Hussey, Susan Kenney, Mitchell A. Leaska, John Lehmann, Jane Lilienfeld, Jean O. Love, Jane Marcus, Regina Marler, William McBrien, Andrew McNeillie, Selma S. Meyerowitz, Madeline Moore, Vara Neverow-Turk, Nigel Nicolson, Tillie Olsen, Ian Parsons, Roger Poole, Phyllis Rose, S. P. Rosenbaum, Sonya Rudikoff, Lucio Ruotolo, Brenda Silver, Frances Spalding, George Spater, Frederic Spotts, Susan Squier, Peter Stansky, Stephen Trombley, Douglas Blair Turnbaugh, Duncan Wilson, and Alex Zwerdling.

For D. H. Lawrence, Ottoline Morrell, and their circle: James T.

Boulton, Sandra Jobson Darroch, Herbert Davis, Paul Delany, Emile Delavenay, Elaine Feinstein, Robert Gathorne-Hardy, Martin Green, Michael Holroyd, Robert Lucas, Jeffrey Meyers, Harry T. Moore, Elizabeth Mansfield, Edward Nehls, Warren Roberts, Andrew Robertson, Charles L. Ross, Keith Sagar, Miranda Seymour, E. W. Tedlock, Jr., John Tytell, Lindeth Vasey, John Worthen, and George J. Zytaruk.

For Djuna Barnes and her circle: Alyce Barry, Shari Benstock, Paul Bowles, Elyse Marie Blankley, Mary Lynn Broe, Lynda Catherine Curry, Anne Beatrice Dalton, Andrew Field, Noel Riley Fitch, Gillian Hanscombe, Angela Ingram, Karla Jay, Louis F. Kannenstine, Nancy J. Levine, Jane Marcus, Frances McCullough, Douglas Messerli, Hank O'Neal, Marie Ponsot, Bonnie Kime Scott, James B. Scott, Catherine Stimpson, Virginal L. Smyers, and Ann Marie Wagstaff.

For Henry Miller, June Miller, and their circle: Deirdre Bair, Mary V. Dearborn, Kenneth C. Dick, Lawrence Durrell, Robert Ferguson, Noel Riley Fitch, Erica Jong, J. Gerald Kennedy, Bettina L. Knapp, Norman Mailer, Jay Martin, Alfred Perles, Bern Porter, Tom Schiller, Robert Snyder, Gunther Stuhlmann, John Tytell, Brenda Venus, and George Wickes.

For writers on creativity, revenge, and the effects of incest, who provided the background against which to view these specific creative acts: David Aberbach, Harold Bloom, Andrew Brink, Janine Chasseguet-Smirgel, Howard Gardner, Judith Lewis Herman, Susan Jacoby, Arthur Koestler, Ernst Kris, Myrick Land, Rollo May, Alice Miller, Thomas Moore, Camille Paglia, James W. Pennebaker, Albert Rothenberg, M.D., Roger C. Schank, Leonard Shengold, M. D., and Anthony Storr.

For biographers of subjects who have described other instances of the issue I take up here: Deirdre Bair (Simone de Beauvoir), Neil Baldwin (Man Ray); Barbara Belford (Violet Hunt); Curtis Cate (George Sand); Gloria G. Fromm (Rebecca West); Victoria Glendinning (Rebecca West); Arianna Stassinopoulos Huffington (Picasso); Herbert Lottman (Colette); Kenneth S. Lynn (Hemingway); Diane Wood Middlebrook (Anne Sexton); Arthur Mizener (Ford Madox Ford); and Anne Stevenson (Sylvia Plath).

Members of the Women Writing Women's Lives Seminar of the New York Institute for the Humanities who have helped through the years by spirited discussions into writing biography include: Sallie Bingham, Adrienne Block, Norah Chase, Ellen Chesler, Bell Chevigny, Gloria Erlich, Francine Du Plessix Gray, Gail Hornstein,

Dorothy O. Helly, Carole Klein, Brooke Kroeger, Nancy Mathews, Joan Mellen, Nell Painter, Nancy Rubin, Sue Shapiro, and Joan Weimer. I owe a special debt to the friendship and work of Deirdre Bair, Louise Bernikow, Blanche Wiesen Cook, and Honor Moore. Knowing these writers through the long years that their works have been in progress has been inspiring; their willingness to take time from their own work to discuss mine has been an act of generosity that I gratefully acknowledge.

Members of the Department of English at Hunter College, and the Hunter College community have been supportive and helpful. Former presidents Paul LeClerc and Donna Shalala were staunch supporters. I owe Allan Brick and Richard Barickman a special debt. They have always arranged for me to teach courses based upon my current research interests, and have been good friends. Thom Taylor and Megan Brereton have helped in many ways. Meena Alexander, Fred Bornhauser, Marlies Danziger, Karen Greenberg, Alan Holder, Harriet Johnson, Eve Leoff, Mildred Kuner, Estella Majozo, Charles Persky, Gerald Pinciss, Ann Raimes, Neil Tolchin, Sylvia Tomasch, and Barbara Webb have been the best of colleagues. My students through the years, at Hunter College and the Graduate Center of the City University of New York, have been eager to discuss the works of my subjects; they have provided a wonderful forum in which to test my ideas; their insights have enriched mine.

Staff members at various libraries and manuscript collections were supremely helpful. I wish to thank the staffs at the Teaneck Public Library, particularly Claudia De Matteo, for assisting me with interlibrary loans; the Fairleigh Dickinson Library; the Hunter College Library; the late Lola L. Szladits at the Berg Collection of the New York Public Library; the Rare Book Collection at the Louis Round Wilson Library, University of North Carolina at Chapel Hill; the Ohio State University Library; the Monks House Papers, University of Sussex, Falmer, England. Beth Alvarez, Curator of Literary Manuscripts Archives and Manuscripts of the McKeldin Library, University of Maryland at College Park, Maryland, was most helpful with the manuscripts of Djuna Barnes. Timothy D. Murray, Head, Special Collections of the University of Delaware Library, Newark, Delaware, was most helpful with the letters of Emily Coleman. Lilace Hatayama was most helpful with the Henry Miller Papers at the Department of Special Collections, University Research Library at UCLA.

Friends, family members, and associates, who have helped by providing rare books as gifts, discussing my work, reading it, helping with professional matters, or accompanying me on jaunts to track down the places where my subjects lived or where their forebears were buried, include Ken Aptekar, Deborah Jean Wernick DeSalvo, Ernest DeSalvo, Frances DeSalvo, Jason DeSalvo, Justin DeSalvo, Janet Emig, Kennedy Fraser, Warren Friss, Elizabeth Harlan, Norbert Hirschhorn, M. D., Tom Hutton, John Koster, Charles Lemert, Elizabeth Lerner, Suki Lesard, Burgess Levin, Eunice Lipton, Temma Kaplan, Paulette Kendler, John Koster, Nick Lyons, Charles Naylor, James McCourt, Roger McIntyre, Charles Naylor, Carol Newman, Paul Newman, Susan Osborn, Katherine Hogan Probst, Mary Saily, Louis Sciacchetano, Mildred Thaler Sciacchetano, Susan Shapiro, Nan Talese, Vincent Virga, Nina Thal Warfield, Jack Warfield, Mindy Werner, and Joanne Wyckoff.

During my writing of this book, my mother, Mildred Sciacchetano, died. I want to remember her here, and acknowledge the support she always provided; I have missed our ritual of reading proof together, and her pride in my work.

Halfway through the writing of this book, I developed a mysterious and disabling illness, which lasted for close to a year. For his skill in diagnosis and treatment, and for enabling me to finish this work, and resume a normal life, I wish to thank John R. Edsall, M. D.

The staff at the Elaine Markson Literary Agency has provided a lively support group. I owe a special thank-you to Elaine Markson and to Sally Wofford Girand. I also wish to thank Sara De Nobrega, Caomh Kavanaugh, and Stephanie Hawkins.

During the early stages of this project, Suzanne Sadlier Stroh was my research assistant. Her work allowed mine to proceed more quickly than it would have otherwise.

My relationship with my publisher, NAL/Dutton, has been greatly rewarding. I especially wish to thank my editor, Rosemary Ahern, for her care and concern for my writing, for helping me grow as a writer, for careful, respectful editing, and for championing this work. To her assistant, Julia Moskin, my thanks for tending to numerous calls and problems with care and cheer. To Barbara Perris, copy editor, I am extremely grateful for her attention to detail, finding mistakes, and untangling sentences. To Jennifer Romanello, publicist, who worked skillfully and cheerfully on behalf of my work, and to Lisa Johnson, publicity director, for her support. To Judy

Courtade, Carole DeSanti, and Arnold Dolin, gratitude for their enthusiasm for this project. To Elaine Koster, publisher, I owe a special thank-you. Robin Locke-Monda and Eve L. Kirch are responsible for the handsome design of this book, and I thank them.

Special thanks are due those to whom this book is dedicated. To my husband, Ernest J. DeSalvo, for more than thirty years of friendship and partnership, for being my first, and most critical reader, for patience and help during my illness, and for keeping me well-fed, happy, working, and focused on my aim in writing this book. To my friend Elizabeth Harlan, for nearly daily discussions on our work (hers, on George Sand) that inspired and sustained me, for helping me through hard times, and for celebrating joyous ones. To my friend, and first editor, Frank McLaughlin, for insisting that I focus on the telling details and anecdotes that illuminate a life, and that I keep my sentences short enough for everyone to understand. To my friend and agent, Geri Thoma, who helped me imagine this book, plan it, and write it, who listened to endless progress reports with the greatest cheer, and who did not flinch when I decided to scrap a completed version of the Lawrence section, but supported my decision to begin yet again.

And, finally, to those publishing companies and literary estates who have allowed me to quote from the works of my subjects, I am extremely grateful. For permission to quote from the following published works, thanks to:

Alfred A. Knopf, for Frieda Lawrence, *The Memoirs and Correspondence*, ed. by E. W. Tedlock, Jr. (Copyright © 1964 by Frieda Lawrence Ravagli); for *Memoirs of Lady Ottoline Morrell* by Lady Ottoline Morrell, ed. by Robert Gathorne-Hardy (Copyright © 1963 by Julian Vinogradoff, reprinted by permission of Alfred A. Knopf, Inc.); and for *Ottoline at Garsington* by Lady Ottoline Morrell, ed. by Robert Gathorne-Hardy (Copyright © 1974 by Julian Vinogradoff, reprinted by permission of Alfred A. Knopf., Inc.)

HarperCollins Publishers, for Paul Delany, *D. H. Lawrence's Nightmare* (Copyright © 1978 by Paul Delany, reprinted by permission of HarperCollins).

Capra Press for Jay Martin, *Always Merry and Bright* (Copyright © 1978 by Jay Martin).

The Putnam Publishing Group for Alfred Perles and Lawrence Durrell, *Art and Outrage* (Copyright © 1959, Alfred Perles and Lawrence Durrell).

Simon & Schuster, for Mary V. Dearborn, *Henry Miller: A Biography* (Copyright © 1991 by Mary V. Dearborn).

Southern Illinois University Press, for *Silence and Power* ed. by Mary Lynn Broe (Copyright © 1991 by the Board of Trustees, Southern Illinois University).

The University of North Carolina Press for *Women's Writing in Exile*, ed. by Mary Lynn Broe and Angela Ingram (Copyright © 1989, the University of North Carolina Press).

The University of Texas Press for Andrew Field, *Djuna: The Formidable Miss Barnes* (Copyright © 1983, 1985 by Andrew Field).

The University of Wisconsin Press for *D. H. Lawrence: A Composite Biography*, ed. by Edward Nehls (Copyright © 1957, 1958, 1959, reprinted with permission).

W. W. Norton for Robert Ferguson, *Henry Miller: A Life* (Copyright © 1991 by Robert Ferguson).

William Morrow for Henry Miller and Brenda Venus, *Dear, Dear Brenda: The Love Letters of Henry Miller to Brenda Venus* (Copyright © 1986 by Brenda Venus and Corwin/Sindell Productions).

The Viking Press for D. H. Lawrence, *The Collected Letters of D. H. Lawrence*, Volume Two (Copyright © 1962 by Frieda Lawrence Ravagli), ed. by Harry T. Moore, and Frieda Lawrence, *"Not I, But the Wind. . . ."* (Copyright 1934 by Frieda Lawrence Ravagli).

I am grateful to the following institutions, literary estates, and literary agencies, for permission to quote from the work of my subjects, to:

Beth Alvarez, Curator of Literary Manuscripts, Archives and Manuscripts, University of Maryland at College Park, Maryland, for the manuscripts in the Papers of Djuna Barnes.

Laurence Pollinger Ltd. and the Estate of Frieda Lawrence Ravagli for the typescript of D. H. Lawrence, *Women in Love,* the letters of D. H. Lawrence, and the work of Frieda Lawrence Ravagli.

Herbert Mitgang, president of the Authors League Fund, for permission to quote from the manuscript of *The Antiphon;* from the letters of Djuna Barnes to various correspondents; from the manuscript of *Nightwood;* from *The Book of Repulsive Women,* from Djuna Barnes's article in *Brooklyn Daily Eagle* (7/9/13); from Djuna Barnes, "Giving Advice on Life and Pictures" (Copyright © The Authors League Fund, Literary Executor of the Estate of Djuna Barnes).

Aitken & Stone for Andrew Field, *Djuna: The Formidable Miss Barnes.*

Timothy D. Murry of the University of Delaware, Newark, Library for the letters of Emily Coleman.

Joseph Geraci, Executor, Estate for Emily Holmes Coleman, for the letters of Emily Holmes Coleman.

The Douglas Duncan Collection, The Thomas Fisher Rare Book Library, University of Toronto, for the manuscripts of D. H. Lawrence, *Women in Love.*

For permission to reproduce the photographs in this volume, I would like to thank the following:

Chatto & Windus/The Hogarth Press and the Estate of Virginia Woolf, for the photograph of Virginia and Leonard Woolf.

Rupert Pole and Gunther Stuhlman, for the photograph of June Miller. Courtesy The Anaïs Nin Trust. All rights reserved.

New Directions Publishing Corp. for the picture of Henry Miller. Reproduced by permission of New Directions Publishing Corp.

Berenice Abbott/Commerce Graphics Ltd, Inc. for the Berenice Abbott portrait of Djuna Barnes.

A. M. Goodman and P. H. R. Goodman, for the photographs of D. H. Lawrence and Ottoline Morrell.

INDEX